EATON'S

During The
Second French Revolution

Working with writers since 1998

Other Books By Golden Quill Press

Working with writers since 1998

Shamrock's Story — From Hurricane Katrina
To Doggy Dementia & Alzheimer's

Tell it to the Future — Have I Got a Story For You -
About The Twentieth Century

Tell it to the Future — Book 1 - 1900's - 1930's

Tell it to the Future — Book 2 - 1940's -1960's

Tell it to the Future — Book 3 - 1970-2000

New Horizon's

Code 47 to BREV Force – Cracko

Code 47 to BREV Force – QuizMaster MixMatcher

Code 47 to BREV Force – Controller the Final Battle

From an Idea to Your Finished Story

How to Write Your Book - Book 1- Let's Get Started

How to Write Your Book - Book 2 - Writing on the Super-Highway

How to Write Your Book - Book 3 - From An Idea...
to Your Finished Story

See an additional list of Books published by Golden Quill Press at the back of this book

EATON'S

During The Second French Revolution

By

Kenneth A. Bray

Golden Quill Press, a division of Barish Stern Ltd.

This is a Historical Fiction publication. Some of the characters have been fictionalized and/or names have been changed to protect and preserve their right to privacy and the rights of all parties involved.

Copyright @ 2023 by Kenneth A. Bray

All rights reserved, except for appropriate quotes in reviews or scholarly works. Printed in the United States of America. No part of this publication may be reproduced or stored in a retrieval system or transmitted in any form or by any means, electronic, mechanical, photocopying, recording or other means without the written permission of the publisher.

Published by Golden Quill Press,
a division of Barish Stern Ltd., Virginia

ISBN 979-8-9860776-1-1
Printed in the United States of America

Cover design by Portraits on Gold Inc.

Editing and Interior Design by Golden Quill Press

Illustrations by Portraits on Gold Inc.

ACKNOWLEDGEMENTS

As with any first-time author the fear of displaying one's literary inexperience is paramount in the creation of his or her manuscript. However, to those of us who are fortunate enough to have a support group of valuable professional authors, editors, and publishers to guide our path to successful completion, we extend our heartfelt appreciation.

In my case two individuals have held the position of assisting me in every aspect of writing this *"Eaton's During the Second French Revolution,"* a book chronicling my experiences working at Eaton's Montreal, Canada department store during the turbulent 1960's.

My wife, Francine, author, poet, photographer, and publisher was the most influential in prodding me along when I would get lax in continuing this arduous and daunting task. She offered encouragement as the manuscript progressed and researched historical information for accuracy. Without her, this book would never have been completed.

Additionally, to my good friend, Bobbi Madry, a professional New York editor and author, who brought my words to life with her years of professional editing experience.

And, to all my family and friends who extended moral support during my writing days.

DEDICATION

Eaton's During the Second French Revolution, is dedicated to all those brave souls who lived through the turbulent 1960's in the Province of Quebec, Canada. To all whose homes were displaced, whose liberties were stolen and who sustained personal losses, or injury resulting from the French attack on Canadian democracy. And, to my valued comrades who worked with me, and for me, at the legendary Eaton's department store in downtown Montreal.

This book is especially posthumously dedicated to our founder, Mr. Timothy Eaton, a Presbyterian Ulster Scot immigrant, who arrived in Canada just two years after Canadian Confederation and turned several unsuccessful retail ventures into the greatest department store chain across all of Canada, and possibly the world.

And, to my grand Eaton's store, that stood so proudly on Sainte Catherine's Street, in downtown Montreal, and defended herself against the onslaught of the Second French Revolution. This is her special place in this historical story!

EATON'S – During the Second French Revolution

⚜ Prologue ⚜

In a 1954 speech, then Canadian Prime Minister, John Diefenbaker stated, *"Freedom is the right to be wrong, not the right to do wrong."* His Canada of that time did not reflect a long history of discord, and he couldn't fathom that years later, those very words would be put to a tumultuous test in the Province of Quebec.

Earlier, British Prime Minister, Sir Winston Churchill had stated, *"There are no limits to the majestic future which lies before the mighty expanse of Canada with its virile, aspiring, cultured, and generous-hearted people."*

Ever since the confederation, in 1867, Canada had always been known to be a peaceful and passive nation. Her people, remarkably diverse, her vibrant cities, sprawling urban communities and vast uninhabited frontiers, are all a testament to untethered growth. These regions combined as one, with a national pride of being a multicultural people who lived together harmoniously; a caring people.

In 1642, **Montreal was founded** by pioneer Jeanne Mance **as a** missionary colony, rapidly flourishing due to its strategic shipping location on the St. Lawrence River and its lucrative northern fur trade based in the Hudson Bay.

By 1840, Canada East and Canada West were unified by the British Parliament into the Province of Canada. Later, this territory was to be re-divided into the Provinces of Quebec and Ontario under the **Canadian Confederation**, which created the federal Dominion of Canada in 1867. This land annexation was the result of years of battle with France, which united Canada's mere three million people as a dominion protectorate within the British Empire.

KENNETH A. BRAY

For many amicable years, the French and English of Quebec lived side by side, respectful of their ethnicity, differences, and cultures. The original early French Quebec settlers were desperately poor and cut off from the decision-making centers of both Canada and Great Britain. However, their rural society remained incredibly prolific, growing impressively in population, while continuing to nurture their French national identity and language.

For over one hundred and fifty years, from the Hudson Bay to the Gulf of Mexico, and from Labrador to the Rockies, these peasants and adventurers were writing a proud history all over the North American continent. They had been the discoverers, the fur-traders, and the fort-builders, while in the St. Lawrence lowlands, they developed an identity quite different from their original France heritage. As the French-Canadian colonization transformation materialized, it survived primarily through their perpetual faith around Catholicism, and its industrious country landowners. The general acquisition of land was confined to small farm holdings throughout Quebec, with the major growth of commercial and manufacturing industries centered in the industrialized cities, eventually developing into progressive resource development centers. This economic growth was the exclusive and undisputed action of, "Les Anglais" [the English], who controlled most of Québec under the compact leadership of Montréal-based entrepreneurs, financiers, and merchants.

The St. Lawrence River valley settlements grew into large cities like Montréal and Québec City, with hundreds of small towns and villages stretching from the U.S. border to the mining centers and power projects in the north. English Canada economically flourished over the next 100 years, but French Québec only survived because of a strange demographic term called, la revanche du berceau *("the revenge of the cradle")*. This translated into a theory that high birth-rates among French minorities promised that French-Canadians could, in time, become a majority population, thus establishing political control within their province.

At that time only the French elite, were made up of doctors, politicians, lawyers, and priests, ostensibly considered, "essential services," for the bodies and souls of cheap labor, whose miraculous birthrate kept the French citizen supply continuously overabundant.

For the average French Quebecer, education had been primarily a modest collection of church-run seminaries, where the emphasis was on recruiting for the priesthood, and which, for over a century, led to just one underdeveloped university. For ninety percent of the French children there was only a grammar school education offering classes in reading and writing, which relegated them to the single option of seeking any employment from any enterprise willing to offer them a steady modest job.

EATON'S – During the Second French Revolution

The old cliché, *"What the hell does Québec want?"* is steeped in historic Canadian political folklore. After World War II, the term had been used whenever Québec's attitudes made it seem like the French Quebecer was the *poor second cousin* in the ever-constant battle in federal-provincial relations.

Originally, as one of four, and eventually one of ten provinces, Québec was incorporated without trouble or resistance, until the nineteen sixties!

While Quebec City was then considered rural in nature, alternately the city of Montreal grew into an impressive thriving metropolis. Her downtown became a hub for major shopping, including department stores such as Eaton's which had achieved unprecedented success in the Provinces of Ontario and Manitoba. Once shopping became a major attraction, specialty boutique shops, restaurants and international corporate offices emerged throughout the quaint downtown core. Montrealer's, both English and French, lived a peaceful life of a peaceful people filled with positive aspirations for the future of their great united nation.

However, in the early 1960's, Quebec's subtle political rhetoric transformed into unprecedented revolutionary acts of mayhem and violence. To understand the modern-day feelings of oppression of the French Canadians we must consider their outgrowth since early confederation. Looking back, it is clear to see that there was a definite outline of an emerging nation in that original French colony taken over by the British Empire in 1763, leading to what they perceive today as a depressed minority.

"What do the Francophones want, and how the hell did this all happen?" This question has been repeated nationwide, time, and again, without a clear answer. French Canadians have always been a people who considered French as their primary language, but at what stage in history did Canadians become separated into a divisive Francophone and Anglophone entity?

In reflection, there must have been a smoldering of discord amongst the more radical French community, which most Canadians never really saw coming. A prominent Montreal newspaper once reported that one McGill University political science professor stated, *"It wasn't like on one particular date someone in power declared war, but, that a definite war began without any formal declaration; but it was indeed a war!"*

Had Anglophones been more cognizant of the needs of their French brethren, we should not have been surprised by the ultimate outcome. To identify a commencement time frame, we surmise that it began by way of the revolutionary rhetoric of political activist, Rene Levesque, combined with a revolutionary political declaration by French President, General Charles de Gaulle.

As in any uprising, to fuel the flames of Francophone discord, a prominent and familiar figure needed to emerge to take up the mantel of unrest. Rene Levesque, a magnanimous political reporter and minister of the Legislative

Assembly of Quebec, was just the person to command that role. His political intellect, shrewdness, and charisma were exhibited regularly in his lectures to French college students. This propelled him to instant national prominence as the principal leader for Quebec independence from Canada. In the early '60's, he gave an incendiary speech to a student gathering at Sir George Williams University, where he preached Quebec independence through political resolve, while supposedly condemning violence. But his nationally publicized statement of, *"We must fight to achieve our goals of an independent Quebec,"* was meant to motivate aggressive French students to do whatever was necessary to achieve French dominance, a statement that completely contradicted his previous insincere admonishment of non-violent actions. His majestic performances were incisive and riveting, stirring his audiences with rallying cries of, *"Do we want to live in an independent Quebec."*

During the same time as Levesque was expounding on utilizing only political remedies, Lévesque and his supporters failed to condemn the murders, kidnappings and bombings by the Front de Libération du Québec, (FLQ), or even, the group's subsequent heinous kidnap and murder of Quebec politicians. Levesque's incendiary statements made him the instant leader of what was to become *"a bloody battle for French independence."*

The goal of Lévesque and his Parti-Québécois government became the independence option termed the *"sovereignty-association."* The concept envisaged Quebec enacting its own laws, collecting taxes from its own people, and establishing relations with foreign countries. All this while simultaneously forming an economic union with the rest of Canada based on a common currency. With Lévesque's formation of the Mouvement Souveraineté Association, which later became the infamous Parti-Québécois, his popularity increased significantly in the Quebec independence movement, culminating in his eventual election as Premier of Quebec.

However, the real spark that gave international legitimacy to the independence movement was encased in an anti-federalist speech given by President General Charles de Gaulle at the opening of the 1967 Expo World's Fair, held in Montreal. Historians agree that "Levesque may have gathered sufficient brush for the political fire, but it was de Gaulle who lit the match." With de Gaulle's well-known animosity towards Canada, history reflects that the Canadian government made a critical error in extending an "open, no strings attached," invitation for him to attend the opening of Expo 1967.

Even before his arrival, the Canadian federal government had been concerned about de Gaulle's visit since previously he had not accepted an invitation to attend the 50th anniversary ceremonies commemorating the Canadian forces World War II victory at Vimy Ridge. With this concern over the potential political interference of France in domestic affairs in the already unstable Province of Quebec, the Canadian Secretary of State was dispatched to visit de Gaulle in France to mend the two countries' strained relationship. Speculation was that de Gaulle was incensed over a perceived slight dating back to World War II era when, then Canadian P.M. Mackenzie King, was slow in recognizing de Gaulle's newly formed post-war French government.

As a courtesy, the Canadian government sent de Gaulle a formal invitation to attend the opening of Expo 67. Alternately, de Gaulle received a separate invitation to visit Quebec from Quebec's Premier Daniel Johnson. As a visiting head of state, conventional protocol dictated that de Gaulle was to arrive in the Canadian capital city of Ottawa, but instead he sailed up the St. Lawrence River on his French navy flagship, so that he could arrive in Quebec's capital, Quebec City, instead. There de Gaulle was greeted with enthusiastic cheers, while Governor General, Roland Michener, was booed by the same crowd when, the English anthem, "God Save the Queen," was played at his arrival. In de Gaulle's speech, he emphasized his country's, "evolving ties with Quebec," openly showing support for Quebec sovereignty over Canadian federalism.

The final insult came later, in his speech at the Montreal City Hall, where de Gaulle managed to seal his commitment to the fate of Quebec's sovereignty efforts by articulating the infamous words that were to become the catchphrase of the Parti-Quebecois, and the battle cry of the French terrorist revolutionaries for the next decade,"Vive Montréal!" *(Long live Montreal)*; "Vive le Québec!" *(Long live Quebec)* and then followed by an even louder distinct revolutionary battle cry, "Vive le Québec libre!" *(Long live a free Quebec)*. With his microphone booming across the throngs of listeners de Gaulle made sure to place particular emphasis in the word, "Libre" *(Free)*, to the delight of his Francophone audience. Never since early Canadian Confederation, has any other world leader ever set foot on Canadian soil to sanction approval for an internal uprising. But Charles de Gaulle, in that one speech, almost 100 years after the struggle to put together an incredible Canadian Confederation, verbally started the war that would virtually tear the Confederation apart and set neighbor against neighbor; Frenchmen against Englishmen!

The, "Vive le Québec libre!" slogan was to become an everyday slogan for French speaking Quebecers who favored Quebec sovereignty. Charles de Gaulle's use of it hinted at extending France's support to their separatist movement. The speech sparked a diplomatic incident within Canada's government, and was condemned by the Canadian Prime Minister saying, "Canadians do not need to be liberated." However, in his homeland of France, many were sympathetic to the cause of Quebec nationalism, and supported de Gaulle's speech and the prospect of Quebec independence, maybe even a Quebec / France alliance.

The days that followed the speech saw Quebec ablaze with bumper stickers, T-shirts, billboards, and TV ads all heralding the now infamous axioms "Vive le Québec libre!"

For resident Anglophones, the events were shocking and fearful since they had never considered the remote possibility of insurrection on Canada's soil. Gone was the peace and tranquility, replaced by constant threats and violence. Gone was the security of living in a once passive country, replaced by constant fear and trepidation. Gone were their rights dictated by the Canadian Constitution, replaced by mandatory Quebec specific laws favoring Francophones, and, most importantly gone was the heritage Canadians had known and cherished. Even their English language, their native tongue, was being threatened with extinction and all that remained for the Anglophone Quebecer was a sense of national hopelessness.

The English-speaking Canadians living in Montreal, were no longer a majority in an English-speaking country of thirty million, but rather a targeted minority in a province of six million. And, with Anglophones as a provincial minority, their rights were being systematically stripped away. They no longer enjoyed their native English language but had to succumb to the forced unilingual language of French. It wasn't just a matter of becoming bilingual with French as a second language, it was the provincial enforcement mandate of French as the *only* business and educational language. Under a Quebec Bill #101 legislative enactment, English was excluded entirely from the provincial legislature and courts. The Bill restricted access to English schools to anyone other than children whose parents had attended English schools, thus making French schooling compulsory for English speaking immigrants, even those from other Canadian provinces. Additionally, the language bill required policies, signs, menus, and jobs to *only* be permitted in the French language. This was a calculated strategy to dominate and destabilize the English-speaking citizens of the province. And, with the law expelling the English language from commerce, business administration and schools, Anglophones lost their rights to constitutional protection to use their native English language in their own country.

The French were winning, or so they thought, but in effect they were creating a severe economic climate of recession throughout Quebec. Although strongly supported by the French public and the ruling Partie-Quebecois, the law triggered an exodus of more than 130,000 Anglophones, most fleeing westward; as well as dozens of large major Montréal-based companies, including Sun Life Assurance Company, Bank of Montreal, Royal Bank of Canada, and numerous manufacturing facilities; all who relocated their head offices to Ontario and the western provinces.

We remember that the 60's were turbulent times with many other countries experiencing daily violence, but Canadians had held to the optimistic credence that their country was different in content and culture. However, as the decade moved forward, they eventually had to surrender to the actuality that with the new internal terrorist threats, Quebec, and even Canada, would certainly experience both economic and political upheaval!

During this melee of political unrest, citizen violence and bombings became a feared daily occurrence in English Canada. But the primary physical target of resentment by radical young Francophones became the prominent downtown core of Montreal and its major department store, Eaton's of Canada.

Eaton's was the largest department store chain in Canada and the single largest in Montreal. With its proud Union Jack British flag flying high above the nine-story downtown store, Eaton's symbolized all that the revolutionaries found wrong with federalist Canada. Eaton's was considered by the revolutionaries as the bastion of Anglo-Canadian power and thus, the prime target of the radical separatist.

The store employees consisted of 90% Anglophone management and 65% Anglophone support staff, and, because of the English / French disparity, this was a thorn in the side of Quebec independence supporters and became the brunt of actions of political discord. The FLQ chose Eaton's to vent their disdain for Anglophone dominance with their focus directed at perpetrating violence. But the battle scars were more than the effects on the store, the emotional and physical casualties to employees and customers who defended Eaton's in words and actions proved them to be the heroes of that time. Unfortunately, these heroes were also the ones to suffer life-altering consequences.

Everyone from coast to coast agreed, distinct lines had now been drawn, and The Second French Revolution had begun; and God help and protect the English citizens living within the turbulent borders of Quebec, and those poor isolated souls working at the Eaton's Montreal department store!

Subsequently, Eaton's became the primary battleground for the revolutionary events of the 1960's. In a world divided by nationality, British Canada was being torn down by her French counterparts placing the entire country in chaos. Violence raged in the streets of Montreal as the war came in through Eaton's front doors.

These events were witnessed first-hand by Montrealer, Richard (Ricky) Dean, a prominent young Eaton employee of the time. Beginning with his first job, he was fortunate enough to find treasured friends within the bustling daily operations at the T. Eaton Company, Canada, Ltd., in downtown Montreal.

Ricky, one of the young basement store managers, was caught at the forefront of the fight; everything was spinning out of control, his chaotic home life, his beloved country, and his treasured historic Eaton's department store -- nothing would ever be the same, again!

The Second French Revolution had begun!

⚜ One ⚜

Ricky spread the wet Morning Gazette newspaper that he'd retrieved from his snow filled front steps, on the floor in front of the heat radiator to dry. The last big snowstorm was just two days ago, depositing nineteen inches of wet, slushy snow, snarling traffic, and taxing the already depleted Montreal snow removal budget.

As he gazed out his front window, he could see the sidewalks and driveways still piled high with the ugly graying remnants of the once beautiful white blanket of snow. The blizzard had buried the parked cars and the plows had packed snow up against all the car doors making entry all but impossible. As if that wasn't enough, the overnight freezing temperatures had turned much of the slush to ice, making shoveling an arduous, if not, impossible task. With his parents and sister permanently relocated to Florida and his brother serving in the U.S. Air Force, Ricky remembered his father's farewell statement, *"Montreal has a great climate, nine months of winter and three months of cold weather, get used to it!"*

Today was Ricky's regular Eaton's day off which only heightened his disgust at the prospect of having to eventually brave the weather to free his car from the grip of Montreal winter. He went to the kitchen to get his first cup of coffee before settling down to check out the morning news. His eleven-month-old daughter, Darlene, was happily playing at his feet. He was thrilled to spend time with her, especially when her mother was not around. They had married at an early age, but it had been a disaster area ever since.

Gathering the damp front page of the Gazette, Ricky settled into his favorite winged-back armchair and put his feet up on the ottoman to read the ever too common front-page headline:

"HAS THE WAR BEGUN?"

Ricky slowly sipped his coffee as he read the article:

Today, the separatist factions of the FLQ unleashed yet more terrorist vengeance on several innocent neighborhood communities throughout Montreal. Ten bombs had been placed in Canada Poste mailboxes throughout the city.

These attacks added to the long list of violence perpetrated by the Front de Libération du Québec, *that began on July 1, 1962, Dominion Day, when the statue to Sir John A. Macdonald was vandalized in Dominion Square, where the words "Je suis séparatiste," [I am a separatist], were spray painted on it. It appears that the FLQ wants to completely denigrate the English Canadian identity. Sir John A. Macdonald, who been the first prime minister of the Dominion of Canada (1867–73, 1878–91), was heralded as the Father of Canada, through its early*

EATON'S – During the Second French Revolution

growth period. As such, he is regarded as the symbol of English federalism, making his statue a prime target for the FLQ vandalism.

This seemingly harmless defacement was just the tip of the iceberg. From that day in 1962 on, marches, rallies, and violent protests replaced the accepted relatively peaceful anti-government demonstrations, usually enacted by peaceful political dissidents.

In the first 5 months of 1963, the violence escalated significantly, creating a threatening air of outright warfare which regularly erupted throughout Montreal. The year began with Molotov cocktails being thrown through the window of the English language radio station, CKGM, subsequently followed by a succession of random bombings that rocked the foundation of Montreal. Three military barracks were attacked with FLQ incendiary bombs, while another three separate bombs exploded at a Federal Tax building, the Central Railway Station, and a commuter train. These events signaled that a war was now in full force and could no longer be ignored by the federal government in Ottawa, Ontario.

Continuing their reign of terror, the FLQ placed 24 sticks of dynamite at the foot of the Radio-Canada transmission tower on Mount Royal, in an massive attempt to totally disrupt national, and international, communications. Fortunately, a technical defect in their timing mechanism prevented the potentially devastating explosion. At the same time, a bomb that was set to explode on the Canadian National Railway line that was transporting Prime Minister of Canada, John Diefenbaker, was discovered and disarmed before his passing train arrived.

Miraculously, up to that point, with all the FLQ anarchy that had taken place, there still had been no fatalities, that is, until April 21st, when everything changed. A bomb exploded at the Canadian Forces Recruiting Centre killing a night guard, Donald Renquist, the first of many casualties to come. This signaled the official beginning of The Second French Revolutionary War!

However, with the placement of these ten bombs in a single day, the war has accelerated to new heights."

Ricky placed the newspaper back beside the heating register to dry. As he refilled his coffee cup his thoughts focused on the news article, realizing the fact that living in Montreal had become a very hazardous place.

He placed a baby rattle in Darlene's hands, and turned on his old Motorola console TV, to watch the local morning news about the bombings. As the screen flickered to life, a bold banner flashed announcing,

"BREAKING NEWS ALERT."

What else is new, Ricky thought. *Just about every day now has brought some news of terror in Montreal or elsewhere in the province.*

The studio T.V. reporter began, *"While we prepare to go live to the scene, we have a recap of the events leading up to our location report."*

Richard watched the backdrop of flashing emergency lights from numerous police vehicles displayed on a separate video screen, as the reporter continued.

"The early morning hours were perforated by a succession of violent explosions cascading through the usually tranquil town of Westmount, Montreal's affluent west end suburb. As emergency vehicles descended upon their town residents realized it had been only a matter of time before their English Quebecer's heritage would make them the prime target of Quebec separatist wrath.

Radical political dialogue had escalated to fever pitch over the past two years, inciting French college students to take drastic measures to bring their cause to the international forefront. Although most Francophones did not condone the violent separation tactics administered by the FLQ, most did believe in the principles of a sovereign Quebec. And now, with total disregard for life and property, the assault on the innocent had begun in earnest."

"Just weeks after the tragic bombing event at the Canadian Forces Recruiting Centre that killed a night guard, Allied Television TV Canada is reporting that the FLQ has placed ten bombs in residential street mailboxes throughout Montreal, and particularly, the usually tranquil Town of Westmount. The Canadian Army has been asked by Montreal police to assist in searching every Canada Poste mailbox in the city."

"In a moment, we will be going live to the site of the eighth bomb. We are being told that the Montreal Police have secured the area around this one mailbox bomb. A small, enclosed RCA bomb squad van has entered the empty street and parked some twenty yards from the mailbox. The armored van was moved into position as a barrier between disposal personnel and the mailbox. Three members of the Royal Canadian Army ordinance disposal unit have exited the van and are now seen assessing the situation. They have also unloaded their equipment and strung communication lines from the suspected bomb to the van."

The newscaster motioned towards his producer, *"Is DesOrmeaux ready to go remote?"*

An off-screen voice replied, *"... in three, two, one."*

The announcer continued, *"We are still awaiting our set-up with ATV Canada reporter, Robert DesOrmeaux, to give us a live on-scene report."*

At the bomb site, Robert DesOrmeaux was preparing for his live on-air report. This was his first field assignment since being hired away from a Toronto all-news radio station. He tried unsuccessfully to remove the apprehension that centered in the pit of his stomach knowing that he was only given this major assignment because the lead anchorman was covering the international monetary conference in Vancouver, B.C. With all the FLQ happenings, there was

EATON'S – During the Second French Revolution

no other reporter available to be tasked with reporting the bomb disposal efforts in Westmount.

Robert knew that this was a life and death situation, but he tried to calm his nerves before going live. He told himself, *this assignment could well be my big break into primetime investigative reporting*. He had a lot to live up to, and a lot to prove, and this could be his one big chance.

While the station was waiting to present the live scene, Ricky got up to put Darlene in her playpen so he could pay attention to the news broadcast. He had followed so many of these terror events recently, he was numb to the fact that they were getting worse.

Having followed the bomb squad through several bomb locations during the early hours, Robert recognized one of the Army's ordinance disposal unit officers as Sergeant Major Andre Carpentier. Earlier in the day he had filed verbal reports to the station on two other bomb disposals by Carpentier, one that almost became critical.

Robert started making notes to be able to give the TV audience a recap of the day's events, as he wrote, *"bomb number seven incident."* He also made a note to discuss protective clothing and body armor.

Realizing that his remote crew was almost ready for his live telecast, Robert positioned himself strategically so that the camera had a panoramic view of the army van ensuring the subject mailbox was visible over his right shoulder. He combed his hair and brushed lint from his blue suit coat, waiting for his cue from Jacques Gauthier, his ATV Canada cameraman, to begin the broadcast.

"Jacques," he called out, "make sure that you have Commander Lalonde ready to join me after my intro, okay," Robert directed.

"He's ready boss, and the studio is already on standby," Jacque replied. "Oh, no pressure, but remember, either Harvey Kirk, or Peter Jennings, is going to do the national lead in for your Cross-Canada report, tonight. They'll be using this video as their basis of reference."

"Yeah, right! No pressure! This damn wind is blowing my hair to shit, even with the extra Brylcreem," he complained.

"It just makes the scene that much more realistic, boss. Relax, this will be going coast-to-coast. Tomorrow, you'll be getting offers from all the TV networks in the states," he teased, checking his watch. "Two minutes to air and counting."

"I'm still shaking. I can't believe that bloody bomb didn't go off when it hit the mailbox this morning. It's lucky I had another pair of underwear with me," Robert joked.

"Yeah, me too! When the box fell over and Carpentier dove for the army van, I thought it was all over. Even Lalonde and his crew hit the ground. I'm glad we were doing on-scene audio only."

Listening to his earphone Jacques added, "One minute to air. Next countdown in ten seconds. Look pretty for the camera, boss!"

Robert stiffened his posture and waited for Jacques' final countdown. "Who's filming over by the army van?" he shouted.

"That's the army media division. They filmed all bomb disarming and disposals for their training program. Live in ten, nine, eight, move one foot to your left Bob. Four, three, two ..." Jacques pointed his finger indicating that they were live.

Ricky got up and turned up the sound on his television, then tensely sat back down in his chair to listen to the breaking news.

"This is Robert DesOrmeaux of ATV Canada, your up-to-the-minute source for late breaking news. For the third time today, we are reporting to you from Montreal, the scene of another FLQ bomb that was discovered in a Canada Poste mailbox.

"Earlier today we observed the disposal of two other bombs by Sergeant Major Andre Carpentier, of the Canadian Army ordinance disposal unit, one which turned into an extremely dangerous situation. After carefully removing the bomb from the mailbox, because of its' proximity to the surrounding buildings, the Sergeant Major decided that it would be safer to move the bomb away from the buildings. To accomplish this, he had a fire truck extend their ladder to him, to which he secured the mailbox. As the fireman raised the ladder, the top rung caught the handle of the mailbox, toppling it sideways onto the concrete sidewalk. Carpentier and everyone else in the surrounding area dove for the ground, fearing an explosion, which fortunately did not occur. Eventually, the ladder truck swung the bomb into the center of the street, where it was safely disarmed by Carpentier.

Jacques silently pointed to the mailbox alerting Robert that he was off camera. As the camera panned the cautious activities around the bomb disposal van, Robert continued his reporting.

"Now, we see that Carpentier is being briefed by his commander who is viewing the bomb site through binoculars. He is pointing to the front access door of the mailbox and handing Carpentier a set of keys. The access he's pointing to is where the Canada Poste mailman retrieves mail, not the upper levered door, where mail is dropped in by the public."

Pausing a moment, signaling to his cameraman that he is ready for Lalonde, DesOrmeaux continued.

"While we await the bomb disposal efforts, we are fortunate to have with us Commander Lalonde, of the Montreal Police Bomb Squad, to gives us some expert insight into the procedures surrounding disarming a terrorist bomb."

"Thank you for joining us today, Commander Lalonde."

"Vous êtes les bienvenus." (you are welcome)

"Commander, what is the most important factor in handling these dangerous bomb situations?"

EATON'S – During the Second French Revolution

As the camera panned full face on Lalonde, he answered in impeccable English. *"Initially, we must secure the scene to ensure there is no danger to our citizens. This is done in cooperation with the local police who set up a perimeter, out of reach of any residual fallout from a possible explosive detonation. The subject bomb site is then surveyed from all angles by several disposal experts to determine if there are any exterior wires, secondary explosive devices, or possible booby traps that could hamper the disarming. When we are given a green light by our lead supervisor, the selected disposal officer will be briefed on the various possibilities of bomb type and given the required tools to approach the sight. Many bombs that we encounter are either static devices, which are much easier to approach, or motion sensor explosive devices that can explode with the slightest of motion disturbances. These recent mailbox bombs we have encountered have all been static timer bombs, meaning that they can go off at any time, preset by the bomber. These are extremely dangerous because until we get to see the timer, we have no idea what time it is set to detonate."*

Jacques panned the camera to include the subject mailbox along with both Robert and Lalonde in the foreground.

"Commander Lalonde, is there any way to accurately estimate how much time is left on the bomb before the officer approaches the bomb?"

"The simple answer is, no! It is a matter of careful deduction by the whole disposal team. For example, in the case of these recent bombs, five actively exploded prior to 5:00 A.M, and two were disarmed by Carpentier this morning. This gives us potentially solid intelligence as to what types of bombs we are dealing with. This information, coupled with the FLQ claims of responsibility, and their modus-operandi of always using simple timer bombs, affords our teams the ability to surmise the actual type of bomb we are faced with, and ..."

Robert interrupted, *"But you're still faced with the unknown timing aspect. How do you handle that?"*

Lalonde smiled, *"I was just getting to that. From what happened today with the previously disarmed bomb, we have recovered two undamaged timers and from a bombing last night, we recovered one intact timer face. The others were all destroyed. But, from these three remaining timers we can discern the actual times that they were originally set for detonation. And, considering the geographic locations, we can estimate the approximate time the perpetrators needed to travel between locations. Also, considering that they are using simple watches as timers we can calculate a maximum window from bomb placement, to bomb detonation, to be a maximum of twelve hours."*

"But what if more than one bomber were placing these bombs?" Robert asked.

"That is where it gets more difficult." Lalonde paused to collect his thoughts. *"That is where we must fall back on our experience of multiple bomb sights and hope that our calculations are correct. The one thing that is usually constant in multiple bomb placements, is that they will allow sufficient timer-spread to permit*

them to escape the area before any bombs detonate. With this information we can calculate a parameter of time for all the placements. Their goal is to create chaos, and to do so they will either set the timers for simultaneous detonations, or more realistically, set them for an average advanced detonation, of say, one hour between each detonation. But again, these are not stupid people, they may be taking our calculations into account and therefore setting the timers to explode randomly. Believe me, the goal of these criminals is to endeavor to harm, or even kill, to further their cause".

"If you, or your squad, were handling disarming this bomb instead of the Army Disposal Unit, would you do anything differently?"

Lalonde peered into the camera, shifting his weight from side to side, before continuing. "Ahhh, that's a difficult question, and the answer is based wholly on procedures, training, and experience. Carpentier has been successfully disarming bombs for more years than any of my squad. He knows what he has been trained to do, but more importantly, he has his years of ordinance disposal experience to draw upon.

Noticeably displeased with the answer DesOrmeaux re-asked the question. "But Commander Lalonde, my question was, would you do anything different under these circumstances?"

Lalonde's face flushed in anger as he pointed a menacing finger at Robert. "At a time like this, you are not going to get me to make a comparison between the Canadian Army procedures, and that of the Montreal Police Bomb Squad. Each agency has developed strict guidelines for disarming explosives, and who is to say which one is safer than the other. Believe me, Carpentier is an expert, and knows what the hell he is doing. Even though he may not have disarmed terrorist's bombs in a metropolitan area, his experience in military ordinance readily compensates for that inexperience."

"Sorry! I wasn't trying to get you to criticize Carpentier's methods," Robert quickly postured, trying to quell Lalonde's anger. "I guess I just wanted your overview as to how the Montreal Police Bomb Squad procedures might differ from what Carpentier is doing. For example, would your squad approach a live bomb without protective clothing? I'm sure our viewers are all wondering about that procedure."

Lalonde hesitated. "Well, no, rightfully, or wrongfully, our procedures differ significantly. In fact, we had a situation many years ago, when one of our disposal squad was badly maimed when an explosive device, consisting of a single stick of dynamite, detonated prematurely. This tragedy prompted radical safety changes in our procedures. In fact, the New York Bomb Disposal Tactical Squad provided us with a consultant who thoroughly modernized our approach to handling potential explosive situations, be they bombs, gas leaks, or other devices. The primary change was that of protection of our squad members, whereby new protective coverings were suggested for approaching an explosive device. This protective gear consisted of a heavily matted top, pants, gloves, and boots that were interlaced with inner metal plating. Also, full cover metal head gear, with half inch protective glass, was required for face protection. It was also suggested that we use a combination of sandbags and protective matting to limit the force of any potential explosion around the bomb site. Additionally, a heavily armored bomb detonation and/or transport vehicle was to be used when bombs could not be disarmed on site. All these suggestions were implemented within our procedures, three years ago. We have not ..."

Robert interrupted Lalonde, again.

"But, respectfully, without making comparisons, what do you make of Carpentier not wearing this type of protective clothing?"

Lalonde again looked annoyed at the interruption. "I was just getting to that. The first major problem with the protective gear is the cumbersome weight, which seriously affects traversing mobility and visualization of the officer. A typical disposal unit outfit can weigh as much as 110 pounds, and combined with demolition suppression tools, this is an incredible weight to carry. Secondly, the protective gloves, because of their bulkiness, make handling disposal tools, and fine wires connected to most bombs, an exceedingly difficult challenge, if not dangerous. Third, and most importantly, the head gear viewing plate, because of its thickness, tends to distort the officer's vision. This negative vision factor is paramount when working with the intricacies of bombs in small, enclosed spaces. Just imagine thick gloves trying to maneuver around the wires connected to a small watch face. And, to answer your question about Carpentier's lack of protective apparel, he is not alone in his decision not to wear this gear. Although it is mandatory for our squad to wear the gear, many other squads throughout Canada, and the states, have chosen not to do so. The controversy centers around whether the gear is more of a liability than an asset in bomb disposal. Apparently, Carpentier has, with his vast experience, weighed the value of the gear and elected not to use it. He has the final decision in this matter, considering it is his life at stake."

Lalonde paused as he listened to Carpentier's commander advise him that the front leg of the box was a quarter inch off the sidewalk and could cause a rocking motion, if Carpentier disturbed it. Carpentier slid a small wooden shim under the leg.

As Lalonde returned his attention to Robert, the camera focused exclusively on Carpentier as he picked up his small metal box of bomb disposal tools and cautiously viewed the mailbox from all angles.

Ricky glanced over at his daughter now sweetly sleeping in her playpen, her head resting on Ruggles, her treasured teddy bear. He thought of all the tragedies that had gone on in his beloved Montreal and held his breath as he watched the officer begin the bomb disposal.

Ricky looked down at his sleeping daughter and sighed. *"Darlin', I am really not sure what kind of a world will be left for you when all this madness is finally over."*

The Second French Revolution had begun!

Two

Ricky was overcome by the Westmount and Montreal area FLQ bombings. As he waited for the continuation of the live T.V. report, he watched and prayed for the all-clear notification that everyone so needed to hear.

Ricky's mind sought refuge in thoughts of an easier time in his life; his beginning days at the Eaton's Montreal store.

Little Ricky, as he had been affectionately referred to by the older basement department employees, had been the envy of all the other carrier boys servicing the selling floor. At just fifteen and a half he could do the work of three of his peers. His job was to collect parcels in his large wooden roller cart, which were slated for delivery to customers, bringing them to the shipping room, where they would be sorted and loaded onto delivery trucks. The one thing everyone noticed was that *Little Ricky* always ran to do his pickups in each department. With his flaming red hair, skinny build and smiling freckled face he was the dream child of all the elderly lady employees.

He was an aggressive, non-complaining boy who would do anything, for anyone, while always displaying a pleasant smile on his face. Whether it was picking up goods from the cleaners for a basement manager, going to Ben's Delicatessen to pick up smoked meat sandwiches for the late-night staff, or simply going to the cash office for change for the cashiers, *Little Ricky* was totally dependable. He could be counted on to arrive at work on time, to always ensure that the holding bins were kept empty and the last-of-the-day delivery parcels got to the delivery room on time.

What *Little Ricky* did not reveal was that he hated high school and constantly chose working at Eaton's over his curriculum. This choice resulted in bad grades and constant reprimands from his parents and teachers. Eaton's offered him an escape from the drudgery of school, and the welcome escape from his verbally abusive, and domineering mother. However, as he reached the age of 18, he was free of school, and available to work full time at Eaton's, which became his focus in life.

Initially, Ricky began his rise in the basement store with his promotion from carrier to stock boy, then to lead stock boy and finally as a commissioned shoe salesman in the men's shoe department. He loved working with customers and excelled in sales results. To make himself a more valuable employee, Ricky studied to prefect the much-needed French working language.

His aggressive work ethic favorably noted on his every performance assessment, and by the age of 19 he had again been promoted, this time, to assistant manager of the shoe department, which included control over department buyers, creating advertising and handling full department duties when his manager was absent. With his department manager's retirement, he again made company history by being promoted to full department head, the youngest in the Eaton cross country chain of stores. Ricky's cross Canada buying responsibility, his history of making historic annual shoes sales revenues, and most notably, the sheer volume of footwear purchases, identified him nationwide as, "The Shoe King of Canada."

By the age of just 21, Ricky's historical success at Eaton's continued as he achieved merchandise manager status of several basement departments, ultimately controlling a staff of more than 125 employees.

Although in his professional capacity, Ricky felt very capable, in his appearance, he was less than secure. He felt that the traces of boyhood that still lingered made it harder for him to lead. His build was still on the skinny side, and his auburn red hair made him standout in a way that made him uncomfortable. He wore his hair above the ears and back, as company policy dictated, but his long sideburns were his signature rebellion against the archaic Eaton dress code regulations. His skin showed subtle traces of an acne problem from his youth, while his faint childish freckles gave his face the appearance of a 14-year- old.

But there was something imposing and disarming about Ricky. Although his appearance and body proclaimed young and inexperienced, his commanding aura and interaction with others displayed intelligence and control way beyond his years. One of Ricky's greatest attributes was his stellar knowledge of retail merchandising, and in particular, his fashion expertise, which was meticulously favored in his personal attire.

For Ricky, achieving so much at such a young age was a miracle since his life up until that time had been disappointing. Ricky had zero athletic abilities. He couldn't pitch, hit, or catch a baseball; he was frightened of football contact; and most extraordinary, living in a country obsessed with hockey, Ricky never learned to ice skate.

When he was given an opportunity to work at Eaton's, his whole life changed. This was more than just a job; this experience was a new beginning in an adopted family atmosphere. It was as if his goals mirrored that of Eaton's, and as such, they experienced growth together.

Ricky felt enormous pride to be amongst Eaton's architectural treasures. Whether it was the ornate metal ceiling panels, the old-fashioned lighting with wooden paddle fans, the hundreds of 1940's sale tables, the hand controlled antique elevators or, the last of its kind, narrow wooden escalators, his pride of involvement was consistently overwhelming. *Little Ricky* was now a pivotal part in continuing the commercial legacy of the T. Eaton Company, Canada, Ltd.

After several unsuccessful business ventures, Timothy Eaton had bought a retail store location in Toronto, originally, *The Timothy Eaton Company, of Canada, Ltd*, a dry goods and haberdashery store, with the motto, *"sound goods, good styles and good value."* That first Eaton's store was only 24 feet by 60 feet, with two shop windows, and a miniscule staff of only two men, a woman, and a young boy. That first foray into the retail business that was to earn him a place as one of Canada's greatest and most successful businessmen. He earned his company a place in the growth and history of this fast- developing nation.

Under Mr. Eaton's superb expert tutelage, his empire grew to become a mega-retail and social institution in Canada, encompassing stores throughout the nation and buying offices across the globe.

As a retail trade leader, The T. Eaton Co. Canada, Ltd. pioneered numerous retail innovations that later became standards in the industry. In an era when haggling for goods was the norm, the chain proclaimed, *"We propose to sell our goods for CASH ONLY, and in selling goods, to have only one price."* Also, Eaton's slogan, *"Goods Satisfactory or Money Refunded,"* was capitalized upon by other future retailers."

In 1883, Eaton's moved from their original small store to one with three full floors featuring an impressive varied 35 departments. History records that it had the largest plate-glass street display windows in Toronto; the first electric lights in any Canadian retail store and became the first store to install an elevator in a retail establishment in Toronto.

During this phenomenal growth period, Timothy Eaton introduced his first ever mail-order catalogue to Canadian consumers integrating the vast expanse of the nation, which remained a largely rural country. These catalogues offered everything from clothing and furniture, to farming equipment, and even prefabricated houses. In the rural settlements, isolated communities and small towns that dotted the Canadian landscape, the arrival of Eaton's catalogue was a major event. It allowed people to avail themselves of the opportunity to purchase an array of products that were otherwise unattainable. Soon this home-shopping catalogue was found in the homes of almost every Canadian.

In 1907, John Craig Eaton, the son and eventual heir of the Eaton dynasty, was largely responsible for expanding Eaton's business from its primary Toronto birthplace by building a new combined retail store and mail order operation in Winnipeg. This landmark store became an overnight success. Within weeks of the store's opening, the staff grew from 750 to 1200 employees. And by 1919, the Winnipeg complex covered 21 acres and employed 8000 people. For years, the store was considered the largest and most successful department store in the world and was said to be the true forerunner of the modern mega-shopping malls. The store would come to boast its own hospital clinic, water supply, library, restaurants and even its own fire department.

In 1911, Saturday Night magazine declared, *"Never before in the history of the world has it been possible for a store to be run on this humanitarian basis of beauty, use and efficiency. All of Canada was proud of Eaton's; and Canada should be, for here we find a store that has set the world pace in modern merchandising."* Also, the Illustrated London News stated, *"The T. Eaton Co. of Toronto can now claim that their stores are the greatest in all of the British Empire." The* Canadian Magazine estimated that, *"Winnipeggers spent more than 50 cents of every shopping dollar, (excluding groceries), at Eaton's. And that on any busy day, one out of every ten Winnipeggers would be visiting the Eaton store."*

From his fascination and tireless research of the overall company history, Ricky had discovered that, "his" Eaton's store, as he affectionately referred to it, began its Montreal operations in the spring of 1925 with the purchase of the old six-story Goodwin's Department Store. Subsequently, it expanded to a full nine stories, and an unprecedented million plus square feet, in the early 1930's.

The downtown Eaton's Montreal store was more than just brick and mortar, it became home to thousands of employees and millions of loyal customers; a place where dreams and aspirations survived, eventually manifesting into reality. A place Ricky Dean could call, "home." Ricky often thought that *with continued commitment to his merchandising career goals, perhaps, one day, he too would become a small part of the perpetuation of Mr. Eaton's dream and legacy.*

As he was reliving the legacy of Eaton's, Ricky heard the ATV reporter's voice launching him back to the frightening reality of present news events.

⚜ Three ⚜

Reporter, Robert DesOrmeaux was the youngest reporter in the ATV Canada news lineup. Coming from a prominent family of vast wealth, Robert had rejected a journalism scholarship at McGill University, in Montreal, alternately choosing the prestigious Arthur L. Carter Journalism Institute at New York University. His ultimate career goal was to become a reporter with a TV news network in the states.

After his cum laude graduation, Robert landed an intern position at station, WENY, in New York City, where he excelled as an investigative street reporter. This position was short lived, when, reporting on a violent teen rape in Central Park, he mistakenly disclosed the name of the juvenile victim. Fearing legal retribution from the victim's family, Robert was dismissed from the WENY news bureau.

To resurrect his career, Robert became a freelance reporter for several Canadian radio and newspaper outlets. With hard work and perseverance, he was eventually able to overcome the stigma of his U.S. reporting disaster.

He was eventually given an opportunity to write a prime investigative article chronicling the high-level corruption in Quebec's Water Authority. This journalistic piece was picked up by the national wire services, which ultimately brought him to the attention of ATV Canada news department. For the last two years, Robert had been relegated to reporting minor events such as: school construction, dignitary visits, and traffic reports. These assignments became his regular beat, until today when fortune smiled down upon him.

While observing Carpentier's advance on the mailbox bomb, Robert continued his questioning of Commander Lalonde.

Ricky breathed a sigh when he finally heard the reporter's voice. Once again, he sat on the edge of his seat watching the horrific events of the day unfolding before him.

"Commander Lalonde, can you tell our viewers the protocol Mr. Carpentier's will use in his attempt to disarm the bomb?"

"Yes," he replied, "as you can see, he made his approach very cautiously, his full attention directed at the path towards the bomb site. Although he is convinced the bomb is another timer explosive device, he can't take any chances of tripping or dropping his toolbox just in case the explosive device is motion sensitive. He has now placed his toolbox to the left of the mailbox and is carefully walking around it, inspecting the area, looking for any foreign object not visible through the binocular surveillance."

The camera was centered on Carpentier as he finished his inspection and gave a "thumbs up," indicating there were no other visible explosive devices, or booby traps. Then, it homed in on him kneeling cautiously in front of the mailbox.

Lalonde continued his observation. "Andre is now carefully opening his toolbox, selecting each of his tools, and placing them on the ground to the right of the mailbox. He has no idea if the explosive device has been secured to the bottom access panel, which would cause detonation when the panel is opened. He has placed the master key in the panel and with his other hand he will carefully open the panel, only slightly so he can see if any wires are connected from the bomb to the door panel."

"This next move is a crucial step," Lalonde continued. "He will make a visual examination through the small opening while continuing to maneuver the panel, inch by careful inch. Again, everything seems to be clear, Andre just gave another, 'thumbs up!' Next, he will fully open the panel access door, exposing the device, which as you can see, is partially covered with parcels and letters."

"Jacques, see if you can get a close-up view of the contents inside the box," Robert directed his camera man.

EATON'S – During the Second French Revolution

Lalonde continued his explanation. *"There is definitely a bomb in the mailbox. Andre is taking a moment to appraise the situation before extricating the device from the mailbox. So far, no booby trap wires have been detected connected to the access panel. He is lying on the ground to get a clear view all around, and under the explosive device. He must remove the several mail envelopes and parcels that had been placed in the box, so he can get a clearer view of the total contents with his mirror tool."*

"After placing the mail and parcels to the far left of the box Andre has given another, 'thumbs up' indicating that the area around the bomb is secure. He has gotten back into his kneeling position, and he is now showing signs of intense tension and concentration as he prepares to remove the bomb from the mailbox."

"Wouldn't it be safer to disarm the bomb without moving it?" Robert inquired.

"Normally it would be," Lalonde responded, *"but because of the confined working area, Andre doesn't want to get his tools hung up on the sides of the mailbox. Also, he needs a clear view of the whole explosive device before he can begin disarming it. It looks like he's ready. He placed his right hand to the side of the explosive device and now, his left. At this point he will carefully elevate the bomb from the bottom of the mailbox, fixing a firm grip, as he begins to ..."*

Ricky could not believe what he was watching on the TV. There was a single loud sound, like a clap of distant thunder, a body flying through the air, then the screen went blank. Ricky felt panicked. He wasn't sure what had just happened. Within a few minutes the T.V. screen flashed back on, and the surreal scene came back into view.

Ricky sat horrified by the scene that he was witnessing.

Chaos had broken out at the bomb sight. The thunderous explosive sound was followed by an immense fireball with searing heat that permeated over the officers and ATV staff. The camera Jacques was holding was violently hurled to the ground, taking him along with it, and rendering the camera feed silent.

Most of the hordes of onlookers were thrown or propelled as screaming was heard everywhere. People were fleeing as fast as they could to outrun the flames and shrapnel which burst forth from the disintegrating mailbox. The intense heat enveloped those closest to the explosion, followed by a severe gust of hot wind. Those closest to the blast would only have heard the ear-piercing sound for less than one second with most experiencing a temporary loss of hearing, followed by a painful ringing noise that caused them to fall to the ground clutching their ears. Pandemonium broke out throughout the blast area.

Jacques regained control of himself instantly searching for the camera, finding it buried in piles of debris, under the van. He cautiously slid his body under the van where he grabbed the camera. Once he was able to remove it completely, he staggered to his feet. He couldn't believe the camera was still functioning. Jacques immediately panned the scene of destruction before him, his head shaking in disbelief.

In his viewfinder he saw Robert lying face down, on the ground. *"Are you okay, boss?"* he asked.

"Yes," Robert moaned. *"I think I just got the wind knocked out of me."* Robert opened his eyes to see his cameraman standing over him. *"Forget about me! Where is the damn camera? Is it still working?"*

Relieved, Jacques answered, *"Yes boss, I got it out from under the van, and somehow it seems to be able to transmit."*

"Get that goddamn camera running. We can't afford to miss any of this!" Robert sputtered, as Jacques began filming.

Robert got to his feet and shouted, *"Over there Jacques! Over there! Carpentier is on the ground. Get a close up, then pan the whole area."* Robert began to brush the soot from his previously immaculate suit, but it was impossible. Then, he realized this is what he should look like in this scene. Though he wanted to choke, to run, he knew this was his job to report what was happening. He surveyed the area as he told Jacques, *"Zoom in on all the scraps of metal, then back to Carpentier and hold. I'll voice over your shot."*

Robert found Lalonde and heard him muttering, *"Mon dieu! Mon dieu! Ils ete morte,"* My God! My God! He is dead, he wailed. He got up on his knees and made the sign of the cross on his chest. *"Ils ete morte, pour vous!"* He is dead, for sure!

"The scene is still active," Lalonde shouted, placing himself between the advancing officers and Carpentier, who was lying contorted on the ground. He had been propelled yards away from the mailbox. One of his arms was lying several yards beyond his lifeless body, *"Bring the ambulance up here, now! And get the bloody camera crew out of here!"* he directed a dazed police officer.

Jacques continued filming, while being forcibly removed from the scene. He was able to capture the commander halting the rush of his men, as he slowly approached Carpentier's still body. Lalonde knelt beside him examining what was left of his face. Shaking his head in disbelief." *He is dead,"* he shouted back to the stunned officers, with tears streaming down his face. With his head bowed in prayer, he signaled for the waiting paramedics to attend respectfully to Carpentier.

"We're going. We're going for Christ's sake!" Robert shouted at one of the officers who held him firmly by the arm and was escorting him towards the mobile press van. Another officer realized that Jacques was still filming and grabbed for the camera.

"We're the bloody press, ya' know," Robert protested.

The officer unhanded him while the other gave Jacques the camera with a look of warning to leave the scene.

Robert continued shouting at them as the officers walked away. *"We're supposed to be covering stuff like this. We are the free press! Our viewers want to know all the bloody world wants to know!"* But, his angry words of protest fell on deaf ears, as an ambulance screamed towards the scene of carnage.

EATON'S – During the Second French Revolution

"My one big chance for international exposure, and I end up with only half a story!" Robert thought.

All the TV viewing public where aware of was that the T.V. signal had been interrupted. After what seemed like an eternity, Ricky finally heard an ATV announcer say, *"There has been a temporary interference to our signal. We will update you as soon as service is restored."*

Ricky, and millions of Canadians, had been left in the dark as to what had really happened at the bombing scene.

⚜ Four ⚜

Ricky sat in shock. The images that had appeared on the TV before the screen went blank were horrifying. The deafening explosion that was heard at that moment was enough to panic all of Montreal.

"What the hell!" Ricky mumbled, as he sat, eyes glued to the screen, watching the return of the broadcast news.

At the forced insistence of a shaken MPD officer, cameraman Jacques Gauthier, moved the ATV Canada mobile transmission van back a half block from the bomb site, where his crew re-setup for his live feed. DesOrmeaux stopped for a moment when he caught a glimpse of his face in the van's mirror. He tried to remove a smudge from his face as he combed his disarrayed hair.

"What the hell are you doing, boss?" Jacques yelled.

"What do you mean, 'what the hell am I doing," Robert asked, angrily. *"I'm getting ready to resume the live feed, that's what I'm doing."*

"You've just been part of a friggin' explosion, part of a historic event, and you want to look like you just stepped out of the studio. What the hell are you thinking? You think that Peter Jennings reports from a war zone in his best dress suit?" Jacques threw up his hands in disgust.

Realizing his error Robert stammered. *"Oh, oh, ... this whole thing has got my bloody brain scrambled. Come over here,"* he commanded Jacques.

As Jacques approached, Robert grasped him in a bear hug, rubbing his body against him.

"What the hell are you doing?" Jacques pulled away in horror.

"I'm trying to get some of that crap off your clothes and onto mine, so I can look the part."

"Okay, okay, but that's not the way. Come over near the van."

Jacques rubbed his hand against the explosion soot that had been propelled onto the outside wall of the van, then spread the dirt on Robert's shirt, tie, and suit. He finished by streaking soot down the sides of Robert's face and forehead, then mussed up his hair.

Standing back, he viewed his efforts. *"Now, you look the part, boss. And it wouldn't hurt if you stammered a bit during your report, like you are still in shock."*

"Thanks, you saved the day. Maybe you should be the one in front of the camera instead of me," Robert laughed, surveying his disheveled appearance, as he wiped more soot onto the back of his hands.

Shaking his head in total incredulity of the carnage before him, he questioned his cameraman. *"Is the bloody feed up yet. We've had dead air for over 8 minutes. Control is going to freak."*

"I talked with them and they're looping your earlier telecast until we can get back on air. Francois has them on the line, right now," Jacques replied, pointing to a crew member talking on a payphone down the block. *"We'll be up and ready in five, boss."*

While he waited, Robert forced his way through the crowded MPD officers asking the question that was in the forefront of everyone's mind, *Is Carpentier dead, or alive?* The consensus among the crowd was that he was dead, but that had yet to be confirmed.

He watched as the paramedics surrounded Carpentier, feverously working to administer medical attention, so hopefully, he was not dead!

Jacques signaled Robert that they were ready again as he returned to the transmission van. *"We're live in two minutes, boss. Control says they have edited the explosion footage, so it is not so gory for the audience. You're going to be doing a voice over when you get to that piece, okay?"*

"Three, two, one." Jacques counted down as he pointed at Robert.

Ricky turned up the sound on the T.V. as the reporter began broadcasting.

"This is Robert DesOrmeaux reporting live for ATV Canada at the scene of a horrendous mailbox bomb explosion in Westmount. Our previous broadcast was interrupted when a bomb that was being disarmed by Canadian Army Ordinance Specialist Andre Carpentier exploded throwing shrapnel throughout the area. As you can see," Robert signaled Jacques to pan the area, *"debris littered the street and sidewalks up to twenty-five yards in all directions. Pandemonium broke out amongst the crowd of watchers, as law enforcement scrambled to restore order. The ambulance core and paramedics were quick to respond, but initial reports stated that tragically Andre Carpentier has been killed by the blast. He was the most recent fatality in the FLQ's bloody quest for French independence in Quebec.*

"Hold on, something is happening," Robert pointed to Lalonde who was running towards his assembled bomb squad.

"Mon dieu, il est vivant," My God, he is alive, Lalonde shouted.

Having witnessed Carpentier's body careening through the air from the explosion, Robert was dumbfounded and speechless in understanding Lalonde's comments. But seeing Jacques frantically waving his hand for Robert to talk brought him back to reality.

EATON'S – During the Second French Revolution

"Ssssorry, ladies and gentlemen," Robert stammered, *"but we've just heard that Andre Carpentier is alive! I repeat Andre Carpentier has somehow miraculously survived the incredible bomb blast. We see that the paramedics are loading him onto a stretcher and a doctor, who just arrived at the scene, is administering something intravenously.*

"I ask the indulgence of the viewing audience as we attempt to get Commander Lalonde to confirm that Andre Carpentier is alive and his current condition."

The camera showed Lalonde shooing Jacques away with a wave of his hand. Jacques ran his hand in a slicing movement across his throat signaling Robert to end his broadcast. He then panned the crowd of shocked observers, the milling MPD officers and the littered debris strewn across the explosion area.

"It appears the Commander is occupied and unable to comment at this time, so we'll turn you back to our regular programing. We will proceed to the hospital to follow up on Andre Carpentier. We will return to live coverage when we have new information. This has been a day of horrors for the citizens of Montreal. Let us band together in prayer for the victim of today's violence." After a second of bowing his head he continued, *"This is Robert DesOrmeaux reporting from the scene for ATV Canada."*

Jacques signaled that they were off air. *"Man, that was totally surreal. And, within hours every news agency in the world will be looking to you for a comment."*

"Yeah, well let's just get this wrapped and get down to the Royal Vic Hospital to see what is happening with Carpentier. We can return to the studio for editing and follow up. I'm sure that either Harvey Kirk or Peter Jennings is going to want to talk to me before they do the 12:00 noon national broadcast."

"Got it, boss," was Jacques' simple reply.

Ricky could not take it anymore and switched off the TV. He walked over to where Darlene was still sleeping and lifted her from the playpen. His hands were shaking as he wrapped them around his precious sleeping daughter. He secured his grip and carried her to the crib in her bedroom. As he watched her sleep, he wondered what was next.

How could ATV allow that man being blown up to be broadcast on live TV. I thought they had a five second delay to prevent people from seeing that horror. Ricky hoped his beautiful girl would never have to see what he had witnessed today.

Ricky caressed Darlene's back as she slept in her crib. *This whole province has gone to hell my little darling, and if your daddy is not careful, he could be confronted with a live bomb at Eaton's one day. But, someday, I promise you that I will find a way for us to escape all this craziness, if it is the last thing that I do."*

⚜ Five ⚜

Ricky was still terribly troubled by the horrific mailbox bombing that he had witnessed on TV the day before. He could not shake the ghastly image of the bomb disposal man hurling through the air as the mailbox exploded. Mercifully, in subsequent broadcasts, ATV had removed the original gruesome scene. The only solace was the later ATV report that Andre Carpentier had miraculously survived the attack but remained in critical condition in a coma.

Being back at Eaton's for his shift also helped ward off these negative thoughts. He was anxious for his lunch break and his cribbage game in the manager's lounge. Over the past few years these lunch hour games had become a financial windfall for Ricky. He had honed his skills and was handsomely rewarded with supplemental income. Even at ten cents per point down, his cribbage winnings provided some extra dollars for a few luxuries he would not have otherwise been able to afford. And today, Pierre Lafontaine, the home furnishing manager, was to be there for the picking.

"How is it possible that every day I walk around my home like a zombie in a horrible foul mood, but when I enter the Eaton's store, my mood is lifted to unimaginable heights." Ricky thought. "I've got to do something about my marriage disaster before I blow my brains out."

"Good morning, Samantha," he stopped to talk to the salesgirl in the cosmetic's department. "How are you handling your new baby duties along with working?"

"That's what mothers-in-law are for Mister Dean?" she laughed.

"I suppose if you train them properly."

A moment later he was startled by a gasp. He looked up and saw a woman ten feet in front of him stepping onto the down escalator, with a baby carriage. "Help," she suddenly yelled.

He could see both her footing and the carriage were not positioned quite right. Ricky ran to overtake her and position himself in front of the baby carriage. He could see the fear in the mother's eyes.

"Ma'am, don't panic, just do as I say," Ricky calmly instructed her, as he looked back at the fast-approaching exit at the bottom of the escalator. "When I lift the front of the carriage, I want you to lift up on the back handle, so the carriage is off the treads, do you understand?"

She nodded.

"Good, then when we get to the bottom just slowly walk off with the carriage held in the air, okay?"

She nodded again. They were almost at the bottom and Ricky could see her hands shaking.

EATON'S – During the Second French Revolution

He carefully stepped backward off the escalator, with the carriage in hand and held on until the frightened lady and her child were safely away from the menacing steel treads. He nodded to her, and they both lowered the carriage to the safety of the floor.

The woman pulled the baby out of the carriage, caressing it to her chest, with tears streaming down her face. "Thank you, thank you so much!" she cried. "I am so, so sorry. I wasn't paying attention and then I was on the escalator and couldn't think of what to do next."

"You are quite welcome, Ma'am." Ricky could see her trembling all over and led her to a place where she could sit down. "The main thing is that you didn't panic, and everything worked out simply fine. I would suggest that in the future that you stay clear of the escalators and use the elevators located against the far walls," he said, pointing in each direction.

She tried to laugh but was still too traumatized.

"Now, are you sure you're okay? Would you like a cup of water?"

The woman clung to her child and just nodded.

"I have a young daughter too, so I know how frightening this was, but you are both safe now!"

A crowd had gathered on the floor above and Ricky called up to say that everything was okay.

As he got her some water he asked Samantha from the cosmetics counter, to come down and sit with the lady, until she calmed down.

She said, "You have already been so kind. I am in your debt!"

"No problem. That is what I am here for."

"Someone needs to invent a device that stops carriages and strollers from getting on these escalators, before someone gets seriously mangled!" Ricky thought as he continued towards his shoe department.

Richard Dean was no longer *Little Ricky*, but the golden boy of Eaton's downtown store. To compensate for his lack of formal education, he attended every available marketing course and found every marketing instructional book he could get his hands on to better prepare him for his career in retail merchandising. Whether it was a simple Dale Carnegie course, or David Townsend seminar, Ricky fought tirelessly to satisfy his insatiable thirst for more business administration knowledge.

Ricky looked over the lady's shoe section with pride, mentally noting any customer neglect, out of place displays or any maintenance requirements. *"We need to get some curtains, or enclosure for the stock room areas so they are not visible to the public. I'll need to include that cost in the next quarter budget,"* he thought.

Today, the whole floor was his. Almost two full acres of selling area encompassing 15 different selling departments; all under his command; at least for today. One Saturday per month he assumed the duties of his boss, Jeremy

Radford, who was the basement floor merchandise manager. Today Ricky's authority was all encompassing. He had full control over all aspects of the basement level operation, including department managers, decades his senior. Ricky loved his job, the fascinating and diverse customers, the loyal staff, and even the historic smell of the basement level. His job was never boring. The constant anticipation of the "trauma of the day," kept the assigned floor manager constantly on their toes. Whether it was a shoplifter, an escalator accident, a medical emergency, or an irate customer; some event was destined to appear every day, without exception. But the best part of his job was that it kept him sane from the never-ending problems of his turbulent personal life.

As he walked around his department, Ricky saw his head cashier Margaret Hilbert, struggling to move one of the antique registers.

"What are you trying to do Maggie, break your back? Let me do it! That damn boat anchor weighs more than you do!"

"Hey Ricky. This monster has given up the ghost again. If we don't get some new registers soon, we are going to be up the creek without a paddle, on sale days. Main floor and second floor all got the new electronic ones and keep passing their junk down to us!"

As Ricky had run to help Maggie, he could not help but reflect on the horrific tragedy that surrounded this incredible woman.

At just under five foot and about one hundred and ten pounds, Maggie had rosy cheeks, a pronounced dimpled chin and piercing blue eyes that were very disarming. Although her electrifying smile and kind facial features projected the image of everyone's grandmother, the strength of her riveting bass voice commanded the attention of all her subordinates.

After over thirty years working in the basement shoe department, Maggie ran her domain with the skill and discipline of an army sergeant major. The one thing Ricky respected most about Maggie, and everyone in her department knew, was that she would not tolerate incompetence or unprofessional behavior within her realm of responsibility.

But her personal story is what got to everyone's heart. Apparently, after a family-day outing at a soccer game to celebrate her son Jimmy's seventeenth birthday, they were involved in a horrendous accident on the Bonaventure Expressway. The Montreal Star reported that they were rear-ended by the driver in a large dump truck. The collision propelled their small car over the three-foot concrete guardrail and sent it plummeting forty feet down through an apartment building roof. Her son and husband were killed instantly, along with two elder seniors who had been eating lunch at their kitchen table.

Maggie had been thrown from the rear seat and suffered multiple lacerations, a broken leg, and a severe concussion. After a difficult operation at Royal Victoria Hospital to relieve pressure on her brain she was mercifully placed into an induced coma for three weeks.

EATON'S – During the Second French Revolution

Once they were able to bring her out of the coma, she had to endure months of extended physical therapy. But the damage to her body was nothing compared to the damage to her life. She underwent grief counseling, and eventually was well enough mentally and physically to return to work. The identity of the dump truck driver was never discovered, and the accident file remained an open manslaughter case.

Now, three years later, at the age of fifty-eight, Maggie's total focus was directed towards her work, and her dreams of retirement where she planned to move to her only daughter's home in Florida.

"Thanks! I know these are ancient, but you realize that neither of us will live long enough to see the newfangled machines, eh?" Maggie responded, cleaning her hands on a paper towel.

"Yes, Maggie, but you realize that we are the basement operation, and that means crap flows downhill right into our department. We'll just have to make do with their hand-me-downs," Ricky commented as he struggled to move the register onto the floor. Amazed that even he could manage moving the awkward 100 plus pound register he said, "Maggie, when you see Serge, have him take this bloody thing up to maintenance for repair, and have him bring down two functioning backups." Serge Koswalski was a shoe department section head, and in charge of the lower stockroom.

Scanning the shoe department Ricky asked, "Is Duane back from lunch, yet?" Duane Hutchison was his assistant shoe department manager.

"I saw him get off the elevator a few minutes ago, but I think he went down to the stockroom to see Serge about the Urban Rubber shipment."

Ricky glanced at the fading battery indicator on his pager. "Can you give him a call and tell him I'm leaving for lunch, and he'll have the floor?" Ricky was always anxious to inject himself into the personal lives of his staff, so he asked, "Are you still going to see your daughter and grandkids over the Christmas holidays?"

"Yeah! Can't wait. Two weeks of sunshine and spoiling."

Maggie got on the intercom. "Duane, Ricky's going to lunch and wants you up here on floor patrol duty, stat." She heard the reply, "Okay, I'll tell him."

"He's on his way up, but said to tell you that once again, we have a major screw up with the Urban Rubber order."

"Oh, crap, not again," Ricky fumed angrily, remembering the nightmare of the last Urban screw up that almost caused a riot.

Ricky remained calm while he waited for Duane, continuing his conversation with Maggie. "It's great that you're going to Florida for the Christmas holidays."

"Yeah, but it's starting to become a major disaster."

"Why? Weren't you just going to fly down, drink in the sunshine and get your grandbaby fix with your daughter?"

"I just wanted to relax, but Myron hasn't seen his family forever, and wants to visit all his cousins that now live in Miami Beach," she laughed.

Myron was the owner and supplier of Gracious Feet lady's footwear, and Maggie's first male companion since her husband's death.

"So, what's wrong with that? You'll have a companion, and he'll be around to spoil you when the grandbaby starts driving you crazy."

Maggie nodded. "Hang on a minute, Ricky," She was getting ready to go to lunch and went over to talk with her relief cashier.

Ricky took the opportunity to talk with Gordon Heinz, who was rearranging the Tana shoe polish display by the register stand.

"Hey, Mister Dean. How are you doing?"

"Hi Gordon. When you get a moment, I want you to straighten and inventory this Tana rack and pass along your list to Carol Levesque to place a fill-in order. With the holidays coming up, we need to make sure that we don't run out of any of these suggestive selling products."

"Sure thing, Mister Dean. Do you want me to include the racks in ladies and children's shoes also?"

"Yes please," Ricky replied feeling a special kinship to this Tana product line, since when he was an assistant manager, he had been the one to introduce this revolutionary product to the Eaton's national merchandising product line. Even with the historically dominant competition of the established shoe polish lines like Kiwi and Esquire, his introduction of the Tana shoe cosmetics line, their unique suggestive selling program and lucrative spiff incentives for the selling staff, resulted in Tana products being sold in every Eaton's shoe department throughout Canada.

"I'll be back in a minute," Ricky called to Maggie as he headed for the stairway to the subterranean stockroom. Just as he was about to descend, he collided with Duane, who had come sprinting up the old marble stairs.

"Don't ask!" Duane quickly stammered, cleaning the perspiration fog from his horn-rimmed glasses. "Every time we get a shipment from Urban Rubber it's either the wrong item, or they back-order half the shipment. I know their prices are good but, if we don't get what we need, pricing doesn't matter much. I don't know what more we can do. I know Carol has talked to their salesman, John Marquette, about these shipment problems on numerous occasions, but it's like talking to a wall," Duane shifted nervously from foot to foot.

Duane was Ricky's longest friend and mentor at Eaton's. He was in his mid-thirties, six-foot tall and rail skinny. To say Duane's attire was unfashionable was an understatement. His wardrobe consisted of baggy navy-colored slacks, brown brogue shoes and a tweed sport coat with leather elbow shields.

Ricky saw floorwalker/detective Katherine Middlestein sauntering towards them, and ushered Duane deeper into the seclusion of the stairwell.

EATON'S – During the Second French Revolution

"What the hell is going on with Urban?" Ricky snorted. "I thought we had that all ironed out and behind us. I've got a feature ad in the *Montreal Star* set for next Thursday, and now I have no friggin' inventory?"

Duane tensed at the rebuke. The job was taking a toll as shown by Duane's prematurely graying hair, but the real problem was that Duane was still old school, and he had no fashionable grooming sense.

Duane continued to explain, "Carol said, that their salesman assured her the back orders would be here no later than Wednesday next."

Carol Levesque was the rubber goods buyer and one of Ricky's newly promoted section heads. Her family had owned a large footwear manufacturing facility where she had worked as a teenager, giving her valuable experience as a footwear buyer. Some considered Carol not overly attractive because of her chunky build, pitch black hair and puffy face, but what she lacked in appearance she made up a hundred-fold in her bubbly personality.

"Yeah well," Ricky interrupted, "Urban's salespeople have made empty promises before. Remember, those pricks hung us out to dry with their failed delivery during our July Dollar Days sale. We were lucky our customers didn't lynch us. As it was, to satisfy the customers, I had to substitute the more expensive Dominion boot, which cost us thousands of dollars and, if you remember, because of our limited inventory we almost had a bloody riot on our hands."

Just then Katherine Middlestein entered the stairwell. "If you boys want some privacy, you could probably find a nice quiet corner down in the bowel room," she quipped, referring to the subterranean stock rooms.

Kate, as everyone referred to her, did not have the commanding appearance that one would expect of a store detective, but her extra weight made her five-foot one tiny stature seem much more powerful. On numerous occasions, Ricky had cautioned Kate about trying to detain a large shoplifter without any assistance, but to no avail.

Kate would regularly transform her appearance from average woman shopper to upscale business executive, just to blend in with the shopping crowd. Today she was outfitted in clothing that looked like her Salvation Army "bag lady" persona. To offset her boredom, Kate loved to kibitz with the staff.

"Actually Kate, we figured you could handle us both right here in the stairwell. So much more excitement that way, don't you think?" Ricky joked, watching the color drain from Duane's face.

"Well laddie, if ye think you gonna keeps me from trolling the harbor for them English frigates, with that fresh meat on board, you're daft. It'd take more than you two lads to wet me whistle," she giggled in her best brogue accent. "Well, you both have a good time, I must be off to keep the Eaton's fortune safe, ta ta," and with that, she began to climb the stairs to the main floor.

"Before you go Kate," Ricky retrieved a paper from his pocket, "does this make any sense to you? I found it lying on my desk when I arrived this morning.

Duane looked puzzled as Kate read the note aloud: *"His body is huge, his hair is red, His eyes search out his prey. He is getting ready to pounce, On his youthful boy selection of the day! The Shadow"*

"Christ on a rubber crutch! The Shadow strikes again!" she exclaimed, grabbing the note, and placing it in her large purse. "This Shadow's information has been great, but his secret identity is driving Tony crazy." Kate was referring to her boss Tony Cartwright, head of Eaton's security.

"What do you mean, have you gotten messages from this 'Shadow' before?" Duane questioned. He was puzzled by what he was hearing.

"Oh yeah! This is like the fifth one, and each one has been right on the money. We have caught two shoplifters, a counterfeit operator and a less than honest section head, all because of his, or her, tips. It's uncanny the knowledge this Shadow has about Eaton's operations. Tony suspects that this informant is an Eaton's employee," and then Kate admitted, "to tell you the truth, either way this Shadow is making our job a lot easier!"

"But what do you make of this message, and why was it put on my desk?" Ricky just could not understand the connection.

"First, I believe the rhyme is regarding a pedophile that we've been trying to catch for the last two months. The creep has been following young boys into the bathrooms where he sexually assaults them. This rhyme may be the first real lead to his identity. I'm going to have Tony put out a watch notice to all departments."

"But Kate, why my desk?"

"All the messages so far have been found in, and concern, specific basement operations. Two messages were found on luncheonette tables, one on the Laura Secord counter, one in Charlotte Henderson mailbox, and now, this one on your desk. Apparently, the Shadow has a special interest in the basement store. Why, I haven't a clue. But I have got to get this to Tony right away. If I find this asshole first, I'll cut his damn balls off, and shove them up his ass!"

Duane, embarrassed by Kate's off-color remarks, was noticeably relieved to see her go upstairs so that he could return to the Urban Rubber topic. "I don't know what else to do. Urban still has the best prices, compared to both Dominion and Acme."

"Pricing doesn't matter, Duane, if we don't receive the friggin' product. I'd rather pay a few cents more, and jack our sales price a bit higher, than must worry about delivery every time we have a sale. I know the owner Sauvignon is having some union problems, but I think if we start cutting back on some orders, he'll get the idea that we mean business. In the meantime, have Carol alert Dominion that we may need at least five hundred pairs of men's rubber overshoes, available for delivery next Wednesday. I'll contact Sauvignon and advise him that if the back orders are not here by close of business, Monday, the order is cancelled, and the total shipment we just received will be sent back to him, collect!"

"Okay, got it. Anything else?" Duane asked defensively.

"Don't take it personally, Duane. I know it is not your fault, or Carol's. I've been dealing with Sauvignon for years, and if we don't take the hard line with him, he'll run right over us. And remember, Carol has only been in her buying position for three months. She needs to firm up to make her suppliers understand that we are the largest purchaser of their products. If they can't keep up, then let them get out of the game. End of Story!"

Ricky felt bad for his friend. *"Duane will never change!"* he thought. *"He takes everything personally and backs away from taking responsibility for anything.*

Duane followed Ricky to the register area. "Anyway, what did you call me for?"

"Oh yeah, I just wanted to tell you that I'm going to lunch, and you have the floor. Check your pager batteries. Maintenance advised that many of the batteries are going bad and need to be replaced. And keep an eye on that back escalator. For some reason, it keeps tripping off and needs to be restarted from the main floor junction box, okay?"

Duane nodded, and immediately began checking his pager.

Ricky passed the register stand as he proceeded toward the north end elevators. He turned and called out to Maggie, "make sure Nora takes over when you leave for lunch. I do not want any of the juniors manning the registers alone. One of them got in trouble with her register last Saturday and had a line of customers backed up to the escalators."

"Yeah, I heard about it on Monday. Got it handled, boss. I now have a permanent back up register just in case that ever happens again. And I set a new schedule so that when I'm not here either Nora or Brenda will be supervising."

"Great! Thanks."

Ricky headed for the basement elevator, "Express to seven, Veronica," Ricky smiled at the operator as he stepped into the elevator.

"Anything for you, Mister Dean," she replied, batting her long eyelashes flirtatiously.

As the elevator ascended, he thought of his upcoming cribbage game. *"Now, it is time to take some money from Pierre."*

⚜ Six ⚜

When Ricky returned from lunch he headed toward Duane who was busy lacing up men's shoes on the display counter. As he approached Duane, he pointed to a sales table on the west side of the men's shoe section. "I need to talk to you about the men's slipper display table over by the wall?"

"I had the display rebuilt and mounted the mannequin high on top so it could be seen from across the different department sections. Why?"

"Well, the display is great, but the positioning is the problem."

"How so?" Duane asked.

"The elevation of the mannequin obstructs the view of the men's bathroom door."

"And?" Duane looked confused.

"You saw the new watch list on the pedophile that security wants us to be on the lookout for, right?"

"Yeah, and I had a staff meeting like you asked, and presented the description the security department came up with."

"That is all fine and good, but with that display so large and high the staff can't see who is entering and exiting the bathroom. The sales staff have been alerted to keep an eye on any suspicious activities, or characters around the men's room area, but when you get over to the register stand or the sections east of there, you can't see the doorway."

"Sorry, I never thought about that. I'll have the display moved immediately." Duane hastened across the department.

Looking back at Ricky, Duane stated, "Before you ask, the Urban Rubber problem has been solved and we should be really proud of Carol Levesque. She really stepped up to the plate this time."

"How so?" Ricky inquired.

"Well," Duane hesitated, "instead of handling Urban myself I told her that we decided that the problem was hers alone to solve. At first, she looked petrified but quickly recovered. And believe it or not, she came up with a remedy that even I would never have considered."

"What? She cancelled Urban and rebought from Dominion?" Ricky guessed.

"Better than that! She contacted accounting and found out that we owed Urban over $8600. in past payables that were due to be sent to them at the end of the month. Then, she pulled a bluff on the owner, Guy Sauvignon, that I would never have had the *balls* ..." Duane seldom used foul language.

"She told Sauvignon that she was packing up all the Urban inventory to be sent back to him, and that his payment would be held up until the offset return was calculated. She then added that Urban would be struck from the approved supplier roster, across Canada. That is when Sauvignon freaked out! He begged her to allow him to fix the problem. This is where it gets interesting. Sauvignon called her back within the hour and advised her that the complete shipment would be sent before close of business, today."

"I thought that he didn't have all the goods in stock and that was why it was delayed."

"Yeah, well, here's the kicker. Carol had intimidated Sauvignon so much that he called his competitor, Dominion, and purchased fill-in inventory just so he could send us a complete shipment. And Dominion raked him over the coals pricewise, so he would never forget that they bailed him out with us. I guarantee Carol will never have a problem with Urban again!"

"That is absolutely priceless, Duane. Tell Carol how proud we are of how she handled this nightmare."

"Already done, boss!" Duane placed the emphasis on the word *boss*, sarcastically regressing to his previous difficulties with Ricky. Duane was still having trouble getting used to his subordinate position to Ricky. At thirty-eight, he had considered that he would have been offered the promotion to manager of the basement shoe department, after the termination of former manager, Reginald Close, for theft. Apparently, Close had uncovered an imperfection in the refund procedure whereby he could arbitrarily issue fraudulent refunds which subsidized his gambling addiction. The fact was, he was just lucky his dismissal was handled quietly, "in-house," to avoid the public relations nightmare for the store if it got out. Ironically, several months after his termination, Close was discovered disheveled and frozen to death in his car at the Blue Bonnets Raceway parking lot.

When it was announced that Ricky, just twenty years old at the time, would be named manager of the basement shoe and teen fashion departments, Duane, after sixteen years of service, felt slighted.

Ricky knew Duane's value and tried at every turn to make him feel important. He gave Duane added responsibilities and told him what a great job he was doing. He knew he could not afford to lose Duane as an employee, or as a friend!

⚜ Seven ⚜

As Ricky was doing his floor circuit Detective Kate Middlestein grabbed his arm. "You look like you're off in Disneyland. Did you hear that we finally got the bastard?" she questioned, keeping pace with his long footsteps.

"You mean the sailor at the docks who stood you up?" he laughed.

She punched his arm again. "No, that disgusting pedophile that's been assaulting those little boys. We caught him in the act, in the bathroom by your shoe department. Now that the police have him in custody, we can't wait to see him convicted and sent to Bordeaux prison. I wonder how he'll like being somebody's bitch up there. Apparently, the *Shadow* saved the day for us, again!"

"How the hell is this *Shadow* getting this information before us?"

"That's what Tony wants to know. He's concerned that whoever this person is, they'll get hurt if they keep giving us information about these crimes." Just then Kate's pager sounded. "Got to go!" She ran for the nearest telephone.

Just as Ricky got to the north bank of antique elevators, his pager went off. He retreated to the closest available telephone which was in the Laura Secord Chocolate department. "I need to use your phone, Marissa," already dialing the page response number. "Dean, 8678," he responded.

"Yes, Mister Dean, security code 88, full evac. Acknowledge please?"

"Code 88, full evac, instructions verified, Dean 8678 acknowledged.

" Ricky replied curtly, dialing the basement area emergency response two-chime alarm. Waiting to hear the subtle chimes he advised Marissa, "Lock your register and then help direct the customers to the north bank escalators. We don't want a panic or for anyone to fall, so keep your voice calm, Marissa, as if this is an everyday routine drill. When all customers have gone up stairs, I want you to immediately follow them outside the store, understood?"

From the frightened look on her face, he added, "listen Marissa, I know this is your first evacuation, but you have already been trained for these measures. We get these threats every couple of weeks, and nothing ever comes of them. So, just do your job and don't worry."

"Yes Sir," she replied timidly.

Ricky ran to the pre-assigned rendezvous point, in the millinery department where the assigned emergency response store representatives, from every basement department, had already assembled.

"Okay, listen up." he began, "this may be just our regular crank call scare, or this may be the real thing. Either way, you are aware of your designated areas of responsibility and the required emergency procedures. The different obstacle we are faced with this time, is that this is a full store evac., top to bottom. So, that means that our customers could be colliding with existing customers coming down from the upper floors as they all are trying to exit. Get them moving quickly, but not so quickly that the customers become alarmed. Just tell them this is a regular drill and to continue in an orderly fashion to the nearest exit. Remember, after all the customers are evacuated, all staff members below section head are also to exit. I do not want anyone remaining on the floor that is not fully trained. Once everyone is safely off our floor, everyone is to meet back here for instructions from the Montreal Police Bomb Squad. Now, let's get going and get everyone out safely!"

Ricky grabbed Duane's arm as he was just about to leave, "I need you to get the cash office to lock everything in the vault, then get their staff the hell out of there, just in case this is some kind of a criminal diversion. Also, on your way, get all the west bank elevators, including the service one, down to our floor and ensure that they are locked down, and the operators also evacuated. Customers will be using the stairs and escalators only."

As Duane started to leave, Ricky hollered, "Oh, and I'll take care of checking that all the department registers are in secure lock down mode and post staff at the top and bottom of both escalators."

EATON'S – During the Second French Revolution

As Ricky saw Maggie helping an older lady onto the escalator, he assisted her in positioning the lady safely. "Have you seen Serge?" Ricky asked.

"Right behind you, boss," came the coarse reply.

"Great, Serge, I need you to make sure no one is in any of the stockroom areas. Then, check and lock all restroom doors and make sure the cooks in the luncheonette kitchen have everything turned off before they leave? We don't need a fire to add to the mayhem."

"Got it, boss," already grabbing the keys from behind the register column, Serge ran to check and lock the nearest restrooms.

Ricky never completely understood the executive directive to have employees participate in the dangerous task of searching for bombs. The consensus was that it was a matter of simple economics. If the task were left to the MPD Bomb Squad professionals, it would create numerous extra hours of lost store revenues. Since all previous threats had been false alarms, senior management had become complacent in thinking that there wasn't any real danger to employees assisting in the searches.

The basement evacuation proceeded calmly and orderly until police and emergency responders showed up on the scene. Customers became agitated at their sight and those exiting the store became panicked, now believing this was not a simple regular drill. Having a bomb suited officer shouting, "Allez, allez vit," *go, go, quick*, did little to settle their minds. Only the gentle prodding and calming assurances of his Eaton staff allowed the evacuation to continue without further panic.

The search itself was daunting. Each sales table had at least six deep drawers; the back stockrooms had thousands of shelves, the fitting rooms, register areas and every conceivable nook and cranny needed to be searched carefully. Even the stairwells, elevators, lockers and under escalators needed scrutiny. On direct instructions from the MPD Bomb Squad, the search staff were only permitted to do a cursory search, careful not to move anything that could disturb a possible bomb. If any suspicious item was discovered, the Eaton's employee was to immediately notify one of the roaming officers and evacuate the area in question. A two-bell alarm would then be sounded signaling searchers to go to a south end staging area, and a three-bell alarm signaling the north staging area, the greatest distance from the possible bomb threat.

Within seventeen minutes, all the emergency response store representatives had evacuated the basement level customers and were reassembled in the millinery department. Ricky spotted an MPD Bomb Squad commander approaching.

"Qui est responsable ici?" *Who is in charge here?* he demanded, in an imposing voice.

"I am, Sir," Ricky replied and then for the benefit of his mostly English-speaking staff he requested, "Anglaise, sil vous plait," *English Please.*

The commander asked, "Your people know the procedures, yes? No one takes chances. Just search and advise, yes?"

Ricky nodded, knowing very well that the commander understood that his staff had been through this procedure numerous times before.

Ricky reinforced the rules given to his people from the bomb squad commander. "Okay, everyone, you all know the drill. Search every possible nook and cranny, inside and out, and from top to bottom. If you see anything that looks unfamiliar, don't go near it, but immediately summon an MPD squad member. Then, get yourself out of there immediately. The MPD will be stationed strategically along the center aisles. So, let's get this done as fast and carefully as possible, and get back to business."

Within ten minutes of the start of the search Ricky heard the unmistakable two bell alarm, followed by a three-bell alarm signaling all searchers to proceed immediately to the staging areas.

Ricky peered from his vantage point in the south end and saw MPD Bomb Squad officers assembling in the main aisle adjacent to the lady's sportswear department. A sergeant was being assisted with donning a cumbersome padded suit complete with facial mask, protective boots, and gloves. Several other officers were lying on the floor, looking under surrounding sales tables, to gain a better insight into the possible threat.

Since none of the assembled employee searchers in the south staging area had sounded the alarm, Ricky had no idea where the possible threat item was located. He was surprised when he spotted Commander Lalonde of the MPD. The only reason he knew who the commander was because he saw him on the TV regarding the mailbox bombings in Westmount. But now, with Lalonde at this possible bomb scare, Ricky realized the gravity of the situation.

An officer approached to talk with Ricky, he struggled with the English, but his gist was hard to mistake. "Commander Lalonde say, Go to stairs."

Ricky thought about what the officer was saying. *"Boy, that does not sound too brilliant! Unless the stairwell has been searched from top to bottom this is the most dangerous area in the store. The shotgun effect of an explosion will catapult up and down the stairwell channel.*

"You mean you want everyone in the stairwells," Ricky questioned.

"Yes, stairs, now," the officer pointed to both east and west stairwells.

Ricky ushered the searchers to the stairwell, as the officer followed behind. Ricky stopped to ask, "What did they find?"

"Paper shopping bag, under table, lady department."

Down the center aisle Ricky could see the disposal expert begin to cautiously approach the possible threat. A long communication cord trailed behind him. "Go now!" the officer ordered, pointing Ricky to the stairwell.

EATON'S – During the Second French Revolution

The seriousness of a possible bomb explosion weighed heavily on Ricky ... he could see the concern on the faces of all his staff as they huddled in the stairwell.

⚜ Eight ⚜

After much posturing by the MPD Bomb Squad, the potential threat package was discovered to have been found to be empty; no doubt, disposed of by a customer. As the basement floor level was determined safe to resume the search, Ricky checked with Duane and Serge to ensure that all satellite areas were secure.

At 2:38, approximately two hours and forty minutes from the start of the bomb scare, the basement level search areas were posted as secure.

Ricky telephoned Security Central to advise them that the basement level evacuation was completed and that his search area was, "Code 99,"' complete with negative finds.

At 2:58 four chimes sounded signaling all floor areas were secure, allowing for the re-entry of all customers and non-essential employees that had been shivering outside on the street. By 3:15 the operations on the basement selling floor were back to normal.

Immediately following the settling of staff and customers, Ricky and Duane met in the luncheonette for lunch. Duane had asked to see him as soon as the crisis was over. Ricky selected two chili hot dogs and a coke, while Duane had his *everyday* signature double burrito, fries and a Seven-up. As they settled into a booth overlooking the selling floor, Duane commented on the bomb search results. "You know, one day, the way things are developing with the FLQ creeps, these bombs may become real, and a lot of our staff and customers could get killed or injured."

"I don't know, Duane, Prime Minister Trudeau seems to have a handle on this whole thing. He is totally unsympathetic towards the French violence to achieve separatism, and, considering he, himself is a Quebec born Frenchman, which takes a lot of balls. He has scoffed and ridiculed the rantings of Rene Levesque, and even lodged a formal U.N. complaint against the insightful statements made by Charles De Gaulle at the Expo opening, where De Gaulle shouted, "'Vive Quebec Libra!' Give me a break. How do you think this jerk would feel if some foreign dignitary went to France and suggested a revolution? Oh yeah, I forgot, they had one of their own in the 1800's and screwed it up royally."

Stabbing his French fry into a gob of ketchup, Duane seemed annoyed, "Well, you know Ricky you've become a bit like De Gaulle!"

Ricky almost choked on his chili dog as it became clear that Duane was on a tirade, as he continued. "Did you ever think that that would be you, Ricky? You came to Eaton's and changed everything and steamrolled right over me."

"Wow, where the hell did all this come from? Ricky wondered.

Ricky tried to get a word in, but Duane persisted. "You made sure to suck up to management and didn't care what 'revolution' *you* started. They loved you with your pretty boy looks and fancy clothes, and your dress boots clicking on the floor so everyone could hear you coming. So, when Close got caught, they didn't even look at my record." Duane needed to catch his breath before he went on. Now his voice reflected a more emotional state. "My years of devotion, my position, no, no they just pushed you in front of me, and you were supposed to be my friend. Some friend you turned out to be! But I took it! I took it all, the same way I take everything in my life, but no more! Today, this bomb scare ... NO, NO MORE!" Duane was almost yelling. I have had it with you and them and putting my life on the line for what? NO MORE! I quit!"

Ricky tried to say something, but Duane got up and took his empty lunch tray to the garbage and left!

Ricky started to go after him as Tony came into the lunchroom. "Hang a minute Ricky, I need to go over the security report from this bomb scare."

"Can't it wait, I really need to talk to Duane?"

"No, the brass and the MPD are all on my tail to get this done, asap!"

They worked on the report for over an hour and Ricky realized that Duane would be gone by then. Ricky hoped he could catch up with Duane later and that by then he would have calmed down, enough to listen to reason.

"Oh, also when I was trying to track you down," Tony continued, "I ran into Christine Guillaume, and she told me she thought you were headed in here. She asked me if I could let you know she wanted to see you sometime today before you leave. I thought it might be about the drill, but she said it was not critical. I think that girl has had some problems cropped up recently because she just hasn't been herself. And I'd keep an eye on her, you know because of that piece of garbage husband of hers!"

"What do you mean, 'keep an eye on her?'"

"Long story, but the quick version when I was in New York, I met Christine's father, William Bankowski. At that time, he was an international foreign trade adviser to the Canadian government. We kept in touch and when I was moving to Montreal, I did some moonlighting for him as an investigator."

"Over the years Bankowski accumulated substantial real estate holdings and became financially independent. When he moved his family to an estate at Deux Montagnes, and Christine got a job at Eaton's, he called and asked if I would keep an eye on her. You know, beautiful, young naive girl! Now, since her marriage to Guillaume, well, her father doesn't approve of him, and I can't say I blame him, so I watch her more carefully. There's something not good about that guy. But I'll tell you Ricky, I can't really put my finger on it, but she used to be smiling and cheerful, but lately, she just seems very preoccupied. It's just not like her."

"You think she's unhappy at work?" Ricky asked.

"No, I think it is something more personal. I tried to find out what was going on, but she just said she wanted to talk to you."

"Okay, I'll go by after we're through here."

As they prepared to leave the luncheonette, Christine entered.

"Your staff performed very well today, Christine. I hope you told them so," Ricky commented.

Christine Guillaume was the twenty-year old manager of Teen Fashions, and subordinate to Ricky. She was a tall blonde with a trim figure and perfect facial features accented by high cheek bones, perfectly applied makeup, and a body to kill for. It was known that she had given up an offer of a promising modeling career with Teen Vogue magazine, to pursue a career in retail merchandising at Eaton's. And she excelled at it, bringing the latest Paris and New York fashions to her small, upscale teen sportswear department.

About 7 months ago, she had married Roland Guillaume, a college student and part time salesclerk in Eaton's 5th floor furniture department. He had been a known party hound and a boozer, but Christine vowed to her friends that she knew his faults but, she felt her love would make him change. Several times employees had pointed out to Ricky that Christine seemed to be hiding facial bruises with extra makeup, and that she had been heard crying in the employee bathrooms. When Ricky had confronted her asking, "How are you feeling?" or "How are things going?" the answer was always the same. 'Everything is great,' or, 'there are no problems at all.' He had left a communication door open with a simple, "If you ever need to talk, just let me know. We're all family here." Now, Ricky was getting the impression that maybe he needed to push her a bit harder to discover what was wrong.

Christine seemed at odds, having bumped into Ricky and Tony. "Thank you, Mister Dean, yes I complimented all the staff on their performance during the drill." Christine replied, as she walked away.

As Tony started to review the report for MPD he commented, "You see. She's definitely acting strange!"

⚜ Nine ⚜

The winds pounded against the old large display windows of the Montreal Eaton's store. It had been snowing for three days straight with no sight of letting up anytime soon. Across the city, roofs had collapsed, schools had been closed and commuters had scrambled to get to work in the icy conditions. Even the activities of the FLQ dissidents had been silenced. But, for Christine, life was very cold and traumatic!

As she sat in Ricky's' office it seemed as if she had been cold all her life. Even as a child, when her friends frolicked in the snow, she secluded herself in the warmth and comfort of her family home. The only consolation to the winter blues of her youth had been the one week, each year, that the family had escaped winter to visit her Aunt Marjorie's home in Bradenton, Florida. She remembered how her depression set in as the vacation neared its end; for her it just meant a return to what was severe cold, as if the winter went on forever. Her dad, long hardened to winter weather joked, "This is Canada, not a Caribbean paradise, so the choices are simple. Either get used to it or leave!" She always wondered why her family had never left!

William Bankowski, a polish immigrant, had been a great father, husband, and family provider. His job with the Canadian government allowed him the luxury of extensive travel and a more affluent lifestyle. When William had first arrived in Montreal harbor with his parents, they had little more than the four large, tattered suitcases that contained the total accumulation of all their personal belongings. For several years they lived in cramped quarters with two other families; and Grandpa Alexy toiling tirelessly as a machinist for the Argon Tool & Die Company. Although his salary was minimal, he always found a way to squirrel away a few dollars from each paycheck towards his goal of, "owning a piece of this country." And in just seven years after his Montreal arrival, he purchased his first piece of Canada in the form of a small, "fixer upper," duplex on St. Hubert street. Christine always remembered Grandpa Alexy's admonishment, related in his broken English, "God no more make any ground, so put money in earth, not in foolishness." Over the years, his motto had worked perfectly for him through the acquisition of numerous apartments, commercial property, and raw land, in and around Montreal. With Grandpa Alexy's early passing at just 52 years old, William, his only child, inherited his vast real estate holdings, and with his superior knowledge of the financial world, he parlayed his wealth through prudent commodity investments. Today, the considerable Bankowski family holdings have made them upper class residents of the small town of Deux Montagnes, Quebec.

Much to the disappointment of Christine's parents, she was the only one of the three Bankowski children to reject a university education. Her brother, Alexander, became a certified public accountant with the Bureau de Transport de Quebec, and her sister, Emily, a paralegal for one of Montreal's most prestigious law firms.

Although Christine was an above average student with a high IQ, she was totally disinterested in a professional career. Her interests rested totally in fashion creation and retail merchandising. This interest stemmed from her early adolescent years of reading fashion magazines and watching TV fashion shows.

EATON'S – During the Second French Revolution

Following her goal, she started working weekends as a junior salesclerk in Eaton's woman's high-grade shoe department. When she began working full-time after high school graduation, her high fashion appearance and knowledge of woman's shoe design quickly propelled her to a department section head position.

She had always been told that her looks were nothing short of breath-taking, thus the original modeling offer. They told her that her features were narrow flawless, accentuated by high angular cheekbones and a small, dimpled chin. Her pixie-like nose, red lips and perfect alabaster teeth added to the elegance of her face. These features were what the camera and runways loved, but it was her deep-set, blue eyes that they specifically talked about. They explained she had a quality of a puppy dog gaze that made most people stare. Also, Christine's silky strawberry blonde hair fell neatly down her back making her height of 5' 4" seem taller and more mature within her hourglass shape. Everything about Christine exhumed, "class." Her impeccable make-up and long manicured mauve nails screamed of perfection. They were willing to offer her a very long and lucrative contract. But she was not interested. All she wanted to do was work her way up to head of a teen fashion department.

Still waiting for Mr. Dean, she thought of the difference between who she was at work; happy, ambitious, almost driven to succeed, and how there was no resemblance to who she was at home. She had now been married for seven agonizing months. Seven months of confusion, frustration, and neglect. Seven months of trying to figure out what she had done wrong and why Roland was always so distant in his interaction with her.

Everything began when she went on a "girl's night out," to the downtown Chez Paris Lounge, to see Joe Tex, a James Brown impersonator. She and her girlfriend, Charlotte, had lined up for two hours to get into the small club. It was loud, smoky, and smelled of spilled beer. Definitely not a place that Christine would normally frequent. Two young men in their early twenties, were seated at the next table which was so close it was almost touching theirs.

Throughout the lively and loud performance Christine found herself uncomfortably drawn to the taller of the two men. During the intermission he introduced himself as Roland Guillaume, a student at Lafontaine University. To Christine he was nothing short of an Adonis, the beautiful mythical Greek God. Roland was not very tall, but his features were striking. His hair was black and curly, and slicked down, so it accented his rectangular face and piercing dark brown eyes that never seemed to blink. Everything was perfect about him, his manners, his personality, his command of the English language, and his interest in current events. These were all the things that Christine admired.

After the concert, the four of them went to Ben's Delicatessen for a smoked meat dinner. Charlotte was getting on very well with Roland's friend, Guy.

Christine learned that Roland was majoring in political science and was heavily involved in student activism at Lafontaine. She also learned that he was an only child of farmer parents in St. Jerome, Quebec. Christine could see that he was kind, caring, attentive and when he told her he was a part-time salesclerk in the furniture department, at Eaton's; everything became too good to be true!

Their courtship had been very formal with some kissing, some minor petting, but generally it had been movies, concerts and drives in the country. Roland, in his very proper way explained that total intimacy should be delayed until both had pledged themselves in marriage.

Six weeks later, after Christine had moved in with Roland, he proposed, asking that they get married immediately. He explained that his parents would not be pleased that he was marrying an "enfant de l' Anglais," *child of the English*, so they would have to keep their engagement secret until he could bring his parents around.

Christine had fallen head over heels in love, and although she had always envisioned a huge wedding at her parents' sprawling estate in Deux Montanges, she agreed instead to a world wind civil marriage at the clerk's office in Montreal City Hall.

Their wedding night together was a disaster as Roland complained that he was having stomach problems. But that was just the beginning. In the months that followed Roland's personality changed drastically. He became rude, verbally abusive, and intolerant. He spent limited time with Christine and never touched her intimately. She pleaded with him, but her cries were met with indifference. Seven months later, still a virgin, she was living with the man that she loved, but a man whose actions she disliked!

Through the long nights that she spent alone her mind took on all sorts of questions. Had he been in an accident? Was he in the bar drinking with his friends, or was he getting into trouble with his university friends? Or maybe he was he out with some other woman?

Christine had no one to talk to about the nightmare of her life since her best friend, Charlotte's answer was, "just dump the bastard and get on with your life." On top of that, her parents were still angry with her for her, "city hall marriage."

As she waited in his office to see Ricky Dean, she wondered whether she should tell him about her situation. She was also personally embarrassed, because for some reason, she could not understand how, on numerous occasions, he had invaded her intimate dreams.

Christine was talking herself out of confiding in Ricky, but because she felt so desperate, she finally conceded that since he had counseled several other members of his staff on matters of a personal nature, if she was going to talk to anyone, he was the logical choice.

She glanced at the office clock; almost five, yes, I must talk with Mr. Dean.

⚜Ten⚜

As Ricky returned to his office, he could not explain it, but every time he thought of the scheduled meeting with Christine, he had a strange fluttering in his stomach. He knew that this was not to be a personal encounter but rather something she wanted to talk to him about. Nonetheless, he was excited about their being alone together.

He saw her sitting at his desk, with her back to the door, but he could still see her long legs. He called out, but he apparently startled her. "Sorry, I thought you heard me coming.

"It's okay, I'm just, well, if this is a bad time, it's nothing that can't wait, that is, if you have something more important to do," she stammered and started to get up, feeling extremely nervous and noticeably embarrassed.

"No, this is fine. Sit down. What did you need to see me about?"

"Well, it's, uh, a personal matter. I know I really shouldn't bother you ..."

"No, not at all. I want you to feel you can come to me about anything. Does it have something to do with the store?"

"Oh, no, well, it's, um," she turned away, tears forming in her eyes. As much as she had convinced herself she needed to talk with him, this topic felt too personal to tell her boss.

"You know what, Christine, I'm just about finished for the night and with everything that went on with the bomb scare, I could really do with getting out of here and getting a drink. Would you like to join me someplace where we can talk?"

"Are you sure that's okay?"

"Yes, and then we can talk without being interrupted. How about meeting me at the Astor Lounge across the street, after closing"

"Ahhh, well, if it's okay with you, could we possibly go somewhere else, more private. You know that so many of the Eaton staff and management go there after closing."

"Absolutely!" He paused to think. "How about the Place Ville Marie, 727 Lounge. Does that sound okay?"

"Isn't that too fancy? I don't think I'm dressed for fancy," she questioned, pointing to her black applique dress.

"Not, at all. You look great. It's just the restaurant and bar on top of the Place Ville Marie. How about if you meet me by the Place Ville Marie elevators, on the main floor, around 6:15, if that's okay"?

"Yes, thank you. I'll see you there, and thanks again, Mister Dean," she almost whispered.

After Christine left Ricky had to get his head back on his shoulders and take care of some business before he went to meet her.

He had been called into an emergency meeting with management, and told that Duane had tendered his resignation, and that Robert Appleton, the no-nonsense store general manager, had accepted it without hesitation.

Ricky was sure that Duane's resignation was not good for the department, or the store, and it was a definite loss for Ricky. He asked his immediate floor merchandise manager, Jeremy Radford if he could convince Duane to consider returning to his position as assistant manager, would Eaton's consider taking him back? After much posturing he got the go-ahead, and Ricky began working through what he would say to Duane. He understood why he felt he had to resign, but he also knew that it was not what Duane really wanted. Duane loved his work, but his pride was hurt; after all he was older and more experienced than Ricky and had given Eaton's years of his life. Most importantly, Ricky understood that Duane should have been the one promoted!

Ricky had thought that with all the responsibility he had given Duane, and all the praise; even seeking out his opinion on major issues, that his friend would have gotten over his upset about being passed over for promotion. But he saw that the bomb scare was the tipping point that had pushed Duane over the edge.

Ricky did not want to lose such a valuable employee, but he really didn't want to lose his friend and that had to be the most important point! But he wrestled with what he could say to Duane. He knew why he was promoted, but that explanation would only put salt on Duane's wounds. Ricky had to come up with something else.

He called Duane and invited him to lunch the following day. He didn't say why, but just made it sound like two friends getting together. He hoped that by then Duane would have calmed down enough to listen to what Ricky had to say. Ricky was concerned that he had to push Duane to accept the realization of his resignation actions, and this was not going to be an easy task. He selected their favorite haunt, Spiro's Italian Bistro, in Notre-Dame-de-Grâce, which was conveniently close to Duane's home in Cartierville.

When he hung up the phone, Ricky was pleased that he had been able to convince Duane to meet with him as he tried to put Duane out of his mind and get ready for his meeting with Christine.

At 6:00 Ricky packed his briefcase and made the one block trek to the Place Ville Marie, where he waited by the elevators nervously smoking several cigarettes. His eyes were totally focused on the revolving doors.

What the hell are you so nervous about anyway? You know the girl is married, for Christ's sake, and in case your forgot, so are you.

At precisely 6:15 he saw the revolving doors spin and heard the familiar click of her high heels against the elegant terrazzo tiles. She'd taken her hair out of the bun and let it flow freely around her face.

"She is absolutely gorgeous!" Ricky thought.

"Hi, am I late?" Christine sounded out of breath.

EATON'S – During the Second French Revolution

He made a gesture to his watch. "No! Right on time," He pressed the 'up' elevator button. Exiting on the top 61st floor, Ricky took Christine's elbow guiding her into the 727 Sky Lounge.

"Wow, this is absolutely beautiful" she gasped. "Look at that view. This is the first time I've been up here."

"Table for two, Monsieur Dean?" the Matre'd asked.

"Yes, thanks Antoine." He looked around and then looked at Christine and suggested, "How about that one over in the corner, it's one of the most panoramic city views?"

Seating them at the table Antoine asked, "Your usual Dubonnet Red, Monsieur Dean?"

"Sûrement," *Certainly,* Ricky courteously responded in French.

"And, for the lady?"

"Choose anything you want, Christine, mixed drink, beer, coffee, or how about something with an umbrella in it?"

"I think I'd like to try what you're having," she replied, sheepishly.

As Antoine departed for the drinks, she gushed, "Mister Dean, this place is just so beautiful. I've never seen any place quite like this!"

"Christine, how about we start with this. No need for the name formality outside the store. Ricky is simply fine."

"Thanks, uh, Ricky. That's going to take some getting used to." It was more difficult to say than the usual formal exchange between them, but she had to admit that it really felt great.

He smiled. "If you look off to the south," he directed her attention to the floor to ceiling windows, "you can see Old Montreal, the docks, and the St. Lawrence River. And, further across the river is Longueil to the west, but unfortunately the view is kinda' blocked by the Bonaventure building. Over there," he shifted her view, "you can also see the Champlain Bridge and Verdun, and to the east you have St. Laurent Boulevard and Montreal East, my second home during my teens." He offered Christine a Cameo menthol cigarette.

"Your second home?"

"Yeah, things were not great with my parents in Rosemont, so my best friend, whose parents lived in Montreal East, became like my surrogate family. Actually, I spent more time there than I did at my own house. In fact, my one and only girlfriend, before my wife, lived there."

"You only had two girlfriends up to now? That is hard to believe," she added in a somewhat surprised way and lowered her eyes from his gaze.

"Well, actually three if you count Maureen Elliot, when I was eleven."

"A Dubonnet Red with umbrella for the lady," Antoine smiled, "and a Dubonnet Red with swizzle stick for monsieur."

"Thank you, Antoine. The umbrella was a nice touch."

Holding her napkin delicately below the glass, Christine took a sip of her drink. Her eyes lit up with delight. "Oh, Ricky, I'm really love this drink, thanks."

"It has a slight bite when it first goes down, but the taste is unbelievable, Ricky hoped the wine conversation would help her relax.

"Is it a French wine?" she questioned, taking a second swallow.

"Actually, *Dubonnet* has an interesting story that I discovered several years ago. It is a sweet, wine-fortified aperitif made with a blend of herbs and spices, including a small amount of quinine. It was developed in 1846 by Joseph Dubonnet, for the French Government, as a way of persuading French Foreign Legionnaires in North Africa to drink quinine which was needed to combat malaria, as quinine alone is very bitter."

"You really know your wines," she was impressed by his knowledge.

"Actually, I can't tell a Chablis from a bulldog. So, the fact is that I only know *my wine*, singular," he laughed. "Anyway, enough of my kidding. I gather you are having a problem that I may be able to help you with."

"No, it's, well, of a personal nature," she offered, sheepishly. "I can't talk to my parents and my best friend gives me all kinds of stupid suggestions that I can't handle." Her previous smile melded into a grim expression.

"And your husband?"

She looked away from him. "He's the problem," she stammered.

"Roland works part time in the Eaton's furniture department, right?"

"Yes, and he's a political science student at Lafontaine College," Christine was surprised that her boss remembered her husband's name, probably from the Christmas party.

"And you've been married, what, eight or nine months now?"

"Well, seven very long and trying months, actually."

"So, tell me, how can I help?" Ricky asked.

"I really don't know where to start. Maybe this was a bad idea to open up to my boss." Her voice cracked as she tried to stem the sobs that were bubbling just beneath the surface.

"Christine, please look at me," he placed his hand over her fingers.

She was barely able to meet his gaze.

"I'm here as a friend, not as your boss. So why don't you just start from the beginning, okay?"

She finally raised her eyes to meet his. "Thank you. I've felt so alone, for so awfully long." Her tears began to flow as she turned away.

Her teary-eyed gaze penetrated his thoughts. *Please let me find the words to help her!* "Look at me Christine," he whispered, staring into her face, "There's nothing that can't be fixed. Let me try to help you, please."

Her eyes darted in panic as she looked around the lounge. "Oh my God, everyone is looking. I feel like such a fool," she whispered as she dried mascara with a napkin. "I'm so, so sorry," she said, as she tried to stifle her emotions.

"You are not a fool, and you have absolutely nothing to be sorry for. Do you think you are the first person to breakdown in this place? Christ, just last week a husband and wife were having a fist fight, and there were cops, and everyone was getting in on the brawl."

"I think I need to go to the powder room." She managed a nervous laugh as got up from her chair and looked around. "Please excuse me."

Ricky quickly rose and pointed towards the exit. "Out the entrance, turn left, and it's the second door on your right."

I told her there is nothing that can't be fixed. I sure hope I can keep that promise, he thought.

Christine returned looking calm and refreshed, but Ricky could see that she had fixed her make-up and combed her blonde hair into a tuck back behind one ear, her expression still displaying immense sadness. "I'm sorry to have run off, but I needed to put myself back together. So, I am just going to spit it all out, while I still have the nerve." She took a large gulp of her new drink, then put the glass down and played with the little umbrella, trying to gather her thoughts.

"I met Roland at a Joe Tex concert at the Chez Paris, about ten months ago, and fell head over heels in love with him that very same night. He was everything a girl could hope for, from looks, to manners, to attentiveness. He was simply perfect. And I'm ashamed to say," she held her breath and somehow got out the words, "...um, just a few weeks later," she took a deep breath and continued, "we moved in together. I thought I was in heaven. I believed our courtship was normal, at least what I perceived as normal, since I wasn't that experienced. Our relationship had some kissing and minor petting, but no intimacy because Roland said nothing more should happen, 'until we both had pledged ourselves before God.'" She put her hands to her face in embarrassment. "I can't believe I'm telling you all this!"

"It's okay, you're doing fine." Ricky prodded.

Christine choked back a sob. "Six weeks after moving in together, we got married at City Hall, but our wedding night was a total disaster."

Join the club! Ricky thought.

"Roland said that he was sick from something he ate. But as the weeks and months followed, he never came near me in any intimate way. In fact, two months after we were married, he began sleeping on the foldout in the living room, using the excuse that the bed was hurting his back. And his personality changed drastically. He became rude, verbally abusive, and intolerant. I pleaded with him to tell me what was wrong, but he just ignored my pleas. I did everything possible to interest him in me. I read books on intimacy, I bought sexy lingerie, but he just scoffed at my advances," she began to have trouble getting the words out, and the sobs began in earnest. "I ..., I even tried to wake him up one night, you know, sexually," shame filled her eyes, followed by sadness. "That was how I got the bruise on my cheek," she shuddered with that thought. "It's like he hates me, and I've got no idea what I've done," her shoulders shook, as she placed her head into the crook of her arm.

"Christine," he reached for her hand. "Please, look at me."

"I don't know what to do Ricky," she sobbed.

Ricky took his handkerchief from his pocket and handed it to her. "Believe it or not, I can personally relate to your dilemma, but that's a story for another day. Right now, we need to face your problem. Like I have trained you in merchandising, we need to identify the problem, and formulate a comprehensive plan to arrive at a favorable solution. So, can you set the tears aside while I ask you some questions?""

"Yes Ricky, I'll try!"

"You mentioned the bruise on your cheek. Is Roland normally physically abusive to you?" he cautiously asked.

"No, that was the only time, and he claims it was an accident. I, um," she faltered, "I tried exciting him while he was asleep, hoping I could overcome his problem with me, but he woke quickly and flung his elbow back which caught me on my cheek. At the time he didn't say a word, he just darted from the bed, got dressed and disappeared for three days. When he did come home, he didn't even speak to me and since then he sleeps on the sofa."

"Do you think he has a girlfriend on the side?"

"At first, I thought that was the case, but I've never smelled any perfume on him, nor have I found any lipstick or makeup on his clothing. He has a bunch of French college buddies that he hangs out with almost every night until two o'clock, or three in the morning. When he invites them to the house, they sit around drinking beer, smoking joints, talking solely in French, which I don't understand, and they totally ignore me."

Something was coming together for Ricky, and he asked, "Tell me about his parents?"

"They have a farm in Saint Jerome, and they are extremely strict Catholics. In fact, he told me that his parents would not be pleased with him marrying an 'enfant de l' Anglais,'" she smiled, as she struggled with the French translation. "Um, a child of the English. In all this time he has never even taken me to meet them."

"Christine, you are an extremely attractive woman, and must have had numerous boyfriends whose actions you could compare with Roland's. Did you notice anything different from your other encounters?"

"I guess that's the main problem, Ricky. I grew up in a Catholic household in Deux Montanges. We went to church every Sunday, and I was taught by stern nuns in school, and my father made it clear that dating his daughter came with an introduction to his treasured Louisville Slugger baseball bat. "So, no, my teenage social skills were limited, or probably best described as non-existent."

EATON'S – During the Second French Revolution

Ricky stopped for a moment and lit another cigarette. "I don't want to offend you, but I need to ask. Has there been any indication at all," he cleared his throat, "that um, Roland could be a homosexual?"

She reacted swiftly as if the words slapped her in the face. "No, he can't be! The guy looks like a movie star. Whenever we do go out women can't keep their eyes off him. So no, he would not have married me, if he were, well, queer!" she winced at her use of the vulgar word connotation.

"I'm sorry, but I needed to ask if you ever considered that possibility."

"Oh, I thought about it once, when I saw him exiting from his friend's car and kissing him on the lips, but I quickly dismissed it as being ridiculous. My friend Charlotte calls him a 'dandy,' believing that he is just that way. But it would not make any sense, would it?"

"Do you know that many pretty boys, even Hollywood's Rock Hudson are homosexuals, and there are many others."

"No way," she blurted, in shock.

"Yes, so if Roland is indeed a homosexual, in today's society, it's still something that he must hide. Do you understand?"

"But, if he is like that, why would he lead me on, and even go through the whole thing of marrying me?"

"It's all for show, maybe to protect his public image. Maybe Roland needs the lie to deal with his strict family, and probably even his friends."

Tears again welled in her eyes, as her head hung in disbelief. "So, I could be married to a homosexual! This can't be! I'm a Catholic, so I can't get a divorce and any possibility of a normal life, with a real-life partner, and children is impossible . . ."

Ricky thought for several moments before asking the most delicate question of their conversation. "I've had a thought," he again hesitated, "but this is difficult to ask, but it might be the answer," he prefaced, "Uh," he labored, trying to find the right words.

"Please, Ricky, just ask your question! Right now, you know more intimate details about me than anyone else in the world, so if you have a possible answer, please let me hear it."

The color rose in Ricky's cheeks. "Okay, here goes. Are you still a virgin?"

"Whew! I didn't see that coming. Is that important?"

"It may be."

"Yes," she mumbled, "twenty-two and still a virgin, and destined to die an *old maid* virgin," an expression of disgust was encased in those words.

"That will never happen!" he assured her.

"Is this something you could feel comfortable talking about to your parents or even your parish priest," he asked.

"God no! My parents would freak out and Father Delvechio is like eighty years old. He still thinks women should always wear hats, dresses up to their chin and anything else that denotes extreme promiscuity."

"All right then. I'll have to come at this from another angle, but you'll need to be patient." He paused. "Christine, you'll have to have faith that there is a resolution, and we'll find it together given enough time. You need to trust me."

After paying the check and descending to the main floor of the Place Ville Marie in silence, Ricky put Christine in a cab and bid her goodnight. She told the driver the address to her home in Verdun and waved as the cab drove away. Ricky made his way to Central Station, and his dreaded train trip home.

Tonight, he didn't mind the long ride since he had so much to think about. He reviewed his conversation with Christine, and one thought kept running through his mind. *Wow how when you least expect it, life can change, even in just a single day!*

⚜ Eleven ⚜

Sitting in the cavernous Canadian National Railroad, Central Train Station, waiting for the last 9:40 train home to Ville St. Laurent, was a solemn and traumatic experience for Ricky. His thoughts of anxiety and depression grew as the time got closer to his arrival home. Whether his daily mood at work had been happy, or sad, he could count on walking through the door of his home and becoming immediately depressed.

Trying to curb his anxious negative thoughts of what lay ahead at home and to stop dwelling on Christine's problems and the Duane lunch the next day, Ricky concentrated on reading the Mount Royal Tunnel's historical plaques. They detailed construction of the tunnel as a measure for north city Montrealers to gain ready access to the downtown core.

The Mount Royal Tunnel - A Marvel of Engineering

The tunnel was conceived in 1910 by the Canadian Northern Railway to gain easy access to downtown Montreal. In 1911, the Canadian Northern Montreal Tunnel and Terminal Company was incorporated to build the tunnel and terminal. It was renamed Mount Royal Tunnel and Terminal Company in 1914 and was a wholly owned subsidiary of CNR.

On December 10, 1913, crews from the east and west portals met beneath Mount Royal. They were only out of alignment by 1 inch.

On September 6, 1918, the insolvent CNR was nationalized by the federal government. On December 20, 1918, the Privy Council issued an order creating

EATON'S – During the Second French Revolution

the Canadian National Railways (CNR) to operate CNR, CGR and eventually other bankrupt private-sector railways.

The new terminal, begun in 1931, opened as Central Station on July 14, 1943. In the late 1950's, the remainder of the CNR lands, acquired in downtown Montreal during the Mount Royal Tunnel project, were developed by CNR, including the signature Queen Elizabeth Hotel, which opened in 1958, followed by the Place Ville-Marie, in 1962.

Ricky finished reading the plaque and realized that until *someone spends the time travelling the three- and one-half miles through the tunnel, they can't truly fathom the immensity of the project, completed utilizing the equipment of the early 1900's.*

Two years earlier, at the age of nineteen, Ricky let his pride, rebellious nature, and his guilt over being a victim of a sexually abusive past, propel him into making the biggest mistake of his young life.

As a gangly, somewhat awkward high school student, Ricky had never been popular with girls. In fact, during his late teens he had had only one girlfriend, and never attended a single dance at Rosemount High School. In eighth grade, Ricky met a fellow student, Johnny Baker, from Montreal East. Ricky spent all his after-school time and weekends with Johnny, and his group of east-end friends. Johnny had been Ricky's savior because, not only did he help Ricky out of his introverted anti-social nature, but he became a confidant and best friend, both of which were sorely missing in his life. With his home life being strict and loveless, Ricky gravitated towards Johnny's hip parents, and took them as his surrogate parents.

Ricky's first adventure in developing his sexuality came with an introduction to sexy sixteen-year-old, Sandy Robertson, Johnny's next-door neighbor. Sandy was everything Ricky could hope for. She was pretty, caring, and, most importantly, completely in love with Ricky; an emotion he had never encountered.

Sandy was slim, full of fun, and at the time, had the "largest set of boobs" he would hopefully ever see. But she turned out to be just a tease. She would be an active participant in passionate necking and clothes to clothes rubbing, but would never allow any actual, "real skin" petting. The closest Ricky ever got to actual sexual contact was occasionally being allowed to touch Sandy's ample breast through her clothes. Even with these ongoing sexual frustrations Ricky and Sandy's puppy love continued into Ricky's senior year.

Seemingly, in every school environment there are those girls who gain a negative reputation as being "lose or easy," and such was the case with Kathleen Sanders. Kathy was short and thin with long dark hair reaching halfway down her back. Her large blue eyes and immaculate makeup accentuated her small pug nose, tiny chin, and full lips. Her personality was always upbeat, making her exceedingly popular amongst her peers. She had been one grade behind Ricky, and because of her big mouth boyfriend, it was common knowledge that they were having regular intercourse. This was the big gossip around school at a time when *proper girls* were expected to remain virgins until they married.

Ricky had just broken up with Sandy when he learned that Kathy had also broken up with her boyfriend. Still a virgin, Ricky pursued her hoping to become her next sexual partner. He discovered that she lived just two streets over from his home.

As the school year ended, Ricky waited outside the school's Beaubien Street exit waiting for Kathy, and when he saw her, he acted as if he had just happened to be there and asked if he could walk her home.

He found that Kathy was not shy and surprisingly forthcoming about her sexual exploits. Within the first week, casual goodbye kisses progressed to longer and more passionate kisses. And, after attending his first school dance with Kathy at Montreal High School, the kisses thankfully progressed to heavy petting with Ricky finally being able to touch skin; his first real breast! He was ecstatic. By the end of the school year, he and Kathy had become an inseparable couple. What began as a simple adventure for Ricky to experience his first sexual encounter had developed into something that Ricky thought might be love, but what did he know? Their sexual activities, although somewhat awkward, were plentiful, and from Ricky's standpoint, extremely rewarding. He could not consider the possibility of being deprived of such pleasure.

When they were not engaged in sexual activities, Ricky and Kathy both confided in each other about their mutually troubled home life. Kathy's father was a strict, cruel dictatorial individual, while her mother had a passive, "everything will be okay," personality. The conflicting personalities of her parents made for constant strife within the Sanders household and made Kathy the brunt of much criticism and mental anguish from her father. Her only remedy was escape and Ricky had become her vehicle of choice. That escape came months later when both parents found out that they had been having sex in their houses. Their parents demanded that they not see each other anymore.

Ricky immediately rebelled and had a huge fight with his parents, but no matter what he said, he couldn't make them understand his relationship with Kathy. They were so adamant that Ricky break up with her, that when he refused, they took away Ricky's car; still registered in their name. In retaliation Ricky moved out of his parent's house. With the money he had saved from his part-time job at Eaton's he was able to get a small apartment.

Ricky believed he was making very mature decisions and decided to elope with Kathy to the neighboring province of Ontario. He borrowed a car from Eaton's friend, and drove three hours to Cornwall, Ontario, where they were married by an unfriendly traffic court magistrate. When they returned to Montreal, they immediately got on a Greyhound bus to New York City, for a planned weeklong honeymoon excursion.

However, the honeymoon debacle began almost immediately. Two hours into the nine-hour trip, the bus driver handed out blankets to everyone, because the bus heater was not working, and the temperature was well below zero outside. With still seven hours to go before they would arrive in Manhattan Ricky tried unsuccessfully to cuddle with Kathy to combine their body heat. He was shocked when she became totally adverse to any personal contact.

They arrived at the Port Authority bus terminal in New York City at 1:30 A. M. Ricky found a cab that took them uptown to the Frazier Hotel where they checked into an extremely small room. Ever the romantic, Ricky had pre-planned the honeymoon night carefully. He had packed scented candles, bubble bath, a bottle of Dubonnet and a collection of breads and cheeses. He wanted everything to be special for the beginning of their new life together. But Kathy rejected all Ricky's planning and romantic advances, instead stating that *she was too tired* and just wanted to get some sleep. Although he was disappointed, Ricky chalked everything that happened up to the whirlwind nature of the events of their previous 24 hours.

The next day turned out to be no better. After eating bagels and coffee at a Broadway deli, they returned to their hotel room, where Ricky began romantic advances that he understood were normal honeymoon activities. Again, Kathy thwarted his advances, this time without reasonable excuses. She explained, she just didn't want to "do it."! After two days of no romantic activities, Ricky gave up, checked out of the hotel, and they began their 9-hour bus ride back to Montreal. Once they arrived in their new home, the apartment Ricky had rented, nothing changed. It took three months and the alcoholic effects from a party they went to before Ricky and Kathy ever had married sex. Ironically, this one sexual act produced a pregnancy, which became the new excuse for Kathy's abstinence.

Saddled with the constant guilt of the sexual abuse of his youth, and now coupled with his feelings of inadequacy in his marriage, Ricky eventually sought the help of his family physician, Dr. Albert Lambrere. After performing numerous tests and getting very extensive history of Ricky's sexual life, Dr. Lambrere told Ricky he was in exceptional good health, and aside from his smoking habit, there was nothing physically wrong with him. The examinations also concluded that Ricky's equipment was all in good working order and suggested that Ricky see Dr. Julius Markovitz, a psychologist who specialized in sexual issues.

As Ricky heard the call over the station loudspeaker, for his 9:40 train and his dreaded ride home, he felt released from his unpleasant thoughts, his thoughts returning to present day as he wondered,

Will my life ever get any better?

✣ Twelve ✣

The following morning Eaton's had been extremely busy, but Ricky made time to think about, and go over, what he was going to say when he met z0Duane for lunch to discuss his resignation.

As he left Eaton's heavy wet snow was falling, severely snarling the downtown core traffic. He pulled up the collar of his London Fog overcoat as a shield against the penetrating blast of cold winter air. The street was encased in crusting snow layered over slippery slush, while the sidewalk was peppered with powdery snow which concealed the dangerous patches of ice beneath.

Ricky leapt over a mound of sand and salt mix snow packed high by the snow plows the previous night. He tried to reach the other side of University Street without falling mid-street, where he could secure a northbound taxicab. It didn't help that he was wearing his slick soled dress boots which afforded him little traction in the wet slush. Available taxis were scarce at midday, and he had to wait several minutes before a cab emerged from the throng of traffic and came to a slush spraying stop by the curb. Ricky opened the rear door of the taxi and grimaced as he sat down on the cold vinyl seats. "Eight-six seven five Decarie Boulevard. Take Guy Street over Mount Royal, Okay?" Ricky commanded.

"A votre plaisir, monsieur," *at your pleasure, sir,* was the simple curt reply from the 400 plus pound, cigar smoking driver.

The cab began to navigate the treacherous 30-minute trek; north on University; left on Sherbrooke Street and then passed the elite Holt Renfrew, six story department store which catered to the high society shoppers of Montreal. When the driver turned right onto Guy Street, Ricky smiled as he remembered that the restaurant on the corner had been the famous "Diana Grill Restaurant," owned during the depression by his notorious gambling grandfather, Nicko, known to Montrealers as Canada's, "Nick the Greek. Ricky recalled the descriptions of the grill that he had heard from his grandmother, about his grandfather, who had been anything but a good husband, or father. He was portrayed as a crazy-ass Greek who took his anger out on his wife, daughter, and son. His chronic gambling escapades often resulted in the family losing all their furniture, and on at least one occasion, being forced out onto the street. Ricky's mother had relayed that it was not uncommon for his grandfather to chase his kids around the house in an uncontrollable rage, threatening them with a butcher knife. And, that his mother's brother Ivan had ended up in the Royal Victoria Hospital emergency room, on numerous occasions, with lacerations and broken bones resulted from beatings from Nicko.

The public story was that having won and lost his Diana Restaurant in numerous poker games, Nicolaus Coliopoullos, to escape his gambling debts,

EATON'S – During the Second French Revolution

had abandoned his wife and two kids and fled to places unknown, never to be seen or heard from again.

Now, the law offices occupying the original, "Diana," location was a far cry from the pictures his mother had described, identifying his heritage.

"Would you mind putting out the cigar, please?" Ricky asked, choking on the acrid smoke that permeated the enclosed cab. Ricky was a cigarette smoker, but contending with cigar smoke, in an enclosed cab, was unbearable.

His request was met with a simple, "Huh," followed by the driver raising his hands in an *I don't understand,* gesture.

"Pourriez-vous éteindre le cigare, se il vous plaît," *Would you mind putting out the cigar, please?* Ricky now asked in perfect French.

Without comment, and noticeably annoyed, the driver rolled down his window; driving a torrent of cold air into Ricky's face, and angrily threw the cigar into the middle of the street.

Every time Ricky had to deal with the "FRENCH attitude," he got more and more disturbed about the French-English conflict infecting his normally tranquil Montreal. Before the uprisings began, both French and English Canadians tried, out of common courtesy, to speak in the other's language; particularly those who served the public. But, since Levesque and de Gaulle, and their inciteful anti-English rhetoric lectures, Frenchmen, even those you knew for years, and who spoke perfect English, refused any communication other than in French. And, with each daily newscast, it became perfectly clear that the problem was accelerating to a point of emotional despair for English speaking Quebecers.

Reaching Decarie Boulevard the driver came to a hazardous sliding stop as he slammed on his brakes, the rear wheel crashing into the sidewalk, ending up inches from the rear bumper of a parked Canada Poste delivery truck.

"Vous ete ici. Six dollars, sil vous plait, Monsieur," *You are here. Six dollars, please, sir.*

"Merci," *Thanks,* the driver said as Ricky gave the driver $7.00. "Keep the change," a statement he knew the driver, who feigned a lack of the English language, would conveniently understand.

Ricky skirted around the rear of a stalled electric tram bus while looking around the parking lot for Duane's old green Volkswagen bus. He pushed open the exterior glass door and hung his overcoat on the antique metal coat tree just inside the door.

Spiro's restaurant interior sported heavily draped windows to keep out the view of the outside modern world, and hundreds of plants hanging from the ceiling, offering the restaurant a realistic Greek atmosphere. The faux-marble columns were a complimentary addition to the old European reproduced master's artwork. And the subdued candelabra lighting and authentic music from the Greek Isles all added to the ambiance, giving an illusion of sitting at a little outdoor café table, in downtown Athens.

With Ricky's Greek heritage, he, and Spiro, shared a special bond that was treasured by "true Greeks." Ricky had spent many fascinating lunch hours listening to Spiro talk about Greece. He told Ricky that when at the age of only seventeen, he heard about Hitler's advance into southern Europe, he realized that it would only be a matter of time before the invaders occupied his homeland. So, Spiro left the orphanage, which had been his home for nine years, to join up with the Italian partisans. He relayed the horrors of his early life as a partisan in Mussolini's war-torn Italy. His involvement however was short lived when his participation in his first anti-Mussolini rally found him swept up in a mass arrest by Italian security forces. Because of his young age, he was initially sent to the civilian Ferramonti di Tarsia prison near Cosenza until overcrowding forced his transfer thirteen months later, to the dreaded Montechiarugolo prison near Parma. He was interred there for two years until he was released by the American liberation forces in 1943. With a painful look in his eyes all Spiro would say was that the filth and cruelty of this infamous prison were beyond human belief. As Spiro would tell it, describing each prison, "First one not too bad, second one awfully bad, near kill me! Then I go home, Greece."

Spiro enjoyed telling the rest of his story. "I work in olive oil factory where I meet my Magdelaine. Very young. Very Pretty. Too pretty, for Spiro," he laughed.

Spiro and Magdelaine were married within three months of his return from prison. They subsequently immigrated to Canada sponsored by his distant cousin, Demetrius Terrazopoullos. When Spiro and Magdelaine arrived in Montreal they lived in his cousin's house for three years. Spiro had worked seven days a week at two jobs, as a furniture factory forklift operator and at a foundry as an iron worker, while Magdelaine worked as a janitor, six nights a week at Rosemount High School. They lived very frugally and finally saved enough money to afford their first house in Rosemount, a northeast Montreal suburb. In the spring of 1948, Angelina, their first and only child was born, at which time, Spiro took over Magdelaine's janitor job, in addition to his other two.

Over the years, his hard work paid off and Spiro was able to purchase a triplex apartment, a small convenience store and eventually his treasured Spiro's Restaurant, then situated in downtown Montreal. In addition to these assets, by 1965 Spiro had purchased three more apartment complexes, and bought a share of the strip mall which now housed the new Spiro's Restaurant. But even though they were now considered affluent, they still lived in the same house they originally bought in Rosemount. Spiro Terrazopoullos was the epitome of the true rags to riches Canadian immigrant success story.

Ricky was greeted at the entrance by both Spiro and his portly wife of thirty-two years, Magdelaine. As the three hugged and his eyes adjusted to the low interior lighting, he spotted Duane smoking and fidgeting nervously in a booth at the rear of the restaurant.

"Spiro say you big boss man now, yes? Maybe you give Angelina job?" Magdelaine continued.

Ricky found Angelina an extremely beautiful girl with her riveting brown eyes, long pitch-black hair outlined against her olive tanned skin, which made it easy to see why Greek girls, had a reputation of being the most beautiful girls in the world.

Angelina, balanced school, and her career goals against the more traditional aspects of her parents' generation. Though she was considered, "the sweetest girl around," she had gone through her, 'bad girl,' phase in her late teens. Despite it all, she never seemed to lose her sense of innocence.

Angelina was Spiro and Magdelaine's total reason for living. Their late-in-life pride in their special baby was nothing short of a miracle. Now, five foot seven inches tall, Angelina towered over both her parents. At twenty-two years old, she was a goddess of beauty. Ricky had known her since her days as a busgirl in Spiro's downtown restaurant. Now, she was all grown up and following her passion as a pre-med student at McGill.

"You may have job for my Angelina?" Magdelaine repeated.

"Sure Magdelaine. Have her call me," Ricky replied, handing her his business card. "Maybe I'll find some work for her in our Teen Fashion department. She'd be a great fit there."

"Thank you, thank you, Mister Ricky. She good worker, you no be sorry," she exclaimed again hugging him tighter. "You meet Mister Duane today?"

"Yes, Magdelaine, I see him over there in the back booth."

"Come, sit," she impatiently tugged him towards the rear booth.

"Thank you, Mama".

"I get you nice ouzos, today? Yes?" she asked.

"Just a tall Molson for me, and whatever Mister Duane wants."

This is not going to be easy and going to take hell-of-a-lot of finesse, Ricky anticipated.

⚜ Thirteen ⚜

Ricky walked back to the booth and extended his hand to Duane, who promptly ignored it.

Duane raised his voice as Ricky settled into the booth opposite him. "I don't know why the hell we had to meet. I made my decision and it's final! I've been screwed over, and this whole promotion thing is bullshit." He took a gulp of his Foster's beer. "Sixteen fuckin' years and I get shafted."

Duane swearing was a definite sign that this was going to be one helluva meeting. In all the years I'd known him I never heard him curse like that.

Ricky noticed Duane's eyes watering as he avoided any direct contact. "You know, Ricky that I practically wiped Reggie's ass and covered for him for years, doing his job, and him collecting the big bucks and then blowing it on booze and gambling."

"Please lower your voice, Duane," Ricky commanded. *This is going to be even harder than I thought.*

At six foot two, you would think Duane would have emitted an air of strength and power, but his slight weight of only 175 pounds, and his heavy black bi-focals, suggested an unintimidating college professor. Although generally timid, Duane had a heart of gold. His old-fashioned nature showed in how easily he was embarrassed, especially from off-color language and strong forward women. Normally, he'd slink away to avoid controversy and was the peacemaker amongst his peers and subordinates. This was a different man resembling an injured animal ready to pounce.

And I'm his prey, Ricky thought.

Sipping his beer, Duane hesitated and gathered his thoughts before continuing. "For Christ's sake, Ricky, I've got two kids, a wife with psychological problems, and debts coming out of my ass, and what do I get for all my efforts ... bloody shafted! It ain't bloody fair! I deserved that promotion! I needed that damn promotion!" His voice quivered as it trailed off into silence as he turned his face to hide his emotions.

Ricky allowed the silence to continue. He was anticipating a crescendo build up and an eventual grand finale to Duane's tirade.

Just have patience, let him get it all out, Ricky thought.

"So, why are you here, Ricky? I mean you now have the world by the ass. I suppose Radford sent you to hunt me down and explain the ills of my ways? Well, read my lips. I don't need it, man. I know I'm screwed, but I don't have to take this anymore. I'd rather work for 'Simpson's' or 'The Bay,' rather than put up with this bullshit! Damn, Ricky you're just twenty-one and I'm thirty-eight and I have seventeen-years seniority while you have just five. I taught you the ropes, by the way. Now, how's that fair?

Magdelaine arrived at the table and poured the Molson beer into a tall stein, asking, "You wanna good veal parmesan, today? Maybe, bake ziti?" Magdelaine placed the menus on the table. "I make *Baklava* for after, really good, you like? I make dough and sweet Greek pastry, just for you."

"Maybe later Magdelaine. Right now, we'll just stick with our beers."

"Okee Dokee, Mister Ricky."

"Duane, you know we've been friends ever since I began working for you five years ago. I admit that you graciously took me under your wing and taught me everything I needed to know. And, you must know I'll forever be grateful for

EATON'S – During the Second French Revolution

all you've done for me, and no, I'll be the first to agree that what happened to you in this promotion thing was not fair. But Buddy, crap happens! I know you are angry, but I didn't have anything to do with the selection process. The decision was made between Radford and Appleton, without any consultation with me."

Ricky paused to sip his beer. "Duane there are two really important factors that I believe you are not considering. First, you know that when Levine packed it in as general manager last March, everyone was shocked by Toronto corporate's decision to send down Appleton as GM, especially at his young age. Many times, you and I discussed the fact that Appleton was Toronto's superhero who turned around central division's bottom line. Shit, we spent six years running in the red under Levine, and the powers that be recognized that they needed youth, and not old farts to bring our store into the twentieth century. And Buddy, I'm not suggesting that you're an old fart, but you've seen all the signs. Eaton's stores across Canada still have dress codes dictating only white shirts, conservative ties with drab brown, blue or gray suits. Even the women in fashions are not permitted to wear any of the high fashion items that they are peddling."

Ricky continued, "But, with the arrival of Appleton, everything has changed. As for me, you must certainly have figured that something was afoot, last August, when I was selected to be one of only eight candidates for Appleton's pet project on his, 'Bound for Success,' committee. "Don't you see, Duane, all the committee members, except for Appleton, are under the age of thirty. He tasked us with restructuring our store to reflect the needs of younger buyers. With all that exposure, the 'Super Eight,' are all front and center and under his supervision. We now boast the most under thirty management positions held by any of the Eaton stores, coast-to-coast."

Duane grabbed a cigarette from Ricky's Du Maurier pack. "But, what about loyalty, seniority, dedication, doesn't any of that matter anymore? Has that all gone down the crapper? Why don't they just take all of us older guys out and just shoot us?"

"Don't be ridiculous," Ricky replied. "At only thirty-eight you are an unbelievably valuable, experienced employee. We still see many promotions for older employees, but it's just that now the emphasis is on the younger management, and in case you haven't noticed, also the Francophones. The noise they have been making in provincial politics has brought them to the forefront for accelerated inclusion in Quebec's English industries. Unfortunately, that means preferential treatment in all future Eaton's management selection. I also believe that in the future, with Appleton's, 'bottom line,' mission, we will no doubt see more departments combined so that they can save a buck on managers."

"So, what are they planning?" Duane asked. "Just fire all the old goats.

Ricky caught Magdelaine's eye and motioned for a beer for Duane.

"You think that's enough Ricky? A few bucks, a slap on the back, and sayonara amigo. It is plain bullshit! You're supposed to be rewarded for your efforts and loyalty, not discarded like a piece of garbage."

"I'm not arguing with you, Duane. The whole thing sucks, big time, but they are the bosses. It is the company money they're looking out for. We may not like it, but we've got no choice except to make the best of it!"

"Okay! Okay, you're probably right," He raised his eyes, for the first time, to meet Ricky's. "Man, you know I don't really hold it against you personally, and I am truly happy for you, it's just ..." his voice cracked. "I am just so bloody frustrated. I really don't know what to do next. My home life is screwed with Miriam's illness, my finances are messed up with all the extra medical and daycare expenses, and surprise, surprise, now I'm bloody well unemployed." Tears began to run down his cheeks, as he turned away.

Whoa, I did not expect this, Ricky thought.

Taking a clean handkerchief from his breast pocket he handed it over to Duane. "Listen, we've been buds for a long time and been through a lot of crap together, but you've got to be realistic, man. You talk about getting a job at Simpsons, or The Bay, but you know, as well as I do that The Bay is doing extensive layoffs, and Simpsons is probably going to be bought up by Sears, in the states. And half their employees are coming to us looking for a job. As your friend, I came here to try and convince you to reconsider your decision to quit Eaton's. With the volatile situation in Quebec right now, and the English retail industry under attack, it's both personal and career suicide."

"Ricky, I don't think you truly understand. When I told them that I was going to quit, neither Radford, nor Appleton even tried to talk me into staying. At the very least, I expected they might make some kind of offering, or even a false promise to encourage me to stay, but they didn't. Did I do something to fall into their bad graces?"

"Actually, you did Duane. You know that Appleton was tasked with bringing Montreal into the black, and, to do so, he must trim personnel, and with your resignation you helped his quest. And, for your information, I wasn't sent here by either Radford, or Appleton. I told Radford that I needed you. I told him that your absence would radically affect the continued growth of our department. You know Radford is just marking time 'til his retirement, and he hates controversy. So, he cleared it with Appleton and gave his okay for me to try to get you to reconsider your resignation. So, what do you think?"

Duane took Ricky's hand and surrounded it in his two hands. "So, now my friend, what do you think about what I've just told you?" Ricky asked.

"I'm just embarrassed. How will this look to the staff after they all know I was such an asshole when I quit. I've always led them from a point of respect, and now I'll have to rebuild all that."

EATON'S – During the Second French Revolution

Respect is not the accurate word, but they do follow your lead.

Ricky smiled, "Only Appleton, Radford and I know that you quit. I even delayed your records going to personnel for severance pay, until I had a chance to make my pitch to you. So, all you must do is show up tomorrow like nothing's happened. You had a sick day off, that's all."

Duane was noticeably shocked by this unexpected revelation. "They don't know? How can I ever thank you, Ricky? You've saved my life."

"Be my right hand again. Guide me, train me some more, in turn I swear that I will do everything in my power to see that you get your much-deserved full management position, as soon as possible."

Ricky clinked beer bottles with Duane as a salute to their combined progressive futures. Ricky didn't doubt that the smallest smidgeon of jealousy still might be present in Duane, but he hoped that after their talk it would evaporate over time. Until then, he was certain that Duane would continue as his inseparable friend and loyal employee.

Magdelaine interrupted, "Now eat?

"Yes, Magdelaine, now eat," he teased. "Bring us both baked ziti, some hot rolls, and your great baklava for dessert. Oh, and, more beer, yes?"

"Yes, Mister Ricky," she bowed as she left.

⚜ Fourteen ⚜

The day before the thanksgiving weekend began Dorval airport was swamped with crowds of transient people frantically trying to negotiate ticket counters, immigration, and customs procedures, in an effort to make connecting flights. With Dorval being an international connection hub, the throngs of people overwhelmed airline personnel, and delayed disembarking passengers from across Canada and the U.S. This bedlam made identifying the arriving passengers an absolute nightmare.

Ricky stood patiently at the Air Canada arrivals area. He strained on tip toes to find his brother among the frenzied crowd. It had been eight months since he had last seen him and the prospect of missing him fed deep into his stomach. Norman was catching a connecting flight to Quebec City and had only two hours between connections, but his flight was already over an hour late on arriving in Montreal.

After serving two years in the U.S. Air Force, Norman had been recruited by the Royal Canadian Mounted Police; the equivalent to the F.B.I. in the U.S. He had told Ricky that the R.C.M.P. had assigned him as an English/French translator for visiting dignitaries and traveling members of the Canadian government travelers. This choice of vocation for Norman seemed strange given the fact that his brother had always been a rebel and being a translator just seemed way too tame for him.

Ricky spotted Norman's stocky frame and his signature trademark outfit. He wore a huge red maple leaf embroidered across an oversize Montreal Canadiene hockey jersey, shearling flight boots with the front tongue sticking out and his comical red checkered buffalo trapper hat, with faux fur ear flaps.

No one will ever get him to conform to today's fashion, Ricky thought.

Norman was only about 5' 7" but his stocky build was a lasting feature from his weightlifting and wrestling competition days. His blue eyes and fair complexion were accented by premature thinning light brown hair. He walked like a heavily muscled bouncer and talked like a swearing, fighting sailor but, to his many lady friends he was a teddy bear. Within a split second his disposition could swing from tender, loving and considerate, to alternately, harsh, crude, and violent. Those who knew him knew enough to never get on his bad side.

Spotting Ricky across the airport concourse, Norman's eyes brightened as a large grin spread across his round face. He sprinted through the crowd, weaving left and right, to avoid colliding with other passengers.

"Glad you could make it, Bro," he greeted Ricky breathlessly, wrapping him in a bear hug and lifting him off his feet. Although he was three inches shorter than Ricky, his strength made up for the lack in height.

"This place is a bloody zoo." Norman looked at his signature Mickey Mouse watch. "Let's hit the Igloo Bar in the up-stair lounge." He placed a firm arm around Ricky's neck, directing him towards the escalators.

"Is that all your luggage?" Ricky questioned, looking at the small duffel bag Norman had slung over his shoulder.

"You know me, travel light, ready to fight!" Norman laughed.

"You're lookin' good, even without Mom's cookin'," Ricky chided, squeezing Norman's bicep, as they stepped off the escalator on the second floor. "So, we only have two hours between your flights?"

"*Had* two hours, Bro, thanks to Air Canada. Have you ever seen them be on-time? We were forty minutes late leaving Calgary, then twenty-five minutes late on the stopover in Regina." That leaves only about forty-minutes 'til my Quebec City connection."

"The last time I saw you, we only had half an hour before your flight to Washington, D.C. Are you ever going to come home for a few days?" Ricky opened the glass door to the Igloo Lounge. The bar was crowded with reveling holiday travelers watching a repeat of the previous night's hockey game.

They found two seats at the crowded bar. Norman offered Ricky a Du Maurier cigarette. "I haven't a clue where home is anymore. With Mom, Dad, and Sis in Florida, and you here in Montreal. I guess I could consider myself homeless," he laughed. "Sometimes I wake up in a hotel room and can't remember what city

EATON'S – During the Second French Revolution

I'm in. At least with my six-month training at the R.C.M.P. Depot in Regina, I always knew where the hell I was at."

"A Crown Royal neat and a Seagram's seven and seven, please," Ricky directed the petite blonde bartender. "I never understood why a translator for the R.C.M.P. needed six months of training. That's an administrative position, right? It's not like you'd be chasing crooks all over the country."

As the waitress returned with their drink order, Norman took a big gulp of his Crown Royal. "The popular consensus is that it probably takes them the whole six months to indoctrinate idiots like me to be stupid enough to take a bullet for our assigned charges. Like politicians are really worth giving our lives for, eh!

Lifting his glass in a toast Ricky replied, "Well, here's to seeing you one hour per year and never finding out what you are hiding from me."

Mockingly pounding his chest, Norman feigned being hurt. "We went through this last time, Bro. What do you think I'm not telling you?"

"I don't know exactly, but you never could lie to me. I told you when you were younger that you have a 'tell' in your left eye that twitches when you lie. Remember when you came home one night all bruised and bloody and you told mom and dad that you'd fallen off Erskine's roof, while shoveling snow. Well, they believed you, but I knew that you had been in a fight. I found out the next day that you and the Calabresee brothers cleaned out the Beaubien Tavern of Jimmy MacDonald and six of his Westies gang. How did I know? Because of your 'tell,' that's how!"

Norman avoided Ricky's gaze. "Well, this time you are wrong. Now I'm just a boring guy, in a boring job, with a prime objective of getting laid as often as possible, in as many cities as possible." He checked his watch again, then checked the time against the clock above the bar. "How about you? Are you getting any?"

"Come on, you know quite well that I only get laid on my birthday and that's not until January. She hasn't gotten any less frigid, and I haven't gotten any less horny!"

"What about you? Got anyone special?" Ricky asked.

"Actually, I do. I have a special lady in Vancouver. She is in her third year at the University of British Columbia, majoring in media communications. The sad part is I don't get to see her very often."

"Long distance relationships can be difficult, but it's not like you to settle for just one girl at a time. Before you went in the service you were juggling at least three oriental girls at the same time."

"I think I've matured since then and finally discovered the joy of a monogamous relationship." He waved to the waitress for another round.

"That sounds like love, Norm. Tell me about this special heart throb."

"She's twenty-two, barely five feet tall, with long black hair and a body to die for. Her father owns a Chinese Buffet in Vancouver's Chinatown."

"And I gather she's oriental?"

"Of course."

"What's with you and oriental girls? The only time I've ever seen you with a white girl was with Calabresee's sister, when you were in high school and that almost got you killed."

"Yeah, going out with a mob boss's daughter wasn't one of my finest moments."

"You think?"

"Anyway," he ignored Ricky's sarcasm, "about my choosing Oriental's over white girls, when I was stationed in the Philippines with the Air Force, I dated a lot of young Filipino ladies ..."

"I'm sure you did." Ricky clinked Norman's glass.

Norman ignored Ricky's comment, To continue," I found that oriental girls were just so much more real than white girls, not to mention prettier. Their values were not based on how much money you had, how good looking you were, or how good you were in bed. They liked to spend the time getting to know the true you. My girl is not just pretty, she is kind, considerate and she's genuinely interested in intellectual conversation. What more could I ask for?"

"I'm really happy for you, Little Bro'." Ricky put an arm around him, pulling him tight. "You got the job, the adventure, and you even got the girl. Congrats."

"Thanks."

Gulping the last of his drink Ricky slid from the barstool as he placed fifteen dollars beneath his glass. "Let's get you to your flight." His face was flushed with pride.

Descending the escalator Norman stated, "Ricky you can't keep going on like this. At your age you should be getting laid every night, if not, your dick's going to atrophy and fall off. If you aren't getting it at home and you're not going to leave her, at least get some stuff, somewhere, even if you have to pay for it."

"Sure! Now you are giving me sex advice when you're the one who juggles three broads at the same time. Norm, with the new baby my situation is complicated but eventually I'll solve *my* problem, in *my* own time," he responded with a bit of irritation clearly in his voice.

Norman glanced at the long Air Canada boarding line then wrapped his arms around his brother and kissed his cheek. "Okay, okay. I got it! Anyway, it was great seeing you, and if I can swing it, I promise that I'll try to drive up from Quebec City in the next month or so to spend a few days with you."

"That would be great," Ricky responded as he watched his brother get in line in front of the ticket counter.

Norman yelled back, "And remember, stay in the shadows, Bro!"

That made Ricky smile and wave. Whenever they parted that had been the mantra of the two brothers since childhood.

If you stay in the shadows, you'll never get hurt.

✤ Fifteen ✤

All the madness going on with the FLQ in Quebec, American politics, and events in the states, never figured prominently into Ricky's thoughts, that is, until November 22nd, 1963.

Ricky folded the newspaper he was reading and put it down on the table. "Hey, you're late for coffee?" he said, as Randy settled into the luncheonette booth.

"Yeah, sorry. I got tied up with some shit Appleton wanted."

"For our Bound for Success meeting?" Ricky lit a cigarette.

"No, just some new Fiberform motors that he wants me to look at for our ski boats." Randy sipped his coffee. "That's because he was just up at the lake in Rawdon last weekend with his son and daughter-in-law. Every time he goes out boating, he gets a hair up his ass about what I should be carrying, then he complains that our purchasing inventory is over budget."

"That's because he is an administrator and not a merchandiser."

"Well, he's driving me crazy with his 'wish list' requests." Randy was jumpy and it showed in his tone. "What are you reading?" he asked, turning the paper so he could read the headlines.

"The *Montreal Star* has another follow-up article on that poor bomb disposal guy who got blown up in Westmount. They say that he's gone through numerous surgeries, but he remains in a coma." Ricky pointed to the article.

"All because he was just doing his job, thank you FLQ! Randy was disgusted. "And what did the idiots accomplish. Absolutely nothing?"

"Well, with all the bomb threats to the store, they sure as hell keep us on our toes. My department people are jumpy these days. And, if I'm being honest, me too!"

"Yeah, you and me, both! One of these days those bloody threats are going to prove out and they are going to blow the shit out of us."

"They sure have been working hard all-around Montreal, and I'm sure they aren't finished, yet. Their reign of terror will only get worse until we have all-out war in the streets." Ricky was concerned.

"Well, Ricky, I guess us Anglophones better start looking for some weapons to defend ourselves, eh?"

"With us being massively outnumbered by the Francophones, weapons won't help us. We'd be a lot better off getting the hell out of Quebec before we all have to kiss our goodbye." Ricky never thought seriously about leaving his city until that very minute.

"Well, so much for our uplifting inspirational talk of the day. I gotta' get back to work and make a few bucks."

Ricky watched Randy leave the luncheonette, then finished his coffee and cigarette and headed back to work.

As he headed toward the south end of the store, he smiled and waved at Marissa, as he passed the Laura Secord Chocolate department.

"No chocolate today, Mister Dean?" she asked.

"Gotta watch my waistline," he kidded, rubbing his belly.

"Not from what I see," he heard her say, as he passed by.

As he approached the shoe department a strange calm seemed to come over the whole basement. No one seemed to be moving, or talking, instead whispering to each other in soft tones. The eerie calm was only broken by the odd sound of all the telephones ringing at once.

Dorothea McCurtly, a salesclerk in ladies sportswear ran up to him, tears filling her eyes, "they shot him, Mister Dean they, they," she cried, "they shot him, in Dallas.

Ricky took the elderly woman into his arms, "Calm down, Mrs. McCurtly, who got shot?"

"The President ... Mister Kennedy ... they shot him in his car! Jackie has blood all over her. Oh, those poor children," she kept sobbing, "they shot the governor too, but I don't know if he's dead," she sniffled.

"Why don't you go sit down in my office until you calm down. I'll be there in a few minutes," Ricky said, sending her on her way.

He saw Duane running towards him. "I heard ...." is all Ricky said.

"Everything has stopped. Everyone is in shock. We haven't wrung up a sale in the last twenty minutes," Duane exclaimed breathlessly. "What should we do?"

"First, have Serge get my black & white T.V. out of my office and have him plug it in at register two, that's the most central area. Get a large box to place under the T.V. so it's elevated high enough for everyone to see."

Ricky approached a large group of distraught customers and employees that were listening to a small portable radio that a customer had provided.

"Ladies and gentlemen, this is a horrible tragedy, but if you'll be patient, I'll have a television operational in a few moments," Ricky's voice boomed over the crowd noise.

He signaled Gwenn Robarts, assistant manager of ladies' dresses, "Gwenn, I want you to have someone positioned at the base of both the up and down escalators, so that, as the crowd grows around the television, no one is pushed back towards the escalator stairs."

Gwenn nodded as she returned to her department to secure some sales staff to handle the chores.

By that time, Duane and Serge had the little 13" black and white T.V. highly elevated at the register. A throng of viewers, both customers and employees, were gathered around and glued to the screen.

EATON'S – During the Second French Revolution

The image of Walter Cronkite, the consummate professional news anchor for CBS news, filled the screen as he read a report. Over his shoulder the studio clock showed 1:40.

Cronkite began. *"Here is a bulletin from CBS News. In Dallas, Texas. three shots were fired at President Kennedy's motorcade in downtown Dallas. The first reports say that President Kennedy has been seriously wounded."*

Cronkite reported that a priest had administered the last rites to the president at the hospital.

At 2:38 pm, Cronkite was handed a new bulletin. After looking it over for a moment, he took off his glasses, and noticeably shaken, he made the official announcement:

"From Dallas, Texas, the Associated Press flash, apparently official: President Kennedy, the 35th President of United States was officially pronounced dead at approximately 1 p.m. Central Standard Time."

Cronkite paused briefly, put his glasses back on, and continued.

"Vice President Johnson has left the hospital in Dallas, but we do not know to where he has proceeded; presumably he will be taking the oath of office shortly and become the 36th President of the United States."

Walter Cronkite, with emotion still in his voice and eyes watering, began recapping the events surrounding the Kennedy assassination.

Ricky moved to where the T.V. was placed, to speak to the crowd. "Ladies and Gentlemen, this horrible tragedy will be replayed all day long, so we are asking our staff to resume regular business operations."

As the crowd somberly began to disperse, Duane nodded towards the main aisle and whispered in Ricky's ear, "Here comes trouble, and it looks like Jeremy's loaded for bear."

Ricky quickly intercepted Radford and Appleton, outside of earshot of the crowd. But before Ricky could utter a word, Radford lashed out, no doubt posturing for Appleton. "Do you think it was smart, Dean, to close down selling activities in your departments for almost an hour?" Radford pointed an accusing finger at Ricky.

"I do! And I would do it again under the same circumstances."

Taken back by Ricky's abrupt response, Radford continued, "That T.V. thing stopped everything, and that stunt cost us thousands of dollars."

"With all due respect, sir, it did not cost us a penny!" Ricky readily contradicted his boss.

Flabbergasted at Ricky's questioning his comments, Radford stammered, "Your actions …"

Before he could finish Appleton placed a firm hand on Radford's shoulder. "Jeremy, I'd be interested to hear Mister Dean's explanation."

Ignoring Radford, Ricky spoke directly to the general manager. "Sir, before I placed the T.V. on the counter, selling activities had already come to a complete halt. People, both customers, and yes, employees, were already standing around in shock, listening to portable radios, not buying merchandise in any of my departments."

Ricky looked at Radford before continuing. "The selling down time was less than thirty-eight minutes, as calculated by Walter Cronkite, during his news cast. Our Canadian viewers weren't watching a live CBS broadcast, but rather an ATV edited feed version, which was less time than the total CBS report."

Ricky returned to Appleton. "Sir, I elected to make the best out of a very tragic situation, and I stand by my decision."

"How so, son," Appleton responded, crossing his arms, presumably in anticipation of some lame excuse.

Radford sneered with an expression that implied, *let's see you wiggle out of this one, Dean.*

"Sir, seeing all the people just standing around, I immediately realized that I needed to take some sort of action that would benefit Eaton's in the long run. Just imagine, if you asked the last generation where they were when Pearl Harbor was attacked, almost everyone would be able to pinpoint their exact location, to the minute. And ..."

Appleton interrupted, "Yes, yes, you are right. It was a Sunday, just after eight o'clock in the morning, on December seventh, forty-one, and I was just leaving for church with my parents."

Ricky continued, "You'll find the same recollections of VE day, the end of World War Two on May eighth, the Korean War beginning on June twenty-fifth, these memories will all be permanently embedded into people's minds, for generations to come. And now, these few hundred people will retell their story to thousands of others as to where they were when they heard of the JFK assassination. History will show that this was definitely a moment that they will remember hearing the tragic news while they were shopping at Eaton's."

"Son! I am amazed and, believe me, since I've been doing this job, it takes a lot for that to happen. What you did was brilliant. In fact, it is so outstanding that I want you to explain the whole process at the next store management meeting. Also, I want you to write it up as part of our Procedures Manual. I'm going to take this to the General Manager's meeting in Toronto, next month, and have it instrumented across Canada. Well done my boy, well done! The next time a tragedy of this magnitude occurs, Eaton's will be shown to be putting our customers before our quest for dollars. Thank you, Mister Dean."

They both departed with Radford noticeably disillusioned, but not uttering a single word of apology.

Ricky noticed Christine standing nearby. He was sure she had heard the conversation and she seemed to be beaming with pride.

Well, at the very least I know two people that I impressed.

⚜ Sixteen ⚜

Norman was drinking his Molson's beer in Les Jardins Norde, a neighborhood tavern in St. Micheles, a suburb of northern Montreal. He had just returned from an R.C.M.P. terrorist's seminar in Quebec City. His right leg bounced nervously as he awaited a meeting with several students with ties to the radical FLQ movement. He casually scoured the bar analyzing the faces of the patrons, most of which were of French descent.

The neighborhood bar was owned and operated by Joseph Tremblay; a one-time hood turned political activist. A decade earlier Tremblay had spent several years in Bordeaux Jail on manslaughter charges, surrounding an incident involving the Calabresee crime family. Both law enforcement and Quebec citizens, could not understand how Tremblay had survived after beating to death a Calabresee soldier. The popular belief was that accommodations had been made with the Calabresee's, whereby Tremblay's prominent association with the FLQ would benefit the Calabresee's illegal activities. This placed Tremblay in the pocket of the Calabresee family.

Norman, now operating under the alias, Louis Thibodeaux, looked around the scant cavity of the bar with its three tattered pool tables, naked walls, and frayed carpeting. He knew from intelligence reports, that the bar was a front for Tremblay's drug enterprise, and now the official headquarters of the Montreal FLQ terrorist cells.

The development of the early FLQ in Quebec was directly related to the culture of North America, which at that time was evolving rapidly towards a more action-oriented process of change. The impact of revolutionary philosophy and politics spread the doctrines of violence as a means of legitimate change among young people and particularly university students. Figures such as Che Guevara, Chairman Mao and the writer Franz Fanon were touted for their different interpretations of history and politics where violence played a pivotal role in advancing their causes and ideas.

To achieve their goals, the Palestine Liberation Organization [PLO] had been recruited to train FLQ members in urban warfare and revolutionary tactics, including bomb making and violent civil acts of disobedience. To maintain their anonymity, the FLQ disavowed any members that were captured participating in violent acts throughout the province.

To achieve their new more violent purpose, groups of 10 to 15 members were formed under the guidelines of the movements philosophy and were referred to as 'action cells.' Many cells were formed throughout Quebec including the Viger Cell, the Dieppe Cell, the Nelson Cell, and two of the most radical cells, the Liberation, and the Chenier cells.

The other important vehicle to disseminate their separatist philosophy was ownership and control of their own newspaper which they named the *Revolutionary Strategy*, the backbone of their action plans.

Being an undercover operative in 1960's Quebec was a harrowing experience for young Norman, and his successful infiltration of the FLQ's prominent Montreal north, *Dieppe Cell,* pumped adrenaline through his adventurous veins.

As he sat watching the hockey game on the tavern T.V. Norman was thinking.

Sometimes the hardest part of my job is the skepticism required in the way I perceive the average citizen. I find it harder and harder to trust people. I see the worst of the worst daily. Most of the time I feel like I can no longer even trust myself because of the double lifestyle I've chosen to live. Even though I can revel in the realization that my job as an infiltrator has a greater purpose for my country and its citizenry, it's still hard to cope with and, somehow remain grounded. At times when it gets rough, I just need to forget who I was, and stay focused on who I am. To breach my persona of Louis Thibodeaux, former University of Quebec student, could cost me my life.

Norman, as Louis, had arrived at the tavern 15 minutes early so that he could strategically position himself at the rear of the bar, with his back to the wall, and a clear view of the front door. He had met with these guys before but because he was unknown in the university circuit he was still being watched and treated like an outsider. With his perfect command of the French language and a custom-built background, he had spent months developing a convincing presence within the radical student organization. As such, he played an active part in violent rallies or destruction of public and private property, he stayed focused on his ultimate goals, passing along actionable information to his handler.

He saw the large double doors swing open admitting his two faux comrades who immediately crossed the bar to where he was seated.

"Bon Jour, mon amie," *Hello my friend,* Jean-Claude Allard, the taller of the two bellowed, taking a seat across from Louis. His associate, Adrien Belliveau, did the same.

Jean-Claude was 6' 2", approximately 225 pounds, with broad shoulders like a football player, and a demeanor that struck fear in those who knew him well. He was a no-nonsense guy with no sense of humor and his total focus in life was the elimination of Les Anglais, *The English,* by any means. He had no qualms about inflicting injury or even death, on Anglophones if the FLQ cause benefited in its quest for French dominance.

Louis had seen Jean-Claude in action at many rallies and could only characterize him as ruthless and cruel. Whether it was an Anglophone who lay bleeding on the pavement, or even one of his own, his sense of compassion was non-existent. All that mattered was furthering the cause.

In sharp contrast, Adrien Belliveau, Jean-Claude's inseparable companion, was short, overweight, and plagued with a serious facial pock-marked complexion. With his timid disposition Adrien cowered at the slightest rebuke from Jean-Claude, and stood vigilant to his every command, without question. He was Jean-Claude's treasured puppy dog.

Jean-Claude picked up Louis's Molson bottle, faced the bartender, and circled his hand signifying a round for the table.

Last Saturday night several student cells had united to invade Lafontaine Park, setting garbage cans afire, toppling park benches, and eventually getting into a confrontation with the MPD riot squad. Louis had taken this opportunity to get into an altercation with an officer, by throwing a brick through a police van window, getting him quickly arrested.

Jean-Claude spoke to Louis in French. "So, my criminal friend, you are now an official part of our *Les Montreal North Dieppe Cell*," referring to the branch of the FLQ student cell controlling northeast activities.

"Anything to further our cause," Louis replied, raising his beer.

"But, for future, you should have thrown the brick through the large windshield instead of the small side window," Jean-Claude said critically. "Or better, you should have thrown the brick at the head of that MPD pig!"

"Yeah, and then I would have been in jail for months, instead of overnight, yeah, a loss for *Montreal North Dieppe Cell*, qui?"

"I guess," Jean-Claude relented. "Anyway, we did good, and got good press for our cause."

"How did you get the cut on your head?" Adrien asked timidly, pointing to the multiple stitches on Louis's forehead.

"The cops weren't happy about me mouthing off about my rights and decided to connect my head with the wall inside the police van."

"A battle trophy," Jean-Claude offered. "Don't feel too bad, Guy LaBlanc got kicked in the nuts and will be out of commission for weeks."

"Ouch!" Adrien feigned pain. "Every time I hear that one, it hurts!"

"Okay, so what's our next plan?" Louis prodded, as the bartender arrived with three beers.

Jean-Claude slowly studied Louis's face, then looked to Adrien who gave a sight nod of his head. Jean-Claude motioned Louis to come closer across the small table. "I don't have all the details, but I'm assured that our next attack will cripple the financial markets across Canada, and, let *Les Anglaise* know that we are serious in our quest for French independence. The blow will be dealt by the *Liberation* cell operating out of Laval and I can guarantee that it will be a violent encounter."

Louis's mind raced trying to fathom the scope of such an attack, *could it be a major bank robbery, or an attack on Ottawa's financial services? No, it had to be local but with consequences that would affect all of Canada.* He realized that he needed more information if he was going to prevent such a major catastrophe.

"Wow! That sounds great, but how can a local action have national ramifications?" Louis questioned.

"Let's just say that I wouldn't be putting my money in the stock market, any time soon."

"Is our cell going to be involved?" Louis needed to pump Jean-Claude for additional information.

"I'm sure we will but so far, I haven't been given any details."

"Now that I've proven myself, I'd really like to be part of the operation," Louis offered.

"Patience my friend. Your participation has already been discussed and your talents will surely be utilized, where and when needed." Jean-Claude smiled slyly.

"That is of course, if you check out," Adrien added.

"Are you still questioning my loyalty to the cause, Adrien?" Louis asked in an indignant tone.

"I'm just saying that you might not be who you say you are, that's all. It wouldn't be the first time some asshole tried to spy on us."

Jean-Claude sat back and carefully watched the escalation of the confrontation between Louis and Adrien.

These guys are just testing me to see if I will crack. Norman thought.

Louis's piercing eyes seemed to drill a hole into Adrien's face as he brought his face within inches of Adrien. "Perhaps you and I need to have this conversation out in the parking lot, my friend," Louis challenged.

Jean-Claude made no move to intervene or quell the escalation.

"Are you threatening me?" Adrien responded, moving his hand towards the rear of his belt.

Jean-Claude stiffened as he heard the unmistakable loud click of a switchblade knife from beneath the table where Louis sat facing Adrien.

"I don't think you want to try that Adrien unless you don't care if I cut your balls off," Louis challenged.

Adrien froze in place, his eyes darting to Jean-Claude for help.

Jean-Claude laughed, placing a calming hand on Louis's shoulder. "I think you passed the final test, my friend. Don't you think so, Adrien?"

"Qui, Jean-Claude."

"We'll be in touch, Mon Amie." Jean-Claude downed his beer, as he and Adrien stood up and left Louis nursing his beer.

EATON'S – During the Second French Revolution

Somehow, I've got to find out more details about what their plans are for crippling the financial market, and what is their target.

As an undercover operative it was frustrating to be distrusted by the main principles and to scrounge for every tiny bit of information.

Norman knew that contrary to popular belief, undercover work is a lot more different than the popular perception portrayed in crime novels and on T.V. shows. The average citizen believes that an undercover agent gets out of trouble by extreme measures but in real life they get out of bad situations by being able to talk themselves out of trouble. Many times, their family and friends can get seriously injured, and some undercovers never make it home alive.

Louis cringed at the eventuality of the arrest as a result of his undercover efforts. It was one thing to sit and hear plans for their criminal activities, to take part in their assaults, to listen to their normal conversations of their families, but it was quite another to place the handcuffs on these individuals, feel their wrath of hatred, betrayal, and threats of retribution. At that exact moment you realize that you may be looking over your shoulder for the rest of your life.

Louis left the bar and walked to his old '56 Chevy in the parking lot. He knew he needed to somehow discover the location, day and time of the upcoming financial attack and warn his handler!

Louis drove several miles to a local French restaurant where he found a payphone and dialed the number he'd committed to memory.

"McFadden and Holmes Consulting," a pleasant voice answered.

"Mister Jones for Mister Smith," was all he said.

Louis had met Mr. Smith only once, which was when he'd been transferred from Hamilton, Ontario to the Montreal office, following the completion of his undercover drug sting operation. To say that the encounter was less than cordial would be an understatement. Mr. Smith dictated what he had expected of Louis, regarding his infiltration of the FLQ in a fashion that was emotionless and methodical in its execution. "Here are the parameters, now go do your job," Smith had bluntly commanded.

Mr. Smith appeared to be a total mystery, not only to Louis' Hamilton handler, but apparently also to the staff of the Montreal office. He was a heavyset man in his late 50's with graying hair and matching goatee and moustache. His rosy face was round, sporting a bulbous nose that supported a pair of frameless granny glasses. He spoke with a heavy aristocratic British accent that seemed laced with an Irish brogue. The only thing that Louis heard about his handler was that a rumor floated around that Mr. Smith was a former British MI-6 operative who retired on medical disability, and was immediately snatched up by the R.C.M.P.

The problem Louis had was that he wanted to be confident in the person handling his life, but he wasn't sure Mr. Smith was that person.

"Hold, please," the McFadden and Holmes receptionist replied.

Louis smiled as he listened to the familiar clicking on the line, the bogus consulting firm greeting, and the exact same introduction details of his every phone call.

"The line is secure, sir. Your code verification, please."

"Code 8678."

"Code verified. Your party is on the line."

"Report," came a clipped voice.

"As planned, I met with Jean-Claude Allard, leader of the Montreal north Dieppe Cell, and his flunky, Adrien Belliveau," Norman explained. "The good news is that, after my arrest at the LaFontaine Park rally, I've been accepted as a permanent member of Allard's cell.

"Excellent."

"However, the bad news is that something big is coming down that involves my Dieppe Cell, the Liberation Cell, and the Chenier Cell. So, with three independent cells all involved it must be something more than just a rally." Norman held his breath awaiting a reply.

"How will you fit into this?"

"Whatever the event is, they have made it important for me to participate in some capacity, which they have not clarified at this point. As the event date gets closer, I'll be able to gather further information."

"Any chance at a more accurate timeline?" Smith asked.

"No, if I push any further, I'll blow my cover."

"Guesses on the type of incursion?"

"My best guess is a bombing. Possibly something to do with the Montreal Stock Exchange."

"Anything that you need?"

"You could get me Allard and Belliveau's criminal rap sheet."

"Done! It will be at the dead drop tomorrow evening after six. Resume contact as more information develops." With that Mr. Smith was gone.

If only it was that easy! Norman thought.

⚜ Seventeen ⚜

Vinney Calabresee stood in the center of his 68,000 sq. ft. warehouse, the finest Cuban cigar clutched in his mouth and a 24-carat gold Bronson lighter in his hand. He swiveled his body 360 degrees taking in the variety of cars and trucks lined up in the building. The large walled-in area in the far corner held all his stolen merchandise. There were also sorting and packing tables that his crew used to "modify" the stolen goods in addition to a five-foot tall antique cast iron safe, and a center "boardroom" area where he conducted all his business meetings.

This is all mine, and I don't have to share it with my family, and no one tells me what I can, or cannot do, he thought.

It hadn't always been that way. In some circles people would have believed that because his parents were rich, he was therefore a child of privilege. The difference was that some children of privilege lived on Millionaires Row on Mount Royal, while he lived on a forty-acre walled-in compound in Terrebonne, Quebec, just 15 miles off the east end of Montreal Island. The Millionaire Row kids were surrounded by maids, butlers, and chauffeurs, while his home staff consisted of armed guards at the front gate, men with guns patrolling the property 24 hours a day and regular visits from local and federal law enforcement agencies. Vinney remembered that in times of trouble, his father's 'soldiers' would be sleeping on bare mattresses on the floor, while armed men were perched on their roof. There was a never-ending stream of men talking, eating, and smoking throughout the house.

Until he was of high school age he had never gone to public school. Instead, various nuns and priests would come to the compound daily to school him in all his subjects. When he was finally permitted to attend high school, the only friends he ever had were family members, or children of members of the family crime business. He never played in parks or playgrounds, never slept over at a friend's house, and never went anywhere without an armed escort.

He remembered his excitement when the Monsignor told his father that it was time for Vinney to attend public high school. But his excitement was short lived when he realized that he would be driven to and from school by an armed chauffeur. This limited his access to making friends, playing sports, or interacting in any extracurricular school activities. It wasn't until Vinney reached the tenth grade that his father reluctantly agreed to remove the security detail, allowing him to be schooled unsupervised.

And like a kid let loose in a candy store, Vinney tried everything. He joined everything and experienced everything, including sex. The life he built as a junior crime boss was exciting and profitable!

It wasn't long before he got into trouble at school, and eventually with the law. His response to why he was always getting into trouble was, "I just do what I know how to do."

He ran a bookie operation and a protection racket aimed at the most vulnerable kids. Vinney even ran a mini prostitution ring for the many teens who knew they wouldn't get laid otherwise.

His high school friendships consisted solely of bullies and friends of "the family" who respected and accepted his authority. His mantra was neither the French nor the English could be trusted. Vinney echoed his father's words, "Give me an Italian, anytime." He even structured his "teen mob" along the same lines as "the family" with a consigliere, an under-boss, and several soldiers.

His high school consigliere, and trusted friend, was Peter, "the Wire" Constantine, who was named that because of his talent of being able to hotwire a car in just minutes.

By the time Vinney was in his senior year, he commanded the hallways of Rosemount High School. He would strut down the hallways flanked by at least two of his soldiers. Anyone who valued their health respected him and gave him a wide berth, including teachers who understood his power and that of his family.

He wore the best clothes, drove the best cars, flaunted his ownership of a "party pad" and was envied by his peers for the successful "mini-family" that he had built. In fact, after Vinney and his friend, the Wire, had been caught pilfering money from the cafeteria cash register, the charges against them mysteriously disappeared after a strong conversation between the principal and "the Calabresee family" consigliere.

The event that radically changed the course of Vinney's life came in the form of cohesion between his "teen family" and the Calabresee family when he was hospitalized for a stab wound to his stomach.

It had happened when he and the Wire had been mocking a knife fight in his apartment, which got out of hand. During the faux fight Vinney had slapped the Wire several times across the face causing his friend's temper to surface. Vinney was still playfully lunging back and forth but now the knife the Wire, was holding was extended out in front of him. With one pass the knife sunk into Vinney's chest just below his ribcage.

Vinney collapsed and was rushed to the Royal Victoria Hospital. When his father Giuseppe, and his uncle Carmine, capo of the Calabresee crime family showed up at the hospital they ignored Vinney's explanation that his injury was just the result of playful actions between himself and Peter.

"Allowing this *attack* to go without retribution would show weakness, a fact that would be capitalized on by our enemies," his uncle Carmine had stated.

Vinney's pleaded that Peter was loyal to the family, but his words were dismissed. After he was released from the hospital, Vinney searched for Peter for two weeks hoping that his inability to find him meant that Peter had left the area and was tucked away somewhere safe. However, an article in the *Montreal Star* removed any hope of ever seeing Peter again. The headline simply read, 'Teen Body Found in Laval Landfill.' Vinney hadn't needed to read any further, he knew that his lifelong friend had been eliminated by "the family."

This instilled hatred and disrespect for his father, his uncle, and the whole family organization. From that point on Vinney decided to make his own way and distance himself from the family.

Vinney lit the lighter and brought it up to meet the end of the cigar. He drew in the hot smoke into his lungs until he could feel the bite of that first puff.

The warehouse had been a steal, literally. A client had turned over title to him as payment for his weekly "vig" that had risen to over $12,000. The actual value of the warehouse was ten times that, but the client couldn't meet his obligation, so the client had to turn over ownership to Vinney or put his life and that of his family in jeopardy.

It was a steal for the client because it was far less than his medical bills would have been. Vinney smiled as he thought of what he could have done to the client.

Vinney took another deep draw on his cigar, brushing a single tear from his eye. He would never forgive, and certainly never forget the injustice that the family had unleashed on Peter, his innocent beloved friend.

The solitude of the empty warehouse was both soothing and sobering. What Vinney saw was not a vast cavern, but rather, a strategic blow to his father and the whole Calabrisee empire. His expulsion from the family, because of his actions of skimming funds for his personal portfolio, had only added to his determination to get even for Peter's murder.

Vinney was startled from his thoughts when he heard footsteps approaching behind him. Instinctively, he reached for his gun, un-holstering it to confront his attacker.

"Jezz boss, it's just me," his second in command, Frankie, exclaimed with fear in his eyes.

"For Christ's sake, Frankie, do you have to sneak up on me like that?" Vinney returned the gun to the holster.

"I'm sorry, boss. I thought the place was empty," Frankie stammered uncomfortably.

"So, if you thought the place was empty, what the hell are you doing here, in the middle of the night?" Vinney walked Frankie over to the boardroom.

"I was coming to pick up 'da small black van to help with the Imperial Tobacco delivery." Frankie pointed to the van by the north wall.

The Imperial Tobacco heist had been planned for several months based on intel from an informant inside their Montreal headquarters. The company had over 400 employees and some 22,000 retailers throughout Canada. The heist was to be for a large shipment of cigars and cigarettes being sent to their Toronto distribution center. The plan was to hi-jack the delivery truck in L'Ile Cadieux before it crossed the bridge into St. Lazare-de-Vaudreuil. The van would then enter the Trans-Canada Highway. From there the driver was to be neutralized and the truck driven to a vacant barn on L'Ile-Perrot, where the goods would be transferred to one of Vinney's box trucks and brought to his warehouse.

"Why do you need the van when you already have the 24-foot box truck?"

"Aw boss, the Imperial truck was a 40-foot semi-trailer instead of the box truck that our snitch told us." Frankie was concerned because the information came from *his* snitch.

"What the hell are you paying him for if he doesn't give us the right information?" Vinney admonished.

"I called him when I found out and he tol' me dat they changed trucks at the last minute, combining two box trucks into the semi. And there will be a lot more product in the shipment."

Vinney hated it when his great plans went awry. "Okay, okay. So, is the semi in the barn now?"

"Not exactly, boss," Frankie replied. "The whole truck wouldn't fit in the barn, so, after we unloaded it, we separated the trailer from the cab, and I had Aldo and Marcus abandon the tractor at a truck stop on the Trans-Canada. Nobody will notice it for days," Frankie smiled.

"What a fuck up!" Vinney replied exasperated, "Just get the goddamn cigars and cigarettes back here before nine A.M. I've got to get a shipment down to Nova Scotia."

"Sure 'ting, boss," he replied, running for the van.

I'll be so glad when I don't have to work with these imbeciles, Vinney thought. And then yelled across the warehouse. "And tell Marcus I want to talk to him about his shoplifting operation. His figures are down, and I want him to move the crew to a different department store."

"Will do, Boss," Frankie hollered back, as he jumped into the van.

As Frankie drove the van out the large bay doors Vinney propped his feet up on the desk reformulating his plans for the two upcoming Eaton heists.

Maybe it's time for a radical change, and to get rid of all my idiot employees? Vinney thought.

⚜ Eighteen ⚜

Ricky stepped off the elevator on the fifth floor, on his way to a meeting with Tony Cartwright, in the security office located in discreet area hidden behind the sporting goods stock rooms.

"Hey, Agatha. Is the boss man in?"

"Do you have an appointment, Mister Dean?" she responded, not looking up from her old Underwood typewriter. "Mister Cartwright is a very busy man, you know."

"Well, Mrs. Marchant, I just ripped off the basement cash office and I came to turn myself in," he answered in a sarcastic tone.

She scoffed as she pressed the intercom button. "Mister Dean is here, Mister Cartwright, but he doesn't have an appointment."

"Send him right in," Ricky heard Cartwright reply.

"Mister Cartwright will see you, Mister Dean," She pointed to the door, as if he hadn't heard Tony's response, or didn't know where to go. Then she added,

EATON'S – During the Second French Revolution

"I'd appreciate, in the future, if you would call for an appointment. Mister Cartwright has a busy schedule," she reaffirmed.

"I'll make a note in my calendar."

Entering the small office and closing the door behind him Ricky said, "Christ Tony, you could get more warmth out of a prison guard matron than Agatha. That bitch needs to get laid, or something!"

"Yeah, Yeah. I've heard it all before." Tony replied in exasperation. "But, if I got rid of her, they probably wouldn't let me replace her and I'd be doing my own typing, and all that other crap."

"You may be better off."

"She types eighty-five words plus a minute, has exemplary filing skills, keeps the books, keeps flakes like you out of my office, makes great coffee, and I still believe I can give her an attitude adjustment."

"It's been four years Tony, and her friggin' attitude still sucks."

"Anyway," Tony waved his hand, dismissing any further Agatha conversation, "so the boss sent you down here to hold my hand, right?"

"How the hell did you hear that already? I only found out from Appleton fifteen minutes ago."

"I'm an investigator in case you hadn't noticed the sign on my door. I know things about people before they even know them, themselves."

Tony's ex-military, provost marshal mode he learned during his stint in the U.S. Marines during the Korean War, and his homicide detective mode always kicked in when he got defensive.

"It's not like that, Tony. Appleton is gravely concerned about the acceleration of this shoplifting epidemic. You've got to admit that all efforts so far have not resulted in anyone being apprehended and he just wants me to give you some assistance from the department managers. This is not a slight on your investigation abilities, uh, just strictly support."

"And what investigative experience makes you the professional candidate to be involved in this fiasco." Tony questioned'

"Come on, Tony. I'm young, good looking, and I'm the first to pick up the tab at the Shamrock Bar & Grill. What more could you want?"

"And why does Appleton suddenly have a hard-on for shoplifting? Until now, that has always been an everyday cost of doing business. In fact, since I've been here, we've caught more shoplifters than ever before."

"Have you seen the stats over just the past four months?" Ricky asked.

"Of course. And they show only a point four percent increase."

"But did you analyze them by department?"

"Well no. I am usually just concerned with the total store, why?"

"The stats include the large ticket departments like furniture, sporting goods, fur salon, etc., and realistically, no shoplifter is going to be trying to get out of the store with a sofa or bedroom set under their coat." Ricky laughed. "When you remove the figures for those departments the shoplifting losses change radically. The loss figures are six-point three percent, not the point four that you are looking at."

"Really?" Tony replied, while thinking, *And just because we have this shoplifting epidemic, Appleton has this kid busting my balls.* Tony continued, "Well, let me fill you in on a recent collar that changes your numbers and might even change your need to get involved. On your day off, we hit it big. Kate Middleton collared one of LeClerke's staff's wives walking out of the store with seventy-five dollars' worth of luggage."

Just then, Ricky got a notice on his pager. "Tony, I need to go and check this out. It's a supplier that I need to ream out. It shouldn't take too long, but with other appointments, I probably won't get back to you before end of day."

Tony nodded.

"Then you better tell Agatha to schedule me an appointment or she may bar my entrance!" With that Ricky laughed and left.

⚜ Nineteen ⚜

Ricky made his way on his regular circuit and as he passed the Laura Secord Chocolate department, the salesclerk thrust three fruit flavored chocolates into his hand. "No need to choose today, Mister Dean. Here's three of your favorites," she smiled.

"You're going to get me fat, Marissa," he replied, biting into a raspberry cream.

"I hardly think so," she blushed. "By the way, I know you love Eaton history, but did you happen to see the article in the Toronto newspaper about the Laura Secord history? I found it fascinating."

"No, but I'd love to see it. Do you have a copy?"

"I surely do." She reached under the counter. "I never knew that our name derived from an 1812 war heroine."

"Really? I'll be interested to read it," he replied, placing the article in his breast pocket. "I can read it on the train home, tonight."

Continuing his trek Ricky stopped at the leather goods department to talk with manager, Charlotte Henderson. "Are you all set on the kidskin gloves for Saturday's sale, Charlie?"

"Yes, I have five hundred pairs on hand and an additional fifteen hundred pair on backup with the supplier that we can use to fill phone orders, if necessary," she replied.

"Let's hope we need them," he laughed, continuing towards his office.

EATON'S – During the Second French Revolution

As he passed through the ladieswear department he asked a salesclerk, "Have you seen Mrs. Rousseau around? Oh, never mind, I see her," bumping into Monique Rousseau as she left the basement offices.

"Just the person, I was looking for. I need you to come to my office at three thirty, and bring your sales reports from the past two quarters?"

"Sure thing, Mister Dean."

Ricky proceeded passed his office to the desk of Jeremy Radford's secretary. "Is Mister Radford free," he asked noting the closed door.

"Yes, just go ahead and knock."

Ricky knocked lightly.

"Enter," Radford called.

"Hey Rick," He put down his newspaper while taking his stocking feet off the desk. "What can I do you for."

What the hell does this guy do all day? If he's not out of the store, he's sitting in here with the door closed.

"I just have a couple of things to bring you up to speed. First, I'm switching managerial positions between Rousseau and Snyder. Both ended the year in the red and aren't doing any better in the first two quarters. I'm going to give them the rest of the year to get back on track or I'm going to make permanent changes."

"Any ideas why their sales are off?"

"In lingerie, I believe it is just a matter of a particular product, such as corsets, going out of style. I reviewed the last ten-year stats and found a systematic reduction in corset sales every single year.

"And ladieswear?"

"I believe this is a buying problem. Our buyers are just not up on today's ladieswear fashions. I need to get them on New York buying trips."

"What's the second thing?"

"I requisitioned two of the new electronic cash registers that they started installing on the upper floors. I want my staff and the whole basement for that matter, fully trained in operating them before they just drop them on us. These mechanical monsters from the nineteen-forties are simply falling apart, so we can make an easy transition from one to the other with no problem."

"Great! Sounds like you got it all covered," Radford responding picking up his paper, and placing his feet back on the desk.

Ricky just turned and walked out. He returned to his office and called the shoe department. Tom Bryant answered, recognizing Ricky's voice. "Is Mister Hutchinson on the floor?" he asked the salesclerk.

"Yes sir, but he's with a customer right now."

"When he's finished have him come to my office, please."

Several minutes later, Duane entered the office and flopped down into the chair opposite Ricky.

"I got approval from Radford to requisition two of the new electronic registers so we can get the basement cashier staff trained in operating them immediately. Have Maggie set up a training schedule for her group, and we'll put the other one with LeClerke for training the north-end staff."

"That's great. When will they be arriving?"

"Before the end of the month. I want both units operational. We'll need two cashier teams, very well trained, special events."

"Did you hear about Boulanger getting fired?" Ricky asked.

"Yeah, hasn't everyone! Why?"

"I want you to select two of your staff to interview with John for the replacement section head position."

"Sure, that's great."

"Also, Duane, I've decided to make some changes in our lingerie and ladies sportswear departments."

"Yeah, something really needs to be done there, both departments' sales revenues have been going down the crapper for far too long. Are you going to get rid of management?"

"Something, like that. I'm actually going to switch managers with each department. Becky's going to go from lingerie to ladieswear and Monique from ladieswear to lingerie."

"Isn't that still going to leave us with two ineffectual managers operating in different areas?" Duane asked.

"No Duane," Ricky continued. "I believe this change will be a wake-up call for both of them. They'll realize that if they don't get their revenues in line their future management will be in jeopardy. They were both initially promoted because of their exceptional performance as assistant managers, so they have the capability, I think it just got lost somewhere."

"You realize that this is going to go over like a lead balloon. They both think of their present departments as their own fiefdom, and any change is going to be met with resistance," Duane insisted.

"But they'll also be made to understand that the alternative is not so attractive. I think they'll both understand that it is their last chance. Either they can be part of a progressive management team, or they can go!"

"I like both these gals and would hate to see them get canned or demoted, so yes, giving them another chance will be great. When you give me the go, I'll spend more time getting them oriented to their new positions," Duane responded, rising from his chair, and heading out.

Ricky left the office to find Christine applying price tags to some teen sweaters. "Can I speak with you for a moment Miss Guillaume," he asked.

"Yes sir," she replied, hurrying to his location.

"Would you like to meet me in my office after closing? I have some news on our discussion at the Place Ville Marie last week."

EATON'S – During the Second French Revolution

"Okay, I'll be there shortly after six," she responded, returning to her tagging chore.

Ricky went back to his office where he returned a few calls, scheduled an appointment with Doctor Markovitz, and gathered statistical files for his three thirty meeting.

At 3:30 sharp, both Rousseau and Snyder entered his office looking very worried.

"Ladies please take a seat and wipe that apprehensive look off your faces," Ricky told them. "We're here to set a plan to get your departments out of the red. Follow along in your own department sales books as we review your past revenues." Ricky opened his master sales book.

"One year ago, we note that both your departments were seriously running in the red. Next, at year end, again in the red. Finally, this year to date you are both still in the red. Monique do you have any thoughts?"

"Ahhh," she hesitated, "perhaps the problem in ladieswear has to do with our buying selections. I hate to say this 'cause I love her to death, but my buyer, Mrs. Richfield, doesn't seem to be up to date on today's fashions. She can't grasp the new designs and she's intimidated by her own suppliers. We lost more sales just because we ran out of product."

"Good point, Monique. Becky, what about your department?"

"I believe my problem, as I've discussed with you, is that we're still trying to sell the horse and buggy years after the car has become the staple of transportation. The corset market is all but non-existent today. Additionally, our store policy of allowing us to only carry lingerie staples such as push up bras, padded bras, conventional cotton underwear and heavy silk panties, puts our competitors years ahead of us. I believe that there has to be some product latitude between the Victoria Secret brand and our Eaton's selections."

"All right." Ricky displayed his stern look. "You both seem to have identified your respective problems, but you are still running in the red." He opened their two employment files. "Becky, I see that you've been managing your lingerie department for twenty-seven months, and Monique you've been managing your ladieswear for thirty-two months. With the fact that neither of you have ever been out of the red I ..."

Becky interrupted, "Oh, Gee, Mister Dean, are you going to fire us?" She burst into tears, "please I have two kids in coll ..."

"Whoa," Ricky put up his hand to stop the confusion, "no one is getting fired. Calm down."

"Sorry, Mister Dean," Becky whimpered, drying her eyes.

"I have a two-year max manager policy whereby I try not to allow managers to remain in the same department longer than two years. So, starting Monday morning you will each switch departments, with the idea that you can bring new thoughts and ideas to build new revenues. In the next four days before you begin your new assignments, I want you to think about the negative growth obstacles we talked about here today. I want you to meet with each other about what needs to be done to achieve sales projections. Give me your thoughts, no matter how radical or off the wall they seem. I want each of you also to give me a growth marketing plan for your new department first thing Monday morning. Think about the positives of this opportunity. Each of you can be the motivator to make the other succeed. Questions or comments, Ladies?"

Ricky stood and extended his hand to his *new* managers, "Thank you both. Remember, Monday is a new beginning for all of us."

It was getting late, and his next meeting was to be after 6:00 with Christine.

⚜ Twenty ⚜

As Ricky arrived for his appointment with Tony, it was apparent that Tony wasn't thrilled with having to be overseen by him. Although Tony realized that Ricky was smart and was certainly upwardly mobile, he felt that his investigative abilities and qualifications were being questioned by Appleton. Tony also realized that when the old man's directive came down from on high, he had little choice but to grin and bear it.

Ricky sat down, "Tony you look upset about something."

"I'm totally frustrated. I've had homicide investigations that were less complicated than these fuckin' shoplifters," Tony pushed the intercom button. "Agatha, could you bring us a couple of cups of coffees, please."

"Sure. Would you like me to go out and get some French pastries with that?" she responded sarcastically.

"No, and I'm not in the mood, Agatha", he curtly responded, releasing the intercom button.

Swiveling his chair towards his one small window overlooking the Woolworth Five & Dime store, Tony became lost in thought for a moment. "Okay, let's exchange ideas and see if we can figure this shoplifting thing out!"

He pressed another intercom button, "Denis, I've got Ricky Dean in my office. Could you bring in the 'Liftermob' file, and the incident board?

"'Liftermob'?" Ricky quizzed.

Tony explained. "From my days in homicide, we always gave our cases nicknames so we could easily remember them. For example, instead of saying the Jones case, or the Hernandez case, where duplicate names could develop, we used the Central Park case, or the Wall Street attacker case. In our case here, these shoplifters are like mobs."

Ricky looked confused, "Like mobs?"

"Yeah, you know, people intent on causing trouble, thus the 'Liftermob' case, Yes? Like the two yahoos who tried to rip off an eleven-hundred-dollar stereo television console system out of Heidi Mullin's department on Friday night."

"A console TV! Shit, those weigh over one hundred and fifty pounds," Ricky replied in disbelief.

"That's right, so it fits only a mob would try something so stupid! Especially since the department was jammed packed with customers. These two geniuses, wearing coveralls, stick a sales receipt to the top of the console, pick it up, and take it to the freight elevator. You wouldn't believe they got that far, but luckily the operator started asking questions about something that didn't look quite right on the receipt. Long story short, when the elevator reached the freight level, they hi-tailed it out, without their console. But unfortunately, we didn't get the alert in time to catch them. The elevator operator gave us a description, but …"

Just then, Denis entered the office with a brown accordion file under his arm. He kicked the door closed and struggled with a large white chalk board, teetering from a wooden easel.

Ricky jumped up to grab the easel before it fell over.

"Merci," Denis acknowledged.

Ricky knew that Denis Charbonneau was a true Frenchman. His politics were especially sympathetic to the Quebec separation cause, while his previous MPD employment left him with a permanent chip on his shoulder. Although not a registered FLQ member, when conversations developed, Denis chose to have little, or no normal criticism of the terrorist tactics. He was a strong proponent of a 'French only' business language in Quebec. At times he inappropriately exercised his unpopular beliefs within the English confines of Eaton's leaving him ostracized amongst many of the English-speaking employees.

He was a handsome bright young man who was plagued with rumors about his exodus from the ranks of patrolman of the MPD. The most credible story was that he had pissed off an influential and connected crime family boss. The story followed that he had disrespected and pushed for the arrest of the son of Don Calabrisee in an incident at the Montreal wharf. Following the incident apparently, Don Calabrisee, who had strong influence inside the MPD upper echelon, demanded his termination. To placate the Don, and eliminate union dissention, Denis was instead transferred from patrolman to an office position as a dispatcher. With his life stripped of any upwardly mobile aspiration, after four months, he resigned from the MPD.

Denis, needing income to support his wife and two young children, capitalized on his police training, and applied for his private investigator license. Within a short time, he realized that with his limited investigative skills, no experience, and extremely limited funds for advertising, made it impossible for him to succeed. In desperation, he made the rounds of all the department stores searching for any job that would pay the bills. Fortunately, Tony recognized his police background and offered him a position as a security floor walker. Two years later, after exhibiting outstanding arrest results, catching numerous shoplifters and a major employee thief, Tony promoted him to assistant manager of security.

Denis set the board on the easel in the corner, handed Tony the brown accordion "Liftermob" file and stood in front of the chalk board.

"Comment allez-vous, Monsieur Dean, *How are you, Mister Dean?* he purposely asked in French.

"Pas mal, Denis, et vous," *Not bad, Denis. and You?* Ricky politely acknowledged.

"Très occupé tout le temps," *Very busy all the time,* Denis responded.

"Okay guys, lets knock off singing the Quebec anthem, and get to it, Eh?" Tony interrupted, showing that he hated the French business language referendum. "Here's what we have so far." He approached the board, taking out a file from the folder.

"First of all," Tony began, "we know they're operating in gangs because we're getting alerted to multiple shopliftings at the exact same time. Except for bulky items like luggage and furniture, they always cop multiple items like ten pairs of gloves, a dozen tubes of lipstick, and so on. They always pick the most expensive items off the shelves. They either work alone, or as husband and wife, or a mother with children. These people are smart, or I believe they must have at least been trained in precision timing. Aside from the one guy we nailed in the notions department, with five sewing kits down his pants, we haven't apprehended anyone else that we can prove is part of the gang operation. And we couldn't squeeze this guy enough to get him to roll on anyone else. He insists that this was a one-time thing, and he is not part of any gang. Denis checked the guy out. Tell Ricky what you found," the conversation shifted to Denis, catching him off guard.

Denis stiffened, as he looked at his notes. "Uh, the guy's name is Ronaldi Morenzo, thirty-nine, living in Montreal North, and ..."

"Just the facts, Denis," Tony insisted.

"Okay, he has a long rap sheet for petty theft, including multiple counts of shoplifting, assault and battery, grand theft auto, and a manslaughter charge for which he just completed a six-year term in Bordeaux Prison. This is one bad dude. But the most interesting part of his sheet is the rider from the MPD Major Crimes Bureau which ties him to the Calabrisee crime family. From what my contact says, he had some problems within the family a few years ago and was eventually thrown out on his own. Maybe he went out and formed his own organization?"

"I can't believe that" Tony countered. "I grilled this guy and to me he doesn't have the brains to form his own bowling team, let alone a shoplifting organization. No, if it is organized crime, it's farther up the food chain."

EATON'S – During the Second French Revolution

"Could this be all part of this FLQ crap, developing funding for their organization?" Ricky asked, noticing the grimace across Denis' face.

But Tony didn't wait for what might be Denis' colored view regarding the FLQ. "We gave that a lot of thought and decided that this would be too small potatoes for the FLQ, if they wanted money, they'd just blow up a bank or kidnapped another million-dollar hostage."

"Are we the only ones being targeted by this gang, I mean 'Liftermob' gang?" Ricky smiled.

Denis looked at his files. "No. In fact, I had a meeting with my counterparts at Simpsons, The Bay and Dupuis Freres and they've all been hit bigtime. The consensus is that the gang only targets one store at a time, for one or two months, creating as much havoc as possible before moving on to the next store. They are all as baffled, as we are."

"I hate to admit it, but" Tony looked over at Denis, "with the evidence we've been able to gather, we just don't have enough information to formulate a viable plan for their capture. Their appearances change regularly, their interaction with store personnel varies, it's a friggin' nightmare. I'm taking a lot of heat from both Appleton, and now, Toronto corporate."

Ricky thought for a moment then asked, "Why don't we look at it from a different angle? What do you think they do with all the merchandise? They're certainly not stealing ten-dollar gloves to sell to some fence."

"That's the easy part," Tony replied, throwing his hands up in exasperation. "They can sell the shit back to us at a hundred cents on the dollar. That's the beauty of their operation."

Ricky shook his head. "Huh?"

Tony's frustration led him to get up and pace around his desk. "You know that Eaton's has a *Goods Satisfaction, or Money Refunded* guarantee, and as you also well know, that means, with or without a sales receipt. This is a license to steal! I can cop a pair of shoes from your department today, and if the Eaton's price tag is attached, I can bring it back tomorrow, for a full cash refund. Ain't life grand?"

"Yeah, but Tony, now you are in my realm of expertise. If we start to have large and unusual amounts of returns, especially without receipts, my staff would be jumping on it! And our policy is that a supervisor must sign off on every single refund."

Ricky continued. "Which brings us to how we also make life simple for criminals. Eaton's prides itself on our network of truck drivers who come to your home to either pick up or deliver parcels, Eh? So, now you can steal those pair of shoes, call for a pickup and sit in comfort of your home watching the fuckin' FLQ blowing up all our mailboxes." Tony looked straight at Denis as his anger free flowed!

"Don't you see, Ricky, it can't get any better for the thief. They come into the store and steal, then they get **our store policy** accommodations **by way of** an Eaton's pickup. Then they return the merchandise without ever having to come back into the store."

Tony finally sat back down. "I talked to Appleton about changing the policy to require dated receipts for refunds and he laughed me out of his office, telling **me** to go dig up old Timothy Eaton, and convince him of that. So, we're screwed, unless you have some miracle up your sleeve."

"Well, you were right earlier, Tony, I don't know crap about investigation, but I do know store products, my customers, and my staff. And I believe therein lies a possible solution. Since we spoke earlier, I've given this a lot of thought and believe the key may be to get into their heads, understand their habits, and what you call their modus operandi and that is where we have a chance of picking them off."

"I'm confused. I thought we covered all that," Tony replied pointing at the board.

"Where I believe we can capitalize is in identifying their structured diversionary tactics. When these criminals enter any department, they are going to be approached by a salesperson, Right?"

"Okay, go on," Ricky acknowledged.

"These people cannot steal anything as long as that salesperson is there with them. So, to remove the salesperson, and allow the items to be stolen, these people must create a diversion. The diversion can be as simple as asking for an item or size, that these guys know will require the salesperson to go to the rear stock area, leaving them alone to gather the bounty. There is also a more calculated diversion in utilization of a team to create physical diversions that will draw staff and everyone's attention away from the shoplifter."

"Sorry, I got the first, but got lost on the calculated diversion," Tony quizzed.

Ricky explained. "Think about what happens when unusual events happen on any given selling floor. For example, a stroller comes crashing down an escalator, someone passes out on the floor, a salesperson is being yelled at by a customer, and on, and on, The one thing that all these events have in common is that everybody's attention is drawn to the event. Ergo, the thief has complete freedom to complete his, or her, theft. The beauty of our having this knowledge is that it is completely controllable on our part. Now we can level the playing field."

"Shit, when you put it that way, Ricky, yeah!"

"How the hell did we miss this, Denis," Tony asked accusingly.

Denis just shrugged.

"The point is Tony," Ricky continued, "our staff has had extensive training in selling and only minimal training in security. We must change that. Because of the uptick in thefts in my area I implemented what I labeled as the 'eyes on' program. It's simple. Using a buddy system, each salesperson is required never to leave any customer without someone having 'eyes on' them. That means when I go to the stock room, 'my buddy' is keeping an eye on my customer. The customer is never, ever, without 'eyes on'. My section heads and managers are required to regularly check the 'buddy system' and see it in operation. They look for any holes that might allow the thieves the advantage. I believe this makes so much sense because these are skilled unconventional shoplifters and using your standard floor walking procedures are just not working."

"I understand that" Tony interrupted. "It sounds great, but how would you handle the big diversion, as you call it, the stroller careening down the escalator, or some customer screaming at one of your employees?"

"This requires education and military style enforcement by both management and staff. I had the electricians install a buzzer at each of my register areas last week. Whenever an event happens, be it large or small, the duty cashier at the closest station rings the buzzer alerting all employees to scan their area for suspicious customers. That puts hundreds of eyes searching for an offender, instead of gawking at the event. Minimal responding management are directed to rapidly resolve the event, freeing others to extend investigative assistance, within the subject department. Additionally, the duty cashier is to immediately alert security and request your detective's presence. With any luck, and hundreds of 'eyes on' we will catch these crooks in the act. It really isn't complicated, and a viable plan to nail these crooks."

"It sounds excellent, Ricky. What do you need from us?"

"I did this in my departments," Ricky explained, "but we need this to go into effect store-wide if it's going to work. I suggest that you present this whole program to Appleton and insist on full implementation in all departments. I feel so confident that I'm tempted to say that this is guaranteed to work. Additionally, we'll need to develop a training dialogue for all your detectives, to present to the selling staff."

"You want me to present *your* plan to Appleton and take all the credit. That is not me, Ricky."

"Just present the plan as the result of our joint collaboration on the 'Liftermob' problem and leave it at that. I don't need any credit. We are both after the same goal, to put these guys out of business. One last thing that I neglected," Ricky continued, "from what I've put together I believe the other way these guys operate is through what I call crowding. That's where they get rid of a salesperson, then a whole group of the gang crowds around the faux customer to shield the thief from view. This allows the stolen items to be quickly shoved into a bag, or on his or her person. My duty cashiers are instructed to ring the buzzer when they see, or have reported to them, any suspicious crowding activity.

"This is really great, Ricky. I see that pooling our expertise can really work to get these bastards." Tony extended his hand.

Tony looked over at Ricky, and thought, *This kid ain't so bad after all!*

⚜ Twenty-One ⚜

Ricky had been dreading his encounter with Dr. Julius Markowitz for over a month. He felt very uncomfortable and had already cancelled two previous appointments.

"So, Richard," Dr. Julius began, reviewing his notes, "I see your physician, Dr. Albert Lambrere, referred you to me, yes?"

Dr. Lambrere was Ricky's general physician who he had been seeing for many years about is sexual performance problems.

Ricky wasn't convinced whether any of this psycho-babble junk was going to work for him. Dr. Lambrere had tried everything in the medical area to help Ricky but had failed. Finally, he told Ricky he needed help, as he put it, "from a mental health professional."

"Yeah. Dr. Lambrere doesn't think I'm medically sick, he just thinks I'm nuts," Ricky joked.

"The notes Dr. Lambrere sent over indicate that your problems are sexual, leading to depression and insomnia, is that correct?"

"Yes, I can't get any sleep and I can't get any sex and it depresses me," he laughed.

"Richard, if this therapy is really going to help you at all, you are going to have to take it more seriously. Both of your issues are treatable with positive results. But you must be a willing participant, yes?"

Ricky was having a difficult time getting the comic image of Groucho Marx out of his mind as he considered Dr. Julius Markovitz, sitting before him. It wasn't just his hooked nose, or extra bushy eyebrows, but his whole stature. He had a cylindrical face with a bald head and gray tuffs of hair above his massive ears. He was a pudgy five foot three with a protruding Buddha belly, large enough to hold his notepad.

"Yes, I understand. I just tend to joke when I get nervous."

"Then, we shall proceed, yes? It appears from your patient intake questionnaire here, that there have been difficulties in your marriage, originating from the day you got married. And, for reasons unknown to yourself, you and your wife have settled into a 'partial platonic' relationship. Please explain your definition of a 'partial platonic'?"

"It's just that ..." Ricky stammered from embarrassment, "that we only have sex every few months, actually, probably more like every six months. Even then it appears that I am the only one participating."

"How many times have you had sex during the two plus years that you have been married?"

"Maybe four or five times. I can't remember for sure."

"Of those sexual encounters, have they been fulfilling to either of you?"

"To her, definitely not, to me, it was just a necessary quick release."

"Explain please, 'quick release'."

"The act never takes longer than a couple of minutes. Dr. Lambrere calls it premature ejaculation."

"But I see that Dr. Lambrere finds no physical ailment for this situation, yes?"

"He ran all kinds of tests and says, in that area, I am perfectly normal. He prescribed some numbing cream for me to use, to delay things, but it had no effect."

"You are both healthy young people, so what does your wife say about the lack of sex in your marriage."

"Well, first she blames everything on me. Then she says she has absolutely no desire for sex and can live without it for the rest of her life."

"Do you compensate for this missing sexual release with personal masturbation?"

Ricky's face totally flushed in humiliation.

"It's nothing to be embarrassed about Richard, it is a normal function that people engage in."

"Yes, I do," Ricky answered reluctantly.

"Good. Good. Is your masturbation done with enough regularity that it is sexually satisfying to you?"

"At first, I did it a lot, but as time passed, I needed it less, and less. It just felt so cold and impersonal. I guess I've come to the point that I put sex out of my mind as something that is just not going to happen."

"That is quite understandable. Now, getting back to your wife. I see here, that before you married you classify your sexual activities with her as normal. What do you mean by normal?"

"We petted a lot and had sex whenever and wherever the opportunity arose. It didn't matter if it was the back seat of a cold car, or my mother and fathers' bed. For me, and seemingly for her too, the sex was great!"

"And the sex tapered off, how much after you married?"

"No! It ended on the day we *got* married. There was no sex on the honeymoon night, and no sex until three months later when she got drunk at a party that we attended. And our daughter is the result of that one single encounter," Ricky looked away in disgust. "My daughter is everything to me, and, having her is worth anything I need to endure!

"Tell me. Has your wife ever been checked out by a medical doctor or a psychologist?"

"She was under the care of her gynecologist for nine months, but everything was normal. As for her, or us, going to a marriage counselor, or phycologist, she doesn't even want to discuss the matter. She insists the problem is all me!"

"Yes. That is a very typical denial. Does she exhibit any other abnormal behavior in her relationship with you?"

"Her mood swings, as I call them, are constant, even in the limited time we spend together. One minute she is talking calmly, and the next she's off on some tangent that doesn't make any sense. She's most content when she's by herself or, watching television."

"Do you know of any major traumatic incidents in her past that could be affecting her behavior towards you?"

"Well, she came from a verbally abusive environment with an extremely strict father, and an overly passive mother. In fact, her father used to tell her he hated her and wished she were dead. And he constantly accused her of being responsible for the death of her three-year-old brother. Her only escape was when she would faint because his words became so abusive, that the next step was physical abuse from him."

"Her father holds her responsible for the death of her three-year-old brother? Explain."

"Apparently her brother had some sort of medical issue from the time he was born. But, since the child died while Kathy was babysitting him, her father squarely placed the blame for his death on Kathy."

"My, my, my," the doctor exclaimed, noticeably disturbed by this revelation. "So, you say that she refuses any sort of mental health assistance, yes?"

"That's right, and she seems to be getting even worse, the longer we are together."

"It is really sad that she won't get help because from the sounds of it, without my actually examining her, all I can conclude is that she has the A-typical symptoms associated with Schizophrenia, coupled with a possible anxiety disorder. It is sad to say, but although these conditions can be treated with early diagnosis and medication, without such treatment they will continue to worsen." Dr. Markovitz hesitated a moment, then continued. "So, Richard, this places the problem and the resolution, solely in your hands."

"I guess that's why I'm here."

"I'm sure you've talked to her about her lack of sexual drive and the effects on you. What does she say?"

"To be blunt, she tells me, 'that if I need it that bad, I should go and pay for a hooker'."

"Apparently, she's given you her permission so, why haven't you visited with a prostitute?"

"I don't know. But I guess, it's my upbringing that dictates that you don't cheat when you're married, and my mother's favorite saying that 'I made my bed, so I better lie in it.'"

"That's very admirable Richard, but even if we take into consideration personal negative views on infidelity, or your aversion to prostitutes, it appears clear to me that you are backed into a corner with few options. You are young and virile, and need normal sexual activity in your life, yes. You need to feel the healthy emotions of love and caring. You need to experience feelings of close companionship, and somehow you need to make these necessities happen in your life."

Ricky was shocked by these statements. "So, you're saying I need to go out and get laid?"

"Not in such crude words, but yes! If you want to stay in your marriage because of your daughter, you need to explore other avenues. Since you do not feel comfortable seeking out a prostitute, you can explore other possibilities. Of course, you do not need to rush, or jump into bed with the first woman you find attractive, but if there is someone you are comfortable with and you develop a relationship, and then if it progresses to a sexual desire, then that is good! Do you understand?"

"Yes. I know I need to do something, I just never thought that would be the answer."

Dr. Markovitz looked at the time and suggested, "Now, perhaps we should expand upon this problem at a future session. Let's explore your insomnia problem for a bit, yes?"

Ricky glanced at his Bulova wristwatch, "Isn't my time up?"

"Let's not worry about the time, today. You're my last patient and we are making *great* headway. Anyway, I stopped charging you ten minutes ago. "So, to begin with, can you tell me if you have experienced problems with insomnia at any other times throughout your life?"

"No, it began about two years ago, when I first got married."

"I see," he responded making notes in his file. "And, during that period have you had occasions when you did not have trouble sleeping.

"Yes, when I was alone on a vacation to visit my parents in Florida, or away on a business trip."

"I see," making more notes. "Let's move on then, yes?"

"I guess so," Ricky replied sounding exasperated, and thinking, *if this guy gives me one more "I see" or "yes" I'm going to strangle him, yes?*

"We must have patience, Richard. This is only your first session, and I must get to know you to understand your problems, yes? Now we've already explored the sex issue in your marriage, so now you can tell me about your childhood."

"My childhood story is short, and not so very sweet" Ricky began. "I was the oldest of three children born to a mentally and physically abusive mother, who spent her life demeaning all her children. I had a passive father who constantly worked away from home, so remembering the early years with him is a problem. Between the age of eight and ten, I was sexually abused by two different men, one being my grandfather, the other a family friend. I had a grandmother who was verbally abusive and a Christian fanatic. During my elementary school years, I was very shy, awkward, and unpopular with my peers. In high school I was a below average student because I hated school and had only one serious girlfriend during my teen years, but no sexual intercourse. Late in my final year of school I met my future wife and experienced my first sexual relation at the age of eighteen. I married my wife because I felt an obligation, not because I loved her, but because I had slept with her."

Ricky paused in thought, "Correct that. More likely I married her because my mother told me not to marry her. Boy, does that sound sad! Anyway, on our wedding day, I realized that I'd made the biggest mistake of my life and that I would forever suffer because of it. Also, my previously, very sexual wife, immediately became frigid on our wedding day. But to end with some positive thoughts, my grandfather died when I was eighteen and I went out and celebrated. I am now considered extraordinarily successful in business."

"I see, my boy. Really very extraordinary. You are very eloquent and concise in your description. Opening yourself up, which is particularly good. But you present some of these horrors as if you are making a business presentation. Are there no emotions, feelings of anger or sadness? It is as if you are relating the story of a third party. We must get you to let, *you*, be the person we are talking about, yes?"

"We may need to talk about this more, so I better understand what I need to do, or say, here in the future," Ricky replied sarcastically.

"There are no rules, Richard. You are free to do, or say, what you please, I am only here as your director, the person who hopefully guides you to a satisfactory resolution of your problems."

Looking at the grandfather clock in the corner of the small office, Doctor Markovitz added, "as you requested only half hour sessions, your time is ended for today. But as an exercise I wish you to relate the childhood story you told me to yourself. When you do, I wish you to try and generate at least one tear, one tear for at least one of the tragic events that you related to me, yes? And try to tell the story as if it happened to you and not someone else."

"Yes, Thank you, Doctor. I'll set up my next appointment with your wife in the outer office."

As Ricky braved the cold back to Eaton's, he thought,

I'm thirty bucks poorer, and I sure as shit don't feel one bit better!

EATON'S – During the Second French Revolution

⚜ Twenty-Two ⚜

It was 8:45 A.M. and as Eaton's would open in 15 minutes, the staff were busy primping displays, opening registers, and straightening sale tables.

"Marge, can you tell all the section heads and managers that I need the staff assembled by your register for a short meeting?"

"Sure, Ricky. Do you want the stock personnel, too?" Marge asked.

"No, just the sales staff."

He watched as his employees quickly gathered.

"Good morning, ladies and gentlemen," he began. "I just have a few words before we open. Everyone needs to keep an eye out for customers approaching the escalators with strollers. We've had two accidents in the past week of strollers toppling over on the escalators. Also, all section heads, please make sure that all your temporary staff are aware of the kill switch location for the escalators. I asked two of the weekenders last Saturday and neither of them knew what I was talking about."

"Now, as you are all aware, the FLQ have escalated their cause with increased vandalism, robberies, bombings, and anti-English rhetoric which we've all in the media. This has resulted in increased animosity of the average French speaking people towards the English." Ricky noted the embarrassment on faces of several of his French employees.

He continued, "And since our downtown store symbolizes their complaints concerning English Federalist Canada, we have become the prime targets of the separatist movement. We have all been made a part of the increased bomb threats directed at our store over the past few months, and as such, we must be much more cognizant of the feelings of our French Quebecers. With that in mind, we have been advised by our executive office to make special efforts to accommodate our French speaking customers. This means making sure that none of our actions will make them feel uncomfortable while shopping at Eaton's. Therefore, for those of you who have only a limited working knowledge of French, you are directed to turn over any French customers to a salesperson who is fluent in French. We don't want you trying to muddle through a conversation in broken French, which will irritate the customer. Just say to the customer, 'excuszee moi, Madame or Monsieur,' *Excuse me, madam, or sir,* and find a bilingual person to take over. Now, for those of you on commission, I'm sure that you are worried about your sales figures. To overcome any losses, the person that you hand off a customer to will, as they say, owe you one. That means that he, or she, will pass along the next available customer to you. Therefore, no one will lose any money and our French customers will be kept happy. These are trying times for all of us, and we need to make these concessions if we are going to weather the political storms in Quebec."

"Also, our 'eyes on' program to address the increased shoplifting is now in full effect. Make sure that everyone in your control area is up to speed, and that all weekend staff are totally familiar with the program."

"So, thank you all, and let's have a great selling day. Section heads please stick around for a minute."

As the regular staff dispersed to prepare for the store's opening, Ricky addressed the remaining section heads. "I realize this commission thing is not going to go smoothly with the older sales staff. They are going to be reluctant to turn over any sales, and ultimately, they are going to overwhelm the younger ones. You are going to have to be more diligent and observant, to ensure this doesn't happen."

"Also, we are finding that many of the older sales personnel are running out of here at night without straightening up or putting the protective covers on the sales tables and leaving that chore to the younger staff. That has got to stop immediately. If you have problems with any of the older staff not toeing the line, let me know and I'll handle them.

"Finally, as you are all now very aware from our security meeting last week, the whole store is being plagued by a serious rash of thefts. It seems no department is safe from these thieves, which security believes to be an organized shoplifting ring. Now, organized doesn't necessarily mean the mob, but be careful anyway. Get your staff to always keep an eye on the customer, even when you go into the stock area. If they are going to be in there for any length of time, be sure to have someone else keep an eye on the customer. I'm sorry for all these new procedures, but we can get through all these issues if we do them together! Have a great selling day!"

"Duane, stick around for a minute," Ricky requested.

As everyone else dispersed, Ricky pulled a paper from his inner jacket pocket, and handed it to Duane.

"This is an investigative report from security about a menswear weekend staffer by the name of Andre Benoit. Apparently, they suspect him of passing free clothing to his friends. They are going to insert an undercover operative into the menswear department this weekend to keep an eye on him. I want you to let Amed Darzada know that this security agent will be working with him. I also need you and Darzada to keep this information to yourselves."

"Got it boss!"

⚜ Twenty-Three ⚜

Rather than sleeping on the uncomfortable sofa, Ricky lay restless in his king size bed listening to the baby fidgeting in the next room, and knowing that his wife Kathleen was there, in her usual position, crowded to the left side of the bed. It was only 9:32 P.M. according to the clock on the stacked cardboard boxes that served as his nightstand.

Moving from his one-bedroom basement apartment in Rosemount, Ricky had settled on a second-floor duplex apartment in Ville St. Laurent, adjacent to the railroad tracks, to conserve money. Being only 25 feet from the train tracks meant that every train, commuter, or freight, going by at all hours of the day or night, shook the entire apartment as it passed. The upside was that you eventually got used to the trains. The downside was that anyone visiting your house freaked out as each loud train passed by.

Aside from his daughter, Darlene, his home life was non-existent. He believed that without his life at Eaton's, he wouldn't have any life at all. According to his phycologist's impressions, regarding Kathy's abnormal mood swings, the doctor had diagnosed her as schizophrenic.

For Ricky, every night was the same; come home from work, endure silence from his wife, eat supper alone, play with the baby, watch T.V., and go to bed. He'd go to sleep at 10:00 and be awake by 11:00, that's how it had been since he'd gotten married. He joked to himself that, *"when I said I do, I really, really did."* He knew what the problem was, he just couldn't control it.

Ricky thought, *If we are lucky each of us makes one colossal mistake in their life and thank God, I got mine out of the way early in life!"*

Ricky reached for his Pepsi on the nightstand just as the 10:00 final train to St. Eustache rumbled through his back yard, violently shaking the apartment. The baby whimpered, and the wife stirred, but both returned to sleep. This was going to be another long night.

Ricky got up to check on the baby. She was sleeping peacefully but had kicked her blanket off, which he tucked in around her. Turning the thermostat higher, he walked aimlessly around the small apartment as he had done so many nights in the past. From the upstairs front window, he could see that it had begun to lightly snow. It looked so peaceful, yet in minutes it could turn treacherous. He hated the cold, hated winters, and hated his life.

Ricky returned to bed. Looking at the clock, he noted it was only 10:18.

He pulled the comforter up to his chin and curled his feet in the blankets. It seemed that his feet were perpetually cold from October through May.

It was now 10:27. He had to lay still, clear his thoughts, and get some sleep. He fluffed the pillow and rolled onto his side. He had just begun to fall asleep when the kitchen phone blared. Throwing the covering back he ran for the phone before it woke the baby. The clock on the stove showed 10:31.

"Hello," he whispered.

"Ricky? Is that you?"

"Yes, who's this?"

"Ricky, this is John Witherspoon. Get down to the store A.S.A.P. There's been an incident, and we need you down here right away!"

"Sure, but what kind of ..." but he never finished, as John interrupted.

"Not now! I still got a bunch more people to contact. Just get your ass down here, stat."

"I'll be there in thirty," he offered, but John had already hung up.

Along with being the manager of the main floor fine jewelry, John was designated as the store's emergency services officer.

Ricky ran back to the bedroom, speedily dressed, and called a cab.

The snow hadn't yet begun to accumulate, and the cab made it downtown in record time. As he neared the store, Ricky could see the surrounding streets bordering Eaton's were ablaze with emergency vehicles, their strobe lights casting macabre images on the building. Although Ricky saw the presence of police, fire, and medical responders, the largest group was that of the Montreal Bomb Disposal Units. As they got closer a patrolman, in the middle of the street was directing traffic away from the store. Ricky rolled down the window and presented his employee card to the officer saying, "I just got a call to come into the store."

"The taxi cannot go any further down the street. You will have to get out and walk to the store," he replied, waving the cab towards the curb.

Ricky paid the cabbie, scooted around the emergency vehicles, and entered the store at the employee's entrance where he was met by Duane.

"How did you get here so fast? You live farther than me," Ricky asked, already heading for the basement escalator.

"I was at my mother's house downtown when I saw the news report. I figured nothing good was going on, so I came right over."

"So, what the hell happened?"

"We finally caught a live one. The bomb went off in the bank of lockers beside the middle escalators by our notions department. It nearly took out old Raphael, the janitor. He had just walked by there a few minutes before the bomb exploded. He was so shaken up that they had to take him up to the Royal Victoria Emergency."

"Has contact been made with our own response group?" Ricky asked, veering away from the damaged escalator, towards the stairwell.

"Yeah, all the senior staff, section heads and up, are on their way in. Once I got here, I spoke with Witherspoon and got the orders to fill them all in. I told them to bring a change of clothes and plan on being here for the next 24 hours."

Exiting the stairwell, both Ricky and Duane stopped speechless in their tracks. The scene of the incredible carnage was beyond anything they could have expected. A smoky mist enveloped the bomb site, a heavy acrid smell permeating the air. Metal ceiling panels, electrical wires and hanging fans dangled precariously above the floor. The area was strewn with thousands of broken products from the notions, sundries, and Laura Secord Chocolate department. Displays were overturned, counters and tables destroyed, and the

EATON'S – During the Second French Revolution

floor was slick with a blend of assorted liquids. The huge antique wood and metal escalator was demolished as were the bank of 25 metal lockers. Products such as scissors, toiletries, cosmetics, glasses, lipstick, pencils, pens, Q-Tips, pills, nail polish remover and more were scattered haphazardly throughout the bomb site.

This is the closest one can get to the scene of a war zone! Ricky thought.

Ricky and Duane were directed by a fireman to remain at the entrance to the stairwell until they finished hosing down the floors and walls of toxic liquids. He advised them that the bomb squad had cleared the area of any other possible bomb threats.

What hit Ricky the worst was the destruction of the historic wooden escalator that lay strewn around the blast area. He frowned as he viewed the damage to the most important treasure remaining from the original Goodwin/Eaton store. This was the last remaining narrow antique wooden escalator that had carried hundreds of thousands of shoppers to and from the main and basement floors. Now it laid twisted and splintered in its throes of death. Of all the remaining store antiques this had been Ricky's favorite and most fascinating. He had researched its history and even been permitted to climb underneath the escalator mechanism during a repair period. He had learned: *the original Goodwin's department store was one of the first stores in Montreal to install the newly invented escalator, called a wooden 'traveling stair', in the early 1900's. It was the first-time shoppers could be automatically ferried between floors without having to ride an elevator. Now, Montreal's first wooden escalator was destroyed by an FLQ bomb in the 1960's.*

Duane pointed towards the south end of the store. "It looks like our crew is already here."

Ricky reached around the corner to a telephone on the counter in the corset department and dialed the 5662 extension for the millinery department where his staff had assembled. Carol Levesque answered.

"Hey Carol. How many people do you have?"

"I've got eight and Serge and Mrs. Robarts are also on their way in. I couldn't get Christine Guillaume, but her mother is trying to contact her. Did anyone get hurt?' Carol asked.

"No, thank goodness. Just a big bloody mess of product everywhere. While we're waiting for clearance, get someone to gather as many buckets, mops, shovels, and brooms as they can lay your hands on from the up-stair department. And also, garbage carts and garbage cans. There's a lot of glass here, so outfit everyone with sturdy leather gloves and rubber boots. Also, make sure everyone changes into their old clothes."

"Got it handled. Anything else?"

"No. Just stand by," Ricky replied, hanging up the telephone.

Steve Fortuna, the luncheonette manager, appeared behind Ricky and Duane. "Mio Dio! Chi farebbe questo?" *My God! Who would do this?*

Ricky looked at him confused. "What?"

"Sorry! Who do this?"

"Our FLQ friends, no doubt," he replied sarcastically.

"They hurt my ristourante?"

Ricky pointed to the large hole in the wall behind where the lockers had been. "It looks like the blast went right through the wall into the luncheonette and probably your kitchen area."

"Mio Dio!" *My God!* he mumbled in response.

At that moment, a group of senior management executives appeared behind them in the stairwell.

"What a goddamn mess," General Manager, Robert Appleton, mumbled. "If this had happened during store hours it would have been a friggin' massacre."

That's the closest I've ever seen Appleton come to displaying any actual emotion, Ricky thought.

"Do you think we can get this cleaned up in time for store opening?" Jeremy Radford chimed in, ever thinking of the 'bottom line' potential sales losses.

"I haven't been able to get close enough to evaluate the actual extent of the destruction, but I sincerely doubt it." Ricky replied, disgusted by Radford's lack of compassion.

"Mister Dean, you will have the full cooperation of all the store assets to get your departments operational," Appleton interjected. Then, directing a critical gaze at Radford, "Mister Dean will decide when and if we can reopen the basement for business, understand."

"Understood, Sir," Radford replied sheepishly.

The fire captain approached. "Your area is all clear but be careful not to slip on the water and glass. We did the best we could, but liquids have still accumulated in the broken remnants. I trust you have suction pumps or shop vacuums to clean up the liquids?"

"We will get them from hardware," Ricky answered.

"Also," the fire captain continued, "the blast area will need to be contained over by where the escalator and lockers were destroyed. And do not allow anyone to enter or clean up that area until the arson investigator gives the okay." He pointed. "Can your carpentry department construct a plywood wall around the area?"

"We will get it handled, captain. Thank you very much," Ricky responded, as they all made their way to the center of the floor, closest to the blast area.

Shaking his head in disbelief Appleton said, "Okay Mister Dean, these are your departments ... your baby. We're here to help. What can we do, and what do you need?"

EATON'S – During the Second French Revolution

During the last half hour, Ricky had been formulating a plan of action to bring some semblance to the horrifying scene. "Well, for starters," Ricky pointed to the escalator area, "I'll need a crew of carpenters to erect a plywood wall to completely close off this area. I'd guess about forty feet across and ten feet out from the wall. Oh, and they'll need an access door so the arson scene investigators can gain access. I'll make sure that my staff have the perimeter around the blast site cleaned up before the carpenters get here. Also, they'll need to build ..." He was interrupted by Appleton.

"Jeremy. Are you getting all this down?"

"Yes Sir," he replied timidly.

"The carpenters will need to build a similar wall on the main floor escalator exit," Ricky continued.

"If you will excuse me," Duane interrupted. "I'll begin to get our crew lined up on the various tasks."

Ricky turned to Duane. "Okay go ahead, but make sure everyone has on rubber boots and gloves. We don't need anyone falling in this mess."

Duane ran to the waiting group in the millinery department.

Ricky continued to address Appleton and Radford. "I'll need maintenance to bring down as many shop vacuums as they can find. They'll need to have a large city garbage truck stationed at the Metcalfe entrance and sufficient garbage cans and carts to get rid of all this stuff. There is no way that we can inventory all the damage, so I'd like someone from the portraits department to come down and photograph every square inch of the blast area for the insurance company. That way we can just shovel up everything without worrying about calculating losses. I have an up-to-date inventory available from our inventory control sheets.

Appleton interrupted, "I already have my secretary chasing down our local insurance adjustor, so he can either take his own pictures or fill out a full inventory by himself." Appleton laughed waving his hand around the deluge of broken products. "My guess is that he'll elect to take pictures."

Ricky continued. "Also, I see a large hole in the wall into the restaurant area, so I suppose there is significant damage in there. I'll need a kitchen crew to handle damage and cleanup in that area. And, since we are going to have a large contingent working here all night, it would be great if we could get the kitchen chefs in the luncheonette to fire up the grills to make some hot food, and lots of coffee."

Steve piped in, "I'lla have alla my people coming here."

"It all sounds great Mister Fortuna. Mister Dean, anything else we can do?" Appleton inquired.

Ricky did a slow 360-degree turn taking in all the potential problem areas. "When the morning news media reports what happened here, if we are open, we are going to be inundated with thousands of gawkers descending to the basement to get a glimpse of the devastation. This presents two serious major problems. Number one, shoplifters are going to have a field day operating within a massive crowd, so I suggest that we have Tony Cartwright temporarily triple his detective staff presence on our floor. It also wouldn't hurt to have three or four uniformed cops available, which may even dissuade ideas by any follow up bombers. Number two, I'm not comfortable with all those *looky-loos* hanging around, so I suggest that we close the basement cash office. It could make things extremely easy for a major hit, at least for the next few days. In the meantime, we can use the fifth-floor cash office."

"Consider it done." Appleton looked to make sure Radford was still writing everything down.

"Just one more thing," Ricky added. "We'll need two freight elevator operators available. We'll bring the garbage to the elevators down here and they can take them to the street level and unload them into the garbage trucks. Someone will have to contact the Montreal Sanitation Department to requisition some extra trucks to be on stand-by."

"You seem to have thought of everything, Mister Dean, so I'll be in my office if you need anything else," Appleton directed at Ricky. "Oh, and keep me advised of your progress."

Soon, more and more employees arrived, even the very apologetic Christine Guillaume. They each joined the arduous cleanup task and over the next several hours: the security walls were built, tables were re-set, shelves restocked, displays rebuilt, garbage shoveled from the floor, floors mopped and waxed, and all the damaged product and fixtures were disposed of. The only semblance of anything out of place was the stark plywood walls concealing the blast area.

"Duane, tomorrow get the carpentry department to paint that raw plywood, and, have merchandise display create some magic on those panels." Ricky glanced around to see what else needed his attention.

"Will do," Duane responded. "We'll also need signage to direct customers to the front escalator or elevators."

As Duane headed for the telephone, Ricky caught sight of Christine who was loading a broken mannequin into the garbage cart. "First thing in the morning, I want you to call the merchandise display department and have them print a half dozen signs that say, 'escalators under repair', and have them plastered on these lower plywood panels and the main floor panels."

"Will do, Sir," she replied.

At 5:10 A.M. Ricky advised a much-surprised Appleton that everything had been completed and the basement sales area would be ready for the regular 9:00 A.M. opening.

Next, Ricky directed Christine to have all the cleanup staff assemble in the restaurant for breakfast.

EATON'S – During the Second French Revolution

Ricky addressed his employees, as they gathered at the tables. "I really can't express how very, very proud I am of each and every one of you. You worked tirelessly, over and above the call of duty. It's just five twenty-five," he checked his watch, "and this place is going to be a zoo today. I want everyone to try and doze off, as best you can, for the next three hours so we can get through the day. You can get some blankets from the linen department and crash in the large booths here. If we run out of room here, section heads and managers can use the manager's lounge upstairs. Now, when we open you are going to be pelted with questions from curious shoppers about the bombing. I want you to downplay the devastation. Just direct the customer to look around, and then say, 'It really wasn't that bad.' If we allow this incident to build into a monster, we'll play right into the hands of what the FLQ terrorists want. Thank you all, again. Now, please get something to eat and then try to catch a few hours' sleep."

Heading towards his office he signaled Duane to follow. He pointed out, "There's still some glass under the watch display. When the fresh staff arrive have several of them make a sweep for debris under all the displays, tables, and counters."

Duane nodded.

Arriving at his office, they both took a seat. Ricky taking off his boots to massage his burning feet.

The office was small, just six feet by nine feet, which Ricky joked was the exact size of a standard jail cell. The office contained a wood desk and three straight back chairs. Cushioned executive chairs were only supplied to the upstairs, elite management. Ricky's desk was always kept neat with a simple file tray, blotter, pen cup and picture of Darlene. The walls were adorned with large fashion posters from *Woman's Wear Daily* and some old *Harper's* catalogues.

"Duane, as you saw, the shelves in the sundries department are very sparse, so I need you to have our buyers contact their suppliers immediately and have them hand-deliver as much replacement inventory as we need to fill those shelves."

Duane began to write in his notepad.

"Also, call Frank McCorcoran, at the Laura Secord corporate office, in Toronto," Ricky directed. "Tell him about the bombing, which he probably already knows, and advise him that his department will be closed until further notice. Advise him that, if he wants, we will meld his employees into our regular staff, until we get an indication of when he can re-open. That way none of his staff will lose any wages." Ricky hesitated as if he were going over his check list. "Oh, and one more thing Duane, most importantly, you handled things great out there today, my friend. Thank you"

Duane lit up with a wide smile. "Thank you."

But Ricky was already on to the next thought, *My poor Eaton's store ... it will never be the same!*

⚜ Twenty-Four ⚜

After getting approval from Christine at their last meeting, Ricky contacted Father Mac about her marital situation, Ricky scheduled a meeting with Father Mac, at St. Patricks' church. As he walked down Bleury Street, Ricky pulled up the collar of his overcoat to shield him against the fierce wind. His thoughts weirdly centered on his strange ties to religion. When his parents first got together his mother was Catholic, and his father was Anglican, but in those days, for them to get married his father had to convert to Catholicism. And, when Ricky was born Father Mac baptized him in St. Patty's Church, as a Catholic. However, years later, Ricky's father, disenchanted with the Catholic religion, convinced Ricky's mother that they should both convert to Anglicanism. This strange occurrence left Ricky the only Catholic in his family until finally, at the age of thirteen, he was confirmed as an Anglican. Years later, Ricky became reacquainted with Father Mac, who became his baseball coach.

As Ricky made it up the hill the massive 125-year-old St. Patrick's Basilica loomed into his view. He always marveled at the beauty and elegance of this historic gothic revival structure, with its twin steeples rising 226 feet from the ground. For every occasion, or service, the ten bells of 'St. Patrick's Chimes,' chimed to welcome congregants, the oldest bell being originally cast in 1774.

Ricky pushed open the heavy wood door to the *Basilica* and was immediately greeted by Father Mac with a big bear hug that lifted Ricky off his feet.

Father Angus Gavin MacDonald was anything but your typical Irish Catholic priest. At 6'3" and 235 pounds of solid muscle, crew cut blonde hair, and the gait of a linebacker, he was an imposing figure. One of his greatest attributes was his community involvement. Not only did he handle his church duties with professionalism, but found time for participation in youth activities, family counselling and charity benefits. He was a priest that you could talk to one on one, without the total conversation falling back to religious rhetoric. With Father Mac you could question passages in the bible without being ridiculed or being told that the simple answer was to "just have faith". He was a man who was not afraid to literally get his hands dirty. Whether he was helping a farmer harrow his fields or sitting on back-alley pavement hugging a homeless person as they threw up all over his robe. Father Mac was always there! Ricky believed that Father Mac was the mold that the Catholic Church should use to cast their legion of future priests.

"Whoa coach, we don't want to crush these tender ribs." Ricky returned the hug. "How have you been?"

"Well, now Laddie, I still got me collar and I ain't become an Anglican yet, so I thinks God has me blessed," he kidded, putting his arm around Ricky. "Let's go to me vestry and get a spot of Irish tea."

Father Mac guided Ricky into his small vestry office. "So, Ricky, me boy," he poured tea from a silver tea set, "have 'ya finally come to your senses and decided to rejoin our church? 'Ya' know, once a Catholic, always a Catholic," he smiled, mischievously.

"Not today, Father," Ricky replied, returning to seriousness, "but I am here on another matter, one which is very pressing involving one of my employees, which I believe you may be able to help with."

Father Mac poured two cups of Irish tea before plopping his ample body on the sofa next to Ricky. "Okay, Ricky. Let's hear the whole story."

Ricky relayed, in full detail, all that Christine had told him about her marriage problems at their meeting at The Place Ville Marie. He ended by asking, "Does that shock you, Coach?"

"You've got to be kiddin'. After all me years sittin' in my little phone booth, listenin' to confessions or counselling people here in the vestry, well, my dear boy, truly little is shocking to me anymore." Father Mac gave a slight laugh and picked up his tea. "As much as your Christine's situation may seem shocking, it is actually quite common these days. These unfortunate people, confused about their sexuality, will go to extraordinary lengths to preserve their anonymity. But mercifully there is an answer to be found within the Catholic Church, which is, no doubt, why you came to see me. You are inquiring about an annulment, correct?"

"You got it Coach. But where I see the obstacle is the fact that she was married in a civil union, not in a Catholic service."

"Aahh, the old civil union versus a Catholic marriage! That debate of Catholic theologians has gone on for over a century. Well, fear not my boy, now canon law recognizes that any legal marriage is acceptable. But, our friend Monsignor Mercer, still has a hard time with that ruling!"

"Well then, how should she proceed?" Ricky asked.

Father Mac walked over to his desk and retrieved a book from his desk drawer, scanning the contents for several minutes.

"So, Ricky, on the surface it looks like your Christine will have grounds of non-consummation of the marriage, deceit of intent on the part of her husband, and abstention of procreation for the purpose of not bearing children. All three are strong points for granting annulment under canon law. But, since the evidentiary area is weak and apparently witnesses are of no probative value, her key witness will be the written testimony stating that she is *adhuc virginem*, or still a virgin. If this is indeed fact, her annulment should have no problem passing the scrutiny required by both tribunals. Within one hundred and twenty days of submitting her forms her annulment could very well be achieved."

"What's the next step."

"That will all depend on how fast Christine is going' to want to move on this. She'll need to tell her parents, if nothing else, for their moral support and she is going' to need an examination by her gynecologist, followed by an affidavit from him certifying her *adhuc virginem*, then, she needs to come and see me A.S.A.P., so I can guide her through the canon forms procedure. She'll need to bring a copy of her birth certificate, her baptism certificate, her marriage certificate and one other form of government issued identification."

Ricky made notes on his small notepad. "Thanks, I'll tell her. She'll be ecstatic."

Father Mac returned to the sofa sitting close to Ricky. "So, now that we addressed her problem, tell me, my boy, how you are getting along with your own problem? Is Dr. Julie treating you all right?"

Ricky had previously spent many hours discussing his home life with Father Mac, before being referred to his psychologist. "It's okay, I guess. Slow going. The dredging up hurts from the past, stuff like that. The Doc is okay if he'd only stop saying *'yes'* as a question after every comment," he laughed.

"Well, Julie's like that at our card games, too. It drives everyone nuts. A pair of threes', yes?" he mimicked, then returning to the topic at hand. "Really, is he helping you at all, I'm concerned."

"Well, I am sleeping better, so I suppose that's good, but I ain't getting none of the other, so that's bad, yes?" he joked.

"You're sure as hell getting more than I am," he roared, "now get your skinny behind out of here, so I can get me Sunday sermon prepared."

They hugged as Ricky turned to leave the vestry and return to Eaton's. "Thanks again, Father Mac, you are always a life saver."

"Then come to services on Sunday and return to being a good Catholic, and we'll call it even," he laughed, squeezing Ricky's shoulder. Ricky smiled as he left Father Mac's office. *If only I could solve all my problems that easily, life could be great!*

⚜ Twenty-Five ⚜

The adoring eyes of the female salesclerks followed the man as he slowly made his way through the cosmetics department, entering the jewelry department, casually offering a seductive glance to each attractive clerk.

"Isn't he just gorgeous?" one clerk was heard to say.

"Yeah, I'll take one of those!" the other responded. "He can put his slippers under my bed, anytime!"

He bowed his head slightly acknowledging their secreted glances. He had always gotten female attention; women, young and old, had been throwing

EATON'S – During the Second French Revolution

themselves at him, all his life. With his wavy ebony hair, olive complexion, chiseled facial features and six-foot height, he was the epitome of the modeled man. Wearing an expensive pin striped suit, he typified the image of the ultra-successful businessman.

Little known was the fact that his small band of petty thieves and con artists had been wreaking havoc on Eaton's profit line, for months.

As he passed the leather goods department, he stopped to question a pretty blonde that was noticeably taken with him. "Please, you can 'elp me, yes?" He faked an Italian broken English accent. For the man, Vincenzo, Vinney "the Trunk", Calabrisee, this was a simple task.

"Yes sir. How may I assist you?" the clerk stammered, as a blush blossomed across her pretty young face.

"I get lira, no, no, money for dis," he replied, pulling a stack of American Express travelers checks from his jacket pocket.

"You want to change those into Canadian money?"

"Si, money."

"You can change those at the Bank of Montreal, across the street," she indicated, pointing to the south-end exit, or at our cash office, downstairs."

"Downa stairs?" he feigned total confusion.

Looking around to ensure that sufficient staff was covering her counter area, she took his arm, directing him towards the elevator.

"Sei molto gentile," *You are exceedingly kind.*

She giggled, not understanding a word, as she pressed the elevator *down* button on the wall.

The shear girth of his biceps sent a shiver through her body. "Come with me, and I'll take you there."

"Gratis, Gratis, Signorina"

When the elevator arrived, she ushered him inside, addressing the uniformed operator. "Wanda, could you take this nice gentleman down to the basement cash office, please?"

"My pleasure," Wanda gushed. "Watch your step, Sir," pointing to the slight elevation difference between the elevator and the floor level.

The antique elevators were circa 1920's, with expensive natural walnut interior wood, which was elegantly trimmed with matching cornice and moldings. Even the impeccable two-piece burgundy uniform and pill box hat of the operator spoke of the tasteful and elegant flavor of the past.

As she opened both doors, she stepped outside pointing towards the somewhat hidden cash office. "The cash office is just over there, Sir.

"Gratis, Signorina. Possiate avere una vita meravigliosa piena di molti bellissimi bambini. *May you have a wonderful life filled with lots of beautiful children.*

Wanda smiled sheepishly. She hadn't a clue what he had said, but she thought, *with those dreamy eyes, he could say that to me all night long.*

Vinney proceeded towards the cash office carefully taking in the surroundings, when he suddenly recognized a familiar face approaching.

Damn, I went to Rosemount High School with this guy. If he recognizes me, it's all over, he thought.

Vinney turned his face towards the elevator bank as they passed. *Whew! He didn't see me!*

Putting the close call out of mind he concentrated on the area layout noting that there were three center-aisle escalators leading to the main floors, but only two stairwells on both the east and west sides.

A small hallway led to the cash office where four wicket windows, with heavy protective antique wrought iron, were currently vacant. Vinney scanned the interior of the small office noting that only three employees were present: two women and an elderly man. He assumed that the man was probably the manager. As the woman approached the window he tensed remembering to revert to his Italian persona.

"Do you wish to cash a traveler's check, Sir?" she inquired, motioning to the checks in his hand. "I just need to see some identification."

He stared at her with a confused look on his face.

She animated holding up a small card, saying, "picture, photo."

"Si, si, foto," *Yes, yes photo,"* he answered in Italian. He made it seem like he was searching, and then produced his trusted forged international driver's license, while tearing a $100.00 check from the traveler's check packet.

"Thank you, Mister DiBenedito," she continued, noting his name from the driver's license. She pointed to the lower left corner of the check, "Please, just sign here," she made a motion with the pen.

"Gratis, Signorina," he signed the travelers check and slid it through the small opening in the wrought iron.

As the woman went to the manager, probably for check approval, Vinney mentally diagramed the interior of the cash office. He noted the approximate dimensions, furniture positioning, and vault location. Vinney was surprised that the clock on the wall showed 2:25 P.M. and the heavy rear vault door was being left wide open.

I need to check back several times, at the same time of day, to see if that vault is always open. That could sure save a lot of time and headaches, he thought.

Vinney also noted that there was an entrance doorway at the end of the small hallway where he stood had an entrance buzzer to the right of it. From his vantage point, staring into the office, he could also see a comparable buzzer by the door inside the office. No doubt, the interior buzzer was the one that unlocked the door.

He reached into his pocket and grabbed a handful of loose change. When he removed his hand, he let the change spill to the floor; making sure the coins rolled towards the cash room door.

Hearing the noticeable jingle of coins falling to the floor the woman returned to the window. "Do you need some help, Sir."

"No, no. Scuzzie," he replied, gathering the coins as he made his way down the hallway toward the entrance door. He noticed that the door, which he originally presumed to be made of solid metal, was a solid core wooden door with a metal plate laminated over the top. What he found most interesting was the fact that he could see light from the office on the left lock side of the door.

Just a single lock that could be easily freed by a quick crowbar entry. But all that was for another day! He thought.

He returned to the window and looked over the office again for any sign of alarm buttons; he couldn't find any.

Well, we'll be in and out so fast their alarm won't do them any good, anyway.

At the window, the cashier gave him five twenties, which he pocketed, as he walked toward the stairway leading back to the main floor.

It was crucial to Vinney's surveillance plan that he return to the same floor position he had before his excursion to explore his secondary target. He needed to clear his mind allowing total concentration to calculate a successful plan to breach the primary target. And an escape route that was both convenient and expeditious.

"You're back. Did you find the cash office?" said the pretty blonde in the leather goods department.

"Si. Gratis, Senorita."

"Can I help you with something, Sir," noticing his concentration on an expensive Buxton wallet.

"Si, Si. How much 'dis?" Although seeming to be inspecting the wallet, Vinney's peripheral vision was directed at the window display on the mid-University side of the store. He noted that the window was approximately six feet above floor level, which was not apparent on his earlier inspection from the outside. Because University Street, ran uphill from St. Catherine Street; the front of the store was at ground level, whereas the middle was six feet below grade and the north end totally below grade.

This could be a problem, he thought.

The one positive was that the selected display window was just 15 feet south of the middle exit doors, where he planned to enter the store.

If I can solve the problem of getting into the window, the rest will be a breeze.

"That's genuine calf leather, Sir, at only twenty-four dollars and ninety-five cents," the clerk offered.

"Okay. I take," he responded, taking two twenties from his pocket.

He thanked the young clerk and took his package and his change. Vinney then proceeded out of the store and went across the street where he sat on a bench in the courtyard of the historic Christ Church Cathedral. Vinney was always amazed at what he felt when he was around the church. That famous church was home to the largest pipe organ in Canada.

From this vantage point he had a clear view of the store and more importantly, a peaceful area in which to solve the problem of entry into the window. The hardest thing to do was to push plans for his number two target which was the main; cash office out of his thoughts and allow total concentration on target number one, the furs in the display window.

⚜ Twenty-Six ⚜

As Ricky arrived at the employee entrance to Eaton's, he smiled as he saw the throng of customers lined up outside awaiting the opening bell. It had taken three months to prepare for this momentous event, and it seemed like the T.V. and newspaper advertising had done their job.

Finally, I've found a historic merchandising vehicle that would make old Timothy Eaton proud.

"Hold up, Ricky," he heard from behind him, looking around to see Duane hurrying to catch up with him.

"Oh, hi Duane. Did you see that crowd outside?"

"Yeah, this is going to really put Jeremy's nose out of joint. He'll revel in the sales volume we achieve, but he's going to be so jealous that he can't take credit for the show."

"I guess he's just going to have to get over it", Ricky stated as he and Duane stepped onto the down stair escalator.

"Have you noticed that for the last few days Christine has been very nervous?" Duane asked. "It's really strange because she's usually '*Miss total in-control*'.

You had better believe that she's got a lot on her mind right now and it has nothing to do with the fashion show, or anything work related.

"I'm sure she'll be fine Duane. Just let her get through the next three days, then I'm sure she'll be back to her normal self."

Ricky made a quick circuit of the selling floor as Duane entered the shoe department.

"Got a sample for me, Marissa?" Ricky asked the clerk at the Laura Secord department.

"Anything you want, Mister Dean," she blushed. "What kind would you like today, your usual lemon in milk chocolate?"

EATON'S – During the Second French Revolution

"So many choices," he pondered, "maybe the orange in milk chocolate, or ..."

Before he finished, Marissa thrust both the orange and the lemon selections into his hand. "Mister McCorcoran directed that we treat you right, 'cause he owed you big time,' as do I," she smiled.

"Thanks," Ricky shouted back, munching on his chocolate as he continued his trek to his office.

"Mister Dean," Ricky heard the call as he entered his office. He turned to see Christine, out of breath, chasing after him. "Oh hi, Chris. Are you ready for your big day?"

"I don't know, Ricky. I've never been so scared in my whole life. Maybe I made a big mistake using my own staff as models?" she questioned, slumping into a chair.

"Now, come on, Chris. We began these plans three months ago, as a team effort. If this thing goes south, it is I who will have to answer for it, not you. So, just relax, everything is going to turn out simply fine. There are already hundreds of customers waiting at the doors. And the training that we've given the staff will make them look like pros. Don't worry. Just get out there and get the ball rolling," he squeezed her hand tenderly.

He felt a slight twinge go through him. *I better not hold on too long.*

"Okay, Ricky," she stammered, leaving the office.

He watched her go and the feel of her remained and it flashed him back to the night months earlier, at the 747 lounge. He and Christine had met after work to discuss what he found out from Father Mac that could remedy her personal problems. Over drinks he explained the details and helped her realize that there was hope for her.

They started with some casual conversation, and he had asked her how she felt about her job at Eaton's. Christine opened about her aspiration to put her teen fashion department on the map, and her frustrations of being sandwiched between the lady's fashions and the oversize dresses departments. She had told him that she appreciated the promotion to manager and buyer for her department and that since her revenues had greatly increased, she was able to show him he was right in giving her a chance. Her concerns were that she was not getting sufficient exposure so that the Montreal public was aware that there *was* a high fashion teen department in Eaton's basement.

She had hoped for increased advertising dollars, for her department, but to her remorse, Ricky had responded that the advertising budget had already been approved for the next year, and no discretionary funds were available. Thinking the topic had ended, he hadn't expected his own words to contradict his explanation.

Remembering it now, he recalled how he thought that was the end of it and how sorry he was to disappoint her, but that Place Ville Marie meeting, between him and Christine, took on a life of its own and a new direction for Ricky.

"But, Ricky," she exclaimed, "you've preached to all the staff, numerous times, to use your motto of 'there's always a way to accomplish that which, on the surface, seems impossible'. There must be something we, no, sorry, I, can do, to make my department an important profit center."

Ricky had been at a loss for words, remaining silent for several minutes, he pondered the problem. He recognized that building a viable teen fashion department could offset the dwindling revenues of his corset department, which had not met its goals in several years. He was also cognizant that the appropriation of increased advertising dollars was out of the question. So, a resolution seemed hopeless until an inconceivable thought entered his mind.

"You know I was just in New York on a buying trip with Marie from hosiery," he stated excitedly.

"Yes, I know. I wasn't invited on the trip," Christine pouted.

He ignored her slight. "And, you know very well that this buying trip was specifically scheduled with Dolores Richfield, ladieswear buyer, to purchase the new nylon 'Combination Stockings and Panty', they call 'pantyhose'. There's nothing like it in Canada, and I wanted our department to be first to introduce them."

"Yes, I know all that, but what does that have to do with me?"

"Don't you see, Chris, you are missing the point! This pantyhose product is going to be more readily accepted as a fashion item with teens, before the older women accept them. I've been watching this new product grow in leaps and bounds in the states for the past two years. I've studied the growth in popularity for the past six months."

"And what do you know about pantyhose that I don't, smarty-pants?"

"I know that these panty hose, which were originally called, *'Panti-Legs'*, were first invented in North Carolina, in 1953, by Glen Raven and Allen Gant, Jr., whose grandfather was the founder of the National Council of Textile," Christine said smugly. "However, in 1956 Ernest Rice invented his own design for pantyhose which he called *'Combination Stockings and Panty'*. The problem was that the major textile mills, such as Burlington Industries in the States, recognized the revolutionary importance of the pantyhose phenomena, and went around Mister Rice's patent, by introducing spandex, which was much cheaper to produce their very own version. And, Ricky, I think you know first-hand all about pantyhose from John Carver, president of Burlington Industries, right?" she smiled, thinking she made an impression with her technical knowledge.

"Meaning?" Indeed, Ricky was impressed by her knowledge.

"Meaning, the scuttlebutt around the store is that you and Dolores were picked up in a long white Burlington Industries limousine. And you were wined and dined by Mister Carver for four hours at the famous Mama Leone's Italian Restaurant on forty-fourth Street, in Manhattan."

"I see that you have quite an investigative pipeline, Miss Guillaume," Ricky smiled.

"Only when it is vital to my teen fashion operation," she pressed. "Without this new pantyhose, my department is going to be way behind the curve in being first to offer top fashions, at affordable prices to Montreal area teens. My counterparts at both Macy's and Gimbels already have these throughout their chain. We're eighteen months behind the fashion trend, and these are not flash-in-the-pan fads, like the bubble blouses that only lasted two seasons. These are going to be around for years to come. This one product alone can bring teens into our department where they'll see our large array of other fashion products."

"Okay, Okay, I surrender," Ricky countered, raising his palms in defeat. "Get a hold of Dolores for the name of the Burlington Industries Canadian salesman in Toronto and order a large supply of these pantyhose things. Then, prepare a product brief for all the teen fashion departments, high grade, and discount, across the Eaton's chain."

"Thank you," Christine submitted.

"So, now let me expand on what you already know," Ricky continued. "Mister Carver invited Dolores and me to the annual Women's Wear Daily fashion show, at the elite Carlton Hotel. There, I met several of the Women's Wear Daily senior publishing staff and had a long talk about our building a teen fashion center in a discount basement environment. They were fascinated that we had the forethought to take on such a progressive challenge. In fact, they specifically introduced me to the general manager of the Canadian Women's Wear Daily publication who expressed interest in possibly doing an article about you and our teen center."

"Really?" Christine's eyes widened in disbelief. "You mean that our department could get free publicity across Canada," she asked.

"Yes, but I want to take this idea much farther, and to a much more daring level. What if we created our own fashion show?"

"You mean like hiring teen models to walk around our department wearing our teen fashions?" she questioned.

"Come on, Christine. You're thinking too small. I'm not talking about just hiring a clown, I'm talking about building a whole damn circus!"

"I'm not dense, but I have to admit that I am totally lost."

"You can find models walking around showing dresses, sportswear, shoes, in lots of stores, but it's not an event, it's just a demonstration that's forgotten as soon as the model passes by. What I mean is to create an event that will be historic in merchandising circles across the country, for years to come. A modeling show that will be written and featured throughout the news media. A spectacle that we can all be proud of."

"But, she paused, gathering her thoughts, "how can we possibly pull this off without money? The cost of the models, doesn't come cheap."

"And therein lays the challenge, young lady. If it were easy everyone would have done it. Our goal is to do it without money, and I have some ideas how to achieve that goal."

"I'm sorry, but it still sounds impossible," she replied, fiddling with the small umbrella in her glass.

"Consider this, Chris. How about if we use your teen salesclerks, and other basement clerks as models for the show? Not only would that be free, but it would give an added dimension to your own unique show." He touched her hand, "Before you say anything, just think about this, wouldn't it be a great opportunity for the staff to participate in an event of this nature? And for the girls to be able to talk about having participated in a fashion show that will set basement merchandising on its ears for years.

"But, but, she stammered."

Ricky interrupted, "No 'buts'. Think of the possibilities, take the challenge, and run with it." He was tempted to say, run with me.

"Just remember what you reminded me about my motto, earlier. 'There's always a way.' We simply need to identify the problems and find the sources, and resources, for resolution. So, let's get started. Have you got a pen and paper with you?"

"Sure," she fumbled in her purse, finally producing a stenographer's coil bound pad. "Can I borrow your pen; I can't find anything in this suitcase?"

"Here," he answered, handing her his treasured Cross ballpoint pen. "Create a separate page for each of the challenge areas that we need to overcome, the first headed 'approvals. Before we can attempt anything as disruptive and unorthodox as a teen modelling show, we will need approval from both Radford and Appleton. We'll also need to touch base with our corporate attorneys to ensure that we are not violating, or bending, any Montreal City ordinance codes. Am I going too fast for you?" he questioned, as he watched her scribbling on the page.

"Not, at all. I can take dictation at 50 to 65 words per minute."

"Okay then, the next heading should be 'geography'. I believe that holding the event anywhere other than in our existing teen center would defeat the purpose of building customer traffic to generate increased sales. Also, each of the surrounding department managers will be advised that they must temporarily shrink their department size, for the duration of the show, to allow for substantial increased space to be allocated to the teen center."

Looking at his watch and worrying about missing the last train home, he continued. "I suggest that the rest of the project be discussed by a project development committee, which you will chair, if that's okay."

"Sure. That's okay with me, but shouldn't you be chairing the committee?'

"Not at all, Christine. This is going to be your baby, and I'm confident you can handle it. I'll attend your meetings and offer all the suggestions and assistance that you require.

"Thank you so much for having the confidence in me to handle such an important project. I'm just so excited, and I won't let you down.

Three days later, Christine presented Ricky with an invitation to the first committee meeting, with a roster of appointed members and an impressive, detailed agenda. This included member's areas of responsibility, project development areas, and notes on pre-resolutions to anticipated problem areas.

The roster identified the committee members as Christine Guillaume, as chairperson and Richard Dean, as second chairperson. It also listed six additional committee members. Cindi Valdez, assistant manager of teen fashions: Gwenn Robarts, assistant manager of ladies' dresses, Marissa Haggerty, clerk at Laura Secord Chocolates, Julianna LaGuiere, clerk in lady's sportswear, Maggie Hilbert, head group department cashier, and Angelina Terrazopoullos, newest clerk in teens fashions, and Ricky's friend Spiro's daughter.

The first meeting was held after store hours with table and chairs set up in the teen center and consisted of a wide array of event topics such as set construction, lighting, financing, teen model training, audio, lighting, etc., necessary for a successful teen fashion show. Each participant was delegated a specify area of responsibility.

When the meeting adjourned, Ricky headed across the selling floor towards the shoe department. He was smiling at how the simple thought of the fashion show manifested into this new working relationship with Christine.

Entering the shoe department his mind returned to the present and the culmination of months of hard work.

"And, what's got you smiling from year to ear?" Duane asked.

"Oh, just thinking about how an idea I almost threw away out of hand, is coming together so beautifully and should make our new Teen Department really stand out, making history across Canada!

Thanks to Christine.

⚜ Twenty-Seven ⚜

Arriving at the luncheonette and pouring a cup of coffee, Ricky settled into his favorite booth where he had a panoramic view of the selling floor, his thoughts falling to Christine.

Before their Place Ville Marie meeting any thoughts regarding Christine had been of a professional nature and only fleeting casual thoughts of personal content. He was attracted to her, but he was her boss, and they were both married. But, after hearing the detailed account of her heart wrenching dilemma regarding her marriage, Ricky's whole consciousness went into "prince-princess rescuer overdrive".

It still amazed him that she had been comfortable enough with him to bear her most private secrets and to release those long pent-up tears. She had allowed him to see her inner soul and begged for his help. For that moment we were totally connected.

He was torn between acting with the familiarity of her boss or letting his walls down and pursuing a more personal relationship. "Boss" won out!

Ricky still had a half hour before his meeting with Christine and nerves began to flutter in his stomach.

This is stupid! She's married, I'm married, and I'm supposed to act like her boss, right!

Ricky extinguished his cigarette, drank the last of his coffee and made his way back to his office. He first stopped at the men's room to freshen up, where he bumped into Jeremy Radford.

"Ahhh, there you are. I was looking for you," Radford said, standing in front of the urinal.

"Why do people always think they can have an intelligent conversation with their dick in their hand?"

"I was catching a quick coffee in the luncheonette, and I have a meeting at six-fifteen, so what do you need?" Ricky countered.

"I'm going to be in Vancouver for ten days at a merchandising symposium, so you'll have the floor during my absence. You'll also need to attend the general manager's meeting on my behalf, next Tuesday."

"Sure thing, anything else?"

"No, that's it," he said, zipping up, and walking out without washing up.

What a disgusting prick.

When Ricky arrived at the basement offices, they were almost empty. The accounting staff had all left at five and he could see Radford's secretary packing up to leave. As he did his final circuit of the selling floor his mind flashed back to his meeting with Christine the previous evening.

It had been just 6:10 when Christine came bouncing into his office. Her eyes were twinkling, and she was wearing a smile that could light up the darkest room.

"Hey boss," she beamed, delicately sliding into the guest chair opposite his desk, "you ready for me?"

If you only knew!

EATON'S – During the Second French Revolution

"Sure, but before we begin, are all the final plans in-order for the Fashion Show. I'm sorry I missed the last few meetings, but I did follow up on all your reports."

"Yes, we are right on schedule, and I have been meaning to stop by and tell you how much I appreciate all the support," she noted, "it made handling this so much easier."

"Well, good! That's what I wanted to do! So, now to other subjects, do you want some coffee? I just brewed a fresh pot."

"Well, since we finished business, if I had my choice," she smiled deviously, "I'd probably choose that fantastic Dubonn … Dubonn … you know, that great wine we had at the Ville Marie," she laughed, "but yes, black coffee is fine!"

"Dubonnet," he corrected, getting up to get two mugs.

Ricky placed the mugs on his desk, reached down into his bottom drawer, where he secured a half bottle of Dubonnet, and poured the wine into the mugs.

"My, my, don't you come equipped for every contingency," she wrinkled her cute little nose in pleasure.

"Well, its after-hours, and our meeting is not work related, so I guess as much as this is, uh unconventional, I believe it is okay, at least, this one time"

"Yes," she hesitated, a smile flashing upon her face, "and I believe that we're both of legal age."

"Ahhh, maybe we better get started, did you give some thought to what we talked about at the Ville Marie?"

"That's all I've thought about ending this marriage nightmare, since we talked."

"I have to ask again, are you positive that you want to permanently end your relationship with Rolland?"

"Yes, there's nothing left there for me."

"And, when you leave him, would you move back home?"

"Oh God, no! My best friend, Charlotte, wants me to move into her two-bedroom apartment on Hutchinson Street. This is great since it is walking distance to work. It'll be great being around someone who doesn't hate me all the time," her blue eyes misted.

"Right then, let's discuss the plan for your freedom," he slid a pad and pen in front of her.

Ricky laid out the full details of his annulment conversation with Father Mac. "He's convinced that you will have grounds of non-consummation of the marriage, deceit of intent on the part of Rolland, and abstention of procreation for the purpose of not bearing children. He says that all three are strong points for granting an annulment under canon law. You'll need to set up an appointment to meet with him and fill out all the required forms A.S.A.P. Part of the package is an affidavit, to be filled out by your gynecologist, certifying that you are still a virgin, 'adhuc virginem', Father Mac called it."

Ricky saw her blush and he grimaced at his invasion into her most private life and at his poor pronunciation of the Latin language. "The annulment requires going through two separate Catholic tribunals, at different levels of jurisdiction, which takes approximately ninety days."

"Did he say what he thought my chances were of getting an annulment?" she quizzed.

Ricky laughed, "Let's just say that Father Mac told me that the next time he plays golf with three senior members of the tribunal, God might miraculously allow all three to beat him for the first time, after-all God works in wondrous ways!"

"Oh Ricky, this is all sounding too good to be true. How can I thank you?" she gushed.

"So, the next thing is how to get you out of that apartment with Rolland, when the annulment is finalized. Do you have a lot of furniture, clothing, and stuff that you need to move?"

"That's the really ironic part of all this. When I moved in with Rolland, Charlotte was just setting up her apartment, so I let her borrow my furniture. So, she's all prepared, and anxious, for me to be her roommate. All the stuff I'll be taking with me will easily fit, in the backseat and trunk of my car." Then she thought for a moment. "What if Rolland is around or comes home while I'm leaving? ...he'll blow a friggin' fuse!"

"No problem, I've got that handled. I talked with Heidi Mullins, Rolland's boss, and explained the parts of your situation that she needed to know. She was infuriated, and wanted to fire him on the spot, but I held her off. Instead, when you are prepared to leave him for good, we've arranged to send him to assist our Eaton's driver with an out-of-town furniture delivery. That's normal procedure, so he won't be suspicious. That will give you over eight hours to get your stuff moved to Charlotte's. Does he know where Charlotte lives?"

"No, and I've kept it that way purposely."

"Great! Now, the last thing is to make certain Rolland never again has the opportunity to lay a hand on you, or subject you to verbal abuse. I had a buddy of mine in our legal department draw up a restraining order that will keep him at least one-hundred yards away from you, or he'll end up in jail. You'll need to take that down to City Hall and sign it in front of the court clerk. The judge will sign it and send a copy to you and Rolland when we are ready."

"Boy, is he going to be mad when he receives that."

"He didn't give a crap how you felt all those months, so don't be thinking of his damn feelings," Ricky commanded firmly.

"Yes, sir," she cowered, shrinking into her seat.

"Sorry," he quickly apologized, "I just get so pissed off when I hear of any man abusing a woman. I want to beat the crap out of him."

She smiled, "And, with those muscles, I bet you could."

EATON'S – During the Second French Revolution

Is she flirting with me?

Ricky cleared his parched throat with another gulp of wine and continued, "When Rolland returns from the delivery he's going to be asked to meet with Heidi Mullins, myself, and Tony Cartwright, in the security office. Possibly Tony's friend, Detective Francois Lafleur, will be there too if he can. At that meeting Rolland will be advised that you have left him, and he will be shown a copy of the restraining order. Heidi will make it clear that his actions are not tolerated, even in his personal life. He will be strongly advised that it would be in the best interest of everyone for him to resign from his post in the furniture department, instead of having a 'being fired' notation on his record. And that's that."

"Christ, he'll be enraged. What will he tell his friends and family?"

"We discussed that too, and we're going to tell him to say that he made a big mistake marrying an Anglo, which will placate everyone on his side."

"How will he handle the details of his homosexuality if that will come out in the annulment documents that he is going to receive?"

"He will not receive any documentation from Father Mac, or the tribunal until after the annulment is granted. And you are to make sure that as few people as possible know about your actions until it is granted. Then, you don't need to care what he says about it, 'cause it'll be too late."

Ricky looked deep into her eyes and started to reach for her hand but then thought better of it. "Can you think of anything I left out?" Ricky asked, relieved that he got through the whole scenario, without showing his emotions.

Christine sat silently for several minutes, nervously crossing, and uncrossing her shapely legs. Then, she began to wipe the tears from her face, as if the whole thing had just hit her. Then the damn burst spilling pent up sobs which racked her whole fragile body, as tears spotted her pink patterned blouse.

Ricky was at odds about how to handle this outburst. He timidly pushed a box of Kleenex towards her, which she apparently didn't notice. He stood and slowly walked around the desk, putting his hand affectionately on her shoulders. Then, he handed her a tissue.

"I'm so sorry. I'm such a baby," she buried her sniffling face into his chest. "I ... I ... I never thought this could happen. I thought my whole life was over. But, but you saved me." More sobs. "You truly gave me back my life," she looked up into his eyes.

Ricky had to get himself into "boss" mode. "Not me, Christine, you! You made the decision to end your nightmare. I just found the vehicles to help you along the road. It's still not over, but hopefully we are on the road where sooner than later, you'll never have to be frightened by Rolland again."

Christine slowly rose from the chair, until her face was at his throat level. She rose on her tiptoes and planted an affectionate kiss on his cheek.

The electricity immediately went through him. He felt her warm breath's breeze on his face and the heat of her body so near him.

She whispered, "Ricky, I've never felt so grateful to anyone, in my whole life."

Ricky put his hands on her shoulders, then quickly removed them. He could feel himself holding his breath.

This is not such a good idea for either one of us now! he thought.

With that, she pulled away from him quickly, but her tears began, again.

Ricky pulled her toward him in a comforting embrace. He could feel her body clinging to him, in perfect alignment with his. He felt his "little brain" come to attention, a reaction he couldn't stop and one he was sure she felt too!

In that moment of closeness all propriety left him, and he whispered gently in her ear, "You know I'm madly attracted to you, but my life is a disaster, and yours is only now straightening out. Perhaps, sometime in the future, we will be in the same galaxy together, but for now …" He tenderly pushed her back hoping he would see understanding in her beautiful face.

But instead, she gazed at him and sighed, "Until then you can be my dearest friend, yes?"

"Absolutely!" he replied. He stared into her eyes a moment longer, then moved her bangs and affectionately kissed her forehead, "Absolutely!"

And how will I live 'til then?

⚜ Twenty-Eight ⚜

Ricky picked at his petrified lasagna that had no doubt been sitting in the oven for the past several hours. His daughter Darlene was sitting in the highchair beside him dipping her fingers in a bowl of strained apple sauce.

"I can't take this crap any longer, Ricky," Kathy ranted. "We've got to make some radical changes, or I'm going to go crazy."

Ricky shouted in his brain, *That's going to be a short trip!* "What do you want from me? I work hard, I put food on the table, and all you do all day is sit around and watch soaps. I haven't a clue what the hell would make you happy."

She threw a dish towel at him that landed on top of his lasagna. "You think that's all I do? I take care of the baby, clean the house, get the groceries, and cook your goddamn food, that you're never here on time to eat. So, don't give me that shit," she banged her fist on the table.

"Knock it off, you're scaring the baby," he threatened, rising from the table to get a wet cloth from the sink to wipe the baby's hands and face.

Ricky returned to the table and pushed his lasagna aside. "And you think that's all there is to being a wife?"

"If you're talking about sex, I can't stand you touching me," she sputtered.

"It would have been nice if you would have thought about that before you agreed to marry me, eh?"

"I never thought you'd be such an animal as to be after me all the time."

"After *you*, all the time? For Christ's sake, Kathy, you didn't let me touch you until three months after we got married. What kinda' *after you all the time* is that?"

"You know I was having a hard time with my periods, and sex just wasn't appealing to me," she simmered.

"Don't give me that shit. You had period problems years before we got married, and that never seemed to bother you. You're just making excuses."

"I don't need to make excuses. It's my body to do as I see fit! It's not yours to own."

"Don't you see that sex is a necessary part of a healthy marital relationship?"

"There you go again, sounding like a bloody lawyer."

"Don't change the subject," he raised his voice, realizing too late that he too was scaring the baby. "I'm sorry, sweetheart," he picked up Darlene and tried to soothe her, then headed with her to her bedroom. "Let's get you to beddy-bye."

When he returned Kathy had thrown the remnants of his supper in the garbage, and was sitting on the sofa, with an angry look on her face.

Ricky poured a glass of red wine and took a seat opposite her on his French provincial wingback chair. He propped his feet up on the ottoman and looked straight at her. "What the hell do you want from me now, Kathy?"

"I want you to stop pressuring me and I want a different kind of life," she cried.

"That's the same line you told me when we were courting, and you wanted to get out from under the thumb of your abusive father."

"Yeah, and I traded one evil bastard for another, didn't I?" she spat.

"So, now I'm fuckin' evil? I got you away from that sick bastard, and now I'm evil?" he sputtered with anger.

"I didn't know it would be like this! I just wanted to be free."

"And you think *free* meant getting married. Marriage is loving and sharing, and yes, sex, not living at Disneyland!"

"But now I'm trapped."

"Because of Darlene?"

"Yes, if it wasn't for her, I could do something about this insanity," she shouted.

"So, our baby is the reason for your depression, is that right?"

"I never wanted a baby."

"Oh, that's rich. We talked about marriage, kids, buying a home, all before you agreed to marry me."

"I don't remember that."

"So, why did we have a baby, then?"

"Because you raped me."

"What?" Ricky bolted out of the chair, frightening Kathy, as he wagged an angry finger in her face. "What did you fucking say?"

"I don't remember having sex with you, so you must have raped me," she cowered.

I can't bloody believe this shit, and I'm sitting here arguing with a Looney Tunes.

"Give me a friggin' break. You don't remember coming home from Nicky and Brenda's party, loaded. You were all over me in the car, and when we got into bed you couldn't wait to get laid."

"I don't remember, and anyway, how come you didn't wear a condom?" she challenged.

"Oh, please," he settled back in his chair. "You were the one controlling everything, that night. It was extremely exciting and stimulating. But you were the one on top, and you are the one who began having sex with me, without a condom. So, don't put the blame all on me."

"You always see things in perfect logic, don't you? You're never wrong, right? Well, I don't see it that way. I'd never have taken a chance at getting pregnant, so there," she pouted."

"Listen Kathy," Ricky placated, "talking always gets us nowhere."

Ricky rose from his chair. "Figure out what the hell you want to do, and, let me know. I'm going to bed. Someone in this bloody house needs to go to work."

"Don't you walk out on me," she yelled at the top of her voice.

"Keep your voice down or the neighbors will be calling the cops."

"I'm sorry, okay," she whimpered. "You never even tried to understand me. You profess to know me, but you don't know me at all."

"I've really tried but you never open up to me. I've asked you to consider getting some help, but instead you attack me every time. What more can I do?"

"Your answer is always that I'm nuts, or that I need some professional help. That is not very constructive, Ricky."

"I never said that you were nuts, but let's not argue anymore." Ricky settled back into his chair. "Okay then, I'm listening now. Talk to me."

Kathy looked down, idly picking at her fingernails. "You know my family history with my father. And, you know the story of me fainting when he became abusive with me. What you don't know is that I purposely brought on my fainting by concentrating on the fact that I was dying. The reason I did that was, first fear, but when I fainted it stopped my father's tirade, and usually I would be consoled by my mother. See, problem solved."

"You could actually make yourself faint, for real?" Ricky asked.

"It's really not so difficult when you are so frightened that you lose control of your body and mind. And the more it worked, the easier it was to pull it off. I even did it with my English teacher when she started berating me over some problem that I couldn't solve. I scared the shit out of her, and she never tried that again."

"So, that answers your home life, what happened since then?"

"When I started at Rosemount High, I was all prim and proper, and yet, my classmates shunned me, labeling me as stuck up. I wasn't invited to parties, school dances, girl cliques, anything. So, I decided to get attention by dressing in sexy clothes and flirting with all the boys, which only got me distain from the girls, and a reputation as a 'teaser' from the boys. In frustration, I decided to become the 'easy' radical girl in the school by hanging out with the boys. At first, I was just leading them on, but that soon progressed to much more, and eventually intercourse with several different boys. All that made me the most popular girl in school, at the time. The girls hated me, and called me a slut, but the boys couldn't get enough of me, literally, and even you apparently. As you know, I finally settled down with Roger. He was good-looking, had a nice car and plenty of money, and he was who every girl in Rosemount wanted as a boyfriend. So, even though the girls hated me, they envied who I had as a boyfriend. You see, through these extreme measures I had finally won." Kathy paused to wipe her eyes.

"If it was so great with Roger, why did it end?" Ricky asked.

"First of all, I truly hated everything to do with sex, but I put on a great act. Roger had me do everything there is to do, and even more, that he invented. It was a nightmare, but he also gave me the affection that I really needed and had never experienced in my life.?

"Again, if it was so great, why did it end with Roger?"

Kathy looked off in space, silent for several minutes. "Because the asshole cheated on me with my best friend."

⚜ Twenty-Nine ⚜

Ricky went to work thinking that his three months of planning and training had all come down to this, the actual day of the Teen Fashion Show. It was only 11:00 A.M., but since the store opened two hours ago the people were congregating for the first show, which would be at 1:00 P.M.

The last-minute preparations, like any event, were filled with things that needed to be addressed. At the dress rehearsal held the previous night, one of the teens fell out of her four-inch spiked shoes, the D.J. was playing the wrong music and two girls bumped into each other while entering and exiting the ramp. Other than that, surprisingly, things went very well!

Ricky spotted Christine entering his office, which was temporarily the official models changing room. He followed her. "Is it safe to come in, Christine," he asked quietly.

"Sure, Mister Dean, nobody's changing in here, just yet."

He was astonished by the total make-over of his office. He couldn't believe how many pairs of shoes, garments and beauty products could occupy his small space. He greeted three of the teen models who were sitting at one of the desks. "You all did a great job at rehearsal, and you are going to be great today. And Christine, don't forget to commend your group, they are making Eaton's history today. I'm sure, Mister Timothy Eaton will be looking down favorably upon all of them."

"Well, I hope he puts in a good word for us up there, 'cause we're going to need it'. Can you figure out anything that can give us some breathing room in here. When the girls start rapid changing, they're falling over each other trying to get from the back-office door up the stairs and onto the runway."

"I thought maintenance had straightened that out. Give me a minute, I'll be right back." He sprinted for the footwear department, where he caught up with Duane. "Duane, I need some help. The girls and their assist team are all squeezed into those offices that were added to mine, but it really can't hold more than four or maybe five people tops! I've got to make more room for them, stat. Is Radford still in Toronto?"

"Yeah, he'll be back tomorrow afternoon," Duane replied, while being led by Ricky to the stock room elevator.

Ricky caught hold of Serge as he came up the stairwell, "Good, Serge, you can hear this, too. I need the stock elevator to remain on stand-by for our use only. We need four more guys out of the stockroom. And we need three flatbed carts, with the eight-foot-long beds to be brought over to my office as fast as possible."

Ten minutes later, Ricky had the Radford office area stripped of four desks, four file cabinets, seven chairs and Radford's favorite redwood credenza. All the furniture was taken down to the storeroom.

He heard Duane mumble, "Damn, I don't want to be around when Radford finds out we stripped his office.

By 12:15, the 100 seats surrounding the runway were filled and more people were standing around the perimeter. Media reporters had secured strategic positions throughout the area. The girls were getting dressed and all the support personnel were already at their posts. Ricky couldn't help but smile as he noticed many familiar faces that he knew were upper floor employees who had arranged their lunch hour so they could attend the show. He also noticed that none of the executive brass had arrived yet.

Ricky spotted Tony Cartwright and Denis Charbonneau standing by the center aisle escalator. "Hey Tony, Denis!" He walked over to them and shook their hands, "What do you think of the setup?"

Ever the pessimist, Tony responded, "All that you guys put together is great, Ricky, but you know..."

Ricky had to jump in, "I know, Tony, you hate crowds. You shoulda gotta job at de nord pole."

They all laughed.

EATON'S – During the Second French Revolution

"Seriously though," Tony gave his professional opinion, "this close quarters setup is a recipe for disaster. My people are already having trouble penetrating the crowd, and it's still forty minutes to show time.

"I knew that would be your response, but we've done everything to keep the risks down!" Ricky felt confident and continued. "I have eight of my own people, four from menswear and three women I use as extra cashiers, dressed in their outerwear, already in the crowd. And the systems you outlined have been driven into their heads at every meeting for the last two weeks. I even saw two MPD over there, leaning on the wall by the elevators. Are they yours?"

Denis responded, "No they are just two of my MPD buddies who work undercover, downtown. I told them if they came to see the show where I was working, you would buy them lunch." He snorted a little laugh.

"I can tell you this, Ricky, I've been at this long enough to say that we are not going to get away with this clean. It's not if we are going to get hit, it's where and when. Anyway, that's my problem." Tony stopped a moment and then added, "Good luck with the show and catch up with me afterwards for a briefing."

"Speaking of MPD," Tony added, "have you guys heard anything about the MPD thinking of going on strike? One of my associates in our department stores' security network told me that his brother-in-law was drunk at his bar-b-que over the weekend and was spouting off about MVP getting screwed over concerning parody wages and they were going to '*show the city*' by going on strike."

Ricky was shocked by this news. "Christ, that'll never happen. They can't leave millions of people unprotected, especially with the F.L.Q. just itching to take their violence to the streets unencumbered."

"I've heard rumors, but nothing positive," Denis cautioned. "Like Ricky, I can't believe they'd pull a stunt like that."

By 12:50 Ricky noticed that there was full media representation and the crowds had now doubled in size spilling over into the neighboring departments where people were attempting to stand on the sale tables for a better view. "Get those people down from the tables before someone falls and gets hurt," he directed a nearby section head, "and, make sure nobody gets back up."

A contingent of several top-level brass arrived, including general manager, Robert Appleton, assistant general manager, William Porter, and, to Ricky's surprise, none other than, Mr. Jack Eaton, from Toronto. Ricky shook hands and welcomed them as he led them to an area near the beginning of the runway, out of sight of the media.

By 12:59, the overhead fluorescent lights were turned out. The music came on transforming the audience as the song began, "*It is the dawning of the age of Aquarius.*" A single spotlight shot up and down the length of the bright red runway, and finally came to rest on a black curtain with the single word, "*Aquarius,*" illuminated in sparkling silver and gold glitter. The show was about to begin.

As the music level slowly lowered, from off-stage the familiar voice of CWHC radio news anchor, Betty Caruso, could be heard as she announced the beginning of the festivities.

"Ladies and gentlemen, this is Betty Caruso, and I have the pleasure and privilege of being your MC today. Welcome to the historic Eaton's 'Age of Aquarius Teen Fashion Show,' created by teens, for teens and modeled by teens, for your enjoyment. You are going to witness a spectacle of immense historical magnitude, my friends. This is the first time in North American history where such a merchandizing feat has ever been accomplished. The production, directed by our own department manager, Christine Guillaume, has transformed these everyday teens into professional models, with the assistance of a battery of backstage assistants. Without further ado, let's enter the mystical world of the 'Age of Aquarius!' Music please."

"When the moon is in the Seventh House, And Jupiter aligns with Mars, Then peace will guide the planets, And love will steer the stars, This is the dawning of the age of Aquarius, Age of Aquarius, Aquarius!, Aquarius!"

As each beautiful girl strutted her way down the forty-foot runway, swaying to the beat of the music, they stopped at the far end, while the announcer gave the girl's name, described the outfit, and gave credit to the manufacturer. The teens then turned and when they reached their starting point, turned back to the audience, extended a final curtsey as exited the stage.

Ricky swelled with pride. *I've done it, Mr. Eaton. I've really done it. I've continued your Eaton's history!*

"When the moon is in the Seventh House, And Jupiter aligns with Mars, Then peace will guide the planets, And love will steer the stars, This is the dawning of the age of Aquarius, Age of Aquarius ..."

Ricky heard the music repeating, *"Aquarius! Aquarius! Aquarius! Aquarius!"*

Betty Caruso knew this was her cue to begin announcing the finale. She got her list of "thank yous" and began to announce each girl again, and, as they came back on the stage, she gave the girl's name and the house or manufacturer of the outfit being modeled. The audience applauded loudly and when all the girls were lined up, each took up an assigned position on the stage. Once all the girls were on the stage, as the music became a low background, the names of each person who helped in making the Fashion Show possible were shared and each person was invited to join the girls on stage. The audience overwhelmingly applauded their approval. The last to be announced was Christine.

As she made her way to the stage the loud applause resounded throughout the basement and Ricky could see the tears welling up in her eyes.

She joined her teens and thanked everyone and gave a marvelous speech about Teen Fashion and what Eaton's has done to provide a place for Teen Girls.

Ricky glanced toward the executives, and he could see that they were all smiling.

EATON'S – During the Second French Revolution

The music subsided to a low whisper, the lights went out, the applause came up and to the audience surprise, the center stage spotlight began to focus on each Teen, and as it did, you could hear, *"Let the sunshine, let the sunshine in, the sunshine in!"*

The room was getting infectious as each girl sang, in her turn, *"Let the sunshine, let the sunshine in, the sunshine in!"* and then the others before her chimed in. When all the girls were singing, the houselights went up and everyone in the audience spontaneously were on their feet, following along:

"Let the sunshine, let the sunshine in, the sunshine in!"

After the last chorus, the applause and cheers were deafening as the girls bowed graciously and started off stage. As Christine was exiting the stage, believing the show was over, she heard a surprise, but familiar voice, from off-stage.

Ricky had taken the microphone and began announcing, "Ladies and Gentlemen, the entire basement staff here at Eaton's would like to thank you all for coming, and we ask that you give a round of applause for our great MC, Betty Caruso, of CWHC news, who graciously donated her time to our cause." When that applause subsided, Ricky continued, and before you all leave, I would like one more round of applause for the show's creator, Christine Guillaume.

He was now behind her, and Ricky turned her back toward the stage and nodded for her to go receive her well-deserved reward!

As soon as she arrived back on-stage, she was given a standing ovation, and after a moment, all the girls joined her on-stage presenting her with a beautiful bouquet of 12 red roses to thank her for all she did. Christine's tears were streaming down her face, and, after a few bows, she and the girls left the stage.

Ricky met with the cast in the backstage room area. "Ladies, if I didn't know any better, I would say you were all professional models. Everything, and I mean everything went off without a hitch; no wait, not even a hiccup!"

They all laughed!

"I am so immensely proud of each, and every one of you. Thank you."

Ricky was feeling tearful, and he wondered, *Could Dr. Markowitz be right? Maybe there is still a spot of actual emotion left in my body, just as he had predicted.*

"Christine, you were incredible, and handled everything like an absolute pro. But first, I need you to come with me because Mister Eaton has asked to meet you."

"Oh God!" She stammered.

"Don't worry it will just take a second, then I need you to get out there to talk to all the press. They are clamoring to, *'talk to the genius'* who created this historic event'."

Jack Eaton was very magnanimous and gracious in his praise of Christine and her team. "Miss Guillaume, as you youngsters say, I was blown away by this historic event that you created. It is easy to see that you and your team are the future of our great company and a credit to all managers across Canada. And you, Mister Dean, better be aware that it is in your best interest to shield Miss Guillaume from the career advancement offers from store manager across our chain, or you will lose this treasure."

"Thank you, Mister Eaton," Ricky replied humbly. "I'm sure your kind words are an inspiration to all of us."

⚜ Thirty ⚜

The lone businessman approached the wrought iron bench, his gaze fixed on the magnificent Christ Church Cathedral, a one-hundred, and fifty-year old Anglican Gothic Revival cathedral. The bronze plaque indicated that the first Christ Church had opened in Old Montreal in 1814, and in 1850, it was designated as the cathedral for the new Anglican Diocese of Montreal. The original cathedral had been destroyed by fire in 1856 and was replaced by the present cathedral, completed in 1859 and consecrated in 1867.

At the sound of the ten o'clock church bells the man's gaze fixed on the imposing clock tower, and then turned toward the large thermometer, across St. Catherine Street, above the entrance to the Birks Jewelry store. The temperature was twenty–four degrees, but with the wind chill it felt more like zero degrees. As the wind howled around the downtown high-rise buildings, he raised the collar of his cashmere coat to shield himself from the bitter cold. The man had been sitting on the cold hard courtyard bench for almost a half hour, diligently surveying the varied activities taking place along University Street. This was his third reconnaissance of the subject area, and he knew every facet was important to a successful mission. This vantage point gave him a clear observation from St. Catherine Street north to Maisonneuve Blvd. and covered the complete east side of the Eaton's store. He had carefully monitored the north end employee entrance, the middle door, and the south end door, noting pedestrian traffic, street vehicle traffic and foot patrol beat cops. Most notable was what seemed like perpetual traffic congestion at the corner of St. Catherine and University St. He knew this area would have to be avoided at all costs if a speedy retreat was required. Of particular interest were the activities surrounding the ten large display windows facing the sidewalk on University St., especially the first window, south of the middle entrance. Although all the windows were dressed in a Christmas theme, this window was specifically dedicated to the display of women's high fashion boots, gloves, and expensive fur coats. He watched as a steady stream of seasonal shoppers stopped to peruse each window. It was important to know how many people gathered at any one window, at any one time, and how long they remained there viewing the displays. He understood this mission must be simple, swift and, most importantly, authentic. Just one slip up and the mission would fail with dire consequences. But, for him, failure was not even a considered option.

Stamping his feet and rubbing his kid skin gloved hands together to regain some much-needed warmth, he casually watched as a Brinks armored truck parked in front of the Bank of Montreal and began bringing bags of money into the bank. Smiling, he thought, *one day I will have to try and relieve them of their burden*. Looking at his Rolex, he noted that it was the ten-thirty-five, morning cash delivery. From past observations, he was aware that the afternoon pickup was shortly after three-thirty. But that information would have to be mentally filed away for future use.

As he shifted his position on the cold bench, he gathered his coat beneath him to eliminate some of the cold radiating from the metal slats. He watched as an older man wearing shearling flight boots and a black bomber jacket approached. His round face was well-weathered, and his slow gait revealed a slight limp in his right leg. The man's most important observation was the clearly noticeable bulge under the man's left armpit, a sure sign that he was armed. Although the man was not threatened by this event, he had been trained by his *capo* to always size up any threat, no matter how insignificant it may seem. As the man approached the bench, he made a sweeping hand motion intended to request an invitation to share the bench.

"Sure, help yourself, there's plenty of room," the seated man said, loud enough to be overheard by other passing pedestrians.

Removing a map from his inside coat pocket he leaned over and whispered softly, "Just look at the map as if we are discussing directions, okay?"

"Sure boss," the elderly man replied.

"And knock off the *boss* crap, we're supposed to be strangers" He was irritated that he had to work with morons like this, instead of a professional crew.

"What the hell are you doing carrying your piece when I told you I just wanted to review the plan?"

"Okay boss, shit, sorry," he stammered, noticeably frightened by the outburst.

"You know I don't go anywhere without Maisy. Shit, just last month, Guido 'Toots' was hit right over there in the park," he indicated, pointing to the park across from *The Bay* department store. "Christ, he was eighty-two and they whacked the fucker just 'cause his kid sang to the cops on the Morelli hit."

"I don't give a shit about any of that. When I tell you no piece, I mean no piece. If we get caught, and they find it on you, we'll get capped for armed robbery, instead of simple robbery. That's a difference of ten years additional in sentencing, capisce?" *understand?*

"Yes, but …"

"Just shut up and listen. Where'd you park your car?"

"In the Eaton's lot on McGill Street."

"Okay, when we are finished here, go back to your car, and lose the piece in the trunk. Then, go into the store by the center McGill entrance and on your right as you enter, you'll see the door for the service elevator. Casually go in there and make sure they are keeping the ladders and the flatbed carts in there. If anyone questions you, just say you are just looking for the bathrooms, okay? I've got to check out the fifth-floor merchandise display offices. Then, I'll meet you back at the car. Got it?"

"I got it, Boss, not boss, but, what about the empty boxes that we'll need?"

"I've got that handled. You just do as I told you and everything will go as planned."

As the old man stiffly attempted to get up from the bench, the young man raised the map to cover his face, "What's the situation with the Imperial Tobacco shipment?"

"We offloaded all the product in the warehouse last night, and this morning Aldo and Marcus are loading the van to deliver inventory to our distributors throughout the province. Because the haul was so large, we are going to have a large surplus left in the warehouse."

"I already have my guy out west contacting distributors to buy any remaining product.

"Good! I don't want that shit sitting in the warehouse for any length of time."

"Okay, boss ... oh sorry, old habit! Uh, I'll meet you at the car in a half hour." The older man, Frankie "The Nose" Rossie, carefully traversed the treacherous slush laden University Street to the Eaton's' store entrance.

Stomping the snow from his highly polished brogues, the young man lingered a few extra minutes before making his way to the same entrance to begin his internal reconnaissance.

This was to be the beginning of a very lucrative venture.

⚜ Thirty-One ⚜

The last four days had been extremely tense for Ricky, not just because of how he was feeling about Christine, but because he had to juggle both his job and Radford's, who was out in Vancouver. To add to this, Ricky had been coordinating plans with Christine about getting her moved into her new home with her friend Charlotte. At first it seemed the move would have to be delayed when her husband Roland had been home sick from classes. But, as the week progressed, Roland got over his illness and returned to school, meaning he would, most likely, be at Eaton's, Friday, and Saturday for his scheduled worktime.

EATON'S – During the Second French Revolution

On Thursday afternoon Christine advised Ricky that everything was a "go" for Friday's move. In turn, Ricky advised Heidi Mullins and Tony Cartwright. Again, Ricky was nervous that everything wouldn't come off as planned, and he feared what Roland might do to Christine.

At 8:30 A.M. on Friday, after receiving the news from Christine that Roland had left for work, Ricky sat in the luncheonette drinking coffee, his thoughts were gratefully interrupted as Tony Cartwright slid into the booth.

"Man do you look like shit," Tony said. "I thought this would be a happy day for you. Today you're going to right a serious wrong. If we handle your plan right that prick, Roland, will be out of Christine's life once and for all."

"Yeah, if, if, if!" Ricky responded, taking a long draw on his cigarette.

"What do you mean 'if'? Captain Tony is at the helm, my boy, and I've got it all covered. The punk arrived for work and Heidi is sending him out on a furniture run to Lachute, which is two hours north of Montreal, and, between the drive there and back, and assembling the furniture, he won't be back until after five, and we'll be ready for him. So, stop worrying."

"I know, but with my luck it seems that something always goes wrong. And, if it goes wrong this time the kid could get hurt."

"First of all, the 'kid,' as you call her, is your own age, and second you're making this too personal," Tony hesitated, scratching his head, "or, maybe it is personal, my little buddy? Is that it? You got the hots for this babe?"

Ricky stammered at Tony's question. "Me and Christine? Don't be ridiculous. She works for me, and I'm concerned for her, just like all my other staff. That was a stupid question, Tony." Ricky lit another cigarette before noticing he already had one burning in the ashtray.

Tony smiled as he put out the one in the ashtray, quoting, "As William Shakespeare wrote, *'the gentleman doth protest too much, me thinks.* And me thinks so too, my young friend," Tony laughed, leaving the luncheonette.

After Tony left, Ricky returned to his office where he spent the rest of the day consolidating the budget projections for the coming year into a master budget that Radford would present to the general manager upon his return.

To Ricky's relief, Christine had called earlier advising that she was totally moved out of her apartment and into Charlotte's. Also, she had retrieved Roland's copy of the court approved restraining order from their mailbox and placed it prominently on the kitchen table.

At 5:10 he received a call from Agatha, Tony's secretary, advising him that the meeting with Roland would begin at 5:30.

Ricky hurried to the elevator and arrived at the fifth floor, breathless, but exactly on time.

"They're in interrogation room one," Agatha directed, not looking up from her typewriter.

As Ricky entered, he shook hands with Tony, Heidi Mullins, and MPD Detective Francois Lafleur. "Where's Roland Guillaume?" he asked Tony.

"I thought I'd put a little scare in the creep to keep him off center," he smiled, "so, I had Ray Archambault pick him up, and he's officially escorting him here."

At that moment, the interrogation room door flew open as Ray roughly pushed Roland inside. "Take a seat!" he commanded, pointing to the vacant chair opposite Tony.

"Do you need me, boss?" Ray asked.

"No, it's already too crowded in here. Why don't you wait in my office, so you can handle the prick after we're finished?

Ray nodded and exited the room.

"Pourquoi suis-je ici?" *Why am I here?* Roland demanded.

"Knock off the French crap," Tony slapped his hand on the desk, "we know you speak perfect English, so just shut your mouth, and listen."

Ricky noticed Detective Lafleur wince at Tony's comment regarding French.

"But I've done nothing wrong. You are treating me like a criminal," Roland protested, ignoring Tony's directive.

Detective Lafleur, who was standing behind Roland reached over and grabbed his shoulder, driving his thumb painfully into Roland's muscle.

"Fermez votre bouche, maintenant!" *Close your mouth, now!* he commanded, releasing his grip, as Roland sank deeper into his seat.

Tony smiled. "To continue, this meeting is of a personal nature, not about you working at Eaton's. Your marriage to Christine is over! Do you understand? You have verbally and physically abused her for the last time! After all these months, you haven't even consummated your marriage." Tony's anger was accelerating to a dangerous level. "I don't give a holy shit if you're a queer, or a transvestite, no one, and I mean no one," Tony wagged his finger inches from Roland's nose, "messes with any of my people, and gets away with it. Do you understand, you scumbag?"

Frightened by the possible violence, Roland nodded, his gaze never meeting Tony's.

Tony pushed on. "First, let me tell you the facts of life. Christine has moved out of your apartment, and where she has gone is none of your bloody business. Second," he indicated on his fingers, "she has a court approved restraining order against you, which means, if you go within one hundred yards of her, your ass will be in jail."

"Third," Tony continued, "you are going to immediately resign your job here at Eaton's. If you refuse, Mrs. Mullins is prepared to fire you, now, on the spot, and make sure your history is known all over town." Tony waited a moment for everything to sink in. "So, are you prepared to resign, right now, Guillaume?" Tony asked, accepting a resignation letter from Heidi, which he threw across the table, with a pen. "If so, sign that son-of-a-bitch, right now!"

EATON'S – During the Second French Revolution

Roland hesitated, as fear spread across his face, his posture tensed as he began to read the letter.

Tony yelled, "Either sign it, or don't, I don't have the patience to screw around with you. I can't stand to look at your face."

Roland instantly signed the letter, timidly pushing it back across the table.

Tony reached across the table, grabbed Roland by his shirt collar, and pulled him to a standing position. Then he moved his face within inches of Roland's. He whispered, "If I so much as hear that you have tried to contact Christine, been anywhere near her or said anything about her, I will find you one night, take you into an alley and cut your queer balls off. Have I made myself perfectly clear Guillaume?" Tony barked.

"You! You can't do this. This is none of your business," Roland stammered. "I'll get a lawyer and ..."

Lafleur ended Roland's comments by slapping him violently on the back of the head. "Listen carefully, you queer bastard, you are not going to do anything. I already have a file on you and your separatist friends and witness statements confirming the abuse of your wife. If you so much as try anything, I'll bury you so deep in a holding cell, you'll never be found! So now, do you understand?"

"Yes sir," Roland was noticeably shocked that Lafleur knew about his affiliation with the FLQ.

Tony nodded to everyone in the room and then pushed the intercom button. "Agatha, have Ray come back in, please."

Ray arrived in two seconds, "Yeah Boss."

"Take this bastard up to his locker, and ..."

Heidi interrupted, "I've already cleaned out his locker," she said, picking up a paper bag from the floor and slamming it into Roland's chest.

"Good!" Tony pointed a 35mm camera at Roland and taking several pictures, he handed the camera to Ray. "Have his picture distributed to all our security staff and posted in both the staff and manager's lounge. If he shows his face anywhere in our store, I want him detained and turned over to Francois for arrest."

"Anything else, Boss?"

"Yeah, get this prick out of my store, immediately."

"Got it, Boss," Ray replied, crudely yanking Roland out of the interrogation room door.

"So, did I miss anything," Tony laughed, sitting back into his chair.

"Yeah, you didn't punch him in the face," Francois joked.

"But you certainly scared the shit out of him," Heidi chuckled. "I don't think we'll be seeing him around here anytime soon."

⚜ Thirty-Two ⚜

The pelting rain, high winds and dark omnibus sky should have been an early indication of the historic mass depression and futility that was to befall the people of Montreal. The problem had begun several weeks earlier when rumors began circulating concerning the discontentment of the Montreal Police Force, regarding their demands for wage parody with the neighboring Toronto police department. Their representatives had been sprouting rebellious talk of sub-standard equipment and salaries that were thirty percent less than their counterparts, nationwide. Union leaders had threatened the Montreal Mayor and city council with a city-wide strike if their demands were not met. Representatives of the Montreal fire department sided with their brother police officers threatening to follow the police if they went on strike.

The media downplayed these threats, assuring Montrealers that the MPD would *never* strike, leaving its citizens without police protection. But, having witnessed the political climate, filled with violence and threats of separation over the last few years, the average Montrealer was taking these threats seriously. As the threatened 6:00 P.M. Friday deadline grew near, schools, government offices and businesses closed early.

With all the craziness Ricky sat in the basement luncheonette, his tired feet propped up on an adjoining chair. He was not focusing on his two chili dogs and fries, instead his mind was going over all the "what ifs" should the strike occur. He spotted Tony searching for a place to sit. Ricky motioned him over.

"Boy, you certainly look relaxed," Tony said, as he motioned to Ricky's feet. "By the way that was a great presentation this morning."

"Yeah, let's hope it's all for naught," he stated.

"I'm not so sure the strike isn't going to happen, Ricky. You know that Denis told us that he still has good contacts in the MPD, and *strike* is the word out on the street."

"Yeah! And, just between us, I'm not so sure he doesn't have even better contacts in the FLQ," Ricky laughed.

"Shh. Not so loud," he admonished Ricky, "they have ears everywhere. Anyway, he says there are serious mumblings that the strike will go ahead at six o'clock tonight. There are already hundreds of cops who have called in sick. The rumor mill indicates that the union leaders and police brass are searching for a way for the cops to leave their jobs, "en masse," without calling it a strike. The consensus is that they are just going to call for a full union meeting at the Paul Sauve Arena 'to just discuss the issues.' These pricks have a perfectly good idea of the bedlam that the absence of law enforcement will cause but, they don't have the balls to take responsibility for it. No wonder people hate cops!"

"Says the New York ex-cop! Look Tony, you know, as well as I do, that Montrealers are resilient people, and we find a way to survive against any adversity. So, a few windows get broken, and another convenience store gets held up, but the next day it's all over and we go about our regular business."

"My, my, young friend," Tony shook his head, "your naiveté is showing. You were pretty young back then, but I'm sure you heard of the 'Rocket Riot' of 1955."

Annoyed at the rebuke, Ricky responded. "Of course, I remember. Christ Tony, I'm this country's biggest hockey fan and I still think the 'The Rocket' suspension was too severe for the infraction.

"Well, that suspension caused a riot at the Forum larger than Montreal had ever seen, but you better believe that if today's strike happens, the Forum one will look like a cake walk."

"I presume that you will be working late tonight?" Tony continued.

"I was on early shift today, so I was supposed to be out of here by five. But, with all this craziness, I figured I'd stick around to see if the strike actually happens." Ricky couldn't shake his concerns.

"Oh, it'll happen, my boy. And, when it does, you'll wish you'd taken that early train home to Ville St. Laurent."

"We shall see, Tony. Anyway, I'm going to be here until at least seven. Want to join me at Joe's Steak House for dinner?"

"Boy, that almost sounded like you were really going to put your hand in your pocket and buy me dinner," Tony laughed. "But no, thanks anyway, I got a directive from the GM's office that my staff and I are not to leave the store, using his words, 'under any circumstances'. But you could bring me a doggy bag."

⚜ Thirty-Three ⚜

After slip-sliding his way from Eaton's to Dr. Markowitz office earlier in the day, Ricky was not in a great frame of mind for his session.

"At our last session, Richard, you summed up all your childhood experiences and major traumas in a two-minute *Readers Digest* condensed version, and without expressing any regrets, or emotions, yes?"

"Yes, Dr. Markovitz. I've replayed the events in my mind so many times, that now the dialogue flows naturally from my mouth. I don't even have to think about it!"

"But, Richard, I must tell you, over my many years of counseling, I have seen that just one of these traumas could be enough to disrupt a person's life, but here, for you, you have had so many traumas, and at such a young age. Richard, can you relate emotions of anger, pity, neglect, sadness, to these traumas, or do you not permit yourself to feel anything?"

"I don't know, Doc. I guess I realized early on that I just didn't have the time, or energy, to dwell on them, so I just filed them away. I'm exceptionally good at compartmentalizing and I can easily decide what is important, and what is not. There just didn't seem to be any productive value in dwelling on events I couldn't change, or control."

"Interesting! So, you believe that because you have filed them away, you have come to terms with what you were subjected to, yes?"

"What's the use of rehashing nightmares that you can't do anything about? I believe it is counterproductive! In short, I don't have time for it." Ricky didn't seem to realize that his normal easy-going voice tone just got several decibels higher!

Dr. Markovitz stroked his bushy mustache as he digested Richard's comments, and the way he presented them. "Think about this scenario. You are a manager of many departments and employees at Eaton's, yes?"

"Yes."

"So, consider this. One day you are walking through one of your departments and you notice that a display table leg is broken. You realize that you don't have the construction abilities to repair the leg, so what would you do."

"That's simple. I'd evaluate the danger to my customers, remove the table from the department and have a carpenter repair it."

"Okay good, Richard. So, to compare this with just one of your more serious childhood traumas, such as the sexual abuse, you would evaluate the dangers of not addressing the event, you would calculate the ramifications of not focusing on it, and you would seek professional services to handle it, yes?"

"I see where you are going with this, Doc, but believe me, that event is not consuming my thoughts, or my life. It's tucked far away so that it has no effect on me."

"So, you say. So, you say, my boy, but I disagree. You are seeing me because you have sexual and insomniac problems. Whether you want to admit it or not, these issues do have a connection to the events of your youth. The child who is beaten may shed the physical scars of the beating, but the mental scars will direct his adult life, unless he gains the complete understanding of the cause and effect."

"Isn't that rather simplistic, Doc. You're saying that I can't sleep because I was sexually abused as a child, and my mother beat me?"

"Believe me, Richard, nothing is simplistic in the mental health arena. What I am saying to you is that yes, your problems today have a direct relationship to the problems of your past. For example, you have a baby daughter, yes?"

"Yes."

"Would you ever consider beating her?"

"Of course not."

EATON'S – During the Second French Revolution

And I'll tell you why that is. Somewhere along the line in your young life you have addressed the beatings by your Mother. You remember how it felt physically. You remember how it made you feel mentally, And, after evaluating all this information you resolved to never do this to your daughter. You attacked the problem head on, and calculated your personal resolution, which is admirable. But the issue remains that you have never taken the time to figure out why the beatings happened to you. You never analyzed why a woman, who gave birth to you, would hurt you. You just buried all that, yes?"

"Do you love your Mother, Richard? And do you believe she loves you?"

"I don't know, Doc. I guess I've not given it much thought. I suppose I love her in some weird way, but I don't like the things she has done to me. As for her loving me, I sincerely have to say that I really don't know."

"Another scenario. Let's say your Mother had a valid reason for her inability to show you love. And let's also surmise, that every time she saw you her mind tripped to an uncontrollable image of her being attacked. Ergo, to her, beating you was a necessary act of self-defense. With that understanding, as an intelligent adult, could you forgive her for not having the mental capacity to distinguish between right and wrong, during your childhood."

"Of course, when you put it that way.

"And that would be possible because you addressed the problem, looked in depth at the cause, and understand the circumstances regarding the beatings. Don't read this the wrong way. The beatings will always be mentally distressing and painful, but once you can understand the complete story, then, and only then, will you allow yourself to file it away, as a completed project, yes?"

"I see what you are saying, Dr. Markovitz. Maybe I need to get it out of the filing cabinet," Ricky laughed.

"Not all of the solutions are that simple, and we may find that the premise is very different, but bringing these issues to the surface, together we should gain a permanent remedy that will, no doubt, make your life so much more rewarding."

"We still have a few minutes left so let's touch on the exercise I asked you to conduct, last session. I asked you to focus on just one of your childhood stories to see if you could generate at least one tear, or a specific emotional feeling, about the incident."

"Honestly, Doc, I tried! But I have to say, that there were no tears, and the only emotion I felt was uncontrollable rage."

"I'm sure you don't see it right now, but this is still progress. No, you didn't shed tears, but emotional rage is still an emotion and that's a start. What event was your focus?"

"My sexual abuse."

"Of course, that's the most prominent of your childhood traumas. As an exercise, for our next session, I want you to revisit that trauma, but this time I want you to feel sorry for yourself. I want you to think of the millions of children who have gone through what you experienced. Then, I want you to visualize totally and vividly your beautiful daughter going through the exact same thing, under the exact same circumstances. And we will discuss the results on your next visit, yes?"

More exercises? And why Darlene? I will never let anyone abuse her the way I was abused! I don't really have time for all this crap! And, I'm starting to have serious second thoughts about this therapy bullshit. Ricky thought.

⚜ Thirty-Four ⚜

Vincenzo, Vinney "the Trunk," Calabrisee, spent numerous hours methodically planning, and replanning, the daring daylight Eaton's display window heist. He analyzed each obstacle that could foil his "clean operation," and developed viable solutions to countermand any possible detection. One such obstacle was the selection of the perfect partner to assist with the operation. Here, he had selected Francesco, "the Nose," Rossi, a fifty-six-year-old associate who also had been part of the Calabrisee organization. Having spent most of his adult life serving many sentences in Bordeaux Prison, Frankie was considered a liability to the family, and therefore eliminated from family operations. Having nowhere to go, he joined up with Vinney, who was also in a similar banishment situation.

Although Frankie was not the ideal candidate, Vinney felt that his aged look would be a definite asset to the venture. With his weathered heavily wrinkled face, slight limp, and outwardly timid personality he would blend in perfectly as an old Eaton's employee. No one would take any notice of him. More importantly, Frankie was totally loyal to Vinney, owing his life and continued freedom to him.

The bond between Frankie and Vinney began in Vinney's early years as an enforcer for the Calabrisee organization. Vinney had been directed by the family consigliere to set an example to a family book maker who had been skimming from weekly numbers takes. Late one night, Vinney and Frankie abducted Joey Brasso at the Chez Paris lounge, taking him to a secluded area in Old Montreal, where they beat him with baseball bats to within an inch of his life. As they knew not to leave any family evidence of the beating, they placed Joey's unconscious bloody body in the trunk of Vinney's Cadillac, and drove two blocks down to the harbor edge of the St. Lawrence River.

It was 3:00 in the morning and the harbor area was totally deserted. As Frankie and Vinney began removing the unconscious body from the trunk of his car, a Montreal police car showed up. Both officers jumped from their cruiser, guns drawn.

EATON'S – During the Second French Revolution

"Get your hands up," the young officer screamed, waving his gun nervously back and forth between Frankie and Vinney. "I repeat, get your fuckin' hands up, now!"

"Okay, okay, take it easy," Vinney let Joey's body fall to the ground, with a sickening clunk. "We are just trying to help this poor guy."

The older officer placed a hand on the younger officer's hand forcing his gun toward the ground, as he approached Vinney. "You're Giuseppe Calabresee's kid, Vinney, right?" he questioned, casually looking at the still body on the ground. "Is he still alive?"

"Yeah, I'm Vinney! So, what of it? I don't know nothin'." Vinney kneeled to check the victim's pulse. "I think he still has a pulse. Then isn't it good we were just passing by and saw this guy laying here and thought we could help."

"That's bullshit," the young officer interrupted. "You were going to throw the guy in the drink." He turned toward his superior and protested. "What's wrong with you, Claude? Why are you just standin' there? We've caught these Goombahs red-handed, and I don't care who his old man is. For Christ's sake, he was taking a half dead guy out of his trunk. What more evidence do we need?"

"Easy Denis. Sometimes there's a logical explanation for even the most obvious situation. So, what's the story, Vinney?"

Vinney noticed Frankie getting nervous. His hand moved towards his rear waistband, that Vinney knew held his 44 Magnum. Vinney locked eyes with him as he gently shook his head indicating not to go for his gun. Fear was evident in Frankie's eyes but having a shootout with MPD officers would be suicide.

"Officer ugh, Plante," Vinney strained to see his breast pocket name tag, "as I told you, we found the guy here and were trying to help. And, contrary to your partner's observation, we weren't taking him *out* of the trunk, we were trying to put him *in* the trunk."

"That's bullshit! Why were you putting him in the trunk?" the young officer sputtered.

"I couldn't find any phone booths around here to call you guys. And, for your information, we were going to take him up to the Royal Victoria Hospital. I sure as shit wasn't going to put this bloody mess inside my new Caddy. So, that's my story."

"Now, that's one damn story! I can't wait for the judge to hear this one! We need to haul their asses in, Claude, and let the justice system sort it out."

"Not so fast, Denis. It sounds like a reasonable explanation to me. Get on the radio and call for an ambulance."

"But, but, ..." Denis protested.

"Now, Denis, before the 'vic' dies and we have a shitload of additional paperwork to fill out."

As the junior officer, Denis Charbonneau, went back to the patrol car to call it in, Claude turned to Vinney, "Now son, you owe me. So, get your asses out of here before our incident commander gets here." As an afterthought, as he walked toward the cruiser, he turned back to Vinney and whispered, "Give my regards to Giuseppe, and thank him for the confirmation party he set up for my granddaughter."

Hours later, Joey Brasso died of severe brain hemorrhaging, at the Royal Victoria Hospital. The reports indicated he was a victim of a mugging in old Montreal. The case remained an unsolved homicide.

After that, the 'trunk' tale was told over and over, and Vincenzo Calabrisee became known in the criminal world as Vinney "The Trunk."

Jointly escaping arrest for Joey's beating, and eventual death, cemented a lifelong bond between Vinney and Frankie. Also, with their eventual joint expulsion from the family, Frankie realized that his survival depended on staying close to Vinney. They were two black sheep building their own crime family.

Having simulated the heist numerous times in the warehouse Vinney had leased, he questioned Frankie. "Did you get the uniforms from the Russian tailor?"

"Yeah. Both are the exact same color and material that Eaton's uses. And the 'Merchandise Display' patch is perfect. I rolled them through some grease and dirt, and then had them cleaned. Nobody'll notice any difference."

"Yeah, well looking the part is one thing, but acting the part is critical. Can you really do this, Frankie? Can you handle it without freaking out, even if something goes wrong?"

"Sure, boss. We have been over it a hundred times."

"Okay, let's go over it again to make sure we haven't forgotten anything. You have the disguises, moustaches and wigs. We'll change into the uniforms and disguises, in the men's room on the basement level, right by the center stairway. We can get the cardboard boxes, at the north end compactor, at the back of the main floor. We can also get a flatbed cart, and a ladder, near the freight elevator by the same compactor."

"Remember, Frankie, we need to walk and talk as if we are employees who belong there. If not, we are screwed. There is a big payday for us when we pull it off, and if we follow the plan, it should be a breeze."

At 8:15, on Thursday morning, Vinney and Frankie parked the blue mini-truck by the Eaton's' Metcalfe Street freight elevators. The truck was painted in the midnight blue Eaton's color and displayed the gold T. Eaton Company [Canada] Ltd. logo on both doors.

At 8:20, they entered Eaton's, through the north end main floor doors, accompanied by a throng of arriving employees. They flashed their simple counterfeit identification badges like all the other hurried employees. With their uniforms and disguises secreted beneath their heavy overcoats, they proceeded to the lower men's room, where they immediately changed into their disguises.

EATON'S – During the Second French Revolution

At promptly 9:00, as the opening chimes sounded, they emerged from the men's room and proceeded to the compactor where they got the cardboard boxes, ladder, and cart. Vinney realized that it was critical to their success that they not bump into any other members of the Merchandise Display personnel, who would not recognize them. He had scouted the Merchandise Display fourth floor office weeks earlier, where he found a duty roster indicating that all display staff were relegated to creating a 'full floor' display, for the upcoming Eaton's Snowmobile Show, on the fifth floor. This would hopefully keep them occupied and away from the main floor area.

Vinney pulled the flatbed cart with the cardboard boxes across the crowded main floor towards the center eastside window, as Frankie dutifully followed, carrying the six- foot ladder.

An elderly salesclerk was busy displaying ladies leather gloves on a lighted display case. "Good morning," she cheerfully greeted, "gonna' work on the windows today?"

Vinney smiled, "Yeah. Gotta get ready for the Snowmobile Show, next week. Can I trouble you to move those boxes from up there, so we can set up the ladder? We'll give you a hand if you tell us where to put them."

"Just hand them down to me, and I'll put them under the counter. We won't need those until the Spring, anyway," she smiled.

As he placed the ladder to remove the surplus glove inventory, which was blocking entry to the elevated window, he surveyed the floor for store security personnel.

"Okay, that's got it," he said, handing her down the last box; then he slid the window panel open. "We won't be long. Just need to break the window down, move the mannequins and return the stock to the right department."

"Okay. Have fun," she chided, returning to cleaning her glove counter glass showcases.

Vinney leaned towards Frankie, lowering his voice, "Now, just like we rehearsed, Frankie. Look natural, and don't rush," Vinney directed, and then smiled at the ironic thought that they were pulling off a daylight robbery in full view of passing customers on the sidewalk side of the display window. He climbed the ladder to the window crammed full of elegant short and full-length mink, sable and brightly, hued fox fur coats; displayed to attract the elite society crowd to the fur department on the sixth floor.

Lending a helping hand to Frankie to climb the ladder, he carefully began packing the coats into the cardboard boxes, as Frankie moved the empty mannequins to the end of the display window. Vinney remained casual returning waves to passing customers outside the windows as Frankie began taking the boxes down the ladder to the waiting cart.

With the window completely stripped, Vinney was bringing the last box down the ladder as a main floor manager, Doug Fargo, approached Frankie.

"How come you're changing the fur window, already? I thought that was going to be permanent through the winter season," he questioned, eyeing the empty window.

Noticing Frankie flush in search a response, Vinney thrust a box of furs into Frankie's hands, and replied, "Yeah, we were told that too, but originally, they wanted us to break down the Sainte Catherine/University corner window, you know the one with the whole Christmas display. Then I guess they realized, with the Snowmobile Show only one week away, it would be better to break down the fur window, instead. I guess they figured that it's a hellava lot easier than messing with all those little ornaments."

"I guess. But it would've been nice if someone in display would have let us know," the manager replied, continuing his stride across the main floor.

"I'll let my boss know that he should send a memo in the future," Vinney shouted.

He removed the ladder and followed Frankie, as he pushed the box laden cart towards the freight doors.

"That was scary. I almost pissed myself," Frankie muttered.

"All in a days-work of crime, my friend."

Pushing through the rubber doors into the receiving area they were greeted by the smartly groomed service elevator operator. "Where to boys?"

"Just up to the street level," Vinney responded.

"You guys moving out?" laughed the operator, whose name tag read 'Andre'.

"Naw, Andre. Just moving a bunch of crap out to the Dorval store, for a new window display.

Eyeing the cardboard boxes piled high on the cart, he questioned suspiciously. "What are 'ya taking out there, now? Your guys just took a large load out there on Monday."

"Yeah, well. The idiots took everything out there except for the stuff they really needed for the main entrance display. So, I get to waste my time fixing their mistakes. Shit happens, I guess," he laughed.

The elevator arrived at street level. As Andre opened the gate to the outer elevator door, he continued, "I guess that's job security, Eh? For thirty-two years I've been on this same elevator, and the only change I get is when the old bugger breaks down. Just leave the empty cart outside the door and I'll pick it up on my next run. Anyway, you guys drive carefully."

"Thanks," Vinney waved, as the elevator door slammed closed, leaving them alone on the sidewalk beside their truck.

"We did it, boss!" Frankie exclaimed quietly. "We fuckin' did it!

"Cool it, Frankie. We're not out of the woods, yet."

Vinney and Frankie loaded the boxes into the truck, left the cart in front of the elevator door and drove towards their warehouse.

EATON'S – During the Second French Revolution

The following day headlines in the *Montreal Star* and the *LaPresse* newspapers highlighted the brazen daylight robbery.

DARING EATON'S FUR THEFT NETS ROBBERS $80,000.00

Vinney laughed as he finished reading the article. "This is total bullshit."

"What's so funny, boss?" Frankie asked, putting down the Blue Bonnets racing handicap form he'd been reading.

"Both the reporters and the cops both have their heads up their asses. It says the haul was over eighty thousand, but you know, I cut all the sale tags off the coats, and they totaled only fifty-six thousand and seventy-five."

"Maybe we should have Eaton's send us the difference in cash that they are claiming," Frankie joked. "So, what are we going to do with the furs boss? You gonna sell them to that prick Russian fence, in Ville D 'Anjou?"

"Naw. We're gonna peddle them ourselves. We'll get more money that way. The Russian will only give us ten cents on the dollar, but, if we sell them, we can make forty to fifty percent, at least. In fact, old Mrs. Arturo wants to buy one of the sables, for three thousand for her daughter in Rome, and Julian Venicee wants two minks, at two grand each, for his granddaughters. That's already more than we'd get from the Russian."

"Maybe, I get one for my Mama, okay Vinney?"

"Sure Frankie. I'll make you a good price," he laughed. "You know what they say in the community, *'Da Anglos buy offa da rack, but Sicilians buy offa da truck!'*"

They both laughed.

"Ya' know Frankie, do you remember that the junior officer, Denis Charbonneau, we ran into the night we put Joey Brasso in the trunk?"

"Yeah, so!"

"He works at Eaton's now, as security. Wouldn't it have been a hoot if we ran into him when we were making our way with those furs?"

"Anyway now, we need to start planning for target number two. And this time we are going to blame it on the FLQ. Those bastards are creating so much shit with their bombings and bank robberies, no one will question that they didn't do this job, capisce? So, we better start brushing up on our French, if we are gonna pull this off," Vinney said.

"So, boss, I gotta wear that fuckin' moustachee, again? It almos' fall off, and it make my face itch."

"No but, we must change your facial look drastically this time. You remember, Isabella Conte? I was banging her, and her sister last year. Anyway, she works as a special effects makeup artist for Vision Productions, and she's agreed to do miracles with changing both our appearances, in exchange for that silver fox coat."

"OK, boss. As long I no gotta wear that fuckin' moustachee again."

That's the least you should be worrying about, you old coot! Vinney thought.

⚜ Thirty-Five ⚜

Because of their work schedules Ricky hadn't yet had an opportunity to talk with Christine about her new living arrangements with her friend Charlotte. But he was more concerned about potential problems with her ex-husband, Roland, since the annulment and the restraining order came into effect.

As Ricky stood by the office entrance, he saw Christine walk briskly into the teen fashion stockroom and followed her. When he entered, he saw her at the far end of the stockroom, straining to reach a box of sweaters on the top shelf. Her dainty designer skirt rose provocatively above her knees, exposing slim muscular legs, as she struggled up on her toes, to get a grip of the box.

"Here, let me help," he offered, gently moving her aside, "I'm taller than you!"

Handing her the box, he bent to whisper in her ear, looking around to see if anyone was within earshot, "I, uh, was wondering if, well, you'd like to have a drink with me after work to celebrate your release from the 'Roland prison'." He heard his words and couldn't believe how sheepish the question sounded.

In response, Christine rose on her toes, softly pushed his hair aside and whispered in his ear, teasingly, "We're all alone in here, so I don't think we need to whisper, but yes, I'd love to have a drink with you."

Putting on a more businesslike attitude, Ricky said, "I think it is important for you to understand how we took down Roland last week, and I wanted to hear how you are getting along at Charlotte's."

"Sounds good! Besides, I need to get my Dubonnet fix," she laughed, playfully punching Ricky's shoulder.

Why the hell am I sweating like a pig, he thought.

"Great! Why don't I meet you in the seven-twenty-seven lounge around six-fifteen? I need to pick something up on the way." A crimson blush was evident on Ricky's face.

"Can I start getting drunk before you get there?" she kidded.

"I suppose, after all, you are a free woman now! You can do whatever your little heart desires." He then turned to leave the stockroom to avoid any further embarrassment.

How can a friendly punch in the shoulder, or the sexy curl of her lips, drive me so absolutely nuts?

EATON'S – During the Second French Revolution

At 6:00, Ricky bought a single red rose at Academy Floral, before heading for the Place Ville Marie. Ascending to the top floor, in the elevator, he carefully secreted the rose into the inside breast pocket of his overcoat.

As usual Antoine greeted him as he entered the lounge. "The beautiful, Miss Christine, is already seated Mister Dean, and she's already ordered drinks," he pointed toward the same corner table they had occupied some weeks earlier.

"Thanks Antoine," Ricky replied, making his way to the table.

"You're here." She rose from her chair, and planted a swift brother-sister kiss, on his cheek.

Boy, that was a hellava lot different kiss from last time we were here. This rose thing may not be such a good idea, right now.

"That I is," he joked, carefully placing his overcoat on an empty chair, before taking his seat. "So, here you are, at last, a free woman. What is the first big plan you're going to tackle?" he asked, taking a settling gulp of his wine.

"That's heavy. I guess my first big plan is remarkably simple. I just want to begin to experience what it's like to live a normal life. I've missed out on so much Ricky, and I have so many inhibitions to get over." She hesitated, as she took a sip of her drink. "I've got to learn to feel good about myself and get all the negativity out of my brain. But you wanted to tell me about how you guys handled Roland," she changed the subject.

Ricky relayed the story in full, ending with, "You'll never see his damn face, again."

"Do you really think he took the threats seriously enough for him to leave me alone?" she quizzed.

"Oh yeah! Tony can be one scary dude when you get him mad. When he told Roland that he was going to take him into an alley and cut his, oh sorry!"

"I'm not totally naïve, Ricky, I've heard that statement before, 'ya know."

"Anyway, I guarantee that Roland took Tony at his word, And, with Detective Lafleur standing behind him throughout the meeting, he was positively intimidated. Were you aware that MPD had a file on Roland linking him to the FLQ?" he added.

"My goodness, no! I guess it doesn't surprise me, though. My French isn't great, but a few months ago I overheard him, and his college buddies, joking about the crippling of that army disposal guy, who got blown up. I couldn't believe how cruel their joking was. They even thought it was funny that he is still hospitalized, can you believe it?"

"When it comes to Roland, I can believe anything. Anyway, let's get onto a more progressive conversation. How are you getting along with your *new* single life?"

"In a nutshell, I love living with Charlotte. I feel so free. I'm not frightened all the time. Father Mac says my annulment passed the first hurdle of the tribunal. And I told my parents everything and they are being overly supportive and really,

I mean overly supportive. Dad came by the other day to inspect the apartment and asked jokingly if I wanted Roland killed. If I didn't know better, I might have thought he meant it, at least a little."

"After he left, I found twenty, one-hundred-dollar bills under the cookie jar. That's two thousand dollars. Anyway, I got upset and called him, but he denied that he knew anything about the money. He also told me, if I didn't want it, I should just throw it away, since it wasn't his at all! Can you believe it," she questioned?

"Actually, I can. It sounds like, with all you've been through, both your Mom and Dad just want to help you get set up in a better life. It just shows how much they really love you. And it is well past time for some real love to be filling your life."

Christine placed her hand over his. "Last time we were here you promised when my issues got resolved you would tell me about your problems, remember?"

"Christine, yours are not finalized yet," his body warmed as her hand remained on his. "Your annulment still isn't final." Ricky wanted to say more but the words wouldn't come.

She spoke in a whisper. "Ricky, if it hadn't been for you, I don't know what I would have done. You saved my life. Whether I get the annulment or not, you helped me get away from Roland and now I am a free woman. For that, I will be forever grateful."

Ricky had hoped for a lot more than gratitude.

"Christine, listen to me carefully. You've just now been given your rightful gift to a new life and happiness. And, you said earlier, that you needed to get rid of the negativity, well listening to my problems and the baggage I carry is more negativity than you need.

"Ricky, please. When we talked about my problems, I could see in your eyes that you understood and you knew my pain, not because of me, but because of you! I was sure you connected to something that I told you about my life with Roland."

She stopped for a moment and took a sip of her Dubonnet, to give her the strength of conviction to push on. As he was her boss, she thought that might be overstepping, but she felt like she had to try to get through to him.

"I know you are married, but you never talk about your wife. I know you have a beautiful baby because there is a picture in your office. So, if I am wrong, and it isn't a problem in your marriage, then I am very wrong and I apologize."

He lit a cigarette and as he blew out smoke, he released all the tension and related the sordid story of his married life. In the end he told her he felt trapped because of Darlene and felt there was just no way out.

Christine sat silent, apparently shocked by this revelation.

"So, that's all the gory details." Ricky gulped down the rest of the glass of his Dubonnet."

"Oh Ricky! I don't know how you can hold that nightmare inside of you, and not burst. I can see that you feel just as trapped as I did. Are you sure there is nothing that can be done," she got a tissue from her bag and dabbed at her tears.

Ricky signaled for another round of drinks.

"I have to say, I don't understand your wife. You're young, handsome, have a fantastic job, not to mention a great ..." she hesitated.

Ricky laughed, as he flushed with embarrassment.

"Well, you have to know you are every girl's dream. All my young teeny-bopper staff are head over heels in love with you."

He just ignored the comment and turned to hail the waiter. He didn't want her to see him blush.

After the drinks arrived, Christine turned serious. "Ricky, thank you for telling me your tragic story, but can I tell you something, you relay it as if it was happening to someone else. You never showed any emotion all the while you were telling the story.

"Now, you're sounding like my shrink," he laughed, accepting a fresh drink from Antoine.

"You have a shrink?"

"Oops, I don't think that was supposed to come out. I was trying to impress you; not let you know you're sitting across from a nut case."

"Don't joke about that, Ricky." This was the first time he had truly seen her show the slightest bit of anger.

"I think you should be p*roud* of yourself, having the strength to seek out professional help. I've never had the guts to do it." She hesitated. "You seem to always be helping everyone else with their problems, including me, can I at least, in addition to your doctor, be there for you?"

Ricky didn't know how to react. For the very first time that he could remember, real tears rolled down his face.

He thought, *Dr. Markovitz would be proud, but I'm so embarrassed.*

He whispered, "I'm so sorry, Christine," taking hold of her hand.

She pushed him away and stared into his eyes, "Damn you, Ricky! I don't want 'sorry,' you've got *nothing*, do you hear me," she repeated, "nothing to apologize for. It's apparent that others should be apologizing to you." Her anger subsided as she wrapped her arms around him. He motioned for her to stand next to him, then he walked her over to one of the large windows in the back of the lounge so they could share the beautiful night sky, alone. Ricky turned her toward him and gently placed his thumb under her chin, guiding her face ever so slowly towards his.

Looking into her face he could see so many things and he just wanted to escape with her by his side. He leaned down and gently brushed his lips against the softness of hers, taking in the scent of her Chanel perfume. He let his lips surround hers, lingering too long, but he couldn't help himself. He could feel his body betray him. He wanted to show his appreciation not frighten her with a sexually charged body pressing against her. But he could feel every muscle, every nerve ending, every piece of skin, heralding the actions begun by that one innocent kiss. Out of the corner of his eye he saw Antoine, standing by the entry, a wide grin gracing his happy face.

The spell had been broken, but the reality remained.

Not knowing what to do, or say, Ricky looked at his watch. "The nine-forty train to my hell awaits!" he laughed. He looked at her for one more moment as he got up to help her with her coat.

He paid the check and without a lot of additional conversation they exited the Ville Marie. The flurries of new snow began falling.

"I'm just five blocks away, so, I think I'll walk."

"Not on my watch," he insisted, hailing a passing cab.

Ricky opened the rear door as she planted a quick kiss on his lips, before sliding into the backseat of the cab. He leaned into the cab and handed the driver five dollars saying, "Pour vous!" *For you!* Then, he eased out and stopped to connect with Christine's parting kiss, but instead pulled the rose from his inner overcoat pocket. He placed it on her lap, "A rose, for the one who tonight opened my heart!"

He heard her choked sigh, and told the driver, "*Rue Hutchinson, alley.*"

His departing vision was of this beautiful creature, rose in hand, wiping tears from her eyes, peering out of the rear window, as the cab sped away.

⚜ Thirty-Six ⚜

The wail of approaching fire and police sirens pierced the roar of the unruly crowd of student dissidents attacking the Black Watch Armory on Bleury St. They had tried to gain access to the armory by ramming a huge commercial garbage container against the heavily planked front door, to no avail. Louis shouted and banged his club against the doors and barred windows, along with the rest of the crowd. He watched powerlessly as a nearby screaming student hurled a Molotov cocktail against the brick veneer of the building, splattering its blazing contents, which fell harmlessly to the concrete sidewalk below.

"You should have aimed for the upstairs windows," Louis told him.

"Yeah, I guess. And, unfortunately, that was my last cocktail," the student replied.

Louis looked at the student, thinking, "*These jerks need to take a riot course if they expect any substantial results.*"

EATON'S – During the Second French Revolution

Realizing that no one was trying to retreat from the arriving authorities, he asked. "Are you guys going to stick around to get purposely arrested?"

"No, we had planned to get weapons from the armory, extend severe damage and get out of here before the pigs arrived."

"So, what now?" Louis asked.

"We wait for the first cop car to arrive, then we all scatter in different directions. It'll drive the stupid bastards crazy."

"And, after that?"

"A bunch of us are meeting up at the Belgium Pastry Shop, up by Mount Royal. Wanna come?"

"Sure. Sounds great." He extended his hand. "By the way, my name is Louis, with the Montreal North *Dieppe Cell.*"

"Francois," he stated, shaking Louis' hand. "I thought I recognized you. Didn't you get nailed by the pigs two weeks ago at LaFontaine Park?"

"Unfortunately, but no big deal." Louis grabbed Francois's arm. "Let's get outta here before we get busted!" They began running from the scene as the first patrol car arrived.

Smiling, and out of breath from running up the Bleury St. hill, both Louis and Francois bent at the knees to catch their breath.

"Let's go. The restaurant is just over there," Francois pointed to a small shop across the street.

As they settled into a booth a young co-ed came over, throwing her arms around Francois and kissing his cheek.

"That was so awesome!" she squealed in delight. "I almost peed my pants when those cops showed up."

"Join us." Francois directed, unfurling her arms from around his neck. "Jacqueline, this is Louis," he pointed. "He's with the *Dieppe Cell.*"

"Enchante," she cooed, batting her eyes at Louis.

As they entered the shop, Francois held up three fingers to the waitress at the counter.

"Is your cell helping us with the exchange?" The co-ed asked, immediately noticing the admonition on Francois' face.

"No. Not that I know of," Louis responded, questioningly. "I heard about it, but only informally."

The waitress placed three expressos on the table.

"Yeah, well, everyone will know soon enough," Francois tried to regroup. "Our *Liberation Cell team* leader told us that we are not going to be given the specifics 'til the last moment'. That way nothing can slip out to warn the pigs about our plans."

"I heard that *it* is going to be really, really big. And could drastically disrupt finances across Canada," Louis responded cautiously.

"Oh yeah! The biggest Montreal has ever seen," Francois boasted, without offering further details.

Jacqueline remained silent trying to disguise her fear of inadvertently revealing that a terror attack was in the works.

"Man, I wish our *Dieppe Cell* group was part of the plan, or at the very least, I'd love to be close by to see what happens."

"Maybe, Francois, Louis could ..." Jacqueline began, then immediately quieted as Francois' angry eyes settled on her.

Francois was searching for a way to recover. "I heard from Allard that you are a photographer. Do you have professional camera equipment?"

"Yes, a thirty-five millimeter, several lenses, tripod, and lots of other stuff. Why?" Louis asked.

"Good, good," Francois thought for a moment. "Would you be willing to act as a photographer for the event?"

"Sure, but what do you mean by *event*?" Louis tested.

"You will be told the details that day, and perhaps only hours before," Francois responded in an annoyed tone. "You will also be instructed as to a position to take your camera shots that is safe from scrutiny. Do you have a telephoto lens?"

"Of course," Louis answered.

"Bring it too! And do you have a pager so I can reach you?"

"Yes."

"Give me your number." Francois wrote Louis's pager number on a small card.

"I will page you within the next six days and you will immediately contact me at this number, understood?" Francois handed Louis a card with his name and a handwritten telephone number on it. "And you must be ready to move immediately."

"I'll be ready," Louis replied, as Francois rose from his seat.

"Let's go, Jacqueline," Francois commanded as he headed for the door. Jacqueline sprinted to catch up to him.

Louis waited several minutes for them to disappear before exiting the restaurant. He carefully scanned the area for any remnants of the protesters. When he determined that he was alone, he sprinted over several blocks to where he knew there was a vacant telephone booth.

Louis dialed the familiar number and was put through to Mr. Smith.

"Go ahead," came a clipped voice.

"I'm ninety percent sure the target is the Montreal Stock Exchange.

"Date and time?"

"Within the next six days, but more information at this time is unavailable."

"When will it become available?"

"Sources indicate that only a few hours before the incursion."

"Ideas on the method of the incursion?"

"My best guess is a terror attack, most likely a bombing on a major target."

"If that is indeed the case, it is critical that you get more information, Dates, locations, anything we can use." Smith directed.

"I'm working on it. And I was able to arrange for them to use me as a photographer for the event. But they won't tell me anything until a short time before," Louis paused.

"On another subject," Smith interrupted, "the powers that be are very concerned that we didn't have any advance intelligence on the locker bombing at the Eaton's downtown store." There was criticism in his voice.

"And that's because there was no advance intelligence to which I was privy." Louis replied, annoyed at the rebuke. "I am positive that that bombing was not involved with either my *Dieppe Cell* or the *Liberation Cell*. I can only surmise that it was carried out by either the *Chenier Cell*, who have a master bomb maker, or the *Viger Cell*, who have considered Eaton's as its prime target for years. However, I'm going to a rally on Saturday night with James Lanctot, team leader of the *Liberation Cell*, and I'll see if I can pump him for information about Eaton's."

"You don't truly comprehend the scope of what would have happened if that bomb had gone off during regular business hours. My God, there would have been hundreds of casualties," Mister Smith responded angrily.

"Mister Smith," Louis attempted to control his temper, "that bomb went off in one of my brother's departments, so this event is personal to me. He could have been one of *your* casualties. The challenge that you have is having only one undercover trying to handle a sophisticated and organized terrorist operation, and I can't be everywhere at the same time."

Mr. Smith was momentarily silenced. "I had another undercover, before you were assigned to me. My nephew. His body washed up on Lac des Deux Montanges, four months ago. So, there *were* two of you undercover at the same time."

Louis was floored by this revelation. "I'm so sorry for your loss. I'll try and find out some information on the Eaton's bombing, that's all I can promise."

"Good. Resume contact as soon as possible." The line went dead.

He put the telephone back in the cradle and began his walk back to his car. He had parked on Bleury, and he dreaded that long, lonely walk. But the walk allowed him time to reflect on his decision to become an undercover cop directly after his three-year stint in the U.S. military. Everyone, including the recruiter, had advised him to take some time off to thoroughly investigate his vocational options. But, true to form, once his mind was set, Louis had jumped into R.C.M.P. law enforcement without considering the consequences to his family, his friends or himself.

Now, he could only see a lonely trek down a secluded street; a solitary trip home in his old car; a meal alone in his drafty basement apartment; and another listless night with no one to share body heat, thoughts, or dreams.

I am so screwed up! I wonder what Ricky would think if he knew what I'm doing. Louis thought.

⚜ Thirty-Seven ⚜

Finishing his 5:00 P.M. supper break Ricky exited Joe's Steak House, where he saw several hundred people mulling around, filling the streets and sidewalks. Joe's manager told him that dissidents had begun attacking a MPD patrol car that had apparently been strategically stationed on the street to control the unfolding mayhem.

The manager told Ricky. "There was a look of fear on the face of the young officer in the car. The riotous crowd began screaming separatist chants as they violently rocked the patrol car back and forth, off its wheels. I called the police, but no one responded. They kept rocking the car until it rolled over on its roof; the officer lay crumpled onto the interior ceiling. To his credit the officer did not accelerate the situation by drawing his weapon. He struggled to right himself inside the overturned car, and to escape, he shattered the driver's side window with his nightstick. Halfway out of the window he froze in terror as he saw two Molotov cocktail firebombs land and explode within inches of his face. It appeared that the officer's legs had gotten tangled in the steering wheel which left him helplessly trapped in a potential raging inferno.

The manager continued, "both English and French spectators began screaming for help, unable to be heard above shrieks of the frenzied rioters, "L'aider à sortir!" *Help him get out!* "Il va brûler à mort!" *He will burn to death*!

"A few of our staff went to help two large men who bravely penetrated the throng of rioters, brusquely shoving them aside. Ignoring the spreading flames, they raced to aid the helpless officer. One reached in to untangle the officer's legs, while the other dragged the officer out of the window. They were able to free him and get him away from the car just as the gas tank exploded.

"There were shards of glass, flames, and hot metal spewing everywhere. The explosion propelled one rioter through a plate glass store window, while others lay bleeding in the street."

Ricky asked about the officer and was told he was safe.

Ricky was totally disgusted with the whole scene, but he didn't have a moment to lose. He knew he had to get back to Eaton's before he got swallowed up in this crowd making return passage impossible.

Trying to keep his mind on his mission, Ricky threaded his way through the crowds. Rethinking the horror story, the manager told him he couldn't believe

EATON'S – During the Second French Revolution

the events unfolding. *"I guess these idiots never considered that a Molotov cocktail would ignite a gas tank!"* he thought.

The sound of fire trucks and ambulances racing to the scene was heard everywhere.

As Ricky made his way back to Eaton's he found his way barred by angry people who had gathered around Simpson's Department Store, just two blocks west of Eaton's. The crowd was yelling and cheering as their dissident leaders spewed anti-English rhetoric over a loudspeaker.

Ricky pushed his way through the crowd and noticed a dozen Eaton's' carpenters hastily assembling plywood over the St. Catherine Street plate glass display windows.

"You better get inside quickly, Mister Dean," the carpenter foreman cautioned, "That crowd is going to descend on us any minute now!"

"Did the police go on strike, yet?" Ricky yelled over his shoulder, as he sprinted for the center entry door.

"Any minute now. They are set to strike at five-thirty." The foreman took a breath. "God help us all! This city will be totally unprotected."

Ricky pushed through Eaton's door, and spotted Tony Cartwright addressing a large group of managers in the center of the main floor.

"... and we've evacuated all the customers and non-essential personnel from the store." Tony noticed Ricky's arrival and waved him over to join them.

There were about fifty managers and assistant managers assembled in addition to about fifteen store detectives, the general manager and assistant store manager. It was a somber scene. Tony continued, "as you've no doubt heard the cops and firemen are officially going on strike, so we are the only line of defense to keep our store from burning to the ground. I've got two of my junior store detectives infiltrated into the crowd to give us a heads-up about when they are going to storm our store. And folks, that's not 'if' but 'when'. To advance their cause, and at the direction of their FLQ leaders, I'm positive that they will rain havoc on our store. Questions so far?" Tony inquired, looking at the anxious crowd.

"Is there any indication that the QPP, *Quebec Provincial Police* or the Canadian Army are going to step in to help out?" asked John Witherspoon, the main floor jewelry manager.

"The only reports I've heard from CBC radio is that Mayor Martin has requested that Premier Lasage mobilize all available QPP officers, with riot equipment, to be immediately dispatched from Quebec City to Montreal, but that could take hours. Also, Martin has communicated with Prime Minister, Pierre Trudeau, in Ottawa, to marshal the army, but that too, is going to take even longer. So, as I've stated before, we're on our own. Any more questions," Tony asked.

Rene Beaudreaux, manager of the boys' wear department, asked, "How are fifty to sixty of us supposed to combat an enraged crowd of thousands of people with weapons and fire-bombs. Most of us have never been in any real altercation.

"Good question," Tony replied. "And the answer is, we are not here to confront them, we are here to stop them from breaking the barriers into the store. I've had all seven entry doors locked and chained, so their only way in is going to be through breaking the display window glass. Our job is to see they don't get any farther than that. And, if they do succeed in piercing that hurdle, our next move is to get our asses out of the store safely."

"If I may, Mister Cartwright," Robert Appleton interjected. "On behalf of the Eaton's organization, coast to coast, I want to thank you all for your dedication and commitment, and for volunteering to help keep our store safe. I also want to say, and I can't state this strongly enough, we don't want any heroes. Nothing is worth sacrificing your life. If things get hairy, just get the hell out as quickly as possible. Remember, there is no shame in escape, when you are outnumbered forty to one. All right now, continue, Mister Cartwright."

"Thank you. As Mister Appleton just mentioned, escape is paramount to our success. I have security guard, Joey Radar, billeted to monitor any potential breach of the perimeter. Since we suspect the invasion is going to come from the west on Saint Catherine Street, we assume that both the North University, and North Metcalfe doors will remain safe for our primary escape route. When Joey determines a breach is imminent, he will unlock one of those doors, and direct you to which door you are to use. I have three of our large Eaton's panel trucks standing by at each door to evacuate you all and get you a safe distance from the store."

"Who's going to handle the potential breach points?" Ricky interrupted.

"Okay. So, we have about sixty-five of us in the store," Tony responded. "What I want is for management to divide up into teams of seven men per entry door, which will leave me with my security staff to fill in at any possible breach point. Each team will select a team leader who will take responsibility for sounding an alarm of a breach and direct his team in specific duties, as they arise. My staff will handle any fire suppression using the fire hoses situated in the middle aisle. These pressure hoses can also be called upon to force any advancing crowd back into the streets. Each team will have a radio tuned to CBC Canada to get updates on the rioters' progress, and two portable fire extinguishers to put out small fires and/or to be used against any potential attackers. As deterrent weapons each team member will have a spray bottle of a heavily soaped caustic solution to spray in an attacker's eyes, and one of these baseball bats as self-defense." Tony pointed at a large garbage cart full of baseball bats.

"Only use the bats as a last resort. And never aim at anyone's head. We're not trying to kill anyone. If someone is putting their arm in to unsecure an entry door, you can hit their hand or arm. If someone gains store entry while you are trying to escape, you can fend them off with a blow to anywhere except their head. Remember, any serious injuries to the attackers will throw the rest of them into an uncontrollable frenzy. Oh, and one more thing, it shouldn't be necessary, but Bill Galatley here was a corpsman in Korea and graciously volunteered to treat any cuts, scrapes, or falls your team may endure. Now, please set up your teams, gather your equipment and be safe. Both Denis Charbonneau and I will be making constant main floor circuits to touch base with each respective team, about every ten minutes."

As the teams were being formed and began dispersing to their assigned locations Mr. Appleton made a point of individually shaking every team member's hand.

The huge antique clock suspended above the main floor read 6:43. But, the present silence sent eerie shivers down everyone's back as they knew that the conflict was about to begin, and the tranquility that was once Eaton's may never be, again.

⚜ Thirty-Eight ⚜

All the defense staff stationed at the Eaton's entry doors could hear the radios blaring across the main floor and the anxious voices of the on-location newscasters.

"I never dreamt that I would be reporting a historic event of this magnitude. For those of you just joining us, this is Mike Duschannel reporting from downtown Montreal, and yes, it's true, the thirty-seven hundred Montreal Police and twenty-four hundred Montreal Fire Fighters have officially gone on strike as of five-thirty this evening. Their leaders are calling it a collective bargaining conference which is being held at the Paul Sauve Arena, in Rosemount. I'm situated on the rooftop of Dunne's Smoked Meat Restaurant, where I have a clear view of the mayhem unfolding beneath my location. I can make out three Simpsons' display windows broken out and the contents being removed by looters. The streets are completely barren of any automobile traffic and have been taken over by dissident speakers perched on step ladders lecturing and agitating them. So far, damage and injuries have been minimal, aside from an incident where an MPD patrol car was over-turned and firebombed by an earlier angry crowd. Luckily, the officer escaped with the help of bystanders, and I'm told he only suffered minor injuries. From what I can estimate there are over two thousand people assembled at this location, with more arriving all the time. Stand by folks, we have a special report coming in."

"What do you make of this?" Ricky asked, as Tony arrived at his position. "Are we ready for this crap, or are we just putting up a dangerous front for the news media?"

"We certainly can't show any substance of force against thousands of punks, but we sure can bust a few knuckles." Tony's further comment was interrupted by the incoming news report.

"Thanks Mike. This is Marvin Caleville, reporting for CBC Canada, from the Ville D'Anjou Bridge in the east end of Montreal Island. Just moments ago, we were on hand when a squad of eight QPP patrol cars, from Quebec City, started across the bridge, with lights flashing, only to be stopped mid-span by two MPD bomb disposal squad trucks, blocking their passage. The MPD are directing QPP to vacate their vehicles. Wait! Now four of the MPD officers have taken over the QPP cars moving them into position to completely block the ingress and egress to the bridge. Wow! This is absolutely insane. Cop against cop. This is not going to end well!

"Now I see one MPD officer going from car to car removing the keys and radios, while it looks like another cop is removing the distributor caps and hurling them into the river below. The QPP officers are making no effort to resist, instead they are making their way to the Quebec City side of the bridge. The MPD have returned to their trucks and seem to be heading back to Montreal.

"Hang on folks, I have an angry MPD officer yelling at me and coming in my direction. Gaston, regardless of what happens, keep the live feed open to central."

"Que faites-vous ici?" What are you doing here?" the officer questioned.

"Anglais please! I am a news reporter with CBC Canada."

"You don't need to be here. Get off the bridge."

"But I have a right to report the news." Marvin responded.

"You have the right to do as I told you, right now or face arrest!"

"Let's go, Gaston. Folks, the officer has drawn his revolver and is menacingly aiming it at me."

"Well, we are now safely on the Quebec City side, and I am going to try and find someone to talk to, just stay with us folks. You are QPP commander, Roger Longueil, is that right?" Marvin asked, looking at the officers' nameplate.

"Oui." Yes".

"Can you speak English for our CBC listeners, Commander?"

"Yes."

"Commander, what do you make of the actions the MPD?"

"The example they set is no better than the message being sent by the disruptive rioters downtown Montreal."

"But commander, downtown Montreal is in flames, isn't that why you are here? And yet you and your officers offered no resistance to the MPD blocking the bridge and confiscating your patrol cars."

"That was certainly not by choice. We were warned by QPP headquarters that MPD patrols would try something like this, but I am under orders not to get into a confrontation with them."

"Then I guess you are not the 'cavalry', coming to their rescue."

EATON'S – During the Second French Revolution

"I am afraid not. But I do want to say that even though MPD are brother officers, because of their ridiculous and dangerous actions, today I am ashamed to be in their company. Believe me, Quebecers will not easily forget!"

"Thank you, Commander."

Marvin continued, "now, we turn our broadcast over to Nicole Lajeuness, from her vantage point atop the Woolworths' store, adjacent to Eaton's department store."

"Damn Tony, did you hear that! Unless the Canadian Army immediately sprouts wings, that was our last chance at some sort of order from this madness. As soon as these pricks get the news that QPP is not coming to control their riot, all hell is really going to break loose!" Ricky exclaimed.

"Take a breath, Ricky. We can only do what we can do."

They both directed their attention to the continuing broadcast.

"Thank you for that report, Marvin. This is Nicole Lajeuness. I can see and hear the large swarm of activists down by Simpsons, but so far, by our vantage point by Eaton's all is quiet except for carpenters boarding up windows. One of the most unbelievable sights is the numerous shopkeepers standing guard with weapons in front of their shops. All the businesses around me are closed, and many have already boarded up their windows. I did notice a contingent of six armed Brinks guards entering the Bank of Montreal across from my location, and three large Eaton's truck positioned at the north end of the store. I'm not sure what that's all about, but I will endeavor to find out. I do know that Eaton's customers and staff were evacuated from the building before six tonight, so the building should be empty, except for the carpenter crew."

"Okay," she hesitated, "my producer just advised me that he looked through the Eaton's Metcalfe Street door and saw numerous people scurrying around the main floor dragging fire hoses and carrying baseball bats. We'll try to find out more information about that as it develops.

"In the meantime, while we wait, let me update you on several related stories. We've been told that the Caisse Populaire Bank in Desjardins de Notre-Dame-de-Grâce in the west end was robbed by armed gunman within minutes of the announcement of the police strike. And, a gang of rioters invaded a north end movie theater threatening over one-hundred patrons, and causing the proprietor to flee for his life, leaving the theatre to the rioters. Also, our sources reported that thieves are breaking into abandoned cars, en masse. This situation just keeps getting weirder and weirder. Now back to you, Mike Duschannel for more updates."

"Well, there goes our element of surprise." Ricky said to Tony, hoisting the two fire extinguishers to the top of the stairs, by the University Street center door.

"Thanks for that report, Nicole. We're going to take you, now, to our Roger LaPetite who is on-scene at a major disturbance at the Murray Hill Limousine Service garage in Griffintown. Roger are you there?"

"Yes, Mike. I'm here across from the Murray Hill garage where a crowd of disgruntled taxi drivers, from competitive taxi companies, just recently arrived in-group solidarity of unionized drivers. We have learned from one of the group that they are protesting against Murray Hill's monopoly of picking up and dropping off fares at the Dorval International Airport, a procedure that has existed for as long as I can remember. They seem to be taking advantage of the unrest in Montreal and the absence of law enforcement. Several attempts by the QPP, Sûreté du Québec, to halt the large procession of drivers descending on the garage were stopped by aggressive striking Montreal police officers. Eventually, the crowd got out of hand and burned down the garage with several limousines and taxis still inside. Sadly, during the mêlée, Sûreté officer, Corporal Robert Dumas, was killed by shots fired from the roof by the taxi company security guards. We believe this to be the first official reported fatality since the MPD strike began."

"I've also had several credible reports about other riot activities around the city. A Chinese laundry has been robbed in Saint Denis; rioters have penetrated security at several hotels and restaurants throughout the city; and a doctor shot and killed a burglar who broke into his suburban home in Longueuil. Believe me, folks, these incidents have shaken my faith in the human nature of some of our Canadian citizens. Back to you, Mike."

Denis Charbonneau approached Ricky. "Your team is at the center University Street door, right?"

Ricky nodded.

"I've just had a report from one of our infiltrators that the speeches are winding down and the irate crowd is getting restless," Denis related. "He also reports seeing several weapons in the crowd, including Molotov cocktails, and what looks like vials of some sort of bottled clear liquid, so be incredibly careful. Several groups have already begun moving east towards our store, so we can expect some trouble real soon."

"Thanks Denis, good work. Keep your people filtering us as much information as possible."

"Will do, Ricky!" Denis replied. "If you must report any breach, you can identify the window breach areas as window U-1 through U-6, starting with U-1 at the corner of Saint Catherine and proceeding north to U-6 towards Maisonneuve Blvd. If it seems like your flank is going to be breached, send a runner to the other closest team for reinforcement."

"Got it. Anything, else?" Ricky asked.

"Yeah, we need the three University Street team leaders, and one additional team member, to go out onto Saint Catherine Street and help the carpenters with boarding up the display windows. They've got all the Metcalfe Street finished and half of the Saint Catherine Street windows, but they need more help."

EATON'S – During the Second French Revolution

"Okay!"

Ricky turned toward his team and found Jerry. "You're with me, Jer. We need to go help the carpenters board up the windows," Ricky directed, racing toward the center St Catherine Street door. On the way, he gathered the other team leaders while he paid special attention to what the current newscaster was saying, in case it pertained to Eaton's.

The news continued: *"I agree wholeheartedly with your last statement, Roger. Canadians will never be able to fathom a government police agency laying down their arms, leaving its citizens at the mercy of a wild mob and allowing all hell to break loose. And to have all the fireman also walk off the job at the same time, is incomprehensible, and reckless. The death and destruction that has and will take place falls directly on their shoulders. Okay, I've just been handed a report that a crowd of rioters have descended on the Montreal City Hall, which is presently totally unprotected.*

"St. Catherine St. is strewn with litter and the large concrete sidewalk planters with trees have been toppled into the street, and, my God, a rioter just threw a heavy metal garbage can through the glass front door of the souvenir store a few doors down from my location. I can't quite tell what happened, but the owner either was just inside the door and got showered with flying glass, or he received a blow from the garbage can. Wait a minute, I see several men dragging the man out of the store, and onto the sidewalk. He somehow managed to get up and just staggered to his feet and is running east on Saint Catherine Street ... what has this world come to?"

Ricky, and the other team members, converged on the anxious carpenters, to render assistance. He could plainly see and hear the large crowd of rioters assembled just three blocks west at Simpsons. Suddenly he was taken aback at the blare of a shouting voice coming over a loudspeaker.

This *was* followed by the familiar Parti Quebecois separatists battle cry, "Vive Quebec Libre!" *Live Free in Quebec!* A wall of angry rioters proceeded to stampede down Saint Catherine Street towards Eaton's, spreading mass destruction in their wake.

"Leave the plywood, grab your tools and get your asses in the building, right now," Ricky yelled for the carpenters and his fellow team members.

As they quickly obeyed, Ricky's singular thought was, *God help us.*

The Second French Revolution has officially begun!

❦ Thirty-Nine ❦

As the carpenter's and Ricky's team members ran for the doors, the security guard was waiting to lock and fasten the door with a heavy chain and padlock.

Ricky saw Tony frantically motioning the group to Tony's command center in the center of the main floor. Even before everyone arrived Tony was already barking orders.

"I just got the news that we are definitely the next target! I want the team leaders and team members back to your assigned locations. Ricky, you stay here a minute. Bobby." He said addressed the carpenter foreman, "I want you and your guys all out of here, stat. Did any of you drive your own vehicle in today?" he looked around the group.

"I did, Mister Cartwright," the foreman said,

Then, one of his crew echoed, "So did I sir."

"Great! Are either of you parked nearby?"

"Yes, Bobby and I are both parked in the underground on Alymer Street above Sherbrooke Blvd."

"Okay, here's what I want you to do. Divide the crew up as to where they live, and each driver will make sure to get each one home safely. Keep your radio tuned to CBC Canada so you can identify where the trouble spots are that need to be avoided. And Bobby, I'll reimburse your guys for your gas expenses, and you are all on the clock, until you both finish and arrive safely at your homes," Tony directed. "Also, Bobby, I want you to check in with me every hour just in case I need your guys back here. Here's my telephone number, now, get your asses out of here, as fast as you can run!"

"And what do you need from me, Tony?" Ricky asked.

"I've already talked to the other teams stationed at the doors to try to calm them down while you guys were outside. However, I didn't get around to your team before all hell broke loose. Can you handle that, please?"

"Got it covered, Tony," Ricky replied, sprinting towards his group.

As he got closer, he saw his team huddled in deep conversation. "Are you guys, okay?" he shouted, noticing the anxious and frightened expressions on all their faces. "Do we need to talk?"

"It's just," Ricky's friend, Jerry Copeland, stammered.

"I know. I know, Jerry. We're all scared and wondering what the hell we're doing here," he interrupted, trying to calm his voice. Ricky couldn't comprehend how Jerry at 6'2" and 245 pounds, a former star quarterback, looked the most frightened. "I think you guys are reading too much into our presence here. We're here, not as a defense force, but strictly as monitors, just making it as difficult as possible for these guys to enter the store. And, if things get hairy, Tony's exit plan will kick in, and we'll be out of here before anyone gets hurt. I want you to constantly be aware of our best exit route and when I give the word, all I want to see is asses and elbows heading towards that exit. Believe me, I'll be right behind you," Ricky joked. "So, guys, we're about to meet the FLQ up close and personal, so let's be on our toes, and make Eaton's proud."

Ricky listened as a new news report came in.

"... *the crowd of 2000 dissidents are heading towards Eaton's. Many of them are carrying clubs, sticks, and chains, and are smashing windows and looting along the way. FLQ leaders have stated that they believe 'Eaton's symbolizes all that is wrong with their lost liberties in Quebec'.*"

"*My producer was just advised by an Eaton carpenter that there is a contingent of fifty plus manager and security personnel defending the seven entry doors into the store. That means fifty brave souls will face off against two-thousand angry protesters. God help them!*

"*We've also had a report that Mayor Martins' union talks are still deadlocked, as our city remains under siege. Sources also inform us that Mayor Martin has been in contact with Quebec Premier, Jean Lasage and Prime Minister Trudeau requesting QPP, RCMP and military assistance.*"

The noise of the thundering crowd barreling down Saint Catherine Street was terrifying. The echo of several shotgun blasts followed by large panes of glass crashing to the sidewalk made the exterior of Eaton's feel like a war zone. The constant chanting of '*Vive Le Quebec Libre*' and the cheers and yelling persisted as looters stripped the windows of everything valuable. After the Eaton's' glass windows were breached, the only remaining barrier was the inner wall of the window compartment which shielded the store from normal street view. The main problem was that although the rear plywood wall might hold back the rioters, the thin hollow core access door could easily be breached with a single kick. The walls, ceiling and floor were all constructed out of thin plywood sheeting and combined with the thin cloth curtains and heavy privacy drapery, it created a setting that would go up in flames like a tinderbox at the first sign of a thrown fire-bomb.

"Breach SC-2," the shout came from the front of the store. SC-2 meaning Saint Catherine Street window number 2.

"Responding," Tony called out over the microphone. "All entry door teams remain at your posts. Security teams A and B respond to SC-2 with fire hoses ready. And report back A.S.A.P."

The security teams dragged the heavy hoses towards SC-2, testing the water pressure and positioning the streams for maximum effectiveness. The 2 ½ inch hoses could deliver 100 gallons per minute flow that was adequate enough to easily knock a person off their feet. Two hoses could throw them across the street.

One of the security team leaders contacted Tony with the news that the breach was confined to looters in the actual window compartment, but they had not tried to break down the access door to enter the store.

The radio by SC-2 squealed.

"... we have reports that more than a hundred shops around Montreal have been damaged and looted, with several fire houses firebombed and wrecked by the rioters. Also, I have just been advised that the angry crowd has descended on Eaton's Department Store, in downtown Montreal, and is trying to gain entry through the large display windows."

Panic was evident in many of the faces guarding the entry doors. Ricky realized that the only answer was to keep everyone busy and focused on their area of responsibility. They could hear the violent pounding of the rioter's clubs against the exterior plywood panels, followed by shouts and cheers as their clubs penetrated the wood. So far, the crowd had not tried to enter the store and no Molotov cocktails had been thrown, but the team members knew that wouldn't last. Without creating substantial damage to "the evil Eaton's," the FLQ spokespeople would be limited in their political and revolutionary rhetoric. Their words were, 'Destruction needs to be taken against Eaton's so that the FLQ cause will prevail!'

"Breach SC-6," the shout came from the St. Catherine/University corner window of the store.

"Responding," Tony called out over the microphone. "Security team B respond to SC-6 with fire hoses ready. And report back A.S.A.P."

The security team dragged the heavy hoses towards the SC-6.

"Command center! We have fire at SC-6, but no breach. Repeat fire, but no breach," yelled the security team leader.

"Copy, Security B. I'm sending Security C to assist," Tony shouted. "Advise when the situation is under control."

Ricky could see the 'writing on the wall.' The rioters had left Simpsons, advancing towards Eaton's where they shattered display window SC-2 at Metcalfe & St. Catherine. The rioters continued their trek eastward damaging the plywood panels on display window SC-4 & SC-5 but hadn't breached the store. Now, they had broken the glass in display window SC-6 and crashed a Molotov cocktail against the back wall, spreading flames throughout the window cavity. He knew from their course that his area would be their next point of advance. Their leaders had three choices for the mob, head south on University St. towards the city hall in Old Montreal, or continue east along St. Catherine St. to the Morgan's/Hudson Bay Department Store, another symbol of English dominance in Quebec. But, most logical, was to direct the rioters north on University St. to reap more damage on the 6 display windows on that side of the Eaton's store. The carpenters had not yet had time to secure all the University St. windows with plywood, making them vulnerable to attack.

EATON'S – During the Second French Revolution

Ricky was confident that the FLQ and student dissident leaders would not be content with just breaking windows and throwing Molotov cocktails, their goal would be to create havoc inside the store to get the most press coverage. To accomplish that, they would need to gain forced access to the interior of Eaton's and create as much damage as possible. That meant the most probable focused breach point would be his, the center door on University St.

"Command," bellowed the security team leader. "The fire is extinguished at SC-6, with minimal damage, but no breach. Team B and C are heading over to U-1 where there is another fire and possible breach. Will advise!"

It began subtlety, at first, with just the rhythmic pounding of clubs against plywood at display window's U-1 and U-2. Then, came the crash of glass and the cheers of thousands of rioters. They *were* heading north on University towards Ricky's location, leaving massive destruction in their wake. Then, just as suddenly, hundreds of glaring riled faces, were staring at them through the glass of the chained revolving entry doors, pounding the glass and shaking the doors to gain entry. The rioter's sudden appearance frightened Ricky's team members enough to have them retreat down the few stairs leading to the revolving doors.

"Get back up there guys," Ricky directed calmly. "Let them see that we are professionals, not the vicious animals that they are portraying. And whatever you do, don't antagonize the bastards, they're already whipped up in enough of a frenzy."

Just as Ricky started up the four steps to the door, he was met with a crashing brick and flying glass showering him with sharp shards. Quickly inspecting himself for injury, and finding none, he continued towards the doors, now even more wary that injuries could become a realistic factor. Jerry was already at the doors trying to bang a set of bolt cutters out of the hands of one of the students, with his baseball bat.

"Breach at U6 - Center Doors," shouted Ricky across the main floor.

"Assistance on the way," Tony yelled back.

Ricky yelled, "Guys, direct your soap spray bottles towards the face and eyes of the mob. And keep your own faces sideways to the doors, so you don't get glass in your eyes, and watch out for the bricks that they are throwing, they can really create some damn …"

Ricky's warnings were violently interrupted as a wooden club smashed into the glass door panels, cascading glass over the whole team. As Jerry temporarily retreated from the flying glass, the bolt cutter individual was working vigorously on trying to sever the heavy chain, so he could get the doors to open.

Ricky called out, "Jerry, stop directing your bat at the bolt cutters. Aim for the bastard's hands, or arms. And someone grab a push broom and get rid of all this glass before we fall on our asses."

The doors were swelling inside the store. The mob hurled a metal park bench, then used it as a battering ram trying to force the doors to break open. With each rhythmic push and combined yell from the crowd, the doors became weaker and weaker, straining on their locks and 100-year-old hinges.

It is only a matter of time before we'll be face to face with these idiots! Ricky thought.

Jerry succeeded in knocking the bolt cutters from the hands of the now screaming rioter, who was favoring his damaged left wrist. But as quickly as Jerry stopped, someone else picked up the task of gaining entry.

Ricky noted that two out of the four glass door panels were still intact and holding. *Make that one out of four*, Ricky thought, as he saw the metal park bench come careening into the door, shattering the glass. Now, hundreds of arms and angry voices appeared through the three glassless doors.

It's like what you see in movies of prisoners in crowded cells, all with their arms protruding from the cells, shouting at the guards. Ricky thought.

At the same time, the flimsy access door to the display window on the right side of the center entry doors crashed into splinters, and fell onto the floor below. Three wild-eyed young men pushed in bearing clubs and vials of a mysterious liquid. It appeared they were as shocked to see the waiting large group of Eaton's staffers, bearing crude weaponry, as were the staffers surprised by the successful breach. Each group appraised the other for a minute before one of the older looking students barked, "Merde, jeter maintenant!" *Shit, throw it now!*

"Breach at U6 - Center Doors," Ricky shouted from across the main floor.

Ricky understood what was coming, and quickly retreated. But, Jerry, who's French comprehension was not as good, raised his bat above his head, and continued his advance on the three rioters.

"Jerry, no," Ricky screamed, as he watched the contents of the vial being sprayed directly into Jerry's face.

Ricky dove at Jerry tackling him to the floor and rolling painfully down the entry steps. He twisted Jerry head to the side yelling at him to keep his eyes closed and to try to stay calm.

"Get some water hose spray on Jerry's face," Ricky called out, "then get a double spray on those bastards in the window." He commanded the security detail, manning the fire hoses, "and push back everyone at the entry doors."

The team lightly sprayed Jerry's face and neck, then opened the water stream to maximum pressure propelling the intruders out of the window cavity, and back into the street, as the news report continued.

"This is Michael Murphy repositioned on the rooftop of the Birke's Jewelry building, diagonally across from Eaton's. From this vantage point I can see that the rioters have smashed and looted several of Eaton's large display windows and are now trying to gain access to the store through the center University Street revolving doors. There appears to be some kind of skirmish going on as the crowd keeps attacking then retreating from the doors. I also see three young men kicking *in a door in the third display window north of Saint Catherine Street. Wait a minute. These same three have just come sputtering out of the window area with streams of high-pressure water following them. They've retreated to the security of Christ Church Cathedral, across the street, and now the center door crowd is being dispersed by the same fire hose streams. This is amazing to see. The water is saturating the crowd and knocking them to the ground, totally stopping them in their tracks! Go for it, Eaton's!"* Michael yelled excitedly.

"Oh, Christ, no!" Ricky heard Jerry yelling. "Not my eyes, please! They got my eyes, Ricky," he screamed, lying on the floor covering his face with his hands.

"Get Galatley over here, right now," Ricky barked at one of his team, while struggling to help Jerry. "Tell him we have an acid burn to the face." He forced Jerry's blistering hands away from his face. "Andre, hold his hands away from his face, and douse them with the spray bottle of detergent, then rinse them quickly with water. "Jerry, listen to me. You trust me, right? The acid is concentrated on your right cheek, away from your eyes. There's a bit of acid spray in your eyebrows and a burn on your big ugly nose, but that will probably be an improvement," he laughed.

Reaching for the other spray bottle of detergent, he cautioned, "Jerry, I need to get this crap off your face before it does any more damage. So, I want you to stay on your side with your left cheek to the floor. Now, this is important! I want you to keep your eyes closed, as tight as possible, while I rinse your face, okay?"

"Yeah, Ricky," he mumbled, "but is my face going to be scarred?"

"What do you care, you old fart. With your personality you couldn't get laid if you looked like Rock Hudson," Ricky kept trying to joke with his friend to keep him calm. He began rinsing the soap and water away from Jerry's face. "Remember Jerry there is always good news, and for you, the good news is that you'll get time off, with full pay to recuperate."

Jerry crooked his finger in a motion for Rick to come closer, then whimpered into his ear, "Screw you, Buddy, and the horse you rode in on." That was Jerry's signature expression.

Suddenly Ricky heard another. "Good job, Mister Dean. I'll take over from here," Bill Galatley, sat down next to Jerry and immediately opened his medical bag to retrieve some burn inhibiting salve.

Tony arrived at Ricky's location with Denis trailing behind. "Christ no one was supposed to confront these morons. What the hell happened here?" directing his question to Ricky.

"Calm down, Tony. It's all under control. Three guys somehow pierced the U-3 window without our being aware. When they kicked in the access door Jerry was right in front of them, and got acid thrown in his face, fortunately, not his eyes. Anyway, he's okay, and going home. Everyone here did a great job driving the guys out of the U-3 window with the fire hoses and away from the front door.

It was great to see their asses fly across the street," he laughed. "And the good news is that all is quiet right now!"

"Maybe," Tony pondered, "but it ain't over, just yet." Tony looked over to Denis.

"My contacts up at the Paul Sauve Arena tell me that the police and fireman conference is still going on, but half the cops just gave up and went home. Both agencies have been made aware of the riots in the streets, but as my contact stated, 'they just don't give a shit!'"

"Ricky, you had the last interaction with them, what do you think?" Tony inquired.

"I don't know for sure, but I think I was looking at a bunch of frustrated kids trying to breach my entry door location. They want to make noise, create havoc, and commit any rebellious acts that don't require too much energy. It's easy to throw Molotov cocktails, roll a squad car or break windows, but physically breaking into a fortified building like ours is a lot of work. And the humiliation and discomfort of getting pelted by our fire hoses was, most certainly demeaning and I'll bet it hurt like hell! No, I think they are going to keep up their trek eastward on Saint Catherine Street to find new softer targets, such as Morgan's, or the slew of unprotected shops between here and Bleury Street."

Just then, Appleton, and two other corporate executives, arrived to listen in on the conversation.

Where have you been while we've been busting our asses saving the store? Ricky wondered.

Ricky basically ignored Appleton and continued, "Tony, I've got to say, your defensive action plan was flawless, man. You need to put it down on paper, step-by-step, for the Cross-Canada operations. Your idea of using the fire hoses readily extinguished the fires and quickly pushed back the advancing crowd. The only suggestion I might add is that although you had the doors chained with quarter inch link chain, we saw that they showed up with bolt cutters. A single cut would have gained them immediate entry. However, if we would have had two or three chains on each door pull, our guys would have had plenty of time to bruise some knuckles and discourage them from trying to cut any further."

Appleton interjected, "Great thinking, Dean. You and Mister Cartwright get together when things calm down and write a policy and procedure for this kind of event. I'll see that it gets issued as standard procedure across the chain. By the way, you guys all went 'above and beyond the call of duty' and Eaton's thanks you kindly. Now, how is Mister Copeland doing?" he looked at Ricky.

"Doc says he'll be fine. Maybe he'll have a slight scar under his right eye, but fortunately, no eye damage. Galatley insisted that one of Tony's security people take Jerry up to the Royal Victoria Hospital for a more thorough evaluation. From there, the security man is going to see that Jerry gets home safely.

EATON'S – During the Second French Revolution

"Okay, guys." Tony said, "so far, we have not won the war, but we have certainly achieved a small victory in this preliminary battle. We can't be sure if it's totally over for tonight, or if this is just the calm before the storm. It looks like we will still need to be here all night, so I want each team to split in half, and go down to the luncheonette, where we have coffee and food waiting. Each break will be one-half hour unless I ring the alarm for you to immediately return to your posts."

Except for the reports of devastation, injury, and death throughout the province, and most particularly the City of Montreal, Eaton's department store remained free of further attacks on *"Montreal's Night of Terror."*

Ricky took a deep breath thinking,

"This is not the beginning of the end! The Second French Revolution will continue with more bloodshed, property damage and national disgrace for our precious country!"

⚜ Forty ⚜

The day after the rioting, Eaton's top management made the decision to keep the store closed. They had the staff assist with the main and basement floor cleanup and the carpenters securing the broken windows. There was water all over the main floor along with broken glass and splintered plywood panels. The logic was that the one-day closure should not signal a victory for the FLQ.

Ricky sat quietly in the back corner of the luncheonette, disheveled, discouraged and totally exhausted, picking at a breakfast croissant. The Montreal Gazette that he was reading proclaimed, in bold headlines,

"MONTREAL UNDER SEIGE"

After a 16-hour strike, which left Montreal totally exposed to the rioters, the 3700 police and 2400 firemen triumphantly returned to downtown Montreal, with lights flashing and sirens blaring. It was quite evident they were expecting a warm reception for their return to duty. As they paraded through downtown, strewn with litter, broken glass, concrete planters, and trees, both French and English alike, greeted them with boos and derogatory shouts of disgust, while pelting their vehicles with anything that was available. However, some citizens did give the police a salute, unfortunately it was with their middle finger raised.

During the riot banks were robbed, more than a hundred shops vandalized, looted, and destroyed, twelve fires had been set, including several fire stations, over forty carloads of storefront glass had been broken, and millions of dollars in

property damage had been inflicted, before the army and the R.C.M.P. restored order.

Additionally, the Murray Hill cab company garage had been burned to the ground. Eaton's, Simpsons, and Morgan's department stores had suffered major exterior damage; one police officer, and one private citizen, lay dead; 108 people had been arrested and, thirty citizens had been seriously injured.

We quote our radio and television media comrades: 'Montreal is in a state of shock,' a CBC reporter proclaimed, 'and so is our whole nation. With police abandoning the city, and no one to stop them, students, and separatists united to bring total chaos to all of Montreal.'

ATN Canada reported, 'Montreal's Night of Terror" tested the assumptions that the normally peaceable Quebec citizenry, once realizing that the thin blue line had faded, reverted to conduct that was totally unbecoming of Canadians from coast to coast.'

"Anarchy hits Montreal! announced a French Radio Canada reporter, 'and this anarchy did not look pretty. When law enforcement vanishes, all manner of violence breaks out, looting, settling old scores, ethnic cleansing and petty warfare among gangs, warlords, and mafias.'

"The bank robbers, the looters, and the armed shop owners are all embodiments of this lawlessness. Presumably, the in-group solidarity of unionized taxi drivers, or of Québécois separatists was another example of out-group bias in Montreal. Even the solidarity of 2400 metropolitan firefighters who joined the strike in support of the Policemen's Brotherhood could easily be explained as an instance of reciprocal altruism at best. Perhaps it was just radical-chic street theater. If humans were angels, of course, rulers would be unnecessary. But we require government, which notably includes the power of the police to keep a lid on the violence. Without their oversight, people's true nature seems to come out. Like a child stealing cookies when their parent's back is turned."

Ricky couldn't take any more as he sighed, a long sigh, throwing the newspaper in disgust on the bench seat beside him. *What the hell did they achieve?* He wondered.

"You look awful, Ricky," Amed Darzada, quipped, placing his tray on the table, as he slid into the booth. "I heard that your team had all the action last night. How is Jerry doing with that acid spray to his face?"

"He lucked out that the acid didn't get into his eyes. He'll be off from work for a few days, but otherwise he'll be fine." Ricky was reluctant to rehash the events of last night. "Christ, Al, you're going to build your own bomb in your stomach, with that crap," eyeing the large plate of enchiladas and beans on Ahmed's plate.

"We all need to stay fortified, my friend. My team was stationed at Metcalfe North, where we didn't see any action at all, but from the mess I saw this morning around your location, it looked like your team was engaged pretty heavily."

EATON'S – During the Second French Revolution

"Well, it really looks worse than it was." He continued to try and downplay the whole nightmare. "Tony's plan of directing the two and a half inchers at the bastards, took them by surprise, they moved on."

Just then Ricky's pager sounded. "Sorry, got to take this. Take care, Amed." He exited the booth, swiftly.

The page advised him of his scheduled staff meeting.

"No, this is not my new attire or company dress code", Ricky laughed, looking down at his rumpled, water-stained clothing.

"I presume you've all read or heard, the gory details of last night's debacle with the students and separatists, but I can tell you firsthand that Eaton's *dodged a bullet*, this time. But we all know that there may be five more bullets in their cylinder. Aside from a lot of broken glass, water damage and looted merchandise from the window display, the interior of the store remains relatively unscathed. I'm sure you've noticed the water that has cascaded from the main floor, down the stairwells into our basement area and the lower stockrooms. This should be cleaned up within the next couple of hours." Ricky looked to Duane, who had been tasked with organizing the janitor crew for cleanup. Duane nodded.

"The store is closed today, not just for the cleanup, but to put a happy face on all of us for the benefit of our customers when we open tomorrow. I want every department spit and polished, displays rotated, or rebuilt, staff in immaculate dress, and everyone playing down what has happened. After all the news about the riots, and especially about Eaton's, tomorrow's customers are going to be inquisitive and are going to try to get you to engage in conversation. No doubt the press and media are also going to attempt to get reactions to what happened. This is not going to happen! Under no circumstances are you to engage in political commentary. We are here to serve our customers, so just change the subject. As far as the press, 'no comment,' is all you are allowed to say. No matter what your views may be, no one is to express criticism of the police, fire, or government. You never know who you will be talking to."

"Okay, you all know what to do, and how to strongly present these facts to your staff. Warn them that we will be watching and listening when the opening bell rings tomorrow, and we expect to see nothing but happy smiling faces greeting our customers. Any questions?"

Serge Koswalski raised his hand. "Mister Dean, many of us are wondering why we weren't called to help out in the store last night. We would have gladly volunteered to take on the FLQ, and protect our store, instead of putting just our management, security, and carpenters at risk."

"Great question, Serge," Ricky responded. "We are aware of the unquestionable loyalty our staff has towards our company. We decided to have only senior management, security, and carpentry staff so that we could ideally control the situation against all possible store defense scenarios. If we would have had hundreds of employees defending the store, it would have been almost impossible to create an exit plan that wouldn't have allowed for someone getting trampled, or as they say, hurt by friendly fire."

"If there is nothing else, remember we only want to see happy faces for our customers tomorrow!"

And let's hope we never have to go through that Night of Terror nightmare ever again! Ricky thought.

⚜ Forty-One ⚜

Only those that had experienced war in World War 1, World War 2 or the Korean War could genuinely relate to the activities taking place on the streets of downtown Montreal, following the previous night's destruction. The sight of infantry men poised with automatic Bren guns atop downtown buildings and banks; tanks and 70mm shell Howitzers on the grass surrounding city hall and provincial buildings, and armed soldiers patrolling the streets, gave way to a feeling of catastrophic proportions. This was not the Canada that Canadians loved! This was not the Canada that exhumed pride in their nation. This was a third world event taking place on their own doorstep. The rumblings of the heavy tank treads traversing the usually active asphalt pavement of St. Catherine Street gave way to the foreboding sentiment that life would never again be the same for Montrealers, or the Canadian nation.

Pierre Trudeau, P.M. of Canada, had truly *stepped up to the plate* in representing the interest of Canada over those of his home province of Quebec. In a brazen declaration, he had exhibited his commander-in-chief leadership in communicating direct orders to the army.

Trudeau announced, "*In this grave undertaking, I am giving permission to the military to open fire on any person, or group who attempts to attack the foundation of our democracy. If you perceive that the threat is there, you have the permission of the Canadian government to act to contain such threat.*"

Trudeau's orders must have set fear in those revolutionaries because scenes of the Montreal City Hall and other buildings showed absolute calm, and public desertion. Seemingly, even the pigeons disappeared from City Hall.

John Blakely, of CBC Canada, asked Trudeau how far he was willing to go to stop the FLQ, and the bombings in Quebec, "Just watch me," Trudeau replied, a statement that became a welcome battle cry of Canadians throughout the nation. Three days later, the Canadian Cabinet advised the Governor General of Canada to invoke the War Measures Act. The provisions took effect later that same day, and soon hundreds of suspected FLQ members and sympathizers were taken into custody. This Act gave police the power to arrest people without a warrant and gave police sweeping powers of arrest and detention, after negotiations with the FLQ had broken off.

Simultaneously, under provisions quite separate from the War Measures Act, the Solicitor-General of Quebec requisitioned the deployment of the military in accordance with the National Defense Act. Troops from Quebec were dispatched, under the direction of the QPP, Sûreté du Québec, to guard vulnerable points and prominent individuals at risk. This allowed local police the opportunity to pursue more proactive tasks in dealing with the crisis.

In Ottawa, Canada's capital, the federal government deployed troops under its own authority to guard federal offices and employees. Police officials sometimes abused their powers and detained artists and intellectuals associated with the sovereignty movement, without cause, including the popular, Pauline Julien, a singer, songwriter, actress, feminist activist and *Quebec* sovereigntist.

Historically, the Quebec crisis was the only occasion in which the War Measures Act had ever been invoked in peacetime. The act sanctioned the armed forces to march into Montreal to control the riotous situation. With the FLQ being declared an unlawful association, the military had full power to arrest, interrogate and hold anyone they believed was associated with the FLQ. This meant that "a person who was an FLQ member, who acted or supported it in any fashion became liable to a jail term of up to 5 years and could be held without bail for up to ninety days." Conservative estimates indicate that within the first 24 hours, the Canadian forces along with local police arrested 497 suspects and conducted some 3000 searches. Four hundred and thirty-five suspects were released and of the 62 charged, 32 were accused of such serious crimes that bail was denied. One main point of criticism from human rights advocates was that the act violated the rights of people being incarcerated stating that, "everyone arrested under the Act was denied due process. And, Habeas corpus, right of confirmation of unlawful detainment, had been unlawfully suspended." Additionally, now The Crown could detain a suspect for seven days before charging them with a crime, and the seven days expanded to 21 days with approval of the attorney general. The prisoners were denied consultation with an attorney, and in many cases held incommunicado.

Ironically, the negative events of the crisis created a loss of support for the violent wing of the FLQ movement. But support for political separatist party, Parti Québécois, increased.

Although Trudeau's mantra of "Just watch me" was heralded as a definitive exclamation of federal superiority over Quebec activities, the bombings, kidnappings, murders, and revolutionary political rhetoric did not end.

The Second French Revolutionary War would continue.

⚜ Forty-Two ⚜

As if he had not had enough on his mind with the attack on Eaton's, no sooner had Ricky come through the back door of his house from the train station, than Kathy was in his face.

"We need to talk," she commanded, hands on her hips.

"And hello to you, too. Do you suppose I can remove my overcoat and take a piss, first?"

He went to the bedroom to kiss his sleeping daughter then returned to the kitchen where he got a Molson beer out of the refrigerator.

"So, what do we need to talk about *now*," he inquired, popping the cap on the beer.

"You told me to think about what I want, and I've given it a lot of thought," she began.

"And what great revelation did you arrive at?" Ricky took a long swig of his beer as he settled across the kitchen table from Kathy.

"Don't be sarcastic. This is important to me."

"Okay, let's hear it."

"I want to go to Niagara Falls."

"In the middle of winter, you want to go on vacation?"

"No, I want to move there," she replied sheepishly.

"So, out of the blue, you suddenly decided that you want me to give up my job and move all of us to Niagara Falls. Is that what I'm hearing?"

"No, that's not it," she was flustered. "I want to move there with Darlene. I want a divorce."

"A divorce? So, that's a new one," Ricky was shocked. "And where do you think you are going to live, and how the hell are you going to survive? You can't even make out a grocery list without my help."

"You are so mean! My sister has a big house there and I can stay with her until I find a job."

"Find a job? You've never had a job in your life. You left high school, married me, and never had to work a day since."

"I can find a job," she argued, "and, you can give me some money to get by on, until then."

"And how much money do you figure would be satisfactory for your needs?"

"About three thousand dollars to move and carry me over until I get a job, plus fifty percent of your salary to help raise Darlene."

This broad has gone absolutely off the deep end. Ricky thought.

"So, let me get this straight," he ticked off his fingers, "you take my daughter three hundred miles away from me, and because I'm so grateful to you for removing that burden from me, I'm going to pay you a lump sum of three-thousand dollars, and then, fifty percent of my salary. Have I got that right?"

"Yes. I want a divorce and I'm entitled to compensation," Kathy repeated.

"And where am I supposed to get three-thousand dollars?"

"You could borrow it from Household Finance, or from your family."

"And, if I give you fifty percent of my paycheck, am I supposed to live in a cardboard box under the Bonaventure overpass?"

"Don't be ridiculous, Ricky. You could move in with Jerry. He's got a two bedroom in Verdun."

"Jerry's living with his girlfriend, for Christ's sake."

"So, move in with one of your 'chickees'! I know you've been banging some broad for a long time, and I don't give a crap. I just want out of here."

Does she really know about my interest in Christine? Even though nothing has happened between us, she still could use that information as leverage against me in a divorce action. Ricky hesitated.

"You're out of your friggin' mind!" Ricky's mind was swirling. "I can't handle this right now. I need some time to think. We'll talk about this tomorrow. Right now, since you neglected to make my supper, I'm going out to get something to eat,

"Say hello to Christine for me," she yelled, as he slammed the door.

Oh Christ! How the hell does she know her name? Can things get any worse?

The next day Ricky had coffee with Tony and related all the sordid details of his fight with Kathy, except for any mention of Christine.

"So, she wants a divorce. Isn't that a good thing?"

"Not if she takes my daughter away and cripples me financially."

"You need a good lawyer my young friend, or she's going to beat your skinny ass to death."

"I can't afford a lawyer, Tony. I just finished paying off my loan at Household Finance, and I don't have any spare cash."

"Let me think for a minute," Tony pondered, as he filled both their mugs with coffee. "Have you met Bobby England?"

"No, who is he?" Ricky asked.

"He's Eaton's corporate attorney. He's a partner with Colmes, Richardson, and England, down in Old Montreal."

"So, how does that help me? He sounds expensive."

"First, he maintains an office here, at Eaton's beside Appleton's office. Second, he's here today, and more importantly, third, he owes me bigtime for getting his son out of a drug bust in Laval," Tony smiled.

"And that helps me how?"

"Be back in a minute," Tony interrupted, going to an internal house telephone by the luncheonette register. He returned in just a few minutes.

"So, finish your coffee and get your ass up to the fifth floor. Bobby's waiting for you and there won't be any charge for today's consultation," he laughed.

Ricky's meeting with Bobby England was pleasant and extremely productive. Ricky learned that under Quebec law, Kathy would no doubt retain custody of Darlene, but that Kathy could not take Darlene more than fifty miles from their residence. And that spousal alimony, and child support, was based on defendants' ability to pay. The courts did not generally leave the defendant destitute through exorbitant alimony or support payments.

Lawyer Bobby England also explained the procedures of the archaic Quebec divorces, and the one-year minimum divorce period.

Armed with this knowledge, Ricky was encouraged, and brought up the subject with Kathy as soon as he arrived home that evening.

"I saw a lawyer today," he began.

"Yeah, sure. You have all this money, but we can't afford a bloody diaper service," she countered, on the defensive.

"The lawyer was free through a friend of mine."

"And, that friend is Christine, I presume?" she slid a plate of corned beef hash in front of him.

"Where are you getting this Christine shit from?" Annoyed, Ricky pushed his dinner plate away.

"First, from your demeanor over the last few months, know you never could tell a straight-faced lie, Ricky. Second, I saw how she couldn't keep her eyes off you at the Christmas party, and the Eaton's picnic, and third, from the evidence in your blue suit pocket," she laughed.

"What's my blue suit pocket got to do with Christine?"

"If you're going to have an affair, Ricky boy, you need to know how to play the game better. You don't leave The Royal York Hotel receipt in your jacket pocket that includes room service, and two bottles of Dubonnet," she smirked.

"So, did your fancy-dancy lawyer tell you that you had no choice but to pay up and get on with your life?" she continued.

"Not exactly," Ricky replied, still trying to recuperate from Kathy finding that receipt.

"Let's hear it then. I'm all ears," she mocked, pulling her ears forward.

"First of all, you won't be taking my daughter away from me."

"And why is that?"

"Quebec law dictates that a parent cannot be separated from their children by more than fifty miles."

"I don't believe that" she responded, visually shaken by this news.

"Well, believe it 'cause when you get your own lawyer, he'll quote you chapter and verse about Quebec divorce provisions."

Ricky waited for a reply, but Kathy remained silent.

"And, as for draining me dry financially, Quebec law prohibits a defendant from being levied exorbitant alimony or support payments that could render them destitute. So, as they say in court, deal with it."

"So, Ricky, do you think a Quebec judge is going to rule favorably about a man who takes his bitch on vacation to Toronto, and leaves his wife and kid at home?"

"If that fact *were* even true," he postured, "you have absolutely no proof to offer in court, even if it would make any difference."

"I have a receipt proving it."

"You have a receipt that doesn't identify that I had anyone stay in my room. I paid for and got a single room for myself. And, as for the wine, I was at the show with seven other buyers who came to my room for drinks, and they'll testify to it," he jeered.

Kathy threw up her hands in disgust. "You're just so friggin' smug, aren't you, Ricky?"

"Says the person who is trying to stab me in the back?" Ricky tried to control his anger.

"This ain't over, yet, not, by a long shot," she yelled, slamming the bedroom door.

"But, the way it's going, it will eventually be over, and then, maybe I'll get a chance to commit to Christine honestly and openly."

⚜ Forty-Three ⚜

Because of the riots and his heavy workload at Eaton's, it had been two weeks since Ricky's last visit with Dr. Julius Markovitz. Contrary to his original impression of the doctor, he'd come to look forward to his half-hour visits. Although he didn't believe there were any immediate changes, he left each appointment with a feeling of contentment and a positive prospect of rehabilitating his screwed up personal life.

Ricky entered the office and sat on the sofa adjacent to Dr. Markovitz, who was perched, notepad in hand, in his usual armchair.

"So, young Richard," he began, "last session we discussed three areas of concern: number one, the physical abuse you encountered from your mother; number two, the sexual abuse at the hands of your grandfather; and number three, I asked you to visualize your young daughter going through the same physical abuse by your mother. Let's begin with number one, the physical abuse you encountered from your mother, yes?"

"Okay," Ricky answered, wishing for number three instead.

"So, what have you learned regarding the abuse you suffered from your mother?"

"Well," Ricky hesitated.

"Spit it out my boy," he prodded impatiently. "I'm not a mind reader."

"I met with my Uncle Ivan, my mother's brother and had a very candid and revealing conversation. He told me that my mother was terrorized by her father when she was incredibly young, and even into her teens. He told me of episodes of terrible beatings to both of them, and the insane actions of my grandfather chasing them through the house with a butcher knife, threatening to kill them. Although he didn't know first-hand, my uncle totally believes that my mother had been sexually abused by her father, for many years. Also, when my grandfather abandoned the family, my grandmother laid the blame on my mother for his departure. This guilt was accentuated every time the family faced a moral or monetary crisis. So, my conclusion is that my mother is screwed up because of her past."

"Very good, very good, Richard. This is progress. Why do you believe that your grandfather was so violent?"

"From what my uncle told me, he was a chronic gambler who won and lost thousands of dollars on a regular basis. During that time, he was known to his peers as *'Nick the Greek'*. In fact, he won and lost his *Diana Restaurant* on several occasions, each time leaving his family destitute."

"Was there anything else that could have caused his anger to be directed at his children?"

"Yes. Shortly after my mother was born, my grandmother developed gangrene in her right leg and eventually it had to be amputated. I'm told that after that, my grandfather had nothing to do with his one-legged invalid wife," Ricky paused. "Also, after my grandfather left, my grandmother laid the guilt of losing her leg on the birth of my mother. She told her that she had lost her leg because of her delivery of my mother. This fact turned out later to be blatantly untrue. She actually lost he leg seventeen months *after* my mother's birth."

"Why do you suppose your grandmother lied about your mother being the cause of her infirmary?"

"My uncle had joined the navy, leaving my mother and grandmother to fend for themselves. As my mother progressed through her teens, she dropped out of school to maintain a home for both of them. She began to blossom into a beautiful young woman. With her beauty came the throngs of suitors vying for her attention. I believe my grandmother feared being left alone to fend for herself, which was impossible in her condition. So, leveling the guilt of her being an invalid because of my mother, was a mechanism to keep my mother under her roof, and under her control."

"It sounds like you have accurately analyzed our number one and have drawn a conclusion, yes?"

"Yes, this supports the fact that my mother was both physically and mentally abused and, in turn, lashed out at me in her desperation."

"Excellent diagnosis, Richard. Perhaps you should be sitting in my chair," he smiled. "Now that you understand that the abused became the abuser, can you forgive your mother's actions against you?"

"I've thought a lot about that and can come to a stage of understanding her progression from abused to abuser, but I believe total forgiveness may still take some time."

"And why is that the case?"

"My analytical rational mind can't seem to fathom the fact that I also was abused, yet there is no way in hell that I will ever be an abuser. Shouldn't the pain of the abuse be enough of a deterrent to prohibit any sane person from inflicting the same pain on others?" Ricky asked.

"A good point, my boy. To arrive at a sensible answer, we must examine the lives and personalities of each party in comparison. Your mother was undereducated in comparison to you, and by the sounds of it, you are more worldly and better able to cope with life's changes than she. Perhaps the trauma of her abuse was greater than yours, or just maybe, you made a lifestyle commitment to never be the same as her. Whatever the reason, I suspect, that you are an extraordinarily strong individual who constantly guides his future, rather than being dictated to by the events of his past."

"That sounds reasonable, but I still am having a hard time with forgiveness. Maybe with time ..." Ricky lapsed into silence.

"You have heard the saying, 'times heals all wounds', give yourself time, my boy. Rome was not built in a day. Hopefully, your understanding of your mother's abusive past will someday get you to the point of forgiveness, thus lifting another heavy weight off your shoulders."

The doctor looked down at his notes, "All right, let's progress to our next concern, the sexual abuse at the hands of your grandfather. That is your father's father, yes?" What are your thoughts on that?"

"To be blunt, I hated the old bastard and wished him dead. I was only eight years old when he started sexually abusing me, then the creep followed up by sexually abusing both my younger brother, and my cousin. His gratification was achieved with absolutely no concern for our mental stability. We all agree that he was pure evil."

"You used the past tense 'was', has he since passed on?"

"Yes, thank God. Unfortunately, he died a nice quiet death, instead of a prolong suffering illness that he deserved. Neither my brother, cousin, nor I attended his funeral. Good riddance to bad rubbish, as they say." Ricky had raised his voice.

"Calm down, son." He placed a compassionate hand on Ricky's shoulder. "So, the problem no longer exists, or plagues your mind, yes?"

"No, there is still an open wound. I've spent considerable time reading books about familial sexual abuse and understand that this is very common. I've come to terms with accepting the actual acts, but ..."

"Go on, *but* what?"

"What I can't get by is the actions of the other adults in my life when they were made aware of the sexual abuse."

"By other adults I presume you mean other family members like your mother and father?"

"And my father's brother, my uncle. When I finally got up the nerve to tell them what was happening, my confession was met with skepticism and blame being placed on me. There was no compassion for what I had gone through, but more concern about 'what do we do about granddad'. And, where I was hoping for revenge, I was placated with 'we'll have a talk with him'. At the very least, he should have been ostracized by the family, at the very the best, he should have been sent to jail! But no, he eventually was welcomed back into our homes, where he succeeded in sexually abusing my younger brother and cousin. What kind of people have so little regard for their children that they allow all of us to spend weekends in my grandfather's apartment?" Ricky's hands were trembling. "Hell, I even found out later in life that they all knew that my grandfather was a homosexual. I cannot understand any of that ... and can never forgive it!"

"Not every scenario deserves forgiveness. Sometimes it is sufficient to just understand it and for you to be able to just file it away in an obscure corner of our mind and get on with our life. If you can live with it, don't let it consume your thoughts, or alter your life in a negative way."

"Generally, I don't think about it, but when I do, I can't generate any understanding of their actions, so my emotions take over. If you are looking for a display of emotions by me the thought only generates rage!"

"Hopefully Richard, given time, your anger will fade to a point of being replaced by many happier events, and that will cancel out these negatives. Like the glow that you get when you talk about your daughter. I can see the love in you. So, speaking of your daughter, let's move on to the visualization exercise, seeing in your mind, your young daughter going through the same physical abuse by your mother."

"Do we have to?" Ricky tried to joke.

"Yes," ignoring Ricky's failed stab at levity, "how did that work out?"

"It was really difficult. I am very protective of my daughter and having to visualize her in harm's way was intolerable. I would give my life for her."

"Go on."

"I thought of her being tied in a highchair, as I was, unable to move; having shoes and other objects thrown at her; constantly being chastised for her actions; being belittled in front of her friends, and always being told she's not, *'as good as, anyone else'!* All I gained from the visualization was a sense of intense rage. I would never allow anything so vile to enter her life. Haven't we already covered that with the number one, abuse by my mother?"

"Yes, but I needed you to relive it in the third party. And you've done that very well, my boy." He glanced at his watch. "And was that tears I saw misting in your eyes earlier, as you talked of your daughter?" he smiled slyly.

"I guess."

"Your time is up, so for our next session, I want you to think about the problems in your present home life, your feeling of sexual inadequacy, and any outside interest that may be occupying your mind, yes?"

With all I've got to tell Doc about Christine and the developments with Kathy, I'm certain that I'll need an hour session instead of just my regular half hour, he joked to himself.

⚜ Forty-Four ⚜

"Susan, do you know if Misses Bardot has contacted merchandise display about relocating the hat display, away from the escalators?"

"I heard her talking with them last week, Mister Dean" Susan answered, "but the display foreman, John Derber, advised that unless we erect a plastic shield between the escalator and our display, we will continue to have garbage thrown from the escalator, into our department. Misses Bardot put in a work order for the carpenters to construct the see-through plastic barrier, but we haven't seen hide, nor hair, of them, yet."

"Okay! I'll contact the carpenters and get them moving on it!"

"Oh, hi Andrea," Ricky acknowledged the department manager's arrival. "Susan just told me the hat display problem is in the process of being resolved."

"Yes, Sir, but we have a problem with the new location for our cash register. I totally understand the repositioning of the register areas so that each area has a clear view of the surrounding registers, but in our case, having our register so close to the bottom of the up escalator, I believe, is a security hazard."

"How so?"

"I measured the area yesterday. With the register sitting on that glass display counter, it is less than four feet from the entrance to the escalator, which makes it an easy 'grab and run' and a definite fast escape up the escalator. If we want to maintain observation over the surrounding cash areas, I suggest that we install a separate register base, at the back of the register counter, which would be away from any possible threat."

"I agree. So, what's the problem?"

"The one hundred and twenty-eight dollars estimate from carpentry to build and install the new register base, and since you've put a moratorium on any further expenses for this quarter, we can't proceed."

"Okay. Thanks for keeping that in mind Andrea, but here's what you do. Contact the carpentry department foreman, Bobby Hepler, and tell him what you need is approved by me. Also, tell him that I don't want to see a work order invoice until after the third quarter begins. Got it?"

"Yes Sir, thank you," she responded.

Ricky continued his trek, stopping to talk with his new lingerie and corsets manager, Monique Rousseau.

"Hey, Monique. Did you have any trouble sending that order back to Myron at Star Corsets? He can be really unpleasant when he has to cut a check *back* to us."

"Actually, I decided to go talk to him personally rather than getting my head chewed off by him over the phone'" Andrea explained. "Surprisingly, it worked out better than I had hoped. Apparently, Myron is more intimidated by you than the prospect of having to credit us for hundreds of corsets. He kept asking, 'whether Ricky had to know about the screw up'. It seems that his pattern maker, who by the way, got fired while I was there, forgot to notate the positioning of the boning stays, so the seamstresses constructed the corset without the boning pockets. Myron was furious."

"Yeah, when anyone costs him money, he has no sense of humor," Ricky smiled. "Does he realize that we have a sale advertised next Tuesday, and can't wait for a replacement order from Star products?"

"Oh yeah. I think he was more upset with the fact that Jedediah, at Wonderwear, was going to resupply us with the same corsets as he had. You know, there's been a bloody feud going between those two, since Myron's son, Ben abandoned the family business when Jed offered him a partnership in Wonderwear. And Myron will never forgive either of them. I heard through the schmatte, *rag,* business grapevine that Ben has been disowned by his father and stripped of any further contact with any of the family members. I think it is tearing Myron apart and seems to have aged him ten years in the last eighteen months."

"Well, I feel bad for him, but he has his problems, and we have ours. You did your job, Andrea, in getting the goods sent back. Thanks."

Ricky continued to the Laura Secord where Marissa was busy filling an assortment of crème centers for a customer. The locker bombings had happened three weeks ago, and the floor was just now getting back to normal. He marveled at the fresh modern look of the small department following its destruction. Marissa was 20 years old, brown hair and blue eyes with a short heavyset build that she constantly complained about. Never had Ricky seen Marissa in a foul mood, testy with customers or not willing to pitch in to help anyone in need. Because of this, and her naiveté, many times her generosity was abused. Ricky kept a careful watch over her to avoid this happening.

"Welcome home, Marissa," Ricky greeted, as the customer finished paying for her treat. "How did you like working temp for the last few weeks in Miss Guillaume's junior fashions."

"Thank you so much, Mister Dean, for giving me work after the explosion. If I hadn't had a paycheck for that length of time, I don't know what I would have done. And, my boss, Mister McCorcoran, in Toronto, told me to express his sincere appreciation as well."

"And working in junior fashions?" Ricky asked.

"It was absolutely fantastic, and Miss Guillaume is just so cool. She took me under her wing and made me feel right at home. If I ever decide that I want something more than chocolates, her department would be my very first choice. Thank you, again."

"You don't have to thank me. I heard that you did a great job there. I understand that Christine is considering you for the next show, right?"

"Yeah, well ..." she stammered, "I'm still not convinced that I'm the modeling type. Models are supposed to be tall and thin, and I'm short and not so thin."

"Come on, Marissa. You're beautiful, have a great body and an experience like this can open up a lot of opportunities if you remain in merchandising."

"I guess," she replied, somewhat embarrassed.

"By the way, your new department looks great. How do you like it?" Ricky changed the subject.

"Oh, Mister Dean, it is better than I could have hoped. Not just the modern look, but the back kitchen where I make the chocolates is so much more efficient. With the old kitchen I was constantly fighting the glazing machine where the strawberry filled, and lemon filled chocolates would tumble from the machine where they got all mixed up. And, because of their rolling on top of each other, many times the nib on top of the chocolate would break off. Now, with the new machine, the different groups of chocolates gently slide off the small conveyor without damage. I can make fifty percent more at the same time as before."

"That's great, Marissa. Keep up the good work," Ricky replied, and continued north on his inspection circuit. As he reached the luggage department his pager sounded. He grabbed the nearest telephone and dialed the pager response number.

"Dean, basement one," he called in to the operator.

"Yes, Mister Dean. I have a request for you to meet up with Detective Middleton and Manager Henderson on the west side of the purses and leather goods department, stat!"

"On the way," Ricky replied hanging up the telephone without awaiting acknowledgement.

In less than one minute he arrived at the location where Middleton, Henderson, and the store Detective Raymond Archambault, were secreted from view, behind the down escalator.

"What've we got, Ray?" he asked Detective Archambault.

Archambault was a 31-year-old ex-military officer who had retired after twelve years active duty in the European theater. He followed his tour with four months training at the Sûreté du Quebec, QPP training facility, after which he was posted on the security detail of the Minister of Foreign Affairs, but the position hadn't lasted long. Within the first month of his posting, he had arrived for his shift at the minister's home, and when he exited his support vehicle, he slipped and fell on some black ice, careening headfirst into the concrete sidewalk. After a week in the hospital in Quebec City, he was transported to the Montreal Neurological Institute where it was determined that his extended concussion had caused permanent neurological damage. He had received disability retirement from the QPP and was offered a position as a floor detective with Eaton's security department. Because of his military background, and injury, his boss, Tony Cartwright, felt a special protective kinship with him.

"I'm really not sure, Ricky," Ray explained, "'cause I didn't see it for myself. But Misses Henderson told me that her clerk, Gloria, assured her that the big guy, at the counter with the cashmere overcoat, pocketed a Boxley leather wallet."

Misses Henderson interrupted. "I quizzed Gloria as to whether she was sure of what she saw, and she confirmed that she was certain that the man put a brown windowed wallet in the inside pocket of his overcoat, while she was punching up a sale for another customer."

"How can she be certain if she was punching the register, instead of having eyes on him?" Ricky inquired.

"I asked her that," Henderson explained, "and Gloria said that she had been certain the man was going to grab something just from his strange body language, so she never took her eyes off him from the time that he arrived at her counter."

"What do you think, Ray. It's your call," Ricky questioned.

"Well, I'd much prefer making the collar if I had actually seen it myself, but if the kid is so sure, and we find the wallet on the perp, I guess it's a go. Misses Henderson, would you call up to security and have Tony or Denis come down, A.S.A.P. In the meantime, Ricky, you, and Kate, come up behind the guy in case he tries to rabbit, when I confront him."

The detective quickly, and stealthily, approached the suspect, as Ricky and Kate Middleton took up a flanking position nearby.

"Sir," he said, displaying his store credentials prominently in front of the man's face, "We don't want any problems, so could you please empty your pockets on the counter for me?"

EATON'S – During the Second French Revolution

"I absolutely, will not!" he replied loudly and defiantly with no sign of fear on his face. "What the hell is this all about, anyway? I'm a good Eaton's customer, and this is absolutely ridiculous!"

"Please keep your voice down, Sir."

Denis Charbonneau, arrived on scene, and firmly grabbed the man's elbow. "I need you to come with us, so we can iron out this situation, sir."

"Let go of me," the man shouted, trying to pull his elbow away from Denis's firm grasp. Ricky quickly grabbed the man's other arm, as Archambault made a show of revealing a pair of handcuffs.

"We can do this the easy way, or the hard way," Denis instructed, feigning reaching for Archambault's cuffs, "it's up to you."

With no hope of escape, the man relented. "Okay, goddamn it. I'll go, but I promise that you'll be sorry. I have nothing to hide."

The group commandeered an elevator to the 5th floor security offices.

With Ricky following, Ray and Denis escorted the man into a locked security office interrogation room, then retreated to Tony's office.

"What have you got, guys," Tony questioned, not looking up from the papers he was reading on his desk.

"Got a really cool perp in the box who denies that he stole anything," Denis answered. "But there's something real hinky about him that really worries me."

"Isn't that what they all say, Denis?" Tony replied, leaning back in his swivel chair.

"Yeah, well I think this one is different. For a guy who got caught stone cold, he's just too relaxed, like he knew he was going to get caught or something," Ray piped in.

"You mean like our homeless brigade that every winter fakes shoplifting so they can get arrested and receive two months of warmth and three good meals a day, at taxpayer's expense," Tony laughed.

"This guy ain't no homeless guy, Tony," Ricky interjected, "the prick is wearing an expensive cashmere coat, worth a hundred and a half, and a tailored suit of about the same value."

"Okay, okay! Ray you can go back to your floor patrol. And ..."

Ray immediately protested. "Tony, this is my collar shouldn't I be the one to interrogate this guy?"

"You're right, Ray, and the collar will be credited to you, but with Kate left out on the floor, without any backup, I need to position you where you are of the most value."

Ray was noticeably disappointed, but withdrew from Tony's office, without another word.

"Wow! That didn't go over very well," Ricky commented.

"Not my problem," Tony replied, rising from his chair. "Anyway, let me take a first crack at your perp. You guys just remain quiet and observe his reactions. If he's hiding something, you'll notice his 'tell'."

The three of them entered the room. Tony walked toward the back of the room, with his back turned to everyone, stood for a moment. Click! And then took a chair across the table from the man. Ricky and Denis stood on opposite sides of the room.

"Sir, my name is Tony Cartwright, and I'm head of Eaton's security. And your name is?"

"My name is, 'Mister, You Don't Friggin' Need to Know,' but you can just call me, 'Mister,'" the man replied in a sarcastic voice, maintaining the permanent scowl of defiance on his face.

Tony stiffened, "You're not being very cooperative, uh, *Mister*, for someone who is being accused of theft. We have a witness that swears that she saw you put a brand-new wallet in your overcoat pocket. And, if as you say, you are innocent, why wouldn't you cooperate with the floor detective and reveal the contents of your pockets?"

"Because your witness has her head up her ass, and your detective has no legal right to search me, that's why," the man replied.

Tony looked at Denis and mouthed 'camera,' to which Denis left the room returning with a 35mm camera.

As Tony raised the camera, the man threw his hands in front of his face, and shouted, "you have no right! Get that goddamn thing out of my face. And get the MPD in here, now. I'm not talking to you rent-a-cops any further. I want the MPD."

Tony motioned Ricky and Denis from the room saying, "is this guy bluffing by telling us to call in the MPD, or is he really innocent?"

"Christ Tony. Not only did the salesclerk swear that he took the wallet, but she identified the color, the brand and what pocket he put it in. What more information do we need?" Denis asked. "The perp is just bluffing, and it seems to be working."

"Bluff, or no bluff there's something not right with this guy. He's wearing top of the line clothing, and he's stealing a twelve-dollar wallet? It just doesn't make sense."

"Tony, believe me. This prick is bluffing. He thinks we won't call his bluff for twelve dollars," Denis pleaded.

"Okay, I'll make a call to some friends at MPD and get them in here and let's get this thing resolved. We've got more important issues on the table than spending all day with this guy over a twelve-dollar wallet."

Twenty minutes later, two MPD patrolmen arrived. After telling them the story the whole group joined the man in the box.

EATON'S – During the Second French Revolution

Tony again moved to the back of the room to allow the MPD officers to handle the interrogation. Click! Click!

"I'm Officer Sauvignon and this is Officer Trudell, of the MPD. And you are?"

"My name is Marcus Conti," the man replied casually, without hesitation.

"Mister Conti, Eaton's security, here," Officer Sauvignon pointed to Tony and Denis, "have accused you of theft of a twelve-dollar wallet from their leather goods department. What do you have to say to that, sir?"

"I've never stole anything in my life. That's what I say. These pricks have nothing better to do than accuse innocent citizens. I have my rights!"

"Mister Conti. We need to resolve this situation. I must insist that you empty your pockets on the table in front of you, and then step away from the table," the officer instructed.

Slowly, Conti rose from his chair "It's not right, but I don't want to spend all goddamn day with these pricks."

He began emptying his pockets; first a key ring and loose coins from his pants pocket, followed by some papers from his inner jacket pocket. Finally, an old tattered brown wallet from his rear pocket, and then a brand-new brown wallet, from his cashmere jacket pocket. Upon seeing the new wallet everyone sighed a sigh of relief. They had him!

"I told you so," Denis mouthed silently to Tony.

Officer Trudell reached over and picked up the new wallet, waving it accusingly in front of Conti's face. "Is this your wallet, sir?"

"It is," Conti replied calmly.

"Is this the wallet that your employee alleges that Mister Conti stole?" Trudell directed at Tony.

"Yes, it is," Tony replied confidently.

"What do you have to say to that, Mister Conti."

"I bought that wallet at Morgan's, this morning."

"Can you prove that sir," Trudell pushed more forcefully.

"If you look in the billfold area of the wallet, you will find the receipt for the purchase," Conti smiled confidently.

Tony's heart sank in dread.

The scene was as if all the air had been sucked out of the room, and everyone held their breath, unable to speak. The MPD officers looked at Tony, Tony looked at Denis, then everyone looked at Ricky.

Trudell slowly inspected the receipt from the inner pocket of the wallet. Sauvignon addressed the whole room, "It appears that there has been a serious misunderstanding here, Mister Conti. We will be filing a report, which will be available to you at headquarters, should you need a copy. And, gentlemen," directing his attention to Tony, "I suspect that this is something you will be wanting to handle, 'in house,' yes?"

As Tony shamefully nodded, the officers retreated, leaving Tony, Denis, and Ricky, alone with Conti.

"So, boys. How do you want to handle this?" Conti questioned in a very cocky tone. "I can get an attorney and we can go to court, or I can contact the newspaper and give them my sad story of abuse by Eaton's security department; or we can come to a mutually satisfactory financial arrangement. The choice is yours, gentlemen."

Tony remained in thought, then pressed the intercom button, "Agatha, get me DFS-1, Dupuis Freres Security, on the line, please."

Tony was now resigned to the fact that he had been played by a pro. He determined that this had been a calculated extortion exercise that Eaton's now had lost. The only option left was to try to get out of this situation with the least amount of damage possible. He looked at Conti.

"So, what's it going to take, Conti?"

Click

"That's *Mister* Conti if you please. And I think one-thousand dollars sounds about fair to me." Conti displayed a wide smile.

"I was thinking more like two hundred dollars, and I never see your goddamn face in my store again."

"That's not going to happen," Conti responded, rising from the table.

"DFS-1 on line three, Mister Cartwright."

"I'll take it in my office, Agatha," he acknowledged. Before heading to the door, once again Tony moved to the back of the room. Click! "You sir, remain in your seat," he barked, directing Conti back into his chair.

Tony left the room, leaving Denis and Ricky to watch over Conti.

It seemed like quite a while before Tony returned. When he did, he had a very wide smile on his face. "So, where were we Conti?"

"I said one thousand, and you said two hundred, and I was about to tell you to stuff your offer up your ass. So that's where we are!"

"Yeah, well, Mister Conti, or is it, Mister Forte?"

The group watched as the blood slowly drained from the man's face. But he rapidly regained his composure. "I just want to get out of here, now. Just give me your measly two-hundred dollars, and I'm out of here."

"Listen carefully scumbag! That's not going to happen! But here's what is. It takes three minutes and forty seconds to run down the escalators, and out the front Saint Catherine Street doors. I have two of my detectives stationed at the bottom of the main floor escalator awaiting your arrival, and if you make it to the front door before that time, they will let you leave peacefully. If you don't, they will handcuff you, and deliver you to the Dupuis Freres department store security team. Apparently, they are really pissed off at having paid you five hundred dollars, for the same con. Do you understand what I've just told you, Mister, eh?"

EATON'S – During the Second French Revolution

The man nodded.

Tony pushed the intercom button. "Agatha, tell the boys he's on his way. The clock starts ticking, right now you, despicable little prick," Tony slapped Forte on the back of his head.

The man bolted from his chair, went to grab his belongings from the table, but Tony slapped his hand. "Go! You're wasting time."

With that, the man crashed through the exit door, and made a beeline for the down escalators.

"So, how did you know that the Dupuis Freres boys wanted him?" Ricky asked.

"I just remember from my last security meeting that they mentioned they had just paid off a guy in a cashmere coat, so I gave them a call. I sure as shit don't want to be that guy, Conti, or Forte, Mister whatever, when the Dupuis Freres guys get a hold of him."

Tony folded his arms and settled into one of the chairs, a broad grin crossed his face. "Case closed," he muttered.

"That was awesome," Ricky commented, taking a chair across from Tony. "Do you think he'll make it past your boys in time."

"What boys?" Tony laughed.

"But you said ..." Ricky began.

"Ah," young Ricky, "you gotta learn the game. It's so much fun to con a con man. They're so arrogant that they never see it coming!"

"Okay! I'm totally confused. I think you let this creep off too easy," Denis protested.

"Oh Denis! No doubt our Mister Conti, or Forte will stumble down the escalators in the time I allotted. He'll also exit onto Saint Catherine Street, just as I instructed him. However, to his surprise, there will be a van with three Dupuis Freres security boys waiting for him, 'cause they want to show him their sub-basement security office! Ain't revenge sweet, boys?"

"You are one evil bastard, Tony." Ricky smiled.

"Yeah well, by tomorrow this guy's face will be in every retail security office in Montreal."

Denis looked at Tony. "So how did all the pieces fall in place?"

"After my call with Dupuis Freres, I got a call from another one of my contacts at MPD. He told me his real name, and that his aliases including Conte and Forte."

Ricky added, "Yeah, and I guess now, *Mister*, too!" they all laughed. "But Tony, how were your contacts able to identify him.

Tony smiled, moved to the back of the room, and revealed a hidden camera. He pressed the button, and everyone in the room heard, *Click!*

They all laughed. It was the same sound they had heard when the interrogation had begun, and every time Tony moved to the back of the room!

❦ Forty-Five ❦

Since Christine had moved in with Charlotte, Ricky had tried to distance himself from her, to give her a chance at a new single life. However, after their night at Place Ville Marie, when she tried to get him to open up to her about his home life, he had a more difficult time staying away.

During the same time, his relationship with Kathy had come to a head. Kathy approached him about a divorce and Tony set him up with a lawyer who gave him some facts that helped him realize he wasn't as vulnerable as Kathy wanted him to feel and not as stuck in a dead-end marriage as he had made himself believe.

These things led Ricky to the realization that he could open up to the idea of a relationship with Christine. He decided to invite her out and see what happened, since each time they met, they became closer and closer. He chose to meet at different restaurants at least two or three times per week after work. Because of everything they had both been through, he elected to take things slow, but his, soon to be new freedom, allowed him to open himself up to Christine. He became comfortable in sharing very personal details about his home life, and his aspirations for the future. He even discussed his visits with Dr. Markovitz, and only then did he begin to feel comfortable considering the advancement of their relationship.

"You mean this guy actually bought a wallet at Morgan's, put the sales receipt inside, came to our department and faked stealing an identical wallet, all so that, he could con Eaton's out of a large amount of cash?" Christine stirred more cream into her coffee.

"Yep. And if Tony hadn't followed up with Dupuis Freres security, this jerk would have gotten away with it."

Ricky and Christine were sitting in a rear booth in the coffee shop at the Bonaventure Hotel. They met there because of its proximity to Central Station, and it gave them more time together before Ricky had to catch his train to St. Laurent. Christine had also insisted that she walk Ricky to the train station, so he didn't want her going too far alone!

"But what are these Dupuis Freres security guys going to do to this guy?" Christine asked.

"I'm sure that their main point will be to get their money back and at the same time, teach him a lesson."

"Teach him a lesson?"

"You my darling, don't want to know. There is a reason that their security department is in the basement of Dupuis Freres," he laughed, sipping his coffee.

"You always think that I'm too fragile to hear unpleasant things," she lightly punched his shoulder. "More and more you treat me like a little princess, and you, as my knight in shining armor, always ready to rescue me."

"And I love that role."

"Well, 'Ya know, Mister Dean, you are causing me sleepless nights."

"How so?"

"Since we've been spending more time together, which never seems to be enough, when I go home and try to go to sleep my mind is filled with *what ifs*, about us."

"What ifs?"

"You know, *what if* we could spend a whole day together sometime, *what if* you were free of your marriage, as I am, *what if* I could really tell you how I feel?" She placed her hands over her face. "Geez, I'm embarrassing myself."

"You have nothing to be embarrassed about," he replied, gently taking her hand in his. "You are just stating the same thoughts that I have constantly." He lifted her chin with his finger so that he could stare closely into her eyes. "After all the things we've shared over the past few months, not to mention the fantastic attachment we now have for each other, how could I not have my own long list of *what ifs'*?"

"Really, Ricky? But, how come you never talk about it, or take our relationship to the next level?" She positioned her face within inches of his.

Is she really suggesting what I think she's suggesting?

"You know that I have a hard time opening up to more serious issues, just ask Doctor Markovitz," he laughed.

"Well, maybe it is time we change all that!" she replied, kissing his lips.

"How so?"

"Maybe, we could start by figuring out a way to spend more than a few hours together, like going somewhere special for a whole day."

Ricky thought for several minutes before responding. "Your day off this week is Saturday, right?"

"Yes," she whispered.

"I'm also off Saturday. So, what do you say we plan a trip up to Mount Tremblant? I could pick you up around eight-thirty in the morning, and we could return around five, in the afternoon, which would give us plenty of time together.".

Her eyes opened wide in surprise. "Really, Ricky? Is that even possible. What about Kathy? You know I don't ski," she rambled.

"Whoa, little girl. Slow down. First Kathy is house-sitting all day and taking Darlene with her. If I am back by five when she comes home, there should be no issue. Secondly, we are not going there to ski, just to walk, talk and spend quality time together in front of the roaring fire in the lodge."

"Wow! I can't wait. What do I need to bring?"

"Just some warm clothes for our walk on the mountain, and your beautiful smile that will ensure that we have a sunny day." He pulled her close for a passionate lingering kiss.

Looking at the wall clock he reacted. "Crap, I've got to get going or I'm going to miss my train."

"Not without me you're not." She gathered her coat and hat. "I'm walking you to the station."

⚜ Forty-Six ⚜

It was Monday, two days after the Black Watch Armory riot when Louis was contacted by Francois who directed him to get a 2" X 2" personal photo of himself and take it to a small camera shop on Saint Urban Street. When he questioned why he needed the photo Francois curtly responded, "a good soldier acts, he does not question."

Louis had a photo taken at a local pharmacy and took the photo to the shop where he was told to return in three hours, without any explanation as to what they were going to do with the photo. When he returned, he was presented with an official looking *LaPresse* newspaper identification badge bearing his picture. Upon receiving the identification badge, he immediately found a telephone booth and contacted Mr. Smith to update him on the situation.

Louis explained about the *LaPresse* identification badge, "apparently whatever is going down it is important enough they want on-time documentation of the event. I'm thinking an attack could be on the Montreal Stock Exchange.

"You may be right," Mr. Smith responded, "but it still seems highly unlikely. Remember just three weeks ago a bomb was planted in the building across the street from the exchange, outside the offices of a firm involved in a language dispute in a northern Quebec mining town. Fortunately, a guard threw it down a stairwell before it exploded. I don't believe they would try another attack in such proximity to the last."

"Just maybe, that attack was a prelude, or dry run, to test the possibility of an Exchange attack. Maybe they were just trying to get a sense of the reaction time of law enforcement," Louis suggested.

"Anything is possible, but without concrete evidence of the exact target, and the day or time, we can't close down the Exchange indefinitely based on your suspicions. Neither The Exchange nor MPD would never go for it."

"But I really feel that things are accelerating to a point that this may be the week of the planned attack," Louis prompted.

"I'll pass along your concerns to MPD, and the Exchange security officers, but based on the information that you've provided, as I said begore, they'll not take the threat seriously. If you really believe the target is the Exchange, you'll need to get me more information, even if you must jeopardize your cover. Because, right now, your cover isn't worth as much as this information which could save the lives of hundreds of Canadian citizens."

"Okay, I'll dig deeper and let you know."

Tuesday night Louis met with his team leader, Jean-Claude Allard, at Les Jardins Tavern in St. Michele's.

"So, I approved to loan you to the *Liberation Cell*, as a documentary photographer, for the Exchange attack," Jean-Claude lowered his voice. "This is an important event, so make us proud."

Finally, official confirmation of the actual target.

"Yes, but I still feel like I'm in the dark as to the details." Louis sipped his Molson's. "They got me a *LaPresse* identification pass, but no one has explained my role in this whole thing. I don't know where I'm supposed to be, or even what day, or time."

"Patience my friend. You know how these things work. You will be told these details only when, and if, they determine it is necessary to the success of the operation, and not before."

"So, I'm just supposed to stand around with my thumb up my ass and wait for a call to act?" Louis pressed.

"What is the alternative? You just need to stand by for a few more days and all will become clear," Jean Claude explained.

"Certainly, at least knowing what day I'm needed can't compromise the operation."

I better be careful that I don't push too hard.

"You need to be very careful about asking so many questions."

"Why?"

"I shouldn't be telling you this, but, our FLQ provincial counsel has formed an investigative body to search out a traitor in our midst, and they are very close to discovering his or her identity."

Louis tried to disguise his shock. "After all I've done for our cell, am I considered a suspect?"

"No one is above suspicion. The counsel has gathered statistics concerning each individual cell's activities over the past year to determine who knew about all the activities that have been leaked. That way they are assured of nailing *L'ombre.*"

"*L'ombre*, meaning *The Shadow?*" Louis asked.

"Yes."

"What does this have to do with our cell?"

"From what I've been told, information about upcoming events has been leaked to the MPD, the newspapers or direct to the target event by this 'Shadow' character," Jean Claude continued. "The only way that can happen is if someone in our ranks is passing on the information."

Shit, this is not good news, right now!

"So, this is a witch hunt for one person amongst the thousands of members in the various provincial cells? It'll take years to weed out the culprit."

"No, actually, the counsel has narrowed it down to someone within either our cell, or the Laval, *Liberation* cell. Both of us are the only cells that were privy to *all* the events that had been leaked."

"That still leaves sixteen suspects in *Liberation*, and twenty-nine in our cell which is a total of forty-five suspects, right?" Louis asked.

"Yes, but they've already narrowed that figure down by eliminating new recruits, soldiers who had absolutely no knowledge of *all* the events, and loyal team leaders. So, the remaining total is only nineteen. I've been assured that we will know the identity of the traitor within ten days."

"I trust I've proven myself so that I'm not one of the nineteen."

"Unfortunately, Louis, that's not so. I know you are not the traitor, but that's why I'm telling you to be careful with all these questions you are asking. You don't need suspicion being cast in your direction."

"Well, at least, thank you for the vote of confidence, Jean-Claude."

As soon as their meeting ended Louis raced to the nearest telephone booth which was located on Viau St. He was out of breath as he connected with Mr. Smith.

"I have definite confirmation that the target is definitely the Montreal Stock Exchange," he told Smith.

"Is the confirmation credible?"

"It is directly from my team leader Allard, who is coordinating with the Laval team leader of the *Liberation* Cell."

"Good, good! And the type of attack, date, and time?" Smith questioned, impatiently.

"Type of attack is still unknown."

"Well, that is most important, don't you think?" he asked sarcastically. "We can't have the whole MPD, Exchange security and bomb squad standing by if this is just a rally or sit-in."

"With all due respect *sir*, this is *not* some simple rally or sit-in," Louis raised his voice. "There is too much secrecy connected with this operation. In fact, *if* this were just a rally or sit-in, the rank and file would have full knowledge and be openly preparing for it."

"Okay, but how can you nail down the day and time?" Smith asked.

"I am positive that the attack will be sometime this week, which leaves only Wednesday, Thursday, and Friday as operational days of the Exchange. Furthermore, since they have me as their photographer, somewhere they are going to have to tell me where to place myself and what time the event will happen. The bad news is that I probably won't be told until maybe two or three hours before it happens. And I'm unsure how much scrutiny I'll be under once that information is given to me. So, communicating that information to you could be problematic."

"With forty-seven floors in the building, hundreds of brokerage firms, the main trading floor, and thousands of employees, we *must* get that information to prevent any injury or death, regardless of any concerns about burning your undercover operation, understand?"

"I believe my undercover operation is already burnt or will be within the next ten days."

"How so?"

Louis relayed the story about the provincial counsel investigation into the traitor's identity.

"Okay, so they have made the decision for us. After this operation you will be taken out and reassigned. Let me know as soon as you have any further news."

On Wednesday afternoon, with nothing else to do, Louis drove from Montreal Island to La Brasserie du Laval hoping to bump into Francois or other members of the *Liberation* cell. He spent several hours drinking beer in hopes that someone would show up that he could pump for more information. Strangely no one showed up, and the atmosphere in *Liberation's* favorite watering hole was eerily quiet.

Totally exhausted from the pressures of the last few days Louis went home and slept until his telephone rang at 10:45 A.M.

"Hello," he struggled to get into his robe.

"Louis?"

"Yes! Who's this?"

"Francois. Are you ready to make history?"

"Oh uh, hi, Francois. Make history?"

"Wake up my friend, today your photographs are going to be seen across Canada and all around the world."

"I'm ready," he replied, coming alert. "What do you need me to do?"

"For now, I just need you to get your ass and your camera, down to a telephone booth located on the northeast corner of Victoria Square and wait for further instructions. I'll call you at that booth and instruct you where to go. Got it?" Francois questioned.

"Sure, what time should I be there?"

"Always with the questions. Just get down there within the next hour and wait." The telephone line went dead.

Louis dressed, grabbed a bite to eat, got his camera, lens and film and flew out the door of his apartment. Walking to his car he found a telephone booth and called Mr. Smith.

"I just got a call from Francois, the guy who recruited me for camera work. He told me to wait at a booth in Victoria Square, so I'm positive that the Exchange is the target, and today is the right day. His exact words were, 'today your photographs are going to be seen across Canada, and all around the world'. This is *real*, Mister Smith, not some rally!"

"The Tour de la Bourse *Stock Exchange Tower* is Montreal's third-tallest building. A bomb blast there would be devastating, not to mention cripple the financial institutions across Canada."

The line remained momentary silent, then Smith continued, "Okay, get down there and report as soon as you discover the time frame."

Louis calculated, "Francois wants me there within the next hour and since the final trading bell rings at three o'clock, that means that we have a window of about two and one-half hours before this catastrophe."

"You need to get going. I'll get things moving on my end. As soon as you can pin down the exact time, I want you to call direct to Jack Rollins, head of security on the trading floor, so that he can move quickly to evacuate the area. The number is 555-6000. And use *The Shadow* identity again to call in the anonymous tip."

"Got it," Louis hung up and sprinted to his car.

By the time Louis arrived at Cote du Beaver Hall off Victoria Square, parked his car, and found the northeast telephone booth, the church clock tower down the block showed it was now, 1:17. Louis entered the booth carefully guarding it against use by any passerby's wanting to make a call. He watched the church clock tick off the time. When it read 1:45 he began to wonder if he'd been played, and by 2:00 he was deciding if he should just leave.

He decided to wait fifteen minutes more and then give it up. At 2:10, finally the telephone rang.

"Louis. "Go across the street to the Fredrick building. Go up to the roof, the door is unlocked. Position yourself and your camera facing the Tour de la Bourse and be ready to snap as many photos, as fast as you can. Don't linger more than five minutes after the blast. I'll meet up with you at Des Jardins at eight tonight. Bring the film." The line went dead.

Louis immediately dialed the number that Mr. Smith had given him for the contact at the Exchange.

"Rollins," was the quick answer.

"Listen carefully. This is the Shadow. There is a bomb ready to explode in the Montreal Stock Exchange." Louis hung up quickly.

He made another telephone call and gave the same information to Mr. Smith, after which, he ran to the mining building across the street. He quickly ascended the stairs, exiting onto the rooftop. The wind was howling so violently he had to push his way across the roof to position himself. He needed to remain unseen, below the 3-foot concrete barrier running along the roof edge; and that's where he placed his camera. At 2:36 a violent explosion rocked Victoria Square with the third-floor windows of the trading floor raining glass and debris down upon the pedestrians below. The blast was followed by billowing smoke and screams. Even with all his training, Louis was having a difficult time continuing to photograph the disaster. But he knew whoever got possession of the film would need the pictures he was now recording.

Later, the news stations reported that the blast had occurred 22 minutes before the closing bell and had resulted in approximately 300 people on the trading floor and 50 people in the visitor's gallery being injured. It was reported that no fatalities resulted from the explosion thanks, in part, to an anonymous tip which allowed security time to begin evacuation, probably saving many lives. There was no mention of the tipster being labeled "*The Shadow*."

Montreal Stock Exchange manager, Charles Neapole, stated that because of the millions of dollars of damage to the trading floor, and especially the electronic trading board, that all financial trading would be transacted through the Toronto exchange until further notice.

When Louis got off the rooftop and found a phone booth far enough away to call Mr. Smith, he was advised to prepare a complete report of the Exchange incident and await further instructions. He was to report for reassignment to the McFadden & Holmes Consulting firm, the following Monday.

Perhaps now I can get a week of peace and quiet. Louis thought.

⚜ Forty-Seven ⚜

Things had calmed down considerably since *Montreal's Night of Terror* and *The Montreal Stock Exchange* bombing. The police and fireman strike had been amicably resolved, but the sting of the actions of both agencies, abandoning Montrealers to the FLQ, would resonate with the local citizens for years to come. As the military left Montreal for their regular duties, the FLQ bombings subsided, but their political rhetoric continued to be channeled through the *Party Quebecois* politicians.

Although many St. Catherine Street businesses remained boarded up because of the damage from the riots, and others sported large for sale signs, the downtown core had returned to some feeling of normalcy. But the stigma of that night would live on for generations in the minds of all Canadians, but most vividly the Montrealer's who had lived through that night of horror. Montreal would never be the same!

Ricky was compiling his coming year budget for each department when somewhere outside of his office on the selling floor, there was a loud metal bang, followed by the sound of breaking glass and screaming.

Ricky bolted from his chair, exited his office, and sprinted for the center area of the selling floor, as several "eyes on" alarms sounded. He spotted Ray Archambault and several of his staff, on their knees trying to retrieve hundreds of brightly colored gumballs that were flowing haphazardly across the floor.

"Leave this to us, Ray. You need to get out there and keep your eyes peeled."

"Sure thing, Ricky," he responded, beginning to circle the adjacent departments.

As Ricky stooped to assist in gathering the spreading gumballs, Gwenn Robarts, assistant manager of ladies' dresses, leaned towards him and whispered, "I saw that kid over there purposely topple the gumball machine," indicating a young boy of about seven or eight, casually watching their retrieval efforts. "He walked up to the machine, looked around to see if anyone was watching, then just gave it a strong push."

"Where's the mother?" Ricky whispered back.

"The heavyset woman, with the heavy winter coat, over there, in the bra and corset department," she indicated with her eyes.

"Okay. This looks like a purposeful diversion. Leave a couple of your staff to pick up this mess. Position yourself south of the corset area, behind one of your dress racks, where you can clearly watch her" Ricky noticed Frank, the men's clothing salesman. "I'll get Frank to watch the kid, so he doesn't run. Now go!"

Walking over to the salesman, he spoke quietly, "Frank, I want you to keep your eyes on that kid in the green jacket. Don't let him out of your sight, and if he tries to run, grab him, and take him to my office. Got it?"

"Yes sir," he replied, advancing closer to the boy.

Ricky stealthily approached the assistant manager of the corset department. "What have we got?"

"We've got a live one. She's the woman over there in the long beige overcoat, just below, and to the right of the Star Designs sign. I've got two independent confirmations that she's stuffed several corsets and bras into pockets in that coat. She's definitely our shoplifter."

"Okay. I want you to circle around and get an elevator on stand-by. Be sure the doors are kept open and tell any customers or personnel that we need to check the elevator, so it is temporarily out of use."

Noticing the elevator arriving, Ricky walked over to Ray, "We've got two witnesses that confirm the woman in the long coat has got stuff hidden in the pockets. You grab her, and take her into the waiting elevator, and I'll get her kid who caused the disturbance, and meet you there."

Ray and Ricky both arrived at the waiting elevator, with a protesting mother and frightened child. They proceeded to the fifth-floor security where the mother was secluded in "the box," and the child was taken to Tony's office.

"Another one? That's three shoplifters already today and it's not even lunch hour yet," Tony remarked lazily to Ray.

EATON'S – During the Second French Revolution

"We're just here to serve, boss," Ray replied.

"Yeah. Yeah. I've been in "the box" twice already, Ray, you handle the woman and I'll quiz the kid."

"On asking her to give up the goods, she put four corsets and seven bras on the table, about one hundred plus buck's worth, so this shouldn't take too long, boss."

Ray headed for the investigation room, while Tony gently closed the door to his office. "You want an ice cream bar, son?"

The kid's eyes lit up in surprise, expecting a reprimand. Instead. "Yessss, Sir," he responded, with quivering lips.

"Get this young man a bar from the fridge, Ricky," indicating the small portable refrigerator/freezer kept by the file cabinet.

"What's your name, son?" Tony removed the paper from the bar, before handing it to the boy.

"Mario." he replied. "Mario Petrosa," he added with a mouth full of vanilla ice cream.

"And did you knock over the gumball machine?"

"Nooo, sir. It was an accident. I was running to see Momma and I accidentally bumped into it. I'm sorry. Am I going to jail?"

"No, Mario. You are not going to jail, but I need you to answer my questions honestly. Did anyone tell you to knock over the gumball machine," Tony asked, looking to Ricky.

"No sir. It was an accident," he replied, the melting ice cream dripping down his right arm.

"Do you know that your momma is in trouble for stealing lots of lady's underwear? That could happen to you too, Mario."

"No, she can't go to jail. She must take care of me. My Uncle Vinney told me."

Both Tony and Ricky reacted, in surprise, to this significant revelation.

"Who is this, Vinney?"

"He's Momma's cousin, and he said that Momma would never go to jail. He promised me. He promised," the boy repeated, as his tears began to flow heavily, his ice cream bar now forgotten.

"If you help me, Mario, maybe we can stop Momma from going to jail. Do you want to help me, son?" Tony retrieved tissues from his desk.

"I don't want Momma to go to jail," he was now sobbing in gasps.

Tony handed the tissues to the boy. "Then, you must trust me to help you save Momma." Tony ruffled Mario's head of curly black hair.

Mario just stared at Tony, his eyes full of hope.

"Now, tell me about Uncle Vinney."

"He has a big car and sometimes he drives Momma to go shopping."

"You mean like, shopping for food?"

"No, never for food, only down here, for shopping."

"What else can you tell me about Uncle Vinney?"

"Sometimes we go to his big office, and I ride my bike all around, but I never, never, get lost. Momma says she always gotta see me."

"And what would Uncle Vinney do if Momma goes to jail?"

"Momma can't go to jail, says Uncle Vinney," the boy responded, again agitated. "Uncle Vinney 'tol us that the man would save Momma, so she wouldn't go to jail."

Both Tony and Ricky again perked up at the boy's statement.

"What man is going to save Momma, son?"

"I don't know his name."

"Okay son. That's enough for now," Tony pressed the intercom button. "Agatha, can you bring this young man to your office and get him another ice cream bar, while I talk with Mister Dean."

"Got it handled, Mister Cartwright," Agatha replied, quickly entering Tony's office, and ushering the boy to hers."

"What are you thinkin' Tony?" Ricky asked, with a puzzled expression on his face.

"Geez, Ricky, we are onto something big here. I think the shit is about to hit the fan. When Ray comes in here, we didn't get anything out of the kid, okay?"

Meanwhile in the interrogation room, Ray calmly addressed the woman sitting at the table filled with stolen merchandise. "Your name is Alena Petrosa, right?"

Alena looked shocked that Ray knew her name. "Yes. How do you know my name?"

"I am Ray Archambault. Do you know who I am?"

"Yes, my cousin Vinney told me that Ray Archambault would be the man at the store who would help me if I ever got caught."

"Okay then, I'm gonna help you. So, let's hear your good reason for stealing all this stuff, while I take notes, for the 'record!'"

She quickly recited a prepared speech. "Several years ago, my husband was killed with special Canadian forces in South Africa. We were only given a small pension, and because of Mario's age, only seven, I am unable to get a job. We have limited money for food and our rent is two months past due. I am sorry for what I've done! Now, I'm supposed to show a lot of tears and emotion."

"That's good, but, if anyone else questions you, you better be a lot more convincing, than that list you just narrated."

"Don't worry. I can handle it simply fine. I got nailed at Holt-Renfew, back in March, and had their investigator almost in tears when I told him the same story," she gave a mischievous smile.

"Just don't be so cocky! This isn't Holt-Renfrew. My boss, is an ex-New York cop!" Ray stated, exiting "the box," and heading for Tony's office.

"Did you get anything out of the kid," Ray asked, taking a seat across from Tony.

"Nada. He insists knocking over the gumball machine was just an accident and I can't get him to budge on his story."

"Well, maybe he's telling the truth," Ricky threw in.

"I didn't do much better with the mother," Ray offered. "She claims this was a one-time thing, and she's got a sad story to support it. Dead husband, low-income pension, no food for the kid, rent past due, the usual crap we've heard a thousand times. I've scared her about losing her kid when she goes to jail because her theft was over a hundred dollars, making it a felony. She became a basket case and vowed she would never do it again. I believe we should just kick her and the kid, loose, with the promise that she'll never return to the store. But of course, the decision is yours, boss. That's just my recommendation."

"So, you don't see any possible ties to our 'Liftermob' case?"

"Not at all. She's just some poor mother trying to support her kid. Believe me, she doesn't have the brains to be part of any gang."

"Okay then. You've got all her details for your incident report," Tony pointed to Ray's note pad, "including a clear description, and factual name and address?"

Ray nodded.

"Okay then, take their pictures, kick them loose, and escort them out of the store."

Ray exited Tony's office. Then Tony put his fingers to his lips, signaling Ricky not to say a word.

As they watched the mother and child, led by Ray, leave the security office, Tony chimed, "I think I have just experienced an Epiphany moment."

"Christ Tony, have you ever actually been in a church?"

"Don't test me, Ricky. I was born a Catholic, and they say I'll die a Catholic. The time in between is all mine," he laughed. "Anyway, what I'm crowing about is that I think I've uncovered the answer to our 'Liftermob' crimes, and maybe a confirmation of what I've suspected for a long time."

"Oh yeah, that makes it so much clearer, Tony."

"Bear with me, Pilgram. Since Appleton appointed you to be the liaison between security and management, I need to recruit you to assist me in a delicate investigation."

Ricky hesitated, "Why me? Why not Denis, he's your number two?"

"In short, in this instance, I don't know who I can trust in my department. Is that clear enough, for you?"

"All right, mystery man. What do you want from me?"

"I need you to take this file down to your office." Tony unlocked his bottom desk drawer and retrieved a large brown accordion folder. "I've already been over the files numerous times, but I want you to carefully scrutinize them for anything you think looks, shall we say, out of the ordinary. Anything at all."

Ricky peered at the name on the outside of the folder, and with a surprised look, "these are Ray's incident reports. Can you give me some clue as to what I'm looking for? You realize that these reports are foreign to me, since I have limited knowledge of the procedures that you have in place for your detectives."

"Believe me, Ricky, if what I believe has happened, is actual fact, you will readily discover it. I'll meet with you at the Astor Grill after closing."

"Okay, I'll be there," Ricky responded, hugging the file close to his body so that the name could not be seen. He then made his way downstairs to his office.

Ricky locked the door behind him and called Duane to take over floor duty for the rest of the day. He carefully laid the incident reports out on his desk, and then sorted them by month.

For the next two hours, Ricky read and re-read the reports, making notes as he went along. There was a pattern developing, but until he had more information from Tony, his evaluations were unsubstantiated. This could all be explained away by the detective procedures that Tony had in place for his staff.

At a little after six, Ricky found Tony sitting at a large booth in the back of the Astor Grill. As he headed towards Tony's booth, the owner, Armand Lefance, corralled Ricky by the register. "Mister Dean, it's so good to see you. It's been a while."

"Yeah, I've been pretty busy Armand. I'm pleased to see that you got your business up and running after the riots.

"Yes, praise the Lord. We only had small damage, and no one was hurt."

"Good. I'll talk to you later, Armand." Ricky continued towards the booth where Tony sat. "Whew, what a friggin' day. I'm starved and I need a drink desperately," Ricky slid into the booth. "Do you need a coffee refill, Tony?"

"I'm good," he replied as the waiter showed up.

"Just one greyhound, Hans," Ricky ordered from his regular waiter.

"Yes, Sir, Mister Ricky, and a refill for Mister Tony?"

"No, just for me. Thanks Hans."

"So, what have you got for me," Tony asked sounding impatient.

"Maybe something, maybe nothing. I'll tell you my thinking and you tell me if they can all be explained away, okay?"

"Go for it?"

Ricky reviewed his notes. "The files you gave me covered the last three months. From what I could see, the dialogue of Ray's incident reports looked perfectly normal, with nothing strange jumping out at me. When I reviewed his reports against the analysis sheet you included, his apprehension record seemed outstanding. And, although a 'red flag' went up because his 'cleared cases,' also seemed high, I figured out that with a high apprehension number, those closed without further action, or just closed by letting the shoplifter go, would probably be just as high. That's where I decided to do the math. Where my interest was piqued was when I ran a percentage total of 'cleared cases' against his apprehensions. Ray's percentage was way out of whack. He was more than fifteen percent higher than any of your other detectives. Because of that, I again analyzed the contents of each of his 'cleared cases'. That's where I discovered that almost all of those who received their 'get out of jail free' card from Ray, were people with Italian names, or at the least foreign names. That's too much of a coincidence. My conclusion is that Ray has some serious explaining to do. Am I wrong?"

"You are not wrong, my young investigator," Tony beamed. "You've confirmed my suspicions, without even seeing the other hard evidence that I have."

"Okay, so you have a problem of Ray being too easy on people, and for some reason being sympathetic to Italians. The reports show that Ray is one of your best detectives, so as I see it, you need to smack his wrist and tell him to straighten up, eh?"

"Ah, the innocence of youth," Tony responded, reaching into his briefcase, and producing a tape recorder. "I taped Ray's interrogation of that Alena woman earlier today, so you need to listen to this, without interruption."

"You bugged 'the box'?" Ricky exclaimed.

"Just shut up and listen," Tony commanded, pressing the 'play' button, as he adjusted the volume so only the two of them could easily hear the recording.

Ricky just sat there stunned, as he digested the revelations of the entire interrogation. When the recording was completed, he just sat speechless.

Tony gave him a minute to comprehend what he had just heard.

"Whoa! I sure as hell didn't see that coming. What would make him turn like that?" Ricky finally asked, taking a large swallow of his greyhound.

"It's always either women, booze or money, but I think it's money." Tony raised his hand, signaling for another round of drinks.

"After you left, I went through Ray's locker and found several notes about hockey odds, and an 'odds maker' publication. It's a black book that looks like a ledger of wins and losses, with minus numbers into the thousands of dollars and a phone number of a laundromat which, I'll bet, is his bookie's number."

"Now that you know all this are you going to bring Denis into it?"

"I can't bring anyone in until I know how wide scale, or how deep, this is in my department," Tony replied.

"Thanks, Hans," Ricky acknowledged the new round of drinks. Then, he asked Tony, "So, Is your next step to have a little chat with Ray?"

"Yes, but I need to do it 'off the grid', until I have the full story. If someone sees me grilling Ray in my office, this could spook them into running. And, if there are more traitors in my midst, I want to get every one of these sons of bitches."

"If you want, you can use Jeremy's office, since he's at the Macy's conference in New York. I can arrange to get everyone out of the office area for as long as you need."

"That would be great, Ricky, but I'd like you there to be a witness and play 'good cop' to my 'bad cop.' Also, you can handle the recorder because I want every word this creep says on tape."

"I can do that."

"I'll tell Ray that you have a security issue that we need to discuss at ten-thirty tomorrow morning. We can meet in the luncheonette at nine forty-five, to go over our strategy."

"I'll be there," Ricky responded, glancing at his watch. He picked up his drink and gulped it down, then he reached for a twenty, but Tony stopped him.

"Drinks are on me. If we solve this, then you can buy!"

They both laughed. Ricky put on his overcoat, "Sorry, I've got to run, or I'll miss my train home."

"Thanks again," Tony replied. "See you tomorrow!"

⚜ Forty-Eight ⚜

Because of the scheduled meeting with Ray and Tony, Ricky had taken an earlier train so he could get some department chores completed before they arrived. But, as fate would have it, his train was delayed in Mount Royal tunnel due to an electrical failure. So, instead of being early, he arrived at the store just as the opening bell rang.

After placing his coat in his office, he made his way to the selling floor, scanning for any department heads. He spotted Christine in her fashion department struggling to move a large mannequin display. "Here, let me help you."

"Thanks. It turned out to be heavier than I thought."

"Have you seen any of the senior managers, this morning?"

"I saw Duane disappear into the lower stockroom. Mrs. Rousseau was back by the ladieswear changing rooms and I saw Andrea Bardot heading for the luncheonette, can I help?"

"Yes, I need you to tell Mrs. Rousseau that she has the floor until one o'clock. I'm going to be unavailable until this afternoon, and I've notified the switchboard, in case I am needed. Also, for anyone who asks, the accounting staff will be working in the seventh-floor billing office today. So, until further notice, the basement offices will be *off limits* to all personnel. I need you to convey that message to all department managers, okay?"

"Sure, but very mysterious" she hesitated, with noticeable concern in her eyes, "is everything all right?"

"Yes, it's just a security issue that I need to work out with Mister Cartwright. It's nothing for you to be concerned about." With that said, Ricky headed for the luncheonette.

Steve Fortuna caught up with him as he neared the luncheonette area. "Thank you for advising the management group about employees clearing their tables. It seems to be working out fine."

"No problem, Steve," Ricky responded, smiling at the briefness of the conversation.

When he entered the luncheonette, he saw that Tony was already seated in a booth. Ricky grabbed a coffee and bagel, paid the cashier, and headed towards Tony's booth. He stopped at a table where Andrea Bardot was concentrating on a breakfast of eggs and pancakes. "Hi, Andrea, when you finish could you catch up with Christine to review a few instructions I gave her?"

"Sure thing, Mister Dean. By the way, we got the new register area installed, and it's working out much better. There's no possibility of anyone touching the register from that far away, thanks to your help."

"I'm here to please, Andrea," he laughed, continuing towards Tony.

"Hey, you brought your own chair because you think we can't afford extra chairs in our basement offices," Ricky kidded, pointing to a folding chair leaning against the booth.

"That my young friend is my 'intimidation chair'. It's an interrogation trick I learned from my 'rabbi' training officer, in New York."

"So, now you're going to tell me you're a Jewish boy with a rabbi?" Ricky bit into his bagel, sipped his coffee and lit a cigarette in a few fluid motions.

"No time for humor, my young friend. And, just for clarification, a 'rabbi' training officer is a senior member of the police force that takes a rookie under their wing."

"I'm sorry, Tony," Ricky stifled a laugh, "I just have a hard time visualizing an old fart like you ever being a rookie."

"Back to my 'intimidation chair' explanation." Tony ignored the comment. "There is a whole psychology developed by Columbia University connected with its use. The front legs of the chair have been cut about an inch lower than the rear. When the subject sits in the chair, they are totally uncomfortable and constantly trying to figure out why. This puts the subject mentally on edge and makes them more apt to slip up in an interrogation. It's great to watch as the interrogation progresses. The subject, while concentrating on the chair, gets more and more agitated, and eventually blurts out something they hadn't planned to. You'll see it happen today."

"Okay, I'll take your word for it," Ricky responded, obviously not convinced of the psychology of the chair. "So, what's the plan?"

"I told Ray that you had a security issue with one of your stock people, and I wanted him to handle it. Also, I had a contact at MPD check out the telephone numbers I found in Ray's locker and found out that I was right. Both numbers are to known downtown bookies. One is connected to the Westies Family, and the other is an independent, connected to some new kid on the block." Tony pulled a tape recorder and tapes from his briefcase. "I want you to handle the recorder so that I can concentrate on the interrogation. The tapes are only 30 minutes each, so you'll have to be careful to watch the changeover."

"Okay. What else do you want me to do?"

"As I told you, last night, I need you to play the 'good cop' to my 'bad cop'. What that means is that you are going to feign protecting Ray. You are going to show that you're upset when I come down too hard on him, and you're going to show him compassion and understanding, especially when it comes out why he did what he did. He must be made to feel he has an ally in the room, or he'll close up totally. Remember, Ray's been in the military, and trained by the QPP, not to mention that I also trained him, for that matter. He is not going to crack easily. He knows interrogation tactics, and he knows how to skirt them. I need to get to the bottom of this before Appleton cans *my* ass."

"I'll get your *magic chair* set up in Jeremy's office. Do you want the recorder hidden or in plain view?"

"Closest to where you position the chair," Tony replied. "Does Jeremy's door have a deadbolt on it."

"He sure does, and I've got a key. I think Jeremy's paranoid that someone is going to steal his Playboy collection," Ricky joked, grabbing the chair, and the recorder, as he headed back to the office. "I'll see you at ten thirty."

After Ricky took care of the chair and recorder, he headed back out onto the selling floor. On his way he saw Jerry Copeland in menswear and stopped to talk.

"Jerry, do you remember Mister Grant from Rosemount High?"

"Yeah, we had him for English literature in tenth grade, didn't we?" Jerry continued to straighten the tie rack near the men's suits.

"Yeah, but you won't believe this, he finally got busted."

"What for being ugly in a no ugly zone. Christ, that guy had a face like Boris Karloff, and the personality of a toaster," Jerry laughed.

"No, he got tagged by MPD for molesting a junior in his car, two blocks away from school. Didn't you ever hear the rumors about him?"

Jerry thought for a few moments. "Yeah, now that I think of it, a lot of the kids used to call him a gearbox. They'd say he was 'queerer than a three-dollar bill'. I remember that he used to have parties at his house on thirty-sixth street and invite all the juniors to attend. So, what comes next? First, we had to watch out for the horny priests trying to get into our pants, now we have the damn teachers, too!"

"Now, aren't you glad you became a merchandiser instead of a friggin' priest or a teacher." Ricky laughed. "I thought that you'd enjoy the news."

EATON'S – During the Second French Revolution

Ricky returned to his office where he cleared his mail, reviewed his phone messages, made a fresh pot of coffee, and scanned the morning Gazette for his department ads.

He picked up the telephone and dialed the sundries and notions department.

"Mister Dean for Mister Stevens, please." He straightened his desk as he waited.

"Stevens, how may I help you?"

"Bobby, Ricky here. Did you review the Gazette ad before publication?"

"Yeah, I've got it right here, why?" he asked concerned.

"Do you see the ad for Band-Aids and Kleenex?"

"Yeah, the sale prices are right, and the pictures look great. What's the problem?"

"Look at the picture for the Band-Aids."

"Okay, so?"

"Read me what is says on the front of the box in the picture."

"Chem-lab Band-Aids, plastic strips, twenty-four count, and, oh, shit."

"I don't think it says, 'oh shit', but yeah. The ad is screwed for both items, and you can be sure we are going to be hearing from the Johnson and Johnson lawyers, once again, for infringement of their trademark name. These are not Band-Aids and Kleenex, they are bandages and tissues, made by a competitor."

"Jesus, Ricky, Radford's going to have a cow. This is the second time we've let this slip by us. How do I make it right?"

"I suggest you lick your lips and call up the Johnson and Johnson attorney and be ready to kiss a whole lot of asses. It'll be much better if you call them before they call us, don't you think?"

Bobby hesitated. "Maybe they won't see the ad since it's only in for one day."

"Yeah! Just like your wife won't notice lipstick on your pant zipper. Get real, Bobby. They have a whole bloody department that does nothing else but watch every ad, in every paper, just looking for trademark infringements. How the hell do you think these law offices get so huge?"

"You're right. I'll call them right away."

"Let me know how you make out." Ricky hung up the telephone as he looked at his watch and headed for Radford's office.

At promptly 10:30, Ray arrived with Tony following closely behind, roughly brushing passed him, as he dropped into Jeremy's ergo-comfort executive chair. "Take a seat, Ray," Tony commanded, pointing to the *magic chair* that Ricky had positioned on the opposite side of the desk.

"Yeah, thanks." He straightened his pant creases, as he sat down. "How 'ya doing, Ricky. I hear you have a stockman who may be cutting into Eaton's profits," he laughed?

"Let's cut the small talk, Ray, this meeting is about you," Tony began. "Do you have anything that you want to get off your chest?"

"Me? No. What do you mean, Tony, have I done something wrong?" he questioned, glancing between Ricky and Tony. "Why am I here?"

"Tell me about Alena Petrosa."

"What do you mean? She was the broad who boosted the lingerie yesterday. I interrogated her, and we kicked her loose, as you approved."

"Correction *you* kicked her loose. The question is what is the real reason why you suggested that we kick her loose?"

"I told you before I did it. We kick hundreds of people loose, under the same circumstances. Is my performance in question? I'm your top producer, and I never give you any grief, so what's going on here, Tony?"

Tony nodded to Ricky who inserted a tape then pressed the *pause* button on the recorder.

"Did you know Alena Petrosa before yesterday?"

"Of course not. She's just some skank that I collared. But I followed all our procedures to the letter." He pointed at the recorder, "And what's with that thing?"

"As they say, that is for our listening enjoyment." Tony nodded at Ricky, who pressed the *play* button on the recorder.

As Ray's and Alena's voices boomed from the small recorder. Ray's face washed to a ghostly white, he clenched his knuckles as he struggled to not slip off the metal seated chair. Part way through the recording Ray slowly and deliberately reached for the recorder, pressed the *stop* button. "How? How long have you been taping me?" Ray stammered, his eyes misting with tears. "How, how long have you known?"

Tony slammed his hand down hard on the wooden desk, sending shock waves throughout the tiny office. "Shut up, you miserable coward! You know our interrogation techniques; I ask the questions, and 'you' answer them," Tony yelled, getting up from the desk, and waving a menacing fist in front of Ray's trembling face. "I hired you when I knew that your head was screwed up; I took you under my wing and trained you to be a great detective; I accommodated you when you needed time off for medical purposes; and I invited you and your family into my home, as friends! And what do I get for that, a traitor who stabs me in the back and jeopardizes *my* future?"

"I'm so, so sorry, Tony. It just got out of hand, and, well, uh, then, I was in so deep I couldn't bail out," he whimpered, as Tony settled back into his chair trying to get his anger under control.

"Let's hear what Ray has to say, Tony," Ricky pleaded. "At least give him a chance to explain himself!"

"Okay, okay!" Tony relented, calmly leaning towards Ray. "Here is what is going to happen. Number one, I'm going to ask you questions, and you are going to answer them. Number two, you're going to give me the complete story without me having to drag it out of you. And Number three," Tony's voice raised several decibels, "if you once sprout any lies, I'm going to come across this desk and drive your head through that wall. Are we clear?"

"Yes Tony," Ray replied in almost a whisper, his both hands now grasping the metal chair seat to lessen his forward sliding motion.

"I didn't hear you, Ray," Tony challenged.

"Yes, I understand, Tony," Ray replied louder.

"We've determined," Tony began, pointing at the recorder, "that you somehow knew Petrosa beforehand. How do you know her?"

"I saw her and her kid, when I met with several of her associates about four months ago."

"Knock off the shit of 'associates', you're in the security business call them what they are, criminals," he commanded, again positioning a finger into Ray's face.

Ricky easily recognized Tony's tactic of showing rage, then controlled calm, constantly keeping Ray off balance.

"Sorry, sorry, Tony, yes, criminals," an expression of fear flashed across Ray's face. "I met them at an old warehouse on Des Jardins Street, by the railway tracks, in Montreal east."

"Why were you meeting them? Who arranged the meeting, and how many were there?"

"There were twenty-three total in the gang, and ..."

Tony interrupted, "are we talking about our 'Liftermob' Gang?"

"Yes sir." Ray continued. "The meeting was called by a guy named Marcus Castille, he schedules all the shoplifters to specific areas and directs which particular merchandise to pilfer, oh, sorry, I mean steal," he quickly corrected. "He runs his crew with military precision. He doesn't participate in the shoplifting stuff because he has his own extortion con running on major stores."

"Wait a minute. Isn't Castille the guy you had in 'the box' a few weeks back, the wallet guy?" Ricky asked Tony.

But Ray answered. "One, and the same. Denis told me about the interrogation of the wallet guy, named Conti, so I didn't put it together. But I heard Vinney tearing Marcus down 'cause he got caught. He was really pissed off about that."

"I thought this Marcus guy was the leader, who is Vinney?" Tony questioned.

"The whole operation is Vinney's. He runs the numbers, truck jacking, merchant protection, a few robberies, and this shoplifting racket. He's a *made* guy."

"By *made* guy, you mean he's part of one of the mobs?"

"Not exactly. He became a *made guy* by killing someone for the family. He was bounced from his own family and started his own operation, unbeknownst to the capo."

"And you got sucked in because you owe this Vinney's book operation lots of money?"

"Yes," Ray dropped his head in shame.

"How much are you into them for?"

"Sixteen thousand, three hundred dollars, as off my last payment. But no matter how much of a payment I make I can't seem to exceed the 'vig'."

"What's the 'vig'? Ricky quizzed Tony.

"The 'vig' is the interest on a loan to a bookie. It's common to not pay back the principle, but you must pay the "vig" weekly to keep your legs intact. The 'vig' in no way lowers the principle. This lets the loan sharks get their 'hooks into you' and you'll probably be paying it off far longer than planned. If you ever finally pay off the principle, with the vig, you'll find that you paid double, triple or more, than you originally borrowed. Only suckers get involved with loan sharks," Tony responded, directly to Ray. "What's this Vinney guys full name and what family was he originally from?" Tony demanded.

"His name is Vinney "The Trunk" Calabrisee, and he was from the Calabrisee family, of which Carmine is the *Capo* and Giuseppe, Vinney's father, is the *Consigliere*. They bounced Vinney out several years ago because his criminal escapades were giving them too much negative exposure. He was supposed to keep his activities off Montreal island."

"Have you met directly with this Vinney?"

"Yes, several times. He thinks he's God's gift to woman, and smarter than his uncle and father. He can be really dangerous."

"Is the warehouse on Des Jardins Street his?" Tony asked.

"Yes."

"Tell me about the warehouse, how it's laid out and its contents."

"It's huge, maybe twenty-five to thirty thousand square feet. There are two large rollups at the front, big enough to drive a semi-trailer inside, and a single rollup in the back, exiting onto a loading dock, adjacent to the railroad tracks. The inside is empty of any rooms except for one that has sleeping quarters, a kitchen and combo bath shower. Other than that, Vinney has his large old desk positioned in the middle of the floor, so he can see all the entry areas. His desk is surrounded by four or five new sofas, which Frankie jokes 'fell offa da truck'. There are several folding chairs stacked against the closest column to Vinney's desk."

"What's the warehouse used for, beside his office, and what else is inside?" Tony prompted.

"I know Vinney has it so he can coordinate the activities of his group, but, Ray cringed, "I've seen blood stains on the concrete floor in several places where, I believe, he conducts certain disciplines with rivals, and people who get out of line. He's one scary guy! As for the warehouse contents, they constantly change. Right now, there are two tractor portions of a semi, one very new and one that looks like a scrap antique, a large box truck, and several cars, some stripped, some ready to be repainted. Oh, and there was a dark blue truck by the loading dock that looked a lot like one of our Eaton's delivery trucks. As for merchandise, there are several boxes of sportswear and clothing that I noticed was addressed to some distributor in Hamilton, Ontario, over a hundred different ornate mirrors, large cartons of tobacco products, and two racks of ladies' fur coats. That's about it."

"Hold on a minute," Ricky said, as he ejected the old tape to insert a new one. "Okay, go ahead."

"Describe the ladies coats," Tony directed, moving intimidatingly close to Ray.

Ray hesitated, "They're, well, uh ..." but, he never finished.

"You goddamn piece of shit!" Tony shouted, as he jumped up from his chair and propelled Ray head-first into the wall, where he silently slid to the floor. "Those coats are the furs that were stolen last month, aren't they?" Tony didn't wait for him to answer. "You son of a bitch! I should take you downstairs and put my bloody thirty-eight in your mouth and blow your brains out! I told you not to screw with me."

Ricky was shocked. He had never seen this side of Tony. He grabbed Tony and pushed him back to his chair, then offered a hand to Ray. Ray was dazed as he tried to get back in the chair and not slip off. "Give him a break, he's trying. There's a lot to tell, and he's bound to have trouble telling us some things.

"Roughing him up is not going to solve anything."

Ray looked thankfully at Ricky, while trying to get it all together, again.

"The creep is not forgetting, Ricky, he's purposely withholding, there's a big friggin' difference. And you my friend," Tony pointed an accusing finger at Ricky, "are here strictly as a witness, so stop cozying up to this punk and get out of my face, or get the hell out," Tony winked at Ricky.

With calm restored Ray continued, "Honestly Tony I didn't know anything about it until I walked into the warehouse and saw the furs on the rack. The whole robbery was a big joke to Vinney and Frankie. They bragged about how easy it was and how stupid our employees are."

"Who's this Frankie character?"

"He's Vinney's number two man and I guess he would be considered Vinney's *Consigliere*. He's much older than Vinney, acts like his father, oh, and he also was bounced from the Calabrisee family." Ray hesitated, as tears welled up in his eyes. "What's going to happen to me, Tony. I can't go to jail. Brenda and little Roger will never survive without me."

"As I'm sure you've said many times to perps, 'if you can't do the time, don't do the crime'." Tony recited, with a smug look on his face.

"Tony, if I may," Ricky interjected, reaffirming his role of 'good cop'. "Ray, you allowed yourself to fall into a septic tank, how you get out of the shit is entirely up to you. At this point, if you don't accept a helping hand, and get yourself out of this, you're going to sink deeper and deeper."

"I know," Ray mumbled, "I'll do anything I can to assist, but somewhere down the line I'm going to need protection for my family."

"What do mean by protection for your family? How are they involved?" Tony asked, for the first time, showing some actual compassion for Ray.

Ray shifted in the chair, trying to place his weight on one hip, to solve his uncomfortable sitting problem. "Four months ago, before I got dragged into Vinney's operation, I was two weeks behind in my 'vig' and Vinney sent this big bastard, Aldo Renaldi, to my house in Longueil. He's built like a linebacker with a big ugly scar running from his eye to his chin. Thankfully, my wife and kid were out. Anyway, Aldo says that I've been behind before in my 'vig' and Vinney told him to teach me that, *in his words*, 'time is money'. I told him to take anything he wanted in the house, but he told me that that's not part of the lesson, then, he beat the shit out of me. You remember, Tony, I called in sick for eight days.

Tony nodded, engrossed in Ray's revelations.

"Then, after the beating, with me puking all over the living room carpet, he says that if I don't help Vinney out, 'with a little problem', he'd be back to break my little Roger's legs. To prove that he was serious, as he was leaving, he drove his truck up on my front lawn, purposely rode over Roger's new bicycle. I was scared shitless, for my family."

"So, how did Vinney finally get you involved in his shoplifting scheme?" Ricky asked, fascinated by the developments of the conversation.

"While I was recuperating, Frankie called and told me that Vinney wanted to see me at the warehouse. I met him and Vinney who was all apologetic, telling me that Aldo had gone too far with the beating, and that he was just supposed to scare me, which, I knew, was not true. Then, he says, as a matter of fact, that I was now part of his team, and if I cooperated fully, no harm would come to my little boy, *Roger*. He made a special point of emphasizing Roger's name, and even asking how he liked his Cascade Elementary School. I told him that I was not going to be involved in any stealing for him, and he assured me that mine was to be strictly 'a supporting role'. If any of his crew got caught, I was, to ensure that they walked, or got off with a slap on the wrist."

"Did you receive any goods, or free services, from Vinney, or did he ever pay you anything?" Tony asked.

"Never! Never, I swear, Tony. He never even offered to ease up on my 'vig' payments. I've been able to keep up on the 'vig', and even pay back some of the principle, by working part time, as a bouncer at the Verdun Brasserie. There was no way I was going to jeopardize my family, or endure another beating," Ray sighed.

"How many of the 'Liftermob' can you identify?" Tony asked in a much more pleasant voice.

"By name, probably fifteen or sixteen out of the twenty-three. All of them by sight, I guess, if I put my mind to it."

"Good. That's good. This Aldo guy, is he the enforcer for Vinney's operation?"

"I think he does both the enforcing and leads the robberies for Vinney. A few weeks ago, when I was there, he came into the warehouse with two boxes of Timex watches. I think he knows Vinney for a long time because Vinney told him it was 'just like old times, when they ripped off the principal's office at Rosemount High.'"

"Shit. Shit. Shit. I've had my head up my own ass. I know these guys, both Vinney, and Aldo," Ricky shouted. "I friggin' went to school with them. Vinney went under the name of Vincent, or Vince Caleb. I now realize that the Caleb was short for Calabrisee. And Aldo went by James, or Jimmy Renald instead of Renaldi. These guys were bad dudes in school, and everyone was petrified of them. They ran a protection racket against the juniors, offering them protection to and from home, for just one dollar per week. Incredibly, no one ever turned them in." Ricky thought for a minute and then added, "Damn it, I just realized something else important, but I need to talk to you privately, outside, Tony." Ricky rose from his chair.

"Wait a minute," Tony raised his hand, "if it's a continuation of what we've been discussing, I want Ray to hear it. He's still part of my team."

"But Tony." Ricky protested.

"Ray's going to have to make amends for what he's done, but you must admit that circumstances have now changed. After hearing what he had to say, we need to help him, and in turn, he needs to help us. We can't go forward without him, so he must be privy to all the pertinent details. So, go ahead and say what you were going to say."

For the first time since the interrogation began, Ray relaxed. "Thank you, Tony. I promise this time I won't let you down!"

"Do me a favor Ricky, get him a decent chair. I'm tired of watching him squirm.".

"Yeah, please," Ray responded, "what's wrong with that bloody chair anyway, it looks okay, but I've felt like I was going to slide out of it for the last hour."

"Don't ask," Ricky laughed, drawing up a nice, padded chair for Ray.

"So, Ricky, what's this important stuff that you have?"

"Well Tony, about a month ago I saw this guy getting off the University Street bank elevator, noticeably struggling with the English language, as he talked with the operator. I thought I recognized him, but he was too well dressed for someone I'd know," he laughed. "Anyway, this guy had graying temples, slicked back, pitch black hair and a grayish mustache, and he was trying unsuccessfully to translate Italian into English, but I didn't give it any more thought than that, until just now. The guy was, without a doubt, Vinney Calabrisee."

"So, you saw Vinney. Why is that so important to what we're discussing?" Tony asked.

"Don't you see! You have a known hood, in disguise, casing our basement cash office. I watched him go back into where the customer wickets are and he must have been transacting something, 'cause he was there for a long time. The guy is planning a bloody heist!"

"That's what it must be," Ray jumped in. "Vinney, Frankie, and Aldo have all been joking about the 'big score', but none of the 'Liftermobs' know anything about it. In fact, I heard Vinney say, and I quote, 'we're going to beat our own *record*, with this score'."

"So," Tony realized quickly, "what that means is that they're probably going to hit the cash office during our Record-Breaking Sale, next month. This has just gone from a single problem to a total nightmare. We're going to have to move on this fast."

"Tony, please, let me help," Ray pleaded, "I need to get back in your good graces, even if I still have to go to jail. I am so ashamed of myself."

Ray took a moment to contain himself, and then continued, "I can still be of value to you. They don't know I've been made, and since I just helped Alena get off, they probably still trust me. I can keep gathering information until you're ready to take these guys down. I can also try to get all the names of the shoplifters, and keep my ears peeled for Vinney's movement towards his 'big score' and, I can even get a better layout of the warehouse if you decide to have him taken down there. Unless someone knows what's inside that warehouse, people could die."

"What do you mean 'what's inside'?

"Vinney's got the whole warehouse booby trapped. I told you he has two semi-trailer tractors, well, the old one has a one-hundred-gallon gas tank that is rigged with some kind of igniter. He's also positioned all his contraband around the perimeter of the tractor, so if the tractor goes up, so does all his stuff. He jokes 'let them try to take the ashes to court'."

"Okay, that sounds great Ray, but it's still extremely dangerous. We'll have to work out a game plan to keep you as safe as possible."

Ray needed to clarify his position, and asked sheepishly, "In the meantime what do I do about working here?"

"For now, you are going to continue with your regular duties, No one, and I mean *no one*, but the three of us are to know what was discussed here. When I'm ready we can bring in other parties. You guys got that?"

EATON'S – During the Second French Revolution

Both Ricky and Ray nodded.

"Oh, and if we apprehend any more of the 'Liftermobs,' you need to handle them the same way this Vinney character told you to, but with one big difference. Each time you kick one loose, you will fill us in immediately. No more holding back, Ray. Got it?""

Ray digested that for a moment. "Yeah, but I don't understand. You mean you want me to kick them loose?"

"Yes, if you don't, the gang will get spooked and bolt. But by keeping us in the loop, we can monitor what is going on. Okay, Ray now get back to work, and we'll talk again shortly".

Ray left the office.

"So, what do you think?" Ricky asked.

"Although I fault him for allowing himself to be compromised through his gambling habit, I sympathize with him when it comes to the fact of threats against his family. You noticed that he accepted the beating that laid him up for eight days, but when the threat was leveled against his son, he was ready to cooperate with Vinney. From all my interrogation training, both military and civil, the common 'breaking point' for a victim is generally the threat of harm against a loved one."

"Yeah, you're right. But what impressed me the most was that even with his beating, the threat against his kid and the confrontation with a murderer like Vinney, Ray still insisted that his only involvement was kicking any of the 'Liftermob' gang loose, which is what he does anyway, as a normal part of his job. He didn't accept any payment or even a reduction in his 'vig'. The guy just got caught up and couldn't get out."

"Yeah, what started as a mole hill, ended up as a mountain!" Tony agreed.

"And, a very dangerous mountain, from the sound of it, eh!" Ricky chimed.

⚜ Forty-Nine ⚜

Since Wednesday through Saturday were generally the Eaton "Sale Days," Mondays were great days for cleanup, reorganization and for Ricky, a time to catch up on paperwork, like the regular Saturday Incident Report.

His day began, in the luncheonette, reading The Gazette article concerning the stock exchange bombing. The FLQ were at it again.

The headlines read:

"TERRORISTS BOMB MONTREAL STOCK EXCHANGE"

"The terrorist group FLQ, last week targeted the Montreal Stock Exchange which represents a bastion of Anglo-Canadian power. The FLQ planted and exploded a

highly powerful time bomb that ripped through the heavily crowded Montreal Stock Exchange causing massive destruction and seriously injuring 27 people.

"The Montreal Stock Exchange, MSE is a derivative's exchange, that trades futures, contracts, and options on equities, indices, currencies, energy and interest rates. It is located in the Tour de la Bourse, Stock Exchange Tower, Montreal's third-tallest building. The powerful blast ripped walls open, toppled ceilings, shattered glass, and showered debris over 300 traders on the exchange trading floor More than 50 innocent people in the visitor's gallery were injured, with 7 still hospitalized."

"Reports indicate that minutes before the explosion, which occurred 40 minutes before the 3:00 P.M. closing bell, the Montreal Police Department received an anonymous call saying that an explosive device had been planted in the 47-story building housing The Montreal Stock Exchange on Victoria Square, the heart of the financial district. It was the third such explosion in Montreal and the eighth so far this year. The other explosions happened on Monday and Tuesday of last week and were directed at two Canadian armed forces buildings. Three weeks ago, a similar bomb was discovered in a building across from the stock exchange, outside the offices of a company involved in a language dispute in a small Quebec mining town. A guard threw the explosive down a stairwell just before it exploded.

Although damage and casualties were substantial, Charles Newton, president of the Montreal exchange, advised that regular trading was expected to resume on Tuesday. To remain operational brokers were advised to transact their orders through the Toronto stock exchange. Newton also said that overall damage was extensive, especially to the big electronic board that displays stock quotations. The board was so sophisticated and sensitive that it required dust and humidity control. Aside from building repairs, Mr. Newton said that repairing the board may cost over a million dollars."

Ricky felt enormous anger and threw the paper down on the table. He was getting so tired of the senseless destruction and political anti-English rhetoric heralded in the daily newspapers, TV, and radio.

Ricky was shaken from his depressing thoughts by the familiar Italian accent of *Steve* Fortuna, "Mister Ricky, you look sad today."

"Hey, Steve. No, I'm just fed up with all this separatist crap. It's been going on for years, with no end in sight," he pointed at the newspaper headlines.

"Maybe you just gotta think good thoughts, yes?"

"I try, Steve, I really do try, but every day these FLQ creeps are doing something that makes headlines. Anyway, what can I do for you? Did the pastry oven break down again?"

"No, oven okay, but need another favor from you, please."

"Sure Steve, what do you need."

EATON'S – During the Second French Revolution

"Your Miss Maggie tol me dat we are getting new cash registers and dat you have two for your people to practice. Maybe, I get one for my ladies?"

"Unfortunately, they don't have any extras in supply, but I can let you have one of ours for a few days. Just let me know when you need it."

"Thank you, Mister Ricky. I tell my ladies."

"No problem, Steve." He beamed as he returned to the kitchen.

The luncheonette had been the largest department in area in the basement since the early 1940's. Although much of the major kitchen equipment dated back to that era, the customer service and eating area had been transformed a few years ago. A garden atmosphere with hanging plants, modern tables, chairs, and booths transformed the formerly drab appearance into that of modern artistry. The self-service cafeteria style set-up allowed for easy food selection and rapid check out. The luncheonette was now a speedy alternative to the formal ninth floor dining room.

"I heard you are looking to buy a hearse," chided Randy Ballencourt, dripping his coffee, as he dropped into Ricky's booth.

"Very funny, Randy. Who told you about it?"

"Since I was off last week, I just happened to bump into Nurse Nancy Saunders, you know, the Head Nurse of our wonderful infirmary, and she's bragging about offering you and LeClerke a private 'pulse taking' class," he laughed. "So, what's the real scoop?"

"Okay, as long as you don't embellish the story with your sick humor. It wasn't so funny for the guy involved."

"No promises, good buddy."

"Well, I was doing my normal floor walk last Thursday when suddenly I heard a scream from the north end of the floor and several "eyes on" alarms started sounding. As usual, I'm at the other end of the store, so I rush to where a pile of customers were gathered around a guy lying in the main aisle. This was the third person who had passed out so far, that day." Ricky continued. "Anyway, I get there, clear the gawkers, and find John struggling to remove the guy's coat. Christ, the guy was wearing a heavy nineteen-twenties, or thirties, raccoon skin coat, and I can see he's totally out of it."

"Yeah, I had big woman actually bite the bullet and nosedive into one of my canoes. Now, that was a sight," Randy interrupted."

Ricky ignored him and just continued, "So, I get one of the stock boys to run for a stretcher, or a flatbed cart, and one of the salesgirls to hold an elevator, so we can get the guy upstairs to the infirmary. The kid returns with a wheelchair saying that he couldn't find a stretcher or a flatbed. So, we load this guy into the wheelchair. This isn't easy to do with a person who's fainted. It's just dead weight and the guy weighs a ton."

"Anyway, we get the guy to the elevator, being run by a new, young operator, her first day on the job, and I can see she's totally freaked out."

"She gets us to the eighth floor, opens the door, and John quickly pushes the chair toward the exit only to realize that the elevator is about eight inches below the actual floor level. As John strikes the elevated floor, the guy shoots out of the chair smacking hard on the concrete floor. John goes over the top of the chair landing his two-hundred-and-fifty-pound body on top of the guy, and the young operator begins screaming. Thank goodness Nancy heard the screaming and came running to help the man now lying on the floor under John. John is in a panic thinking he might have killed the guy by landing on him, yelling, 'did I kill him,' 'did I kill him'?"

Randy's body shakes as he is trying hard not to burst out laughing.

"I'm sure this is the part that everyone is chuckling about, even though it's more tragic than funny," Ricky says. "You know Nancy, all business, always serious, she gets up from the floor, looks at the operator who is still whimpering, and tells her to 'shut the hell up'. Then, she looks at John, who is totally distressed, and now sitting on the floor next to the guy. So, she folds her arms and calmly says, 'Don't worry, John, he was dead before you left the basement floor.' With that the operator starts howling again. You had to be there. Anyway, that's the whole story."

"Didn't anyone check his pulse down on the floor?" Randy asked.

"Give me a break, Randy, you know our priority in these situations is to get the subject off the floor and to immediate medical attention."

"Yeah! Yeah, I'm sorry, couldn't help myself," he laughed.

Ricky left Randy, still chuckling as he ate his breakfast, and began his first, floor circuit of the day. He exited the luncheonette into the menswear department, and flagged, Barry Stevens, one of the salesmen, "That broken suit rack has been sitting by the column for over a week, get it off the selling floor, and have someone take it up to display for repair."

"Yes Sir," he sprinted towards the rack.

As he passed the purse counter he pointed to a costume jewelry showcase, "Rosalind, hasn't anyone come to replace that bulb yet?"

"No, Mister Dean. I put in a requisition two weeks ago, called electrical twice, and they still haven't shown up."

"Call them again and tell them that one of our part-timers told us that on Saturday they had smoke coming from the register outlet, and it needs to be looked at right away. Tell them to bring down a four-foot fluorescent showcase bulb, at the same time. Believe me, they'll be here in minutes."

Rosalind looked confused, "but, it's not smoking, Mister Dean."

Ricky winked, "You and I know that, but when they ignore your requests, sometimes we must manufacture a reason for them to do what they should have done in the first place. When they get here, apologize for the misunderstanding, and tell them I looked at it, and it seems fine now. They'll be pissed, but they'll get over it."

"That's awesome, Mister Dean, thank you."

Ricky continued his usual trek to the north end of the store where he was corralled by John LeClerke, "Have you been mouthing off about the dead guy?" he accused.

"Come on, John, you know better than that!"

"Yeah, well, someone's spreading the story around that I was laying on the floor up there, bawling like a baby! Any idea who that could be?"

"Actually, I think I do. I saw Randy Ballencourt while I was having coffee in the luncheonette, and he's all pumped by the dead guy story. I think that he and his fifth-floor cronies are blowing this out of proportion, just to get our goat. They're just getting even for that homo story we spread about Randy, last year, remember?"

"Well, I'm not so sure now that that story wasn't true," John scoffed, heading back into his department.

Trekking back toward his office Ricky passed the purse department, where he noticed an electrician replacing a bulb, "Hey Gus, thanks for taking care of that so quickly."

"No problem, Mister Dean, I'm here to please. By the way, you shouldn't be fooling with the electrical outlets, that's our job, and the brass gets real upset when that happens."

"Got it, Gus. Won't happen again," Ricky smiled at Rosalind.

Before he returned to his office, he made a path to the Teen Department. He spotted Christine with a customer, and displayed a smile, as he kept walking.

Back in his office Ricky reviewed his floor manager incident reports before forwarding them to the general manager's office. It was Ricky's responsibility to go over the daily reports, make any notations and forward them to upper management.

Ricky sat back in his office chair, visions of the Mont Tremblant trip with Christine flooding his mind.

Both he and Christine had had the day off that week. He had picked her up at 8:30, in front of her apartment. It was a beautiful day for a drive and they both had been looking forward to having this private time together.

When he pulled up to the elegant Mont Tremblant Resort, a valet opened the door and took his keys. He in turn went around and helped Christine out. She turned about 360 degrees and smiled joyfully. "I've never been here Ricky; it is truly magnificent."

He took her hand and walked her inside to the lounge area where they sat down by a big picture window near a roaring fire. He ordered hot chocolates for them both as they sat watching the skiers negotiate the various slopes. They talked for hours as they held each other's hand. Finally, as they both succumbed to hunger, they went into the dining room for lunch, where Ricky requested a remote table by a huge window.

After lunch, they donned their parkas, and Ricky led her out to a beautiful outdoor patio that overlooked the frozen lake. The scene was something out of a movie, and he was completely happy. He had his arm around her as they stood together gazing at the view; but he was concerned that standing there she might be getting too cold. He unzipped his jacket and turned her toward him. He then gently pulled her toward him and shared his body warmth and covered her inside with his coat. He could feel the emotions physically rising in him and for the first time, he pressed his body to hers and enfolded her to him, with a passionate kiss.

Realizing he might have gone too far, Ricky pulled back, but Christine moved closer and pulled him to her. She stood on her tiptoes so she could feel the fullness of his warmth and placed her lips on his. The passion rose in both of them, as she threw her arms around his neck, while he pulled her closer to him. Without stopping their embrace, he slowly unzipped her coat and pressed her body against his. The moment seemed to go on forever. Neither one of them wanted it to stop. Their kisses became more intense, but he finally broke the embrace. "I need air! Besides, this is going somewhere we can't go today!"

He glanced at his watch, and she frowned, "No, not yet!"

He smiled. "I'm afraid so, my little princess, remember I need to get back and we still have a bit of a drive!

They left Mont Tremblant with a new concept of their relationship; it had moved in a new direction, and he was ready for this next step.

The car trip back was filled with talking about their day. Christine sat so close she was almost on the steering wheel, but he loved her being that close.

When they got back to her house, the parting was brutal for both of them. The next day would be Sunday and they would not see each other, so they had to hold tight to one last kiss until Monday in the store.

Saturday night and Sunday were a difficult transition for Ricky after his spectacular day with Christine, but he tried to keep himself busy with Darlene. Now, sitting here in his office, reliving the day with Christine, gave him new hope for a glorious future!

His thoughts returned to the present and he knew he had to at least try to get some work done. The reports were due upstairs by 3:00 P.M. and he hadn't even begun to go over them, yet!

Finally finishing reviewing the reports, Ricky leaned back in his chair pleased that his day had been relatively quiet, which allowed him ample time to complete his paperwork. He was looking forward to going home to his apartment, eating Chinese take-out, soaking in a hot bathtub, and crashing by the TV with a tall glass of Dubonnet Red. Kathy had gone to her mother's again with Darlene and would be away most of the night.

He finished packing his briefcase and was just putting on his coat when the telephone rang.

Damn, not now! The friggin' day's over!

"Dean," he barked.

"I need you at the Laurentian Hotel, Caruso Lounge, six-thirty sharp, got it?" a familiar voice commanded.

"What? No kiss before our first date, Tony?" Ricky kidded.

"Knock it off, Ricky! We've got a major break in the Calabresee case, but we've got to move fast. Are you free for the night?"

"Yeah, yeah, Tony, sorry," Ricky apologized, realizing the seriousness in Tony's voice. "I'm clear for tonight, just got to make the nine-forty at Central Station."

"Forget the train, you'll take a taxi home!"

"What are you kiddin', to Ville Saint Laurent?"

"Yes, paid out of my budget."

"Six-thirty, the Caruso Lounge." Tony hung up without waiting for a reply.

I wonder why the Laurentian Hotel instead of the usual Astor Grill. Something big has got to be going down for Tony to be acting so spooky.

⚜ Fifty ⚜

At 6:00 P.M the Eaton's closing bell sounded as Ricky headed for the escalator up to the main floor. "Have a good night Christine," he smiled, "Careful that you don't fall off there," he added, watching her teeter on a ladder by the stockroom.

"Goodnight Ricky!" Suddenly Christine realized she had used his first name, "Oh sorry, Mister Dean."

"No apologies necessary. There's no one around." He walked over to her and took her hand in his to help her descend the ladder.

It is so hard being so close to her! he thought.

"Well, thanks, have a good night!" she cooed, keeping a hold on his hand a bit longer.

I would if I were spending the time with you. After our glorious day at Mont Tremblant, that is all I wish I were doing!

Ricky knew he couldn't rush the next step and was still unsure how to approach it; so, he just said, "Have a good night!" and walked the four blocks to the Laurentian Hotel. Ricky peeked into the Caruso Lounge to see if Tony had arrived, yet. To his surprise, instead he saw Ray Archambault drinking a Molson's at the bar, but Ray had his back to the entrance, and didn't see Ricky arrive.

I thought Tony wanted to talk to me somewhere private and now Ray is here. I better warn Tony before he gets to the lounge.

Ricky bought a pack of Belvedere Menthol at the newsstand and positioned himself just inside the east entry door that he knew Tony would use. He'd smoked three cigarettes before he saw Tony emerge from the alleyway, cross the street, and sprint up the stairs to the posh hotel.

Ricky grabbed him as he exited the revolving doors, "Glad I caught you. Ray is in the lounge sucking up a beer."

"Yeah, I know. I invited him."

"What?" Ricky exclaimed, "Is he part of the secret meeting you concocted here?"

"All in good time, my young friend, all in good time," he repeated, directing Ricky across the lobby towards the dark lounge.

Ray saw them as they entered the lounge and started to get up from the bar, but sat back down as Tony stated, "Be with you in a moment Ray." He then looked to the bartender, "Got me set up, Lou?"

"Sure thing, Tony. Your room is ready, right through the door just left of the restroom sign. As you requested, there is a telephone in there, and if you need me press 'two', or, for an outside line press 'nine'. You won't be disturbed unless you call."

"Great Lou. I owe you," Tony headed for the lounge door with Ricky in tow.

Ricky walked through the small door from the bar and was surprised by the immense size of the room. It was a large banquet hall, which could hold about 150 to 200 people, with large double doors leading off the lobby. A long table with a white covering had been positioned in the center of the room on the plush carpeted floor. There were 10 armchairs around the table, and a set-up on the table of three plates of assorted hors d'oeuvres, water glasses and cups, water pitchers, and two coffee urns, regular and decaffeinated.

Tony settled into a chair at the head of the table motioning Ricky into the one to his right. "I'm sure you're confused about what's going on here, but the fact is, from what Ray found out from Marcus, we confirmed that the Calabresee hit on Eaton's is going to be two weeks from now on 'Record Breaking Day,' just as we thought! I've invited a full complement of MPD law enforcement, plus some of my security staff to formulate a strategy to nail these bastards. I've also included Ray, because of his interaction with Marcus, Vinney, and the shoplifting gang, he is going to be invaluable to the success of this operation. I brought both Denis, Kate and MPD up to speed on Ray's shenanigans with the 'Liftermob' situation and Calabresee's activities. Do you have a problem with any of that stuff?"

"It's your call, Tony. I only want to know if you really think you can trust Ray?"

Annoyed at being questioned, Tony responded, "I've got him by the short hairs, and he's fighting for his life. So, yes, I trust him."

Denis Charbonneau and Kate Middleton entered through the front double doors, and Tony pointed to the barroom door, "Denis, grab Ray from the bar. Kate, you can join us here," pointing to a seat to his left."

EATON'S – During the Second French Revolution

When Denis and Ray returned, they were followed by a parade of MPD, some in uniform, some in civilian clothing. Everyone settled into the remaining chairs, as Tony began, "I want to thank you all for being here. We have a lot to cover, so let's get started. Looking around I believe I've personally briefed most of you on the reason for this meeting and the circumstances we are up against. First, let me introduce everyone and their areas of expertise," he began. Tony pointed to Ricky, this is Richard Dean, he is our security liaison to Eaton's management. Denis Charbonneau is my number two man, and Raymond Archambault is an Eaton's detective, and you're all aware of the situation between him and Vinney Calabresee. This is Katherine Middleton, and she is also a senior Eaton detective. She will be drafting notes for this meeting. Then we have Commander Jacques Lalonde of the MPD Bomb Squad; Francois Lafleur of the MPD major crimes detective squad, Henri Gaston, commander of street patrol officers, Rene Holt, head of MPD organized crime task force, and finally, Phillipe LeSage, commander of MPD, S.W.A.T. Does anyone have any questions before we begin?" Tony asked, looking around the group.

Lafleur raised a finger, pointing at Ray, "Your Archambault, here, has committed a serious crime, should he be included in this discussion?"

"You are all privy to the reasons behind Archambault's indiscretions, but the fact is that he was blackmailed, and his family was threatened, those are the reasons he did what he did. But I know Ray and believe they are also things he never would have considered doing, if not for those circumstances. And I believe that in that same situation, any one of us may have done the same thing! Besides, he has strategically infiltrated himself, at significant personal risk I might add, into a major criminal network, to get us the information we needed. He has my trust, and full confidence, and for the record, it is solely *my decision* on how I handle him, *after* this operation is resolved," Tony stated forcibly.

"If that answers your question, then we are going to begin with Commander Lalonde. He must leave early to attend a previously scheduled briefing on the recent bomb activity. Let's start with looking at possibilities for his bomb squad to breach the Calabresee, Des Jardins Street Warehouse. Ray, why don't you take it from here?"

Ray started to respectfully stand, but Tony motioned him to remain seated.

Ray began. "I've prepared a detailed scaled layout of the warehouse identifying the three rollup entry doors, and the approximate location of vehicles, furniture and stolen goods." He handed the layout to Lalonde. "The two main problems I see are the entry doors and the gas tank which is wired to an old semi-tractor. I observed two feeds of slim bell wiring running from each of the doors, back to the tractor battery, and then continuing to the gas tank. The problem is ..."

Lalonde interrupted, seemingly bored with Ray's presentation. "I appreciate the layout, sir but my people will have no problem neutralizing the simple explosive you have detected."

"If I may continue, Commander, the problem is not with the explosive, it's getting your squad to the actual explosives."

Lalonde was about to protest, but Ray persisted, "Each of the three rollups individually have three deadbolt style locks, and each lock has two bell wires from the lock to a junction box up by the ceiling, before continuing to the tractor." Ray paused to make sure he had the commander's full attention, before continuing. "Why this information is so important is because I've heard Vinney, on several occasions joking about 'taking out the cops if they storm the warehouse'. Commander, the doors are booby trapped, and impossible to enter without setting off the explosives. Vinney may be a crook, but he's no fool!"

Lalonde's interest was now piqued, "So, how does this Vinney guy gain entry?"

"That's the brilliant part of Vinney's security," Ray responded, handing Lalonde two other pieces of paper. "That's the design of the lock positions on each of the doors, You'll notice that there are a total of six locks, but only three on each door, which are two feet from each other. Vinney had it designed so that two keys are necessary on either door to bypass the triggering mechanism. If you insert keys, or try to pick the locks, in the wrong combination of the locks, the whole place goes up."

"So, we just cut the power," Lalonde scoffed.

"Then you better hope that when you cut the wires, it will also neutralize the battery backup system!" Ray responded sarcastically.

"Are there any windows, or possible *soft spots* where we could break through on the perimeter walls?" Lalonde asked.

"There are no windows, Commander, and the walls are eight-inch concrete cinder block laminated with four-inch exterior red brick."

Ray purposely hesitated, allowing Lalonde to stew on the seemingly impossible task before him, before offering some other solution. "But I think that I've figured out a way."

"Go on," Lalonde anxiously piped in.

"The roof," Ray smiled. "Six weeks ago, Vinney had a crew replace four stainless steel corrugated roof panels, which had rusted out and were leaking. It took these guys less than one hour to cut out and replace the panels. Since time would not be a factor in your squad effecting entry through the roof, they could remove a couple of panels and repel down to the floor by the tractor explosives, in short order."

"Good, excellent!" Lalonde crowed, "I'll get my squad simulating roof panel removal at our training site. After we disarm the explosives at the warehouse, the patrol squad and detectives can secure the site."

"Oh, one other important factor, Commander," Ray interrupted, "I know that Vinney is very shrewd, and I wouldn't put it past him to have a secondary booby trap positioned by the trucks that could be triggered if the front entries were compromised."

"Thank you, Monsieur Archambault, but that is S.O.P., *Standard Operating Practice*, training for my squad, but we appreciate the warning."

As Lalonde stood and gathered his papers, as he gazed at everyone, "Tony and I have already discussed my S.W.A.T team's role in capturing these crooks, so I will take my leave."

Tony interjected, "Jacques, the most important factor to us is that you don't breach the building *until after* we have Calabresee's gang in custody."

"Understood. I'll coordinate with Francois and Henri to have patrol and detectives standing close by until we get the call that the squad has successfully apprehended Calabresee and his gang."

"Thank you, Jacques," Tony said, as Lalonde left the room. "That was great, Ray," Tony whispered quietly. "You had Lalonde completely on the hook, then gently let him off," he snickered.

"My apologies, Raymond, I was out of line earlier with my comments about you," Lafleur acknowledged humbly.

"Let's start with an easy subject, the fur heist," Tony continued. "When Francois and Henri's men enter the warehouse, they should find direct evidence of the heist, if the furs are still there. Ray has told me that they still have the Eaton's price tags affixed to the sleeves. Dumb! Anyway, to really nail his ass to the wall, it would be great if we had some witnesses, and that's where you come in, Ricky."

"Francois, can you give everyone a copy of Vinney, and his honcho, Frankie's mug shots, and rap sheet?"

Tony continued, "Ricky, I need you to coordinate with all main floor and basement floor management to show the pictures to all regular and part time employees, to see if anyone recognizes either one of these perps. Francois has also added an enhanced shot of Vinney using your description of black slicked back hair, graying temples, and graying moustache. If we get a hit from any employee, we will need a very comprehensive written statement."

"Got it handled, Tony," Ricky quickly responded.

Tony continued. "Next item, the 'Liftermob' shoplifters. We are positive from Ray's account that this crew is run through Vinney's operation by a guy by the name of Marcus Castille. Ray also told us that they are planning to operate, as a disruptive diversionary force, to aid in Vinney's cash office robbery. To do this effectively they will be required to concentrate their efforts on the main and basement floors, the only areas where the robbers will pass through. To efficiently divert our detective's attention away from the University Street side of the store, where the robbers will most likely enter, they'll need to stage their shoplifting shenanigans to the north ends of both floors, where they are going to be more than willing to be caught."

"Denis, you are going to direct our regular compliment of sale day detectives, twelve additional detectives I borrowed from Morgans and Simpsons, plus fourteen undercovers, supplied by Francois and Henri. Their jobs will be to watch for the disruption, apprehend the shoplifter and get them up to Ray in the security office, as soon as possible. On the sound of three chimes, I want every detective," and looking to Ricky, "every manager, assistant manager, and section head to move all the customers, on both floors, to the other side of the center aisle, away from the southeast University Street side of the store. Use the excuse that we've had a small ammonia spill and are moving them for their own safety."

"Ray, since they think they still have a mole in our security department, you are to continue with that façade. Get them in the 'box', copy their identification, joke with them about the stuff they stole, while your recorder is running, and then quickly kick them loose, with a detective runner I'll give you to get them out of the store."

"You're going to let them go?" Rene Holt questioned, not believing what he just heard! "I thought the whole idea was to nail them in the act."

"The 'Liftermobs' are small potatoes, right now! Our main objective is to take down Vinney's organization and stop the robbery, without any casualties. And we've got a plan in place to get the 'Liftermobs,' at a later time, which I'll explain in a bit.

"The reason I have Ray kicking the 'Liftermobs' loose, is really to protect him personally, by maintaining his cover as an inside aid to the gang. If Vinney ever got wind that he was taken down through Ray spilling the goods on him, he'd put a contract out on him, or kill him himself. Even from prison Vinney has enough juice to have Ray whacked!" Tony noticed Ray cringe at the thought.

"Rene and Francois, when you interrogate Vinney and his cohorts, one of their biggest concerns will be to figure out who fingered them. You need to let slip that I was the one who matched suspect profiles and photos, comparing our competitor's security files to ours, thus identifying many of the 'Liftermobs'. And so, they'll never suspect Ray, we need to let it spill that some Eaton's staff were asked for descriptions of anyone they saw hanging around the basement cash office. Vinney will accept that explanation and it will keep attention away from Ray."

"Oh thanks, Tony, so me and my staff get to be the ones who gets whacked," Ricky joked.

Tony, now all business, ignored Ricky's humor. "The last and most critical item is the actual robbery. We know what day it'll happen, but not what time, which makes it somewhat difficult for advance preparation. I believe that our only advance clue will be when the 'Liftermobs' suddenly become highly active throughout the main and basement floors."

"Phillipe since your guys are going to do the actual take down, what have you figured out from viewing the possible areas?" Tony asked.

Phillipe began. "We've spent two days drawing a comprehensive layout of the main and basement floors, concentrating on the University Street side. We've also reviewed the tapes of your preliminary discussion with Mister Archambault. There are several points to consider. One, from Archambault's tapes we heard that Calabresee still has the blue Eaton's truck that we believe he used in the fur heist. But Ray believes that they have a new Eaton's disguised box truck for this caper. Our thinking is that that will be the easiest way for them to arrange transport for the robbery. They can park it by the University Street curb, carry out the robbery, then escape in the truck, which will probably be a short distance to a waiting non-descript getaway car."

"Two, from our observation, we are almost one-hundred percent sure that entry will be through either the corner Saint Catherine Street doors, or the middle University Street doors. Since the corner of Saint Catherine Street is always so busy, it would make the most sense for Calabresee to park the truck by the middle University Street doors, with direct entry to the downstairs stairwell.

"Three. Since they must travel such a long distance from the street down to the basement cash office, we believe they will enter heavily disguised as customers rather than in face masks. And certainly, they will be wearing long overcoats to hide the various weapons."

"Their weapons most likely will be sawed off shotguns for intimidation, and handguns for practicality. My team will allow them free access into the downstairs stairwell, where they will be confined, and virtually trapped, while my second team will block exit from the lower stairwell. The exodus of customers from both the main floor and basement floor, University Street side, is critical to not getting anyone hit by flying bullets if Calabresee is stupid enough to engage us in a shootout. I'll have my men in place in the cash office, and when the chimes sound, they will herd the actual cash office employees into the safety of the vault, which they'll close and temporarily lock. That's our plan, so far, and I'll be coordinating our efforts with Francois, Henri, and Rene to have their people available for assistance. And, if everyone does their job, Calabresee, and his hoods, will be going away for a long, long time."

"Thanks Phillipe. Okay, that's about it, unless someone has something to add," Tony concluded.

"Just one more thing," Rene offered. "I've talked it over with Henri, and since he has the biggest supply of manpower, he'll have his people involved in the warehouse breach, rounding up all the 'Liftermobs,' when we get their names, and his people will also be available for assist at the store. He's also going to have a city tow truck standing by to tow the faux Eaton's truck when it parks on University Street. That way, if any of the perps do slip through our net, they'll be standing on the sidewalk with their thumb up their ass!"

"Very good, then the meeting is adjourned. Ricky, Denis, Kate, and Ray, please stay for one more minute."

After the MPD left Tony said, "Ray, I've made arrangements for you to meet with Morgans, Simpsons, Dupris Freres, and Holt Renfew security managers over the next few days. They've figured out what months they had a spike in shoplifting and that's the most probable time that they were hit by the 'Liftermobs'. I want you to look over their pictures and files, from that period, and pick out the people that you can identify from the gang. By the time we nail Calabresee I want to be able to have the whole gang picked up. But, and I emphasis this, do not, I repeat, do not, under any circumstances, give any indication to these security people about the upcoming robbery."

"I've already met with Simpsons, and have additional meetings scheduled to begin." Ray responded.

"And I know I don't need to say this, but I will anyway. We can't have a word of this leak to anyone in our store. So, forget your friends, confidants, or anyone else, if this is to succeed, we need to keep this strictly among this group. One leak and Calabresee skates, got it?"

Everyone nodded their acknowledgement.

"Oh, also Denis, I want you to double check the perps that Ray identifies with our files. We need to have a complete list of suspects ready for Henri Gaston, no later than Thursday noon."

"Will do, Tony."

"Kate, I want you to coordinate basement and main floor detective staff with the MPD officers so that we have these floors in full blanket coverage."

"Okay, Tony."

"And, Ricky, tomorrow I want you to go out with Ray, to the other stores, to help him out. After that you'll need to bring your floor managers up to speed and concentrate on your *'Record Breaking Day* Sale' set up. It would make our life easier if you could direct your managers to position their big sale items away from the cash office. I don't want to have throngs of sale customers flooding that area."

"That's already handled, Tony."

"Okay folks," Tony got up from his chair, and stretched his neck, "Let's get ourselves some bad guys!"

⚜ Fifty-One ⚜

Since Kathy's return from her sisters, it seemed that their home had become a perpetual battlefield!

Ricky ate by himself, watched T.V. by himself, and slept on the sofa, every night. Not a word was uttered between them. The only minimal contact was the few post-it notes stuck on the refrigerator stating bluntly; 'leave money for groceries', 'staying at my Mothers with the baby for three days', or 'get an oil change on the car'. Apart from that Ricky saw very little of Kathy, which was all right by him.

Ricky spent those treasured weeks of solitude anticipating the explosion that was eventually going to occur. He was just biding his time. But the good part was that he spent more time spoiling Darlene and formulating a plan for their future, without Kathy.

One day, when he was watching a hockey game, Kathy exited the solitude of her bedroom retreat, came into the living room, and rudely turned off the T.V.

"We need to talk," she plopped down on the sofa.

"Go ahead," he replied with nothing in his voice but ice.

"I've come to a decision," her face was wrinkled in rage, and she was gnashing her teeth.

"Yes," he prompted.

"I've got to get out of here. I don't know how, but I'll crack up if I don't."

"So, what do you propose?" he asked.

"Just hear me out and let me get all my thoughts out, okay?"

"Go ahead!"

"I'm going to move to Niagara Falls. I've already made arrangements with my sister."

Ricky began to say something, but Kathy held up her hand to silence him. "I know I can't handle the baby and a job at the same time, so you're going to have to take care of her. You'll just have to get a babysitter, or something while you're at work."

Kathy looked uncomfortable in continuing. "I'm going to need some money to get set, like I told you before, about three thousand dollars, and probably about two hundred a week for six months. And you will need to pay everything for the divorce. I just want this all over," she began to cry.

Ricky felt a pang of sadness and compassion towards Kathy but recognized that he had to remain hardnose strong in this important life altering negotiation.

"So, you're saying that I get Darlene and you ship off to Niagara Falls? Full custody, right?" he pushed.

"No, shared custody," she corrected.

"I'm not going to be shipping her three hundred plus miles, back and forth, across the country. It's not healthy, and not fair to her."

"Okay, okay. But I need some visitation rights so I can see my daughter," she pleaded.

"You can have reasonable supervised visitation rights to see her anytime you come back to Montreal."

"Why supervised? Do you think I would harm my own daughter?"

"Of course not, but if you only see her sporadically, you'll be like a stranger to her, and I don't want her life turned more upside down than it is already going to be. By the way, have you talked this all over with an attorney?" Ricky was concerned that this conversation would be useless if Kathy hadn't had some direction from a lawyer.

"Yes, my brother got me a lawyer. He will write up anything I want to get a divorce finalized. I told him that I just wanted to get out of here. I hate the weather, I hate Montreal, and I just want to build a new life."

"Okay then, the only problem left is the money situation, and you know very well what my salary and bonuses amount to, and what bills we have. I'm not rolling in dough, 'ya know."

"You could borrow some money, can't you?"

"Yes, but from my family, I can't get a dime. And I talked with Household Finance, and they'll only lend me up to my one-thousand-dollar limit. So, here's what I propose: I keep the car and all the furniture; I'll get you the thousand from H.F.C, I'll handle all the divorce costs and arrangements; and I'll pay you one hundred dollars a month for three months, then fifty a month for the next three months. After that we are through, and you are on your own! That's the only offer I can afford, Kathy."

"Make it one hundred and twenty-five a month for three months, then seventy-five a month for the next three months, then we'll call this nightmare over," she countered Ricky's offer.

"Deal," Ricky extended his hand, which she shook.

After their discussion, it was agreed that Kathy would still watch Darlene during the day, but she would eat and sleep at her parents' house each night, as she prepared for her move.

The irony was that after all Kathy's efforts and deceit to get away from her family, here she was getting right back where she was three years ago.

I need to talk to Tony about this before she changes her mind.

⚜ Fifty-Two ⚜

Vinney had his eyes closed, his hand behind his head on the fluffy pillow, basking in the glow of yet another incredible love making session, with the very accomplished Jacqueline Nadeau. She placed a lit cigarette between his lips, while whispering in his ear, "Mon Cher, *My Dear* you seem very distracted tonight."

Jacqueline was Vinney's number one girl in his stable of numerous, and revolving, girlfriends. She was also the only one that he trusted enough to participate in his various criminal activities, and certainly, the only one who was uninhibited enough to lure an informant, or co-conspirator into Vinney's organization. Whenever Vinney needed an inside track on information about a heist, he would set up a sexual encounter for Jacqueline, usually with the married mark. After she had sex with the mark, Vinney would blackmail him into supplying information, or even, participating in the heist. Since he had numerous sexual partners, Vinney was not possessive about Jacqueline seeing other people. The most important factor for him was that Jacqueline was the most innovative sexual partner that he'd ever had, even though she was not the most attractive by any means.

Jacqueline had breasts that were too large for her body, thighs that were too heavy for her legs and an ass that protruded out so far that Vinney said, "she needed taillights". Her face was pudgy; bracketed by a full head of black, unkempt hair and brown eyes that seemed to wander uncontrollably. Through her sexual escapades with others, Vinney had made her a lot of extra money that amply supplemented her college tuition.

"Not distracted, just have a lot on my mind," he pinched her nipple playfully.

Vinney had no problem talking about the specific details of the Eaton's heist since it had been Jacqueline who had arranged to have her cousin, Julianna Venicee, make the Eaton's driver uniform, and her friend, Isabella Conte, who would handle the numerous disguises and makeup.

"I thought you had rehearsed all that with your guys and had it all under control." She twirled the hair on his chest between her fingertips.

"Yeah, but it's like going into battle with a bunch of kids. They just don't seem to take it seriously."

"But Vinney, they are all scared of you, so they'll come through when the time arrives."

"Maybe you're right. Anyway, enough about me, what about you? Are you still running with those F.L.Q. flakes?"

Vinney hated the F.L.Q., and all they stood for; he hated the student dissidents who brought police scrutiny down upon everyone, including his organization, and he hated the forced conversion from English to French, and the anti-English laws being passed by the Quebec cabinet.

"We are not flakes; we are fighting for a just cause." She slapped Vinney's bare chest.

"You are fighting a battle that you'll never win. Are you still with that Francois guy in the *F.L.Q. Liberation Cell*?" He slapped her ass playfully.

"Yes," she angrily jumped up from the bed. "and I'll have you know that my *F.L.Q. Liberation Cell* has an event in the works that will make your Eaton's job look like children's *Howdy Dowdy Time*." She gathered her clothes and ran for the bathroom.

Howdy Dowdy never had as big a score as I'm going to have! Vinney thought.

⚜ Fifty-Three ⚜

Ricky arrived at the security office just as Tony was about to leave for the day. "Hey Ricky. My day is over so anything you have to say is double time," Tony laughed, grabbing his coat from the rack.

"I couldn't afford you at your regular salary, anyway."

"You got that right, son. What can I do you for?" he added, slipping on his fur collared overcoat, and his comical ear-muffed hat.

"I talked to Appleton to bring him up to speed on the cash office heist, like you suggested, but it didn't go as well as I had hoped."

"Well, that sounds like a conversation that merits extensive libations to digest."

"Yeah, I was wondering if you've got time for a quickie at the Astor?"

"The last time I told my wife, Coleen, that I was stopping for a quickie, she made me sleep on the couch for a month," he chuckled. "Are you buying?"

"You got that right, Pops."

"Then lead on, son. I'll give you my special 'keep the drinks coming' rate." He guided Ricky towards the door.

"Good night, Agatha," Tony saluted, as he passed his secretary's desk.

"Good night, Mister Cartwright, Mister Dean. You boys don't get into any trouble, now!"

"Wow, was that actually a bit of levity from the old crow? I'm impressed!"

"I've been feeding her kernel corn every day, and it seems to be working."

They headed over to the Astor Grill where they were greeted by the owner.

"Good day, Mister Tony, Mister Ricky. Nice to see you both again. Hans is off today, so I take your order, yes?" He walked them to their rear corner booth.

"Scotch neat with water back, Armand," Tony requested, throwing his overcoat over an adjoining chair.

"A Greyhound for me, please," Ricky followed, sliding into the booth.

"So, whatcha got for me, Ricky boy?" Tony asked.

"Well, I've got two subjects to get your opinion on. One personal and one concerning Appleton." Ricky laughed. "But I'm not saying anything until you take off that ridiculous hat."

Tony feigned hurt. "Ridiculous! I'll have you know this is my lucky hat. This is the hat that I wore when Maurice 'the Rocket' Richard scored his five hundredth goal. He owes that goal to me."

"The hat goes before I talk," Ricky warned.

Tony threw the hat over his coat. "You just ain't no more fun anymore, son. So, lets hit Appleton first 'cause I'm going to need more juice before I hear another one of your sad personal stories."

"Your cocktails, gentlemen." Armand placed the drinks on cocktail napkins.

"Cheers!" Tony clinked glasses.

"So, I clued Appleton in on all the plans we have regarding the cash office heist and the 'Liftermob', and I thought he would be pleased and supportive, but he was kind of distant and cold."

"What do you mean by distant and cold, was he pissed off?"

"No, not that. He just seemed to be not quite as interested as I thought he would be. I think he was annoyed that we made all these plans and that he was only being advised, after the fact."

"Did you ever think that just maybe he was looking to the future so that he could protect himself if this whole thing falls out of bed. Do you really believe he is going to step up to the plate and take any responsibility? Not in your life. He'll be the guy who says to corporate that you and I handled this one on our own without his sanction. They all operate on the C.Y.A. principle to protect their own careers."

"What the hell is a C.Y.A. principle?"

"Cover Your Ass. He probably learned that from his GM procedure manual," Tony chuckled. "Did you really think that we would come out of this unscathed if the shit hit the fan?"

"I never even thought of that. Do you really think we could get fired over this?"

"Fired or promoted will all depend on the outcome. But don't worry, Uncle Tony assures you that we will win this war and save the day for Eaton's," he laughed, "and our own asses! Now what is this personal problem?"

"I need to ask you what you know about Quebec divorce law," Ricky asked, making a face at the first bitter sip of his Greyhound. Kathy and I have finally agreed to the conditions of a divorce, but aside from filling out the forms, I haven't a clue what comes next. I heard that it takes over a year to finalize, though."

"More like eighteen months, if you are lucky, that is," Tony explained. "The main hurdle to get over is what grounds you are petitioning for in the divorce. And the key here is to petition as adultery. In Quebec courts you don't claim mental cruelty or irreconcilable differences, like you can in the states or Western Canada. Generally, you must prove adultery, beyond a shadow of a doubt."

"You have got to be kidding." Ricky buried his head in his hands. All seemed hopeless. "And why is adultery the main grounds in Quebec?"

"Answer this, Ricky. Who do you think runs the province of Quebec?"

"I don't know, the politicians I suppose, or maybe now the friggin' FLQ!"

"Close, but no cigar. It's the parish priests, the monsignors, and the cardinals that have the ear of the lawmakers. Therefore, the politicians who are good Catholics themselves, ensure that the laws they enact get tailored to accommodate the Catholic church doctrine. And remember that this is a deeply religious province. The church wants to control all its parishioners and keep them making more little Catholics, so they make it almost impossible to get a divorce. This is another reason so many people leave Quebec for our other provinces, and even the states."

"So, what's the answer?" Ricky quizzed.

"Well, here's where it gets dicey. I'm sure you are aware that these Catholics do not like adulterers very much, so way back when they started their whole club, at a time when their Popes got married, and screwed around with all their concubines, they wrote this book, called the Bible, which made adultery one of the ten deadly sins. I think it was originally carved in stone, and carried around by a world traveler called, Moses, thousands of years before their club started."

"Are you an atheist, Tony?" Ricky asked.

"No, I guess I'm an agnostic."

"What's an agnostic?"

"It's someone who believes, just in case," Tony laughed.

"Anyway, because the Catholic church hates adultery, they had the Quebec divorce laws tailored so that those grounds were the only ones that they'd accept for divorce. Of course, they don't mind if your single and screw twelve virgins each week, because you can go to that little phone booth in the church and confess your sins to a priest who is jacking off in the adjoining phone booth, while listening to your story. Then, once you confess, the priest gives you absolution, and your free for the next week to do it all over again. It's a really great program!" Tony waved his hand at Armand for another round of drinks.

"There's a cute joke about that. This man goes to confession and says to the priest, 'forgive me father for I have sinned', and the priest says, 'what is your sin, my son?' so the man says, 'I've had sex with one of your parishioners, father', and the priest says, 'was it Misses O'Connor,' 'no father,' 'was it Misses McGilly,' 'no father,' 'was it Misses Jenkins,' 'no father', frustrated the priest asks 'do you wish absolution, my son?' 'no father, I was just looking for some new leads."

Ricky burst out laughing. "All right, so how do I get a bloody divorce without leaving town?"

"Ah, this is where the games begin. Since the Catholic Church will sanction divorce, if adultery can be proven, some extremely savvy lawyers came up with a foolproof plan that guarantees the legal acceptance of adultery. It requires the assistance of a hooker and a private investigator."

"You mean like Sam Spade?"

"Kinda'," Tony continued. "The defendant, that's you, hires a hooker and takes her to a motel room where you either get it on with her, or pretend to get it on. Then, the motel door crashes open and in comes a private investigator, that you've also hired, camera in hand, who takes lots of candid pictures of you and your new girlfriend, buck naked in bed. Naughty, naughty!"

"You've got to be shitting me, and this is legal?"

"Not only is it legal, but it's also expected as proof in a divorce action in a Quebec court of law. The Quebec hookers have never been so happy. It's a great new source of easy income for them." Tony sat back and chewed on the ice from his drink.

"Hookers, motel rooms, P.I.'s? This sounds like a nightmare, Tony," Ricky groaned. "I'm totally screwed!"

"Not with my help, son."

"You really get off on this crap, don't you?"

"Just like my old days when I walked the beat back in New York!"

"Okay, so let's say I'm game to go this route, what do I do?"

"First of all, Ricky, if you want a divorce, this is the only way you're going to get one, understand?" Tony turned profoundly serious.

"Got it!"

"So, number one, you need a hooker, right?"

"Yeah, and I don't intend to troll Saint Laurent Boulevard to get one either."

"Don't worry, I've already got one selected for you, and you even know her quite well."

"I don't know any prostitutes, Tony!" Ricky corrected.

Tony thought for several minutes before continuing. "You have to promise me that you'll never breathe a word about what I'm going to tell you to any other living soul."

"I swear, Tony," Ricky replied, crossing his heart.

"I'm serious, Ricky. If word got out this could destroy someone's life."

"Okay Tony, I'll never tell a soul."

"You remember Debbie Stalinski?"

"Sure, she's that cute brunette, tall, big boobs, about twenty-one or twenty-two who works for you undercover sometimes. I helped her and Kate Middleton take down a drunk sailor in men's wear a few weeks ago. She can really handle herself."

"Yeah well, she's not twenty-one, she's twenty-nine and she's had a tough life. She started on the streets, pimped by her own father when she was just sixteen, got popped numerous times for solicitation and eventually ended up in juvenile detention for twenty-four months. That's where I met her. A buddy of mine from the NYPD got a job as warden at the Montreal J.T., and he took notice of this little girl pouring over all the books she can get her hands on, and he decided to help her out. So, when she's due to be released, just after her eighteenth birthday, he calls me and tells me that she's never known her mother, and her father overdosed on heroin, and can I help her out? So, I meet her, Coleen came with me, and we both fell in love with this sweet thing, and, decided to help her out."

"You old softy!" Ricky interrupted.

"Anyway, when she got out, we had her come and live with us. She got her high school diploma and completed two years of college, which we helped pay for. She insisted on supplementing her income by becoming a nude model. We tried to talk her out of it, but she insisted that this vocation allowed her body to be used for visual, rather than physical pleasure. Coleen believes she's trying to atone for her past. During this modeling period she took night classes and received an associate degree in criminology. Then, she decided before going into full law enforcement she wanted to spend some time working undercover, hence, she came to work for me,"

"This all sounds great, but how does Debbie fit in with what I need?"

"Debbie has 'gone undercover as a hooker' twice before, for the benefit of two other persons in Eaton's that I won't name. She'll cost you one-hundred dollars, but she'll give an academy award performance."

"It all sounds great. So, I've got Debbie as my pretend hooker, and I probably can handle renting a motel room, but I can't afford a P.I."

"That's what you have me around for, son," he laughed, rubbing his fingers together. "I always keep my P.I. license current and I have one *boss* thirty-five-millimeter camera."

"So, you would break into the motel room and take compromising pictures of Debbie and I, nude in bed, right?"

"And I won't charge you anything for my services if you let me hang a couple of pictures of your bare ass in the manager's lounge!" Tony put his stupid hat on and reached for his coat. "Now, you can pay the bill and let me get out of here, before Coleen tracks me down."

Another disaster averted!

⚜ Fifty-Four ⚜

Things had not been going as planned, which was bringing Vinney's temper to a boiling point. He hadn't been able to dispose of all the stolen furs as fast as he had planned and shuttered at the thought of giving the best of the heist to the Russian fence, Yuri Petrovski. The prospect of only getting ten cents on the dollar for the remaining stash grated on him. And now, just days before the largest payday of his life, the head of his shoplifting operation gets caught trying to extort Eaton's through a 'bait and switch' wallet caper.

Maybe I should just shoot the bastard, right now, Vinney thought.

Vinney tinkered with his prized 1956 Thunderbird convertible as he awaited the arrival of his crew. He was just tightening the last lug nut when he felt a presence beside him, a long shadow blocking his light and startling him.

"Hey boss," came a familiar voice.

"Jesus, Frankie could you at least whistle, or something, instead of sneaking up on me, and scaring the shit outta me," Vinney yelled. "And, get your foot off that bumper, I just paid eight bills to get it re-chromed."

"Sorry boss," instantly removing his foot. "It's really comin' along good," pointing at the car. "A real pretty Vinney pussy mobile, eh?"

"Just shut up and hand me that hubcap."

"Sure boss."

"Does every answer from you have to end with the word 'boss'?" He banged the hubcap in place with a rubber mallet. "Have the guys sit at the 'boardroom' table while I get rid of these clothes and take a leak."

The four men sat around his desk, as Vinney nervously paced around the group in circles. Assembled were Frankie, Vinney's main man, Aldo Renaldi, Vinney's enforcer; Jimmy Fellini, Vinney's cousin; and Marcus Castille, head of Vinney's shoplifting operation, and now the subject of Vinney's rage.

Aldo *"Shoulders"* Renaldi, had been Vinney's enforcer ever since he left his Trafficante New York crime family, after an unsanctioned botched hit on Anthony Strollo, the under boss of the Genovese family, over a gambling debt. Vinney nicknamed him "shoulders" because he was constantly looking over his shoulder, most likely, fearing the inevitable retribution from Anthony Strollo. In a feeble effort to alter his appearance Aldo had dyed his graying hair stone black, wearing it craggy, and unkempt, at shoulder length. His features were sculpted by his olive-skinned face and wide nose, beaten one too many times. An old switchblade wound left a crimson mark reaching from the bottom of the right cheek, to above his right eye, no doubt a vivid memory of his life of violence. His dead looking brown eyes, set deeply within their sockets, were ever searching, and scanning every place he went.

If ever there was the stereo-typical face of an Italian mobster, Aldo fit the bill. But there was something fascinating about him. Perhaps it was the gliding steps of a dancer, or perhaps, it was simply his south-Bronx accent, but, either one made the ladies flock to him like bees to honey.

Jimmy Fellini had gone to school with Vinney at Rosemount High and idealized his ostracized cousin. He had just gotten out of Bordeaux Prison where he served time for an assault conviction, at the same time, that Vinney was being banned from the Calabrisee family business. Jimmy elected to go with Vinney, forsaking a just position within the family.

With his wild, wavy blonde hair, pulled back in a ponytail, his cheerful face, and steel blue bright eyes, Jimmy looked more like a teenager than his actual age. His frail build and dangly limbs instantly identified him, as a "Scarecrow". There was something sinister about him, perhaps it was his violent past working for the family, or maybe, his need to show off his talents to Vinney, but regardless of his slight built, Jimmy was fierce in battle. Although everyone thought he was crazy, he would pick a fight with the biggest guy in a bar, explaining that it was a win-win situation. If the guy beat him, everyone would feel sorry for the little guy, but if Jimmy beat the big guy, then he would be a hero to everyone. Jimmy wasn't a hero very often!

Marcus Castille had been a heavyweight prize fighter in his younger years, very often performing as a punching bag for his numerous fixed boxing matches. With a career record of 6 wins and 38 losses he was eventually dropped from the competitive roster. With only an eighth-grade education, and a head that remained perpetually puzzled, Marcus chose petty crime over legitimate work. Unfortunately, he wasn't particularly good at it and spent most of his adult life incarcerated in one prison or another.

Marcus nicknamed "the head," had met Vinney while they were both doing time at Bordeaux. Marcus realized Vinney's prominence in the Calabrisee family and instantly befriended him. While still in prison Vinney schooled Marcus in the proper techniques of petty crime, with emphasis on shoplifting and minor cons. After their release Marcus became a member of Vinney's organization, and under his tutelage excelled in shoplifting, and eventually fielded a crew of his own. At 6 foot 3 inches, 287 pounds, Marcus had the body of a linebacker, and the pockmarked, broken face of a war casualty victim. Although his intelligence was a constant source of ridicule, his loyalty to Vinney was unwavering.

Vinney walked around the table and ended up behind Marcus. "What the Christ were you thinking, Marco," Vinney yelled, violently slapping the back of Marcus's head. "You jeopardized our hundred thousand dollars plus operation, for a few lousy wallet scams! I pay you good money, you get a piece of the action, and still, you try to screw me. Is that how you treat me, you fat fuck!"

"I was going to give you the money I collected, Vin, really, I swear," he pleaded.

"Sure, you were. Just like you gave me the money from the Morgan and Simpson store scams, and every other goddamn store you hit, right?" *After the Eaton's heist, this prick is dead!*

"I, I, ..." Marcus stammered, surprised that Vinney knew about the other hits.

"Yes, I know all about the others. You forget, I have lots of contacts in my organization that keep me advised of flakes like you. Believe me, if I didn't need you for the Eaton's job, I would toss your sorry dead ass in the Saint Lawrence River, right now!"

EATON'S – During the Second French Revolution

"I'm sssorry, Vin, I needed the money for, ..." Marco began, but was cut off by another blow to his head by Vinney.

"Shut up!" Vinney kicked Marcus's chair sending him sprawling down onto the concrete floor. "I don't care if you needed it for a friggin' blow job. Shut your mouth and get your ass back in the chair, and just listen."

Marcus quickly scrambled to his feet, righted the chair, and slumped his bulk quietly into the seat.

Vinney turned his attention to Aldo. "Did you solve that repro problem for Mamma Conte?"

"Yeah, I had a chat with the puke who owns the repro operation, and he started giving me shit about how Mamma Conte was five months late on her payments, and how he had bought her note from the finance company."

"I told him to tell his sorry ass story to my Louisville Slugger, and he gets all up in my face about how he's not worried because he's protected by the Westies," Aldo explained. "So, I tell him that I've already talked with Westie's boss, Ryan McDonald, and he gave me the go ahead to do whatever I needed to straighten out the situation. But he insisted that I didn't waste the guy because he was a good earner for the Westies. McDonald also told me to tell the asshole that he should have known better than to repro any vehicle from any people connected with the Calabresee family." Aldo continued. "So, then the jerk starts sputtering apologies, and tells me that he will agree to forego three of the five-month delinquent payments. So, I pick up his phone and he yells, 'who are you calling,' and I say I'm calling my buddy Ryan, and the guy freaks out. He says, 'Okay, okay. I'll wipe all the five months', and I say, 'too late, turd!' You'll turn over a clean pink sheet for Mamma Conte's car. Well, you should have seen this guy's face, he didn't know what to say or do until I started dialing his phone, then he gave up the title. I brought the title to Mamma Conte, and she cried like a baby. She says to send her love to *Little Vinney*."

Everyone roared with laughter.

"So, Ryan was okay with you muscling one of his own?" Vinney asked.

"Oh yeah. He didn't give a shit. He thinks he may have to get rid of the guy anyway, because he's sure he's holding out on him."

"Okay. If we don't have any bad blood with the Westies. We don't want to give Uncle Carmine any excuse to cut both our nuts off."

"Anyway, if there is no other business," Vinney looked at each man before continuing, "this is our final tactical meeting for the Eaton's job, so we need to know that everyone is on the same page. This will also give you enough time to be fully prepared. We may have some short meetings before, just as a quick review!"

"I trust that you had time away from your wallet cons," Vinney questioned, pointing at Marcus, "to set up the diversionary plan with the shoplifting team."

"Diversionary plan, Vin?" Marcus questioned; his brow arched in confusion.

"Yes, the diversionary plan, you moron. The one that we talked about last week where you were to explain the diversionary activities required by each of your team members, between one and one-thirty, when the hit goes down?" Vinney scowled at Marcus.

"Oh yeah, boss," Marcus responded, "I worked with them all week and they all know what to do. I had to buy three of them watches, but ..."

"Never mind the little shit," Vinney interrupted, "the newly painted Eaton's truck is all prepped, gassed and Jack Gordo put the Eaton's company logo on both doors."

"What was wrong with the Eatons' panel truck that we used for the fur heist, it worked perfectly, Vinney?" Frankie questioned.

"I want to use the large Eaton's delivery box truck so that no one puts together any similarity to the fur heist truck.

Vinney swiveled in his old rocker to face Jimmy. "Julianna Venicee has finished the Eaton's uniform for you, so you'll be wearing it while driving the truck. You do know how to drive a stick, eh Jimmy?"

"Course, Vin."

"We need to hit the University Street doors at exactly one-thirty to gain the maximum effect of the disruption caused by Marcus' shoplifting team. The other four of us will be in the back of the truck wearing long overcoats to hide our shotguns. Everyone is to carry a separate burner in a concealed shoulder holster. Isabella Conte will be here on the morning of the heist to fit us with wigs, fake moustaches, sideburns, and makeup to distort our features. We can't walk in there, in broad daylight, wearing masks. Any questions?"

"Yeah boss," Frankie asked, "what about da back up get-a-way car?"

"Aldo is going to park it on the morning of the heist, down around Victoria Square."

"Can I park it the night before, Vinney?" Aldo asked.

"No. It's a hot car, dummy. We can't have the cops finding it overnight and towing it away. So, it must be that morning, capisce?"

"Got it. Can you review the route in and out of the store again, please?" Aldo asked sheepishly.

"Are you an idiot, or what? We've been over this a dozen times. We park the Eaton's rig at exactly one-thirty. When Jimmy gives us the "all clear," we exit the truck and enter the center University Street doors; we go down four stairs to the main floor where we immediately turn left into the stairwell; once there we will remove the guns from our coats; go down the stairwell stairs, turn right, then right again, into the cash office. This is not rocket science, Aldo," Vinney chided. "For Christ's sake, just remember to follow me, and you'll be okay?

"And remember this is their 'Record Breaking Day Sale', and aside from there being a shitload of money in the cash office, there are also going to be thousands of customers to maneuver around. So, anything can go wrong. You need to be alert and keep your eyes open, got it?"

Christ, this is like teaching kindergarten class.

"Sure boss," Aldo replied, and all heads nodded.

"If there's nothing else, boys, we're ready to rock-n-roll to a big payday. I'll see you back here at eight Thursday morning." As soon as the guys started to get up, Vinney added, "stick around, Frankie, I need to talk to you."

"Sure Vin. What you need?"

"I'm worried about Marcus; he seems to have his head up his ass."

"Oh, he'll be okay, Vin. You know him, give him three things to do and he has ta write dem down to remember. I'll stick close to him so dat he doesn't screw up, Vin."

"All right, he's your responsibility, and so remember that if he does screw up, you're the one who's going to have to put a slug in his pea brain, got it?"

"Got it, boss," Frankie replied, heading for the exit door.

I really don't need this shit! Vinney thought. *Two more jobs and I'll be set for life, and I can leave all this crap behind.*

⚜ Fifty-Five ⚜

Although the sex had been a much-needed physical release, the emotional part had been less than rewarding. After meeting with Francois of the *Liberation Cell*, following the Black Watch Armory attack, Louis had made a point of pursuing and seducing the young co-ed he had met, Jacqueline Nadeau, Francois's cell comrade. He figured that her 'loose lips' at their initial meeting at the Belgium Pastry Café, made her a prime source of inside FLQ information. He found the task relatively simple given the fact that Jacqueline was a self-proclaimed free spirit with no qualms about jumping into bed with anyone she found attractive.

To say that Jacqueline was not his type was an understatement. Where he liked a frail thin body, she had a heavyset muscular body; where he liked slight attractive facial features, she displayed large course features with pronounced eyes, nose, and lips, and where his choice of sex was tender and slow, Jacqueline wanted it fast and rough.

But Jacqueline's best feature, which Louis had discovered to his advantage, was that she had a motor mouth, spewing sensitive information about FLQ activities; credible information that Louis regularly passed onto his handler.

"What are you thinking about?" She placed a lit cigarette between his lips.

"Oh nothing," he sighed, blowing a smoke ring into the air. "Just tired of being poor." He waved his hand around the small sparsely decorated apartment.

"You don't make enough money with your day trading and your gambling?" she asked.

Louis's dossier presented him as a personal stock trader with a serious gambling problem.

"Blue Bonnets Raceway has not been kind to me lately, and several of my stocks that I counted on went to shit." He grabbed an open bottle of beer from the side table.

"You need to find something that will get rid of all your money worries, like my *friend*, Vinney," she blurted out.

"Who's this Vinney guy? Should I be jealous?"

"He's a friend of mine that's going to make a shitload of money and take me with him to Florida to live."

"So, I should be jealous if he's going to take you away from me?"

If this guy is going to make a shitload of money, I need to find out how. With a name like Vinney, he doesn't sound like he's one of her regular FLQ cronies.

Jacqueline lit a spent cigarette from the overflowing ashtray.

"So, can I get in on some of the action with your Vinney friend?"

"No, no, no! I shouldn't have said anything," she countered, a worried look flashing across her face. "He already has his own crew."

"So, he does this regularly?" he prompted.

"I can't say anymore. You just need to know that he's connected and extremely dangerous."

"Like a mob guy, 'ya mean?"

"Kinda."

"I presume if he's looking at a big score, he's probably going to hit a bank, right?" Louis realized that he needed to take a chance to gain this valuable information.

"No, Vinney says bank robbery is for morons, whereas his Eaton's ... oh, shit." She buried her head in the pillow without continuing. All Louis could hear was her 'oh, shit, oh, shit' repeated over and over.

Eaton's! This is friggin' big!

She slowly raised her head from the pillow taking his face in her chubby hands. "You gotta promise me that you won't breathe a word about this." Tears filled her eyes. "This could get me killed."

"I never heard a word," he placated.

So, there is going to be a major heist on Eaton's, to be carried out by this Vinney's mob. The 'Shadow' needs to warn them! Louis thought.

EATON'S – During the Second French Revolution

⚜ Fifty-Six ⚜

Ricky found his life incredibly stressful, trying to juggle all his various responsibilities, on top of everything else that was going on. Not only did he have to contend with the pressure of his upcoming exclusive basement *Good Ole Days Sale*, which just happened to be exactly one week prior to the national one day, *Record Breaking Sale*, but he'd had to talk with Christine about his divorce plans. On top of that he had to plan to physically be involved in an illegal deception with a hooker in a motel room. He was trying to juggle everything; his regular store duties, Darlene's babysitter, and his personal life, but he felt completely frazzled and out of control.

The *Good Ole Days Sale* was to be a feather in his cap. He'd pitched the concept to Appleton, and the board six weeks earlier and his proposal had been met with staggering enthusiasm. In fact, the sale results were to be monitored storewide, and if increased revenues were achieved, the sale would then be promoted for Cross-Canada. But the logistics of bringing this unique sale to fruition, would be no easy task.

To accomplish this Ricky formed a basement level sales committee task force to handle the various aspects of the sale.

At the first group committee meeting, Ricky told them, "We'll need someone to create and co-ordinate all the support advertising for the *Good Ole Days Sale*. Do I have volunteers?"

"I can handle that," Monique Rousseau replied eagerly.

"Thanks Monique. You will need to work closely with Gaston Remy in advertising, and our local newspapers, to achieve complete authenticity.

"Every basement department will be represented in full page spreads in the *Montreal Star*, *The Gazette*, and *LaPresse*, but I want circa nineteen hundred themes to be illustrated in each one. I'd like you to have Gaston research the Montreal and Toronto Eaton's Store archives, for vintage pictures and layout ideas. Also, to determine a suitable font for the text within each ad. I'll need preliminary copy from each department A.S.A.P.

"Next, we need volunteers for inter-department and window merchandise display and costuming," Ricky looked around the room, and two hands were raised.

"I'll take merchandise display," Carol Levesque offered.

"And I can handle costuming," Christine added.

"Okay let's discuss merchandise display necessities," he looked to Carol. "Your first priority is to have a sit-down with John Derber, in our merchandise display department, and bring him up to speed on what we're planning. He has a treasure trove of unique displays stored away on the ninth floor, and he's a valuable resource for things that are available elsewhere. Got it?" he questioned.

"I'll contact John first thing tomorrow."

"Any questions or suggestions on the display matter?"

"I have one. Since all our present displays feature either are special sale items, or regular inventory, how will we accomplish the nineteen hundred's theme, when all these products are current nineteen sixties fashion?" asked Rene Boudreau.

"Excellent question Rene. Since our primary goal is to achieve maximum sales revenues, not displaying our regular inventory would totally defeat the purpose. What I envision on every display is a 'then and now' comparison. For example, the ladies' dresses display could show our current high fashion midi-length dresses, next to a nineteen thirties flapper dress. Our hats and accessories could feature standard men's fedoras beside some straw hats. The creativity will come not only from the product displayed, but also the earlier supporting merchandise shown as part of the display. The straw hat could include a raccoon skin coat, the flapper dress, old photos of people dancing the Charleston in a speak-easy. Have fun with it, but be creative. Just remember the goal is record sales of current merchandise, with a twist from the past!"

"Now, if there are no other questions about displays, let's move on to costuming. I've seen Christine writing vigorously," he laughed, "so, I suppose you've already come up with a costuming plan?"

"Yes sir," Christine blushed, consulting her steno pad. "I see several areas in costuming that need to be addressed," she. "First, we have customer costuming and next employee costuming."

"Customer costuming?" Dolores Richfield questioned.

"Yes, to bring continuity, and a unique nineteen hundred's theme, to the whole selling floor, getting our customers involved is paramount. I believe that many of them would love getting dressed in period attire and strutting their stuff across our floor," Christine paused.

"And how do you propose getting customers to dawn their spats and straw hats to join our *Good Ole Days Sale*?" ever the skeptic, John LeClerke, asked.

"You mean besides letting them be part of our family fun event?" Christine shot back.

"Yeah," John wilted at the rebuke.

"I plan on blanketing the outside display windows, and selected columns within the store announcing our *Good Ole Days* event, and inviting our customers, with their family, to join in the fun," Christine continued. "Next, we need to encourage every Eaton to allocate space at the bottom of every full-page advertisement, to invite customers to become involved in our *Good Ole Days*. And finally, I will create five prizes for the best costumes of our participating customers. The prize awards will also be listed on all the advertising that I just mentioned."

EATON'S – During the Second French Revolution

"What are the prizes and who's going to pay for them?" Jerry Copeland inquired.

"Great question Jerry, but I haven't exactly figured that out, yet." Christine admitted. "But I can tell you that the prizes will cost us nothing, thanks to our committed suppliers, as they will also get lots of publicity for their donations. The actual grand prize could probably be a complete male, female, or child wardrobe, then, graduating down in value to a cheap pair of suspenders from your department, Jerry," Christine laughed.

"Second, and most importantly, will be employee costuming. It will be critical that all our employees wear authentic period clothing. I'll work with John Derber, in our merchandise display department, to come up with suggestions that I can present to the staff. Some people might have access to such actual clothing, if not, perhaps we can have our tailor and alteration department give us a hand."

Noticing no further comments, Ricky continued. "Okay, moving along, the final item I have is the event attractions. "He noticed Christine waving her hand wildly.

"Sorry to interrupt …" she stammered.

"No problem, go ahead."

"One other important item that I forgot to mention is that along with the advertising we need to get feature and follow-up articles in the all the newspapers about the event."

"Great Christine," Ricky acknowledged. "Now, as to the event attractions. Since this is such an important part of our overall success, I'll need two people to handle all aspects of its development. Volunteers?" He looked around the room and found *no one* volunteering.

"Thank you, Jerry Copeland and Andrea Bardot for volunteering," he smiled, as the whole room cracked up. "Now, let's help these two folks out with some suggestions, gang. Andrea, I want you to document the suggestions, then, you and Jerry can see about implementing them."

"Sure thing, Mister Dean," Andrea replied, as Jerry nodded.

"So, suggestions, anybody?"

Voices called out, "Can we get some vintage cars and boats as displays; How about a magician; Yeah, and a caricature artist; I know a barbershop quartet that will wander around the floor for free; "My sister works at Planter's Peanuts, and I'm sure we can get Mister Peanut to walk around the floor. The kids would love it." And the suggestions just kept coming.

⚜ Fifty-Seven ⚜

Within a few days of the first meeting for the *Good Ole Days Sale* everything began to fall into place.

Once Ricky knew the plans were moving along, he had to face the next item on his "to do" list. He wanted to tell Christine about his upcoming divorce plans and to share with her what the Quebec law was going to make him do to get that divorce.

Now that they were seeing each other more regularly, first business meetings after hours and then, "just for a drink," he felt they should be a little more cautious.

They planned to meet after work at their new little hideaway, *The Shamrock Bar & Grill*, on the corner of Cathcart St. and Dorchester St., far away from any possible prying eyes of any Eaton's employees.

The authentic Irish pub was owned by Paddy and Agnes McGuirk, a distant cousin of Ricky's, on his mother's side. The exterior of the front of the building on Cathcart Street was a stark comparison to the stone gray surrounding commercial buildings. Paddy, who was the only son of an affluent Northern Ireland family, had learned his trade as a millwright in the family lumber business, and applied his craft to creating an exact replica of Belfast's historic *Crown Liquor Saloon*, an old traditional Victorian pub, which had incredibly survived 42 bombing during the infamous "Troubles" in Northern Ireland.

During the "Troubles," Paddy, and his young bride-to-be, Agnes MacDonnell, immigrated from Ireland to Nova Scotia, where Paddy worked for 19 years as a constable for the Halifax Police Department, while Agnes, ever the good Catholic wife, birthed five healthy boys.

Paddy's career in law enforcement was cut short after a debilitating leg injury that resulted from a high-speed chase. Because of the severity of the injury, and the prolonged rehabilitation period, Paddy was pensioned out of the H.P.D., at which time, he moved his family west, settling in a Montreal East suburb.

Agnus and Paddy were totally dissimilar in character. Where Paddy was silent and withdrawn, Agnes was outgoing and boisterous. But Paddy had a temper that simmered just below the surface, and all who knew him understood that antagonizing this 285-pound hulk of a man could be disastrous. And anyone disrespecting his wife could result in a world of hurt. In fact, Paddy had a favorite Irish saying that he readily quoted to any potential offenders, *"It is often that a person's mouth broke his nose."*

Their biggest contrast was their physical appearance. Paddy was 6' 5" big boned, an imposing mountain of a man. He was attractive in a rugged way, with his graying dark brown curly hair, sallow skin, and penetrating blue eyes. He had a badly crushed nose like that of a prizefighter, and a hint of freckles from his teenage years. Paddy's face showed the remnants of a nasty faded scar running across his face beginning at his right ear then continuing across his cheek.

Agnes, on the other hand, was just slightly over 5' tall, had a very slender build that averaged around 110 pounds. Paddy always joked that she would blow away in a strong wind. She had medium-brown hair with some coppery red in it, pale, almost ghostly-white skin, that revealed cute freckles on her nose. Agnes had a round cherub-like face with green eyes that always appeared questioning, and she was definitely "very Irish," fighting to never lose her brogue accent. Paddy had long ago assimilated his accent to Canadian, only reverting to his native Irish brogue, for the benefit of his pub patrons.

Their greatest common interest was their passion for *The Shamrock* which had developed over a two-year period, from concept to reality. To achieve true authenticity, they had spent five weeks in Belfast, trolling pub after pub, photographing, drawing, and arguing over what was appropriate for their dream pub. Paddy's constant exclamation, "if it ain't real, it ain't coming in our pub!"

This fact was realized with Paddy's meticulous construction of the front entrance to *The Shamrock*.

Ricky jumped out of a cab at the entrance and marveled at the transition of the front of the building from its early days as a brokerage office. Paddy had constructed a set of impressive arched heavy wooden double doors made from weathered dark brown mahogany with precision-crafted panels; two large heavy iron handles and a small peep-door at the top. He had converted the windows using authentic stained glass and finished off the entry doors with a full surround of Old Tuscany red used bricks, from a demolition site in Old Montreal.

Ricky's face lit up when he noticed Christine hurrying to catch up with him, then propelling her tiny body into his waiting arms.

"Why didn't you take a cab?"

"Geez, Ricky, it's *only* three and a half blocks, and I need the exercise to keep my figure," she laughed.

"That'll be the day," he bent down to kiss her lips.

He opened the door to enter *The Shamrock* pub. The small entryway, with its low ceilings, gave way to a set of three stairs entering a cave-like tunnel towards the actual pub area. The 5-foot-long brick faced tunnel exited into a spectacular two-thousand square foot 19th century replica Irish pub, with twelve-foot-high metal paneled ceilings with contrasting cornice edging.

Ricky helped Christine take her coat off then removed his and hung both on the coat rack. He guided her towards the raised table area, near the rear of the room. A long shelved mirror behind the bar displayed a wide assortment of authentic libations including Hannigan's Whiskey, Connemara Irish Whiskey, Peated Single Malt Michter's Rye Whiskey, Bushmills Irish Whiskey, and others. Complimenting this selection was an array of The Best Stouts, Ales, and Lagers

Brewed in Ireland, both bottled and on-tap. The assortment included Beamish Stout, Guinness Draught, Murphy's Irish Stout, Ohara's Celtic Stout, and much more.

Pulling her close to him, he nibbled at her ear, whispering," I've thought about you all day."

She gently squeezed his hand, "And what were those thoughts?"

Distracted, Ricky finally sensed a body standing over him. "Why don't 'ya git a room, Lad and Lassie," followed by a deep laugh.

Startled, Ricky recovered saying, "It's a lot cheaper here, Agnes."

"Hey Ricky, Chris. 'Ya wan your usual?" she asked, in her heavy Irish brogue.

Ricky looked at Christine, who nodded.

"That would be great, Agnes. Where's Paddy, I didn't see him when I came in."

"At 'da mechanic shop pickin' up 'da ole beater," she huffed. "I hate that lorry."

"It beats walking," he replied.

She headed back to the bar. "Two Dubonnet Red coming up."

Ricky sat fascinated as Christine's eyes traversed the whole pub area, taking in the splendor of by-gone years, and the atmosphere of a mystical far-away country that she believed was beyond her reach.

"What?" she reacted, noticing his eyes taking in her fantasy travel.

"You look mesmerized every time we come in here."

"Well, this is my travel dream," she corrected, "after Paris, of course, I'd love to explore the beauty of all of Ireland."

"Including the bombs, kidnapping and murders?" Ricky laughed.

"Oh pooh! They're not hurting tourist, just Catholics and Protestants, and England," she added.

"And you don't think that Canadians, with our British ties, and our Union Jack flag, would be considered a prime target?"

"You are such a spoilsport, Ricky," she pouted. "Just look at this," she pointed around the room, "have you ever seen anything more beautiful?"

"Yes, I'm looking at it," staring at Christine, as he squeezed her hand.

At that moment Agnes returned with the drinks and just looked at the two of them, smiled and walked back to the bar.

Canopy lighting with amber globes cast elegant shadows on the walnut paneled walls accenting the old brick columns and arches, and walnut plank wood tables were surrounded by wooden Captain's chairs occupying the dark stained oak wood floors. Jutting out from the bar wall was a collection of famous reproduction liquor and wine casks and a collection of beer barrels flanked by a large display of pewter steins and mugs. Throughout the pub were old beer and wine signs; printed on aged wooden fence boards, heralding beers of by-gone years.

EATON'S – During the Second French Revolution

"Do you know anything about those three great pictures opposite the dart boards?" Christine pointed to the far wall.

"Actually yes. I originally thought they were just travel posters, then I found out from Paddy that Agnes painted them in oils from some postcards that they bought when they were over in Ireland. She's an incredibly talented lady. The picture on the left is Dunluce Castle, for a time, it was the seat of the Clan MacDonnell, which by the way were Agnes's ancestors. The middle one is Kilmainham Gaol, an old Dublin prison which, Paddy told me, signifies the heartbreaking courage of the men and women who resisted English rule and helped forge Ireland. It played a vital part in every act of rebellion for one hundred and twenty-eight years. Many of the Irish leaders, right up through the Irish War of Independence, were imprisoned there. In fact, the firing squad there is infamous for executing fourteen leaders of the nineteen sixteen Easter Rising, in the prison yard. The picture on the right is Northern Ireland's town of Derry, officially Londonderry, and is the best-preserved walled town in Ireland, and the finest examples of a walled city in Europe. The walls are up to twenty-six feet high and thirty-five feet thick in spots, are flanked with an array of watchtowers and cannons.

"Then, there's my favorite, the one over to the left of the bar. It's called Inishmurray, and it's a small, now uninhabited island with one of the most intact early Christian monastic settlements in Europe. It was featuring stone churches and a beehive hut enclosed in a circular dry-stone wall reaching up to fifteen feet high in places."

"And you know all this trivia, how?" Christine asked.

"Because I've been coming here for years and both Agnes and Paddy always find something new to tell me about these historic sites. And if a customer happens to ask about the pictures, they just say 'ask Ricky'. So, I guess I'm the de facto curator of Agnes's artwork," he laughed.

"Changing the subject, what was so urgent that you only gave me ten minutes notice to meet you here?"

Ricky took a long drag, then hesitated for a moment before responding, "I have some news I wanted to share with you."

"Well, it better be good news, because I'm feeling good right now."

Ricky looked into her eyes, "Two things are good news, and one, well, I'm not too sure yet, news'."

"Okay, tell me," she was anxious and concerned all in one.

Not one to let anything pass, Ricky kissed her lips.

"Enjoy, guys," Agnes placed the two new glasses of wine before them.

"Thank you," Christine replied sheepishly.

"So," Ricky continued, pulling Christine's head to rest on his shoulder, "news number one is our cause for celebration. I submitted my divorce application to the provincial court this morning. And there's only a couple of minor things that I still must do."

"Oh, Ricky? Is it really happening?" she sputtered.

"Yes, it really is."

"I don't need to hear anymore, please," she sighed. "This is all I've prayed for all these months. I know from everything you've told me, how hard your marriage has been for you, and now," she began to cry.

Ricky handed her a cocktail napkin. "But the next news is good."

"Okay, tell me," she whispered.

"Kathy has gone to live with her sister in Niagara Falls. And I've hired Mrs. Cote, my neighbor downstairs, as Darlene's' permanent nanny."

Tears streamed down her face. "Oh Ricky!" was all she could say.

Agnes raced over from the bar, "What did 'ya say ta da Lass to make her cry, Ricky," she demanded, concerned.

"It's okay, Agnes, these are happy tears, a long, long time coming."

Christine lifted her head and smiled, "Yes, Agnes," she sniffled as she tried to stop crying. "Very happy tears!"

"Okay, den," Agnes returned to the bar.

"I need to go to the little girl's room and freshen up."

Ricky stood as she made her way, "I'll just wait here," he joked.

While she was in the ladies' room, Ricky pondered how he was going to tell her the final news. This news was something that would destroy her glow, and maybe even affect her confidence in their future.

Christine returned to the table, her eyes still puffy, "I've never been so happy in my whole life, Ricky," she gushed.

"But Christine, there's more," he hesitated again, "and, it's not going to be as pleasant."

She stared at him, fear darting into her eyes.

"The laws in Quebec are archaic, and weird," he began. "In order to get a divorce, which can take up to eighteen months, I have to prove adultery as actual legal grounds."

"Adultery? How do you do that?"

There was no easy way to break the news, so Ricky just blurted it out.

"No, I have to hire a prostitute, and ..."

"Oh no, Ricky, please don't say that ..." she interrupted.

"Hold on, you need to hear the whole story."

Ricky related the whole conversation he'd had with Tony, regarding the required simulated sexual encounter, purposely leaving out the information about who was going to play the part of the hooker.

"Where do you find this hooker?" she quizzed.

"Tony knows an actress that owes him a favor, and is willing to play the part, while Tony will be the P.I. taking the pictures."

EATON'S – During the Second French Revolution

"This sounds so bizarre. Isn't there any other way?"

"Not unless I want to leave the province. Don't you see? This simulated sex could be our answer!"

"But ..." she stammered, "you're not really going to have to do *'it'*?" She slightly turned away.

Ricky smiled at her concern and gently turned her face back to his. "The only time I'll do *'it'*, as you call it, is when I'm making love to you, sweetheart!" He gently kissed her nose and lips." As the song goes, *'I only have eyes for you'*. Christine, please." He took her hand in his and brought it to his lips. "You don't have to worry. This is only an act to achieve a much higher purpose."

His tender words caused her to cuddle ever closer. "When do you have to do this?"

"Friday night, after work."

"Do you have to spend the whole night with this, uh ... girl?"

"No, the whole façade should take no longer than one hour and a half, with only fifteen minutes in the motel room."

"But you are so sexy. You can get into a lot of trouble in just fifteen minutes." she chuckled, nervously.

"Not this time, Babe," Ricky countered, "and it's time to get some food in your pretty body, yes?"

"I guess," she whispered.

Paddy insisted that *The Shamrock* specialize in traditional hearty Irish cuisine which was to include staples such as corned beef and cabbage, bangers and mash, Irish brown bread, beef stew, boxty, Irish shepherd's pie and Irish cream Bundt cake.

Ricky and Christine both chose the corned beef and cabbage dinner, and a dessert of Irish cream Bundt cake. Neither one wanting to continue the prostitute conversation.

Later that evening, Ricky put Christine in a taxi for home, and stood stationary for several minutes, watching the taillights disappear. He thought about what was, and what was to be, then suddenly realized he only had twelve minutes to get to his train ride home. Just making the train, his thoughts mimicked the sound of the train's wheels; over and over rehashing the upcoming Friday night nightmare... and what its results might be.

⚜ Fifty-Eight ⚜

Ricky just couldn't concentrate on his work, his mind wandering to thoughts of the planned motel tryst that evening. He'd made arrangements with Mrs. Cote to keep Darlene until late that night; retrieved sufficient cash from the bank and had promised Christine to call her when the whole affair was over. But the pit of his stomach conflicted with the simplicity of the plan.

Just then when a firm hand on his shoulder startled him, "What!" he turned his head to see the somber face of Tony Cartwright.

"Hell Ricky, you look like someone just shot your dog!"

"Yeah well ..." He stammered, "I haven't slept all night and I'm just nervous."

"Let's get a coffee," Tony directed, swinging Ricky to the right towards the luncheonette.

They got their coffees and settled into a booth away from any other customers.

"Why are you so nervous? Everything is set and you'll be in and out of the motel in minutes." Tony lit a cigarette and offered one to Ricky.

"Easy for you to say. All you must do is take pictures."

"Ricky, just listen to me," he leaned across the table, lowering his voice. "Debbie is all prepared, you choose the motel, and I'll be there to back you up. So, get with the program, and stop worrying."

"Okay! Okay, so should I go and rent the motel room ahead of time?"

"No. Pick up Debbie at six-thirty in front of Ruby Foos Restaurant, up off Decarie and Metropolitan. You can see the Bluebird Motel from the parking lot. You'll drive over to the motel and check in."

"Why can't I just get a room and have Debbie meet me there?"

"I need to get a picture of you and her registering at the office."

"Okay, then what?"

"You'll go to the room and Debbie will instruct you on what to do. And remember to leave the door unlocked."

"Debbie will instruct me on what to do?" Ricky looked concerned and confused.

"Not that 'to do', dummy. She'll tell you what to do to help her set the scene properly. Trust her, she knows what she's doing."

"Did you pick up the money for her?"

Ricky nodded.

"Give it to me and I'll pass it along to Deb."

Ricky took a bank envelope from his pocket, and handed it across the table, scouring the room as if he were doing something subversive.

"All right," Tony pocketed the envelope. "I'll come into the room at exactly seven, and let the fun begin," he laughed.

"I'm glad you find this funny, you sadistic prick!"

"Never fear, Uncle Tony is here," he responded, as they left the luncheonette.

Ricky spent the rest of the afternoon secreted in his office, trying unsuccessfully to calm his nerves. He'd made a point of staying away from Christine, and what he figured would be her accusatory stares. Fifteen minutes before closing he corralled Christine in her now empty department.

"Are you ready for this?" he asked, casually.

"Oh sure! My boyfriend is going to check into a motel with a hooker, and I'm just fine," she replied sarcastically.

"An actress, Christine, a friggin' actress," he stressed.

"I know, I know, it's just all so unnerving, I can't think straight."

"It'll all be over soon," he touched her hand lightly, ensuring that no one was around to see.

"What time?"

"We meet at six-thirty, and it will all be over by about seven-fifteen!"

"And you'll call me right after?" her eyes pleaded.

"Tony and I will probably get a bite to eat, so I'll call you from the restaurant." Ricky conveniently left out the fact that Debbie would probably join them for supper.

"Okay, Ricky, I'll expect to hear from you around eight, then."

"Later," he replied, heading back to his office for his overcoat.

Ricky had driven to work that day, something he rarely did, but he knew he would need his car for this evening's event. The drive up to Ruby Foos seemed to take forever, and when he finally parked in the parking lot, he began to panic at not seeing Debbie waiting at the entry. He scoured the parking lot for any sign of her. Turning his gaze back to the entryway he noticed a lady making her way across the lot. She had brilliant long red hair, a short black fur jacket, a mini skirt just inches below her crotch, black leggings and high heel boots up to her knees. As she came closer, he saw the face of a woman of about forty to forty-five years old, with heavy blue mascara eyelids, shadowed bags under her eyes and shocking red lipstick. He rolled down his window as she arrived beside his car.

"You waitin' for me, sailor boy?" she laughed.

The deep throaty voice was undeniably that of Debbie Stalinski.

"Get in," Ricky reached across and opened the passenger door. "Christ, I would never have recognized you until you spoke.

"Isn't that the idea?" she smiled.

"I guess," he replied, starting the car, and heading across the parking lot to the Bluebird Motel.

"Tony wants us both to go in and register," he exited the car and came around to open her door.

"Yeah, he's over there, pretending to be a movie director," she pointed to a car three cars away from where Ricky parked. Tony had his nine-year-old Buick's driver's side window open, aiming a camera at the motel entryway, a broad smile spread across his face.

"Let's do it," she commanded, walking up the entryway steps, where she paused, "from now on I'm Daisy, and you are Mister Jones, okay?"

Nodding Ricky opened the glass door into the motel reservation area.

"Need a room?" a man questioned, taking in the ample cleavage exposed through Daisy's open blouse.

No, I'm here for a fuckin' hamburger, you idiot! Ricky thought.

The man was in his fifties or sixties with a round face sporting heavy jowls and weepy eyes; eyes that never left Daisy's breasts, as a cigarette dangled from his puffy lips. He couldn't be any more than five-foot tall with scarce gray hair evident on his scaled head. His stained floral Hawaiian shirt hug over his ample Buddha belly. Ricky just wanted to run.

"Yes," Ricky replied unsure what to say next.

The old guy spun the register towards Ricky. "Eighteen per night. I'll give you a better price on our weekly rate."

Ricky signed the register 'Mr. & Mrs. Jones', then spun the register back, handing over a twenty-dollar bill, "Only one night, keep the change."

"Big spender," the guy commented, "ah, Mister Jones," looking at the name on the register. "Strange! I've had three Mister Jones, one Mister Smith, and one Mister White, this week already," he chuckled suspiciously, reaching for a key. "I presume you want a lower with direct access to the parking lot?"

"That would be great," Ricky replied, reaching for the key.

"Room one twenty-two, it is, then."

As they headed for the door the man stated, "By the way, if you decide to have any visitors," he smiled, "please leave the door unlocked. We don't need anyone kicking in the door down now, do we?" he roared.

Ricky helped Daisy back into the car and drove to the entrance to the room, Ricky asked, "Why are we using Mister Jones and Daisy names?"

"Because someone who is trying to secretly get laid is not going to use real names." Her reply came out as if he was a moron.

They entered the shabby room and were met with a combined acrid smell of mildew and cigarette smoke unsuccessfully camouflaged with the heavy odor of fragrance. The room had peeling, yellowed wallpaper, a small twelve inch black and white T.V., a double bed with a small two by four blocks supporting one leg and a tiny bathroom off in the corner.

After checking the room out thoroughly, which didn't take but a minute, Daisy emptied the contents of her large handbag on the bed and began sorting through the mess.

Debbie pulled off the red wig, shaking out her long hair, "I've got to take this off for a bit. It's making my head itch. Remind me to put it back on before the show starts," she laughed.

Without exaggeration, there was no doubt that Debbie was well endowed. She was tall, with pitch long black hair down to her waist, a perfect figure and piercing blue eyes on what was now an overly cosmetic made-up face.

EATON'S – During the Second French Revolution

Ricky was standing stone-still, like a statue, in the center of the floor, surveying the room and the faded ugly mottled carpet. "Couldn't we have done this at the Queen Elizabeth, or the Laurentian Hotel?"

She stopped her search, placing her hands on her hips. "And you think some judge is going to believe that you shacked up with a two hundred dollar a night call girl, in some swanky hotel, on your salary."

Ricky saw her point. "But this place is absolutely gross."

She leaned over and pulled up the corner of the ugly stained and ragged bedspread, exposing the white sheets. "All we need to be concerned about is that the sheets are clean." She threw the bedspread back in place. "You need to get your ass moving before Tony gets here. You better strip down to your underwear," she commanded.

"Um, I never wear underwear."

"And I'll bet the ladies really like that," she teased. "Okay, go in the bathroom, strip naked and wrap a towel around yourself."

Ricky went to the bathroom, stripped, wrapped himself in a towel, and when he returned to the room, his clothes in his arms, Daisy had stripped down to her bright red half-cup bra, and matching panties, and had her clothes flung all over the bed and by the door.

"Give me your clothes."

He handed her his clothes which she positioned on the bed, the nightstand, and the floor, directly in view from the door.

"There," she reviewed, "now, it looks like a sex den, right."

"It sure does." He felt totally uncomfortable standing semi-naked except for a towel before a total stranger.

"Oh, particularly important. When our paths cross at Eaton's, no sexy smiles, no smart-ass remarks. Remember, I am just an employee, and you are a manager, okay? This never happened. To me, you are just a client, and to you, I am the vehicle that is going to get your life back on track. Got it?"

"Got it!" Ricky replied.

"Okay then, this is for you." She flung him what looked like a flesh-colored rubber bicycle inner tube, about four inches wide by thirty inches long. "And this is for me," she chuckled, holding up a small triangle shaped, flesh colored piece of thin rubber.

"And these are for?" He was at a loss for words.

"Well, this is the delicate part. These are to conceal our equipment." She held up her small rubber triangle.

Equipment' is a strange way to describe genitals.

Noticing Ricky's confusion, she grabbed her hairbrush from the bed and took the thin rubber piece that he was holding. "This is what you do." She placed the hairbrush against her bare inner thigh. Then, pushed it up until it met her panty, and held it in place as she covered it with the end of the rubber piece.

Then, she rolled the piece of rubber tight around her thigh numerous times, eventually totally concealing the hairbrush. "Get the idea? The hairbrush simulates your penis, which I see you brought your own," she smiled. "Also, the skin tone color won't show up in the photo, and there won't be anything dangling, I hope," she laughed.

"Yeah," he blushed, "I get the picture."

He retreated to the bathroom where he wrapped his genitals in the soft rubber, making sure nothing was sticking out of either the top, or the bottom. He wrapped the towel around his waist, again.

When he returned to the room Daisy was naked on the bed, her knees elevated, and her bra and panties on the other pillow. Her genitals were totally concealed by that mysterious little triangle, but her ample breasts lay fully exposed, her nipples firm.

She looked at the bedside alarm clock, "We need to hurry. It's almost seven. Tony will be here any minute." She pulled on the wig then spread her legs open, the triangle remaining in place. "Come here and lie between my legs, but don't crush me," she directed.

Ricky obeyed.

"Okay now, use your right elbow to support your upper body, and your knees to support your lower, so you are not really lying on me."

Ricky repositioned himself according to her directions.

"No, No," she raised her voice, "your equipment needs to be lower down between my legs so that our equipment is *not* touching each other."

Here we go with the equipment, again. Ricky thought.

Ricky scooted down lower.

"Now, this is important to your health," she gazed at him seriously, "if you get a flutter in your loins, or god forbid, an actual woody, remember that my knee is going to come up into your balls so hard that you'll see stars and be talking in a high-pitched voice for a year, understand?"

"Got it. I'm already thinking about Grandma Moses, and baseball."

No sooner had the words left his mouth than Tony walked through the door, a huge grin on his face. "Okay boys and girls, are we ready for our Santa photos?" He slammed the door and turned the lock.

Ricky stared at Tony embarrassed, while Daisy gave a big grin.

"Let's get this done and get out of here," he insisted. "Ricky, point your left hand at me and open your mouth like you're yelling at me, Debbie, ugh, sorry, Daisy, put your hand on Mister Jones' shoulder and look at me with a shocked look on your face."

Tony snapped off the dozen pictures he needed from several different positions. "Ricky, could you lift your ass higher in the air."

Ricky complied.

"Great! Now, put your right hand behind your head as if you're in ecstasy. Good, good," Tony moved around the room looking through the lens. "That's fantastic! One more thing, Ricky ..."

"Just get this done, Tony. Artistic excellence is not a factor, here."

Daisy pulled a pillow over her head to silence her laughter.

Ricky heard the click of the shutter as Tony snapped off several more pictures.

"Great! Got it," Tony squealed.

Ricky slid off Daisy, wrapping a towel around his waist, then sitting on the corner of the bed, while Tony rolled the film in the camera. He noticed that Daisy still had not removed the pillow from over her head, but her body was rocking spastically with laughter.

As Tony slumped into a chair opposite Ricky, he fought unsuccessfully to control his expression, burying his head in his hands.

Concerned Ricky looked to Daisy, then to Tony. "What's wrong? Tony, didn't you get the shots that you needed?" Ricky was concerned about having to do this façade all over again.

Daisy rolled on her side; her whole body now racked with uncontrollable laughter.

Ricky looked back at Tony who fell from his chair to the floor where he too roared with laughter. "Oh yeah! I got the shots, all right! The best one is the shot of your bare ass up in the air, which will be framed in the manager's lounge." Tony grabbed his crotch and ran for the bathroom.

Ricky shook his head in disbelief as the realization finally hit him. *"I've been had, but good! Tony staged these after shots as a prank against me. I'll get even with him one day!"*

As Ricky began putting on his clothes, he thought, *"The only good thing that will salvage the horror of tonight is that I get to hear Christine's voice, after this nightmare is over."*

⚜ Fifty-Nine ⚜

Ricky pulled the motel door closed and was thankful that he would never have to see the inside of that dump ever again. His only hope was that he could scrub the whole nightmare from his memory.

"Are you guys ever going to get rid of those smiles on your faces?" Ricky asked, gazing at Tony and Debbie who were leaning against Ricky's car.

"Not as long as I have the evidence of your ass flying in the air," Tony responded, pointing to the camera around his neck.

Exasperated, Ricky threw up his hands in surrender. "Screw you, Tony. Let me bring the key back.

"Sure thing, stud!" Tony replied, walking Debbie over to his car.

Ricky entered the office and threw the room key on the reservation desk. "Thanks."

"Wow!" The clerk exclaimed.

"Wow, what?" Ricky answered defensibly.

"You set an all-time record."

"Record for what?"

The clerk looked at the reservation ledger. "You were in the room for only twenty-eight minutes. You should have asked for our premium minute price, instead of daily rate," he roared.

"Screw you," Ricky responding, slamming the glass door as he exited.

Ricky found a quaint oriental style telephone booth in the Ruby Foos entryway where he dialed Christine's number.

The phone was answered on the first ring, "Hello."

"Hello darlin'. Are you okay, you sound out of breath?"

"No, no, I think I've just been holding my breath waiting for your call, that's all. Are you okay?"

"Yeah, it's all over without any problems and we are just getting a bite to eat at Ruby Foos."

"I'm really glad that it's all over. I've been a nervous wreck all day. And this last hour of waiting has been from hell."

"Well, no more worries, just pleasant thoughts of our future, yes?"

"Sure Ricky," she cooed.

"Okay, as we planned, I'll pick you up for Darlene's birthday party around eleven tomorrow morning. I told Kathy about the party, but she has an interview planned so she won't be able to come back to Montreal for the party?"

"And she'd miss her own daughter's birthday party?"

"That's Kathy, dependable as ever."

"Well, at least we were lucky enough to be able to arrange to be off two Saturdays in a row. First, Mont Tremblant, then Darlene's party. How lucky can a girl get?" she gushed.

"Anyway, I'd better get back."

"Okay," she replied. "Sleep well and know I'm missing you!"

"Sweet dreams to you too, darlin', and I miss you too!"

Ricky headed back to the table.

"So, did you tuck her in?" Tony snorted, shoveling a pile of food on his already heaping plate.

"Stuff it, Tony, and pass the lemon chicken."

Debbie piped in, "Tony, what's the hush, hush story going around about Fredrickson, the manager of accounting, getting canned. He's been there for like thirty years?"

"There's a reason that it's a hush, hush story, Deb."

EATON'S – During the Second French Revolution

Ricky took a stab at some chicken wings. "Come on, Tony. After all we've been through tonight, you think we can't keep a secret?"

"Okay, okay. But, pass me some fried wontons and crab Rangoon, first. Here's the scoop. It's been common knowledge for years that Fredrickson has been diddling with some female in the store, but no one has ever been able to firm up the story, that is, until last Thursday. Fredrickson was having what seemed like an innocent lunch with his secretary, Mary Jane Cooper, in the fancy ninth-floor dining room, when in walks none other than his wife, Grace Fredrickson. She walks over to the table, picks up Mary Jane's lasagna from the table and dumps it over her head. Mary Jane jumps to her feet and pushes Grace away, Grace grabs her by the hair and flings her into an adjoining table, crushing the table and spilling the contents onto the floor. Meanwhile, she's using every curse word in the book and looking for something else to throw at Mary Jane, who is crying on the floor." Tony paused to grab another chicken wing. "Two of my people rush over and grab her, but she shakes loose and makes a bee line for Fredrickson, who is still sitting stunned at the table. Listen to this. When he sees Grace coming at him, he jumps from his chair, jumps over the top of Mary Jane, who is lying prone on the floor, and escapes down a stairwell."

"Short story. Fredrickson and Mary Jane are called to the executive offices and fired on the spot."

"Wow. And Mrs. Fredrickson?" Debbie asked.

"She told me that, last night, her neighbor saw Fredrickson and Cooper going up to the guest rooms in the St. Francis Hotel, when he had actually told her that he was going to be in Ottawa."

"What did you do with Mrs. Fredrickson?" Ricky piled more beef teriyaki and fried shrimp on his plate.

"I told her that we appreciated her show, that Fredrickson was going to have to pay for all the damages in the dining room and that I hoped that I personally never got on her bad side."

"That's too much information for me," Debbie rose from her chair. "I need to go to the little girl's room."

"Across the room and down the stairs on the left," Tony offered.

As Debbie disappeared down the stairwell, Ricky quietly asked Tony, "Any news from Ray about the possible date and time of Vinney's heist?"

"Not so far. Ray says that Vinney is being very closed mouth about the whole thing, but he did see a box truck in the warehouse repainted in Eaton's colors and sporting Eaton's logos on the doors. So, we are sure it is a go."

"Without a firm date we could be up the creek," Ricky responded, watching to ensure that Debbie was not returning.

"Well, Ray is trying hard to get the details. He's arranged for Marcus to come over to his house to look at the boat that he's selling. He says that this Marcus guy is the weakest link in Vinney's organization, and he's sure he can trick

Marcus into divulging more details about the heist."

"Let's hope so."

After Debbie returned to the table, they finished their meal, and Ricky headed home.

⚜ Sixty ⚜

Ricky had finally gotten over the horror of the experience with Debbie and Tony and the sleazy motel incident, thanks to the compassionate telephone conversation he had with Christine that night.

Fortunately, Darlene's birthday party had also been a welcome diversion. Christine was a natural with his baby daughter; doating on her all through the party. She reveled in the fact that they had another glorious full day together. But the surprise for him was how much Darlene seemed unable to get enough of the affection lavished on her by Christine. And Ricky did not see any value in telling Kathy about Christine's participation in the party.

When the party was over, Misses Cote put Darlene to bed and agreed to stay with his daughter while Ricky took Christine home. "Don't rush you too!" Ricky heard her say as he helped Christine on with her coat. "Nice to meet 'ya."

"You too, Misses Cote."

Ricky drove Christine back to her apartment. "The party turned out great, don't you think," he asked idly.

"Oh Ricky, it was absolutely glorious. I just love that little girl of yours. Did you see how cute she looked trying to wear those big sunglasses?" she gushed, sliding closer to him.

The following week the spectacular results of the on-going *Good Ole Days Sale,* and the developing plans for the upcoming *Record-Breaking Day Sale* and working with Tony on the cash office heist, left little room for personal thoughts.

Ricky headed across the selling floor for a welcome coffee break in the luncheonette.

He adjusted a crooked wig on a mannequin in the teen fashion department, where he saw assistant manager, Cindi Valdez. "Is Misses Guillaume around?"

Like Christine, Cindi exhumed an air of fashion in her dress and mannerisms. Her dark eyes chiseled facial features and slightly olive complexed skin hinted at her Spanish heritage.

"No, she isn't, Mister Dean," Cindi smiled, "she had to run out to Belletown Sportswear, to pick up some bubble blouses. We ran out of them during the *Good Ole Days Sale* and the supplier told us that he'd have four dozen ready before end of day. I know she also wanted to make it clear that we can't run out because he didn't have the stock. We will need plenty for the *Record-Breaking Day Sale."*

"Great! The blouses have really taken off, haven't they?"

"Yes sir, but if Herb Melville can't get his production up, we are going to continue falling short. Angelina told me that she lost three sales on Saturday alone, and Lori lost two. Misses Guillaume was not incredibly happy about that."

"Nor am I. Ask Misses Guillaume to see me when she gets back please," Ricky replied, continuing across the floor.

"Will do, sir."

He almost bumped into Maggie as she headed for the escalator. "Where are you going in such a hurry, Maggie?"

"Oh, hi Ricky," Maggie stopped, "Myron's come downtown to buy me lunch over at Dunne's Smoked Meat, and as usual I'm running late."

"Don't worry Mag, Myron's so smitten with you he'd wait for you all day, if he had to!"

"I know. Ever since our trip to Florida, he's been driving me crazy trying to put a ring through my nose."

"You mean on your finger, don't you?"

"Same difference," she laughed.

"Have you seen Suzanne Flatley around," asking about his ladies' shoes section head.

"She's right there," she pointed towards the stockroom door, as she stepped onto the up escalator.

"Regards to Myron," he yelled, heading for the rear of the ladies' shoe department.

"Sure will," she replied, as she disappeared toward the upper floor.

Suzanne was matching up miss-mated ladies' sneakers.

"Hey Suzie."

"Oh hello, Mister Dean. Can I help you with something?" she offered.

"No thanks. I just wanted to let you know that I loved yesterday's *Montreal Star* ad for the special Stiletto heel shoes. The ad looks great. The comparison pictures between the old flapper pumps and your Stilettos really stands out."

"I sure hope it works. I've never had to make that large of a purchase before."

"Sometimes you just have to go with your gut. The fashion is current, the price is exceptional, and you have plenty of inventory. So, don't worry, it'll turn out great!"

"Thanks for the vote of confidence Mister Dean."

"You're more than welcome," he replied, continuing his trek towards the luncheonette.

He entered nodding at cashier, Josephine Leblanc, "Hi Josephine. A bit quiet in here today?"

Josephine was a mature attractive woman of about forty years old, plagued with the constant concern of handling personal weight problems. Strangely, over the years, Ricky had noticed that, although she ate like a bird, weight continually gravitated to her ample hips. However, what she lost in body attractiveness, she more than made up with a smiling face and infectious personality.

"Yeah, but you shoulda' been here at lunchtime. It was like a zoo," she replied punching up a sale for a waiting customer.

Ricky went to the beverage counter, where he got an empty cup and picked up the coffee carafe.

"Hang on a minute, Mister Dean, I've got a fresh pot, here," offered waitress, Mary Colmers.

To Ricky it seemed like Mary had been with Eaton's, forever. She had the textbook look of everyone's grandmother. Mary ran the luncheonette operation, under manager, Steve Fortuna, in the style of an army sergeant major. Fortuna may have been the manager, but everyone knew that no one crossed Mary and remained unscathed.

"Great Mary," he handed her the almost empty carafe. "How's Bob doing since the ulcer operation?"

"Much better. Thanks for asking. He's still got three weeks of rehab, then he'll be back to work."

"Well, give him my best, and tell him not to be a stranger."

After a quick coffee, Ricky returned to his office and reviewed the sales statistics from Monday and Tuesday of the *Good Ole Days Sale.* They were great! The advertising and promotions they did to get customers to come in costume really brought in a lot of extra shoppers. And once they saw the employees dressed accordingly, and the décor, of past and present, they stayed longer and bought more!

Even with only two days sales results, Ricky smiled as he thought of his earlier conversation with Appleton. Apparently, not only were the early results noticed by local management, but the Toronto board had already decided to make the *Good Ole Days Sale* a national event next year. This would leave Ricky with the chore of developing a comprehensive action plan that addressed all the development details of the sale, to be distributed throughout the chain. He knew his committee would excel at helping him create a great plan.

The one strange thing about his conversation with Appleton was that Appleton did not utter one word about the upcoming potential cash office heist. It was as if he didn't make any comments about it, he would be able to deny any involvement.

Just as he was about to leave Christine showed up in his office, "You wanted to see me?"

"Sit down for a minute." he directed. "I wanted to know how you made out at Belletown," he inquired, looking up from his report.

"I got it handled. I told Herb Melville that I had a supplier in Hamilton that could turn out as many bubble blouses as I needed, and he just about freaked out. Long story short, he's putting on an extra night shift, so we will be sure to have as much stock as we need. Problem solved."

"That's simply great. Who is the Hamilton supplier?"

"What Hamilton supplier?" she smiled mischievously, rising without further comment, and leaving Ricky's office.

Ricky completed the master duty rosters for the coming week, reviewed several upcoming ads, and prepared a quarterly employee evaluation on Rebecca Snyder and Monique Rousseau.

They're not adapting to their new department management responsibilities as rapidly as I expected. Although I don't want to, I may have to place them both on probationary status to light a fire under them. Ricky thought.

Having finished his work Ricky packed up his briefcase, gathered his coat and headed toward the door, where he saw Jerry retrieving his overcoat from the coat closet.

"Going straight home?" Jerry inquired.

"Nah, I've got to kill a few hours, before I do," Ricky replied as they headed for the Metcalfe employee's entrance.

⚜ Sixty-One ⚜

The day before the Eaton's heist, Vinney was noticeably listless and irritable, barking orders and insults at anyone who had the misfortune of entering his space. He hadn't slept well for the past few days, plagued by reoccurring dreams about the robbery. He saw every aspect in vivid detail right down to the five of them sporting shotguns as they descended Eaton's stairs to their ultimate reward. The troubling and confusing part of the dream was the ending where he envisioned two open ebony coffins situated below the steps to the St. Joseph's Church alter. In the dream he could make out many familiar faces within the hundreds of mourners, but hard as he tried, he could not recognize the people in the coffins. Could they be his mother or father, or maybe Frankie, or …?

Finally, in his dream he was in church as the organ music echoed off the lofty ceiling and the priest began his service. Vinney discovered that he was able to see into the coffins, one of which was the serene face of his comrade, Francesco, *Frankie* Rossie, but the other face was obscured by a floral wreath stand. In the dream he tried to move to a different position to be able to identify the second victim, but no matter where, or how, he moved he found the wreath still obstructing his view.

Each day when he woke up, he analyzed the whole dream, including the coffins. He surmised that the second body must be that of Marcus "the Head" Castille. He justified the dream interpretation was that he had followed through on his threat to Frankie about getting rid of Castille, therefore, the second body must be that of Castille.

But why was Frankie dead, too? He couldn't understand it, no matter how he played out the details of the dream. He decided, the only logical explanation was that he had sent Frankie out to ice Castille, but Castille figured out about the hit, a gun battle ensued, and they were both killed.

It's a sad ending, but if one believes that dreams are blueprints of future things to come, better him than me! Vinney thought.

Vinney jogged across the wide expanse of the warehouse shouting at the semi-trailer driver exiting the cab, bearing the name *Mammoth Trucking & Storage*. "Any problems with the 'jacking, Guy?"

"Almost, but no, Sir," Guy replied, moving to meet Vinney's advance.

"I don't like *almost*," Vinney stated, as he followed Guy to the back of the trailer.

"The *almost* turned out to be nothing at all. As I was following the original driver to the shoulder of the highway, we heard a siren coming up on us. I radioed for him not to panic, and just tell the cop that he thought he had a tire going down and that I followed him off the road to see if I could help. So, the guy is settling down and the cop car goes screeching by with lights flashing and siren blaring. Apparently, the cop was just going to a regular call."

"Any trouble with the driver?"

"No! He couldn't wait for me to reach into my pocket for his envelope full of cash. And he knew exactly what to do after he got the envelope, and he handed me the truck keys, let me punch him in the face and then disappeared into the brush beside the road saying, 'I'll rest here for about an hour before I flag down someone and report that I've been high jacked,'" Guy laughed, as he opened the large trailer doors.

"Any idea about the cargo?"

"Yeah, when I stopped at a truck stop outside Isle Perrot for a piss I told Davie, who was following me in my car, to peek in the trailer. So, he finds the trucking manifest identifying the cargo as furniture contents from a Doctor Larson, who lived on Trinity Hill, just outside Ottawa. That's rich country for doctors, lawyers, and politicians, so this stuff is prime Grade A beef, boss!" he hoisted himself up into the trailer.

"Well, remind me to send Doctor Larson a nice 'thank you' card."

"Will do," he laughed, handing a heavy Cherrywood box down to Vinney. "But you better make it a gold engraved 'thank you', 'cause you're really gonna love this present, Vin."

Vinney opened the elegant brass clasp, and the hinged top, and stared in disbelief at the contents. Before him were rows and rows of Canadian twenty-dollar gold pieces, all identified with vintage dates.

"Is this for real?" Vinney sputtered. "There's gotta be twenty to thirty grand here. Who the hell ships a gold coin collection, with his furniture, in a moving truck?"

"An idiot that has more money than brains, that's who! What do you want us to do with the furniture and the trailer, boss?"

"Get those lazy Quaws, *Iroquois Indians*, to unload the furniture from the trailer, and put everything against the north wall, beside the old beater truck. I want you to supervise them and personally go through all the drawers for any other surprises. Don' leave the Quaws alone for one minute, or they'll steal us blind."

"What are we going to do with the trailer after it's empty?" Guy asked.

"I'll get Robin Conrad to bring his torch set down and have him cut up the trailer for scrap. We don't waste anything here, Guy!"

I sure as shit hope that I was right, in my dream, about that being Castille in the other casket.

⚜ Sixty-Two ⚜

Vinney paced aimlessly around the huge warehouse, ignoring his crew lounging on the sofas and chairs by his desk. He had a foreboding feeling that everything was not right with the planned Eaton's heist. He knew that he personally had planned everything down to the smallest detail, but something kept gnawing at him. Vinney finally walked over to his crew and looked each one in the eye.

"So, today is our big day! The getaway car is in position, the disguises and uniforms are on the table and the truck is ready to go. I also bought new twelve-gauge double barrel shotguns from the Westies. But we may have a problem," Vinney moved towards Marcus.

"What do you think, Marcus, do we have a problem?" Vinney bent to eye level with Marcus.

"No boss, we got no problem," Marcus squirmed in his chair.

"No problem, eh? Since when did you develop this great new interest in boats?"

"I ... I ... I," Marcus stammered.

"Shut up and listen, you fat prick. Why were you looking to buy a boat, and with what, money you stole from me!?"

"No, no, Vin. I was looking for a boat cuz my momma loves to fish. And I swear that she was going to pay for the boat." Marcus cowered as he waited for Vinney's next move!

"And I suppose that Archambault is the only guy in Montreal that has a boat for sale?"

"No Vinney, it's not like that. When Ray was here last week, he told me that he was having trouble making his vig and would have to sell off his boat. So, I told him I was interested."

"And you had to go to his house?"

"Yeah. I had to see the boat, right?"

"It seems like you have a lot of time on your hands between your shoplifting crew and our Eaton's heist. Maybe I should find more work for you like painting this whole damn warehouse, inside and out!" Vinney was now screaming at the top of his lungs.

Marcus looked around the huge warehouse. "No boss, It's not like that. I went to Ray's house in the night when his wife and kid were out."

"And how many beers did you have?"

"No, uh, maybe one, or two," he quickly corrected.

"Don't lie to me or I'll blow your fuckin' kneecaps off. Now, tell me, how many beers?"

"Three or four, Vin, I'm not sure," his voice quaked as he eyed the nickel-plated 38 that Vinney had removed from his shoulder holster.

"And how long were you with Archambault?"

"Forty-five minutes to an hour."

"And what did you talk about for this hour?"

"Just the boat, Vinney, just the boat, I swear. He told me about the whole motor thing and how to use the trailer lift, and ..."

"And you talked about nothing else?"

"Nothing boss, I swear."

"If I find out that you spilled anything to Archambault, you won't need a boat because you'll be swimming with the fishes, understand?"

"Sure boss."

"Okay then. With all that bullshit over with, does everyone know exactly what they have to do today?"

Everyone's head nodded.

"And does everyone have their backup piece?"

Again, everyone's head nodded.

"Okay, get into your disguises and pick up your weapons. It's nearly time to rock and roll, gentlemen."

With that Vinney put his pistol back in his holster and tried to shake the negative thinking that kept coming into his mind.

⚜ Sixty-Three ⚜

Ricky sat with his feet up on his desk thinking of all the upcoming events that he would have to deal with.

Preparation for the annual *Record-Breaking Day* event had always been stressful and labor intensive, but with the addition of taking down a major shoplifting ring *and* thwarting an armed robbery; pressure was evident in everyone's routine.

Sale item deliveries needed to be received, processed, and displayed, personnel required extensive instructions, departments required a customer flow change of layout and additional checkout options. In addition to sale elements, the advertising and pricing needed to be checked, and double checked.

To minimize staff anxiety, the decision was made to not let the staff know about the pending criminal actions until the morning of the sale. However, all management, from section heads through department heads, were given specific areas of responsibility regarding the upcoming robbery. Their main mandate was to keep the customers out of harm's way and to instill calm when the robbery became known. These procedures were rehearsed everyday leading up to sale day.

In addition to his normal preparation for the sale, Ricky had become entangled in a purchase decision that could be the biggest in Eaton's history, coast to coast. A ladies sportswear supplier, Bernie Schwartz, of Bonton Casuals, had contacted Ricky directly with information that 7000 men's and lady's full length leather coats had been seized from an arriving Venezuelan cargo ship, by Canadian Customs. The actual owners of the shipment had been contacted 90 days earlier by Canadian Customs requiring them to have all the coats labeled "Made in Venezuela," and to pay the 26% duties required before the shipment could be released. Since the owners had not acted in the allotted time, the shipment was to be disposed of, as a single lot, by the customs department. The main problem with the disposal was that no one single department store, or distributor, needed that many coats. Since Bernie had agreed to have his company create and affix the labels, Ricky quickly contacted all sportswear department managers, across the chain, and the Eaton's Toronto catalogue office, to get a purchase pledge from each of them, keeping the largest quantity for his own Record-Breaking Sale. The combination of the duty, which was $78,000.00, plus Bernie's labelling costs of $1.00 per coat netted the coats an incredible price of only $10.40 each, for coats with a retail value over $100.00. This price allowed Ricky to advertise the coats at an unprecedented ½ off price of only $49.95 each, offering an unbelievable profit margin, while giving his customers fantastic value.

The nail-biting problem for Ricky was that he had the coats advertised as a "feature item" in all the newspapers, but delay in Canadian Customs bureaucracy and document processing, had delayed Bernie's delivery of the coats. He was faced with labelling and delivering 7500 coats in only three days, but he vowed they would arrive, even if he had to run three shifts to accomplish the feat. But for Ricky, this was but one more problem plaguing his mind.

Ricky also had to follow-up on his assignment from Tony for the pre-robbery security. With the assistance of appropriate department managers, they questioned the main and basement floor personnel, showing the enhanced photo of Vinney. Two main floor salesgirls, one elevator operator and one cash office employee positively identified Vinney as the person posing as the Italian speaking visitor, days before the fur heist. Each employee gave a written statement to the security department, which was passed on to the MPD.

Tony spent the harried days leading up the sale day, coordinating efforts with his detective staff, reviewing field reports from Ray and Denis regarding identifying 'Liftermob' members, and meeting with Ricky and department heads, in addition to coordinating bi-hourly communications with various MPD department heads.

During their recent meeting, Ricky handed Tony a note. "What's this?" Tony asked.

"Confirmation that we are not the only ones who know about the robbery."

"Where did you get this?"

"I found it my office mailbox, at the entry to the main office."

"Damn," Tony responded, "Another bloody ditty from our 'Shadow' friend." Reading the note again, "*'Eaton's will be the home of a terrible slight. Of a criminal caper that won't be right. The robbers will penetrate on mass, with guns drawn, they'll enter the store very fast. The 'Shadow.'*"

"Well, he/she is not much of a poet, but at least, we now are sure that it is going to happen," Ricky hurried towards the elevators.

On the Thursday morning of the Record-Breaking Day sale, all Eaton's personnel, including support staff, had been directed to attend a floor meeting, one half hour before the 9:00 A.M. opening bell. This meeting was to communicate and confirm all information regarding the probable cash office robbery, and each of their roles to ensure customer safety.

When the meeting ended, Ricky asked his department heads to remain. "I know we are all nervous about what might happen today, but I see fear on many of your faces, which we must get under control. First, we don't want to alert *anyone*, and I repeat, *anyone*, that we even suspect any problems today. So, you need to act like we are having one of the biggest sales of the year, not like we are anticipating a robbery! Second and more important, once it is obvious that the robbery is in progress, we need to present our customers with a calm, in control atmosphere, and with assurances that they are not in danger. Throughout the day, we must always maintain a maximum compliment of management on the floor. I've had coffee urns, sodas, and an array of sandwiches, strategically placed in the back-stock areas, where you can watch the floor, while you take your breaks or lunch. Also, cut back on employee breaks and limit lunches to half-hour instead of one hour. Security and MPD believe that the robbery won't be attempted until sometime after noon, and more likely between one and four when the cash office has accumulated the most cash, but don't get complacent, it could happen at any time! All the head cashiers have been directed to process change requests, using the pneumatic tubes, to the fifth-floor cash office only."

"And very important," Ricky emphasized, "If it is absolutely necessary to process any large traveler's checks, or a customer's personal check, they are to be done by the department manager, or assistant department manager, *only*.

Everyone nodded.

"Okay, let's all be safe, and have a great Record-Breaking Day sale," and with that Ricky began his floor inspection circuit.

Ricky was thinking. *This whole operation is predicated on our belief that Vinney is going to hit the store today, but if we are wrong, hundreds of MPD and store personnel have been mobilized for nothing. And, with the disruption of the Record-Breaking Day sale, and the massive costs of additional personnel, Tony and I are going to have a hell of a lot of explaining to do*.

He felt anxious, his heart was racing, and his hands were sweating. Ricky barked final orders to various department staff, as he traversed the floor, from the south end to the north end.

"Get those empty boxes off the floor and into the stockroom. You need to get rid of those handprints on the glass of your showcases. Have maintenance mop around the front of Laura Secord. Call the carpentry office immediately and have them remove the 'cash office' sign above the entry. I don't want customers wandering in there," Ricky directed.

God help us all if we end up with a shoot out on the selling floor.

⚜ Sixty-Four ⚜

As the opening bell sounded, a stampede of sale-crazed customers descended onto the basement floor; wildly shouting to the staff, while grasping for the special sale items. The floor was total bedlam, but more so in ladieswear and menswear, where customers physically fought to acquire the incredible offer of the $49.95 leather coats, many attempting to gather up as many coats as they could carry. In fact, Ricky noticed two buyers from Miracle Mart, piling dozens of coats into their shopping carts, no doubt, to resell in their discount store.

The morning progressed typical of past sale days with few critical incidents, thefts, or disturbances.

Tony met Ricky, in front of the luncheonette. "How's it going?"

"Aside from the bizarre customers, everything else is normal. I've noted a large presence of your security people and MPD undercover, which is very reassuring. Also, as you requested, I've got all the S.W.A.T. secreted in my lingerie changing rooms. It's a hellava scene. Six big, heavily armed guys crammed into three small changing rooms, for the last three and a half hours. They've got to be going stir crazy."

"Yeah, I have the other six guys sweating in the small glove department stockroom. That's what we pay our taxes for, I guess" Tony laughed. "Oh, for your information, we've only apprehended five shoplifters storewide, but Denis and Ray, told me that none of them were part of the 'Liftermob' gang. As we anticipated, their activities are going to begin just before the actual robbery begins," he said, not waiting for a response, as he headed for the escalator to the main floor.

At precisely 1:15 P.M. all hell broke loose in the north and west side departments of both the basement and main floors. Several displays crashed to the floor; a fight broke out on both floors; 'eyes on' alarms were being sounded; shoplifters were apprehended walking away with stolen merchandise; and sales staff were being cursed out by supposed irate customers. The play had begun!

Tony immediately contacted communications and had the opening bell rung again, signaling the attention of all personnel and MPD, that the situation had begun. He watched with admiration as everyone took their respective positions, calmly herding customers toward the center aisle of the main floor. His security personnel, MPD undercovers and S.W.A.T. all took up positions as faux customers in the vacated areas of the respective departments, and in the stairwell.

At 1:23 P.M. Tony's radio crackled with news from Henri Gaston, who was positioned with his men, behind the shrubbery wall of Christ Church Cathedral, advising "A blue Eaton's truck had just been spotted on Maisonneuve Boulevard, awaiting the light, to travel south on University." At 1:25 this report was followed by, "The truck has just parked in front of the University Street entrance, and the driver, the only person visible in the truck, is checking his watch."

At precisely 1:30 P.M. the report was, "The driver just got out of the truck followed by four men, in long overcoats exiting from the rear double doors of the truck. They hesitated for a moment, scanned the surrounding area, then quickly proceeded to the middle University Street doors."

Vinney casually glanced around the street to see if there were any threats. He then signaled his men to enter through the revolving doors, go down the four steps and turn left toward the stairwell.

Henri watched the men disappear into the store and reported, "The subjects have entered the store, and their vehicle is now being towed away. I have signaled my men to take up their positions at all the main floor exit doors."

The Eaton's stairwell, like the rest of the building, dated back to the beginning of the century, and whereas the building had undergone significant updating renovations, the stairwell remained in its original state; complete with one-inch marble walls, stairs, and landings. The handrails were large solid walnut accented by ornamental iron spindles. The lighting in the stairwell was poor; illuminated by a simple dull chandelier, hanging high overhead.

The stairs formed a circuitous route from the main floor to the basement, with seven steps from the top entry down to the first landing, then looping right to another seven steps to the middle landing and looping right again to the final seven steps of the basement floor level.

Vinney followed his men into the stairwell and paused to look back towards the selling floor, "Okay, are we all ready?" he asked, calmly and quietly.

"Now, or never, boss," Frankie responded.

"Take the shotguns out from under your coats and position them against your right leg in case we encounter anyone coming up the stairway. When we exit onto the basement floor, we're only about ten feet away from the cash office, that'll put the guns between us and the cash office wall, so no one will see them. Let's do it!" Vinney commanded.

Vinney led the pack, followed by Jimmy Fellini and Aldo Renaldi, with Marcus Castille and Frankie Rossie bringing up the rear. As they rounded the first bend in the stairs descending onto the second landing, Vinney halted abruptly, the unexpected action propelled the huge body of Marcus into Jimmy and Aldo, causing them to almost lose their balance on the stairs.

Vinney reacted with a menacing point of his shotgun at Marcus chest. Finally, lowering the gun, he peered around the corner, down the final leg of the descent. "All clear," he whispered.

At that exact same moment, a loud voice boomed from behind them, halting everyone in their tracks.

"Stop! MPD, Lower your weapons slowly to the ground."

Seeing the lingering startled reaction from the robbers, the voice yelled again, "Put your fucking weapons down, *now*. This is your final warning, next we shoot." This message must have gotten through crystal clear as the five men lowered their sawed-off shotguns onto the marble stairs.

"Raise your hands above your head and continue down the stairs, slowly," the S.W.A.T. officer commanded, nudging Frankie in the back of his head with the barrel of his gun.

As they started down the last seven stairs Vinney saw another S.W.A.T. officer waiting at the bottom of the stairs. With his gun trained on him."

Only one cop, I can handle that! Vinney thought.

Knowing his crew was bunched up behind him in the narrow stairwell, Vinney feigned tripping; then pushed back hard against his crew, sending them sprawling on the stairs behind him, momentarily surprising the upper officer.

That should keep the cop behind me busy.

At that exact moment, he pitched his head vigorously forward, propelling his blond wig towards the face of the officer in front of him, as he simultaneously reached for his holstered gun, inside his overcoat."

Eat that sucker!

Vinney's glistening 38 had just barely cleared the holster when he heard, "Gun!" shouted by the lower officer. Two shots rang out, one shot from the lower officer who quickly regained his focus, firing point blank into Vinney's stomach. Vinney turned slightly back as shots rang out from behind him. One of the shots entered neatly through the back of his head, at the same time as the lower shot hit him in his upper torso. The effect of these two bullets would be spoken amongst police officers for decades to come. Instead of the usual fact of the body fully collapsing, or pitching forward or backwards, from impact, Vinney's dead body went rigid in a standing stance for several seconds, before nose diving face first into the hard marble floor below, his once handsome face now totally decimated.

Probably Vinney's final thought, if he even had one, was that he now knew who was in the second coffin of his reoccurring dream.

Frankie was scrambling to his feet after Vinney had pushed back upon him toward the rest of the gang. In a feeble attempt to take advantage of the mayhem, Frankie reached for his gun, just as one of the officers fired the third bullet, which penetrated Frankie's heart. Like in Vinney's dream, now Frankie too was dead!

The lower officer cuffed Vinney's lifeless body, while the upper four officers secured Frankie's body, and restrained the other three men. They summoned paramedics for one of the robbers whose arm had been grazed by the bullet that had gone through Vinney.

Other MPD officers quickly sealed off the stairwell entrance from the basement floor with pre-built plywood panels that they had stored in the cash office hallway, restricting any possible entry. Once done, they radioed the "All Secure!" to all security and law enforcement personnel.

On both the main and basements floors customers reacted in panic as they heard the amplified explosions coming from the stairwell, several yelling *'bombs'* which only served to instill even more panic. However, the speedy appearance of Kate's security contingent, along with all floor management, quickly quelled their fears by announcing to the customers that on the loudspeakers, "Ladies and Gentlemen. Please remain calm! The loud noise you just heard has been investigated and it was just some kids that exploded M-80 fireworks in the stairwell. They have been taken to security and everything is under control. Please resume your shopping. Our staff are eager and waiting to help you!"

I guess I didn't have anything to worry about, after all, Ricky thought, as he began an inspection tour of the basement selling floor.

Following the processing of the crime scene by MPD investigators; the removal of the bodies and the prisoners, and the subsequent vacating of the

EATON'S – During the Second French Revolution

MPD presence, the store returned to the welcome craziness that was the annual Record-Breaking Day Sale.

In the weeks that followed, the local, national, and international media, directed by information supplied by the MPD public relations spokesman, pressed the events of the armed robbery to its limits, one publication summing up the totality with bold headlines.

MPD BAGS ROBBERS & SHOPLIFTER RING

Montreal: A coordinated combined task force effort of the MPD departments of Major Crimes, Street Patrol, Organized Crime, Bomb Squad and S.W.A.T., successfully thwarted a robbery attempt by five heavily armed gunman targeting the cash office of a major downtown department store. After the exchange of gun fire, two men lay dead, one injured and the other two taken into custody. The ringleader who has been positively identified as Vinney "The Trunk" Calabresee, was killed in the altercation.

Ricky threw the newspaper on Tony's desk. "Did you see the Montreal star article?" Ricky wanted to forget everything after seeing the bodies and gore in the stairwell after the attack.

"Yeah, and after reading it, and remembering that the whole operation was our baby, even I have to question if we really took any part in it at all?"

"Well at least it's over. So, what are you doing about Ray?" Ricky asked.

"Ray is still a good detective," Tony replied, "who unwittingly, got caught in a mob trap. Since only a few of us know what went down, I've reinstated him on a probationary basis. And, with Vinney permanently out of the picture, Ray won't have to worry about retribution from the Calabresee family."

"So, at least, Vinney "The Trunk, Calabresee, is no more."

"Yeah, and by the way you'll find this interesting. Ray told me that when he was a rookie with MPD he and his sergeant rolled up on two guys down by the river, messing with a body that had been beaten to shit in the trunk of their Cadillac. It turns out that the two guys were Vinney and Frankie. So, Ray says that this sergeant seemed very friendly with the Calabresee family and starts chatting up Vinney. When Vinney says that they weren't takin' the body out of the trunk to dump it in the drink, they were picking him up to take him up to the Royal Vic Hospital. And the sergeant believes him and files his MPD report to that effect. See, so that's how Vinney got the name, 'The Trunk' and became a 'made man'. Later it was found out that the guy from the trunk, was Joey Brasso, who was the family book maker who had been skimming from the family weekly numbers takes. Thanks to Vinney, he died of a brain hemorrhage from being beaten with a baseball bat."

"That's incredible! So, all along, he had gotten away with murder?"

"Yeah. Oh, and one more piece of news. Before the attack, we received another note from *The 'Shadow'*, this time in plain English, confirming that 'a major heist was planned for Eaton's by a connected guy; his name Vinney Calabresee!'"

"Great Tony! Now this elusive *'Shadow'* is our main source of information," Ricky laughed. "So, everything is now tied up in a neat bow, Mister Cartwright. I take my hat off to you!"

⚜ Sixty-Five ⚜

The heavy rain pelted the arriving funeral guests. The massive two-ton metal cast bells in the basilica dome tower of the Roman Catholic Saint Joseph's Oratory reverberated its sound against the adjacent hills of Mount Royal. A funeral at St. Josephs was a rarity available only to major politicians, senior clergy, or, as in this instance, a major contributor such as the Calabresee family. Although most guests sprinted for the huge arched entryway of the basilica, others joined both the healthy, and the infirmed, dropping to their knees to climb ninety-nine of the Oratory's two hundred and eighty-three steps, in solemn prayer. The reason for this physically unpleasant gesture was to symbolically share in the pain of Jesus Christ's suffering on the cross prior to his death and resurrection.

Slowly traversing the winding cobblestone driveway to the entryway, flanked by domestic and international reporters, were two long shiny black hearses, 14 flower cars and an endless line of black stretch limousines snaked as far as the eye could see. The only anomaly to the scene was the large contingent of R.C.M.P., Q.P.P. and M.P.D. police and numerous photographers, with telephoto lenses, snapping photos of all arriving guests.

Those watching could not help but have sympathy for the twelve pallbearers who had to maneuver the two heavy caskets, up the long flight of stairs to the basilica.

The front pew in the massive chapel was reserved for the Calabresee family, with the remaining 1000 seats filled with politicians, business associates, friends, and even enemies. The throng of mourners assembled, not because they personally knew the deceased, but strictly out of reverence to the family.

Giuseppe Calabresee sat stoically, a handkerchief perched in his hand, his face expressionless. He was flanked to his right, by his brother, Carmine, and to his left, his wife, Marianna Rose, accompanied by his children and grandchildren. The uncontrollable high-pitched wailing of Marianna Rose echoed off the elegant walls and high ceiling of the basilica. Giuseppe paid no heed.

To the surprise of everyone, Giuseppe slowly rose from his pew and approached Vinney's coffin, extending a silent prayer as he looked at his son one final time, then gently closed the casket lid. He then went over to Frankie's coffin, where he loudly proclaimed, "Tu dovevi proteggerlo, *You were supposed to protect him.* "Può marcire all'inferno, *May you rot in hell!* With that final statement he grabbed the lid and slammed it down with all his might, the crashing sound resonating throughout the chapel. Marianna Rose shrieked even louder.

The pews directly behind the family were filled with every member of the Calabresee organization from underbosses to soldiers. The pews on the opposite side had an array of Westies members, bosses, and soldiers, the M.P.D. commissioner and his subordinate officers, judges, and numerous major business owners and politicians. Whether politically correct, or not, everyone wanted it known that they had paid their respects to the Calabresee family.

At the altar, to conduct the services, were Cardinal McIntyre, Monseigneur Polland, 2 Bishops, 4 Alter boys and the complete Oratory choir and resident organist. The two elegant black onyx coffins sat below the alter steps, surrounded with large beds of white flowers. As in life, with his main comrade Frankie by his side, Vinney Calabresee now rested side by side with him in death.

At the end of the services, the pallbearers carefully carried the coffins down the long, steep stairs and proceeded to Vinney and Frankie's final resting place in Mount Royal's Catholic Cemetery.

If Vinney had been able to speak at that moment, he probably would have said, *"Damn dreams! If I had only known it was me in the second coffin! But, since I am here, it's not that bad! A full Catholic service and the unbelievable turnout of mourners. Finally, me and Frankie have received our due within the family ... like real heroes!"*

⚜ Sixty-Six ⚜

The month before Christmas was always stressful, but with the addition of the FLQ bomb threats, random bombings, kidnapping and murders, the year was already setting precedents.

The biggest disappointment for Ricky this year was not having the annual Eaton's Santa Claus Parade, a tradition that signaled the official arrival of the holiday season for millions of Canadian children.

The tradition began in Toronto and Winnipeg in 1905. Originally, the only star in the Toronto parade was Santa himself, but gradually over the years, floats from schools, colleges, and charitable organizations were introduced and numerous other participants were added.

In 1925, Eaton's presented the first big Christmas parade in Montreal, designed, and produced entirely by Eaton's craftsmen. The parade would originate in Toronto, then the costumes and floats were sent by train to Montreal, where the parade was presented the following Saturday.

With its myriad of attractions for children, the Christmas parade became a firmly rooted tradition in Montreal society and entertainment, over the years. Children applied for the honor of participating in the parade, which was so popular that they often had to wait up to three years to get their turn. They'd be up at dawn and delivered by taxis, hired especially for the occasion by Eaton's, to get them to the beginning of the parade route. There they would put on their magnificent custom-made costumes and receive a special place on any of the elegant floats. They were paid a small salary of hot chocolate and cookies throughout the parade. The youngsters trekked tirelessly and happily from Saint Joseph Boulevard to Santa's Eaton's University St., private entry door.

Although the world was in the throes of the Second World War for the first half of the 1940's, the "Eaton's Santa Claus Christmas Parade," was still presented every year, to anxious Montrealers, without exception.

In the 1950's, with advent of television, the Eaton's parade was in its heyday, with both the English and French T.V. networks broadcasting the parade live.

The Toronto organizers were pleased to see that Quebec spectators were more receptive and enthusiastic than those in Toronto, saying that *"The French Canadians view the event as a sort of a carnival, whereas in Toronto, it's just a parade."*

At each destination, as a conclusion to the massive parade, Santa Claus would leave his reindeer and sleigh, enter the Eaton's store, and moments later magically be permanently available, with his elves, on his throne chair, in the toy department. To many children Christmas did not begin until Santa arrived at Eaton's. where they could sit on his knee and tell him all the treasures that they expected because they were good little boys and girls.

Ten months earlier, Ricky had the distinct honor of being selected as head coordinator for the Montreal Santa Claus Parade. The position required overseeing one full time employee, and numerous volunteers, tasked with bringing all aspects of the parade together. The venture required months of planning and development and, like everything else he had taken on, Ricky attacked this new venture with exceptional enthusiasm. He selected his permanent employee, recruited volunteers, and formed a parade committee. He worked with the Human Resources department on the hundreds of extra personnel needed for the parade and worked with schools and organizations for band participation. Next Ricky arranged for special float construction and all the fine tuning necessary to make parents and children smile, and Eaton's pride!

But, in late October and early November, MPD advised Tony Cartwright, in Eaton's security, there had been rumblings within the FLQ that they were prepared to trash the parade floats being shipped by rail from Toronto. This threat had also been relayed to Ricky in a private note from the elusive *'Shadow'*.

EATON'S – During the Second French Revolution

Although Ricky had hired extra security staff to guard the transient floats, three weeks before the parade MPD advised Tony that they had a credible threat that, *"if the Eaton's parade proceeded, bombs would be placed along the parade route."* Because of this viable threat, the potential for loss of life or property, and with the deteriorating Quebec political climate, Eaton's management elected to permanently and indefinitely cancel the Montreal parade.

The parade cancellation was a terrible blow to Ricky, not just because of his months of work, but also because of some of the revolutionary innovations that he was going to unveil to the Montreal parade watchers.

Things had been crazy at the store with the upcoming holidays, but Ricky found time to meet with Christine at Shamrock's Bar, locked in each other's arms, and happy to share the upcoming holidays.

But things didn't proceed as well as they both would have liked. On the final Saturday evening before Christmas, Ricky hosted the annual basement department's Christmas party, at the Queen Elizabeth Hotel. Unfortunately, instead of it being a joyous happy event, Ricky had endured the most difficult confrontation of his life. For appearances sake, he had reluctantly taken Kathy to the party since she had come to town to handle a medical issue. He could not have known that she would be seated directly across a long dining table, from Christine. Although involved in their divorce action, upper management expected all management personnel to be in attendance with their spouse. The night had been exceptionally tense, to say the least. The only pleasure was the one dance that he had with Christine where only the subtle squeeze of the hand was available during a jitterbug. As usual, Kathy displayed her typical erratic behavior, rambling on about foolish topics that no one was interested in.

By the end of the evening, Ricky escorted Kathy back to her parents and spent the rest of what was left to the evening thinking about Christine. He reflected on the painful memories of leaving her and going home to his dark living room, where he drank wine and replayed the time they'd spent together. For the first time in his life, he had felt truly alive. With that thought, he made a pact with himself to always pursue happiness over tolerance. He would no longer allow himself to be a victim, but would grasp happiness, at all costs. Since the first day he'd gotten married, he slept serenely, his dreams filled with erotic visions of Christine.

A day earlier Father Mac had called him to tell him that he had received word from the tribunal that Christine's annulment had been approved effective December 31st. Coyly Father Mac had given him the news, saying, "Perhaps Laddie, you'd like 'ta be the one 'ta give the lass this special Christmas present, aye?"

Ricky caught up with Christine just before closing as she was at her desk at the rear of her department.

"Do you have plans for, Christmas Eve?" Ricky asked.

Surprised by the question, she responded, "No, Charlotte and I were maybe planning on driving out to my parents on Christmas morning, why?"

Ricky looked around sheepishly. "I thought maybe we could go out for a drink, and a bite to eat. I have some good news for you."

"Sure, what time?"

"The store's closing at five on Christmas eve, so I thought we could meet in the Place Ville Marie lobby, around five-fifteen."

Without mentioning it, both were still aware of the necessity to keep their meetings secret.

"I can't wait," she beamed.

⚜ Sixty-Seven ⚜

Ricky struggled with his anxiety all through Christmas Eve day. He questioned himself about his upcoming date with Christine, his motives and how he was going to handle the evening.

At 5:00 he donned his overcoat, bid everyone a Merry Christmas, and began his short trek to the Place Ville Marie.

What are you doing, Dean? This may be something you may never be able to undo.

Smoking a cigarette as he entered the PVM lobby, Ricky spotted Christine and quickly picked up his pace to catch up with her. He caught her just as she arrived at the giant Christmas tree.

"Oh, hi," she rose on her toes to give him a peck on the cheek. "I really love Christmas. Well, this Christmas, anyway." Her eyes danced mysteriously.

They stood side by side gazing at the beauty of the remarkable tree as Ricky read the plaque beneath the tree, "The Place Ville Marie Christmas Tree, a Montréal holiday tradition, stands sixty-three feet high and measures twenty-six feet wide, illuminated with over thirteen thousand Christmas lights."

 Wow! Want to count them?" he teased.

"Do we have time?" She responded. "That's about five-stories high, right?" she questioned, grabbing his hand, and giving it a tender squeeze.

"Not too bad at math, I see." Returning the squeeze, Ricky led her towards the bank of eight elevators. As they entered the empty elevator, he pushed the "P" button for the penthouse, which was home to the Altitude 737 Restaurant Club Lounge.

The doors closed and the elevator made its speed assent. Christine put her hands around Ricky's face drawing him closer to hers. "That wasn't a proper kiss in the lobby, let me correct that major error." Softly, her lips brushed his, her face moving back and forth tickling his in a teasing action, then with lips slightly parted she extended the full weight of an intense kiss. "That's better."

EATON'S – During the Second French Revolution

"Ahhh, I think that was better, than better," Ricky reacted, breathlessly.

They exited the elevator, 45-storeys up, and 617 Feet above sea level. Antoine was standing at attention at the entrance to the lounge.

"Merry Christmas, Miss Christine, Mister Dean. As you requested, I reserved your special table by the window," he led them to their table, where he removed a "Reserved" sign. "The usual, today?" he asked, looking at Christine.

"Yes, thank you, Antoine," she responded shyly, then, "Can you answer a question for me."

"Certainly, if I can, Miss."

"If the Ville Marie is listed at six-hundred and seventeen feet high, why is the lounge called the Altitude 'Seven Thirty-Seven Lounge?"

He smiled broadly, "The building itself, Miss, is indeed six-hundred and seventeen feet high, but the radio antenna on top brings the height to six-hundred and thirty-seven feet high, therefore, welcome to the 'Seven Thirty-Seven Lounge'."

"Thank you, Antoine, and Merry Christmas to you and your family," Ricky extended his hand with a ten-dollar bill secreted in his palm.

Without even examining what Ricky had pressed into his hand, Antoine smiled broadly, "Thank you Mister Dean, I'll be right back with your drinks."

Christine began removing her coat but was halted by Ricky. "Keep your coat on for a minute. I want to show you something special," he said, taking her hand in his, walking the breadth of the room, and leading her through a set of double glass doors onto the outdoor terrace observation deck.

"Oh, Ricky," she swooned, "why didn't you show me this before? It's absolutely awesome. I can see the whole city, the lights of Old Montreal, everything." She leaned back against him, his chin resting on the top of her head. "I've never been so happy," she sighed. "It's so much, that I feel I don't deserve all this."

Ricky opened his overcoat and wrapped her in it, her tiny firm buttocks grinding into his manhood. "Shh, just enjoy!" he whispered, folding his arms around her, just below her breasts. "What you're experiencing is the ultimate definition of true beauty. Even with all its faults, Montreal will survive as one of the most beautiful cosmopolitan cities in the world."

They stood embraced for several minutes in silence, their warm breath forming clouds of steam from their mouths, as it collided with the cold air.

"You must be cold, you're trembling. We should get you inside," he stated, turning her towards him.

"I'm not trembling from the cold," she murmured, reaching to kiss his waiting lips. "It's much, much, more than that!"

Hand in hand they returned to the warmth of the lounge and their waiting Dubonnets.

Helping to remove her coat, then his, he sat across from her. Christine was wearing a stunning short black dress accented by a single gold locket on a chain around her neck and knee-high black leather boots. The tight-fitting dress took Ricky's breath away. He sat admiring her when suddenly he noticed a small tear escaping from her left eye. "Are you okay?" he questioned, lighting two cigarettes.

"Oh, Ricky, it's, it's just ... I don't know," she stammered, "I think I'm in ..."

Ricky interrupted abruptly, "You don't need to say anything, just enjoy our time together."

"Yes, you're right," she faltered, brushing the tear from her eye. "I'm just being so foolish. So, tell me the big news you've been holding out on me, for the last two days," she laughed, purposely changing the subject.

"By the way you look absolutely gorgeous!"

"Thank you. I'd only dress like this to be with you," she gushed.

"First, tell me how you are progressing in your new home."

"It's absolutely terrific. Charlotte and I get along great and with Daddy's money I splurged and bought a brand-new oriental bedroom set. Things couldn't be better. And best of all, I haven't seen or heard, a single word from my creep ex-husband."

Christine went quiet, then continued. "I have to tell you something, Ricky, and I hope you don't get offended."

"I don't think anything you could tell me would offend me. What is it?"

"The company Christmas party was surreal, sitting across from Kathy. Not only was it awkward, but she kept trying to get me into conversations that didn't make sense."

"About us?"

"No, not at all. It's just that one minute she was talking to me about some apple tree that you had at your house in Ilse Perrot, and within a second, she changed the subject and was talking about how you should leave Eaton's and become an accountant. She told me that if you hadn't left Rosemount High School early, you could have become Prime Minister of Canada. I just didn't know how to handle her. Was she trying to trap me into saying something?"

"Not at all. You just met the 'real' Kathy Dean."

"Is she like that all the time?"

"No. As a schizophrenic, she has lucid moments and off the wall moments and it has gotten worse over the years. I never knew who I will be meet with when I went home."

"You've lived with that for the last three years?"

"Every day."

"And I thought that I had problems with Roland."

"Anyway, enough of these negatives," he took her hand in his. "Now, for your Christmas present."

They both took a drink of their wine.

"Should I close my eyes?" she cooed.

"No, this is something that money can't buy. And closing your beautiful eyes would just be punishing me."

"I'm intrigued."

"What would you say if I told you that seven days from now, you will never have been married?"

She was shocked, "You mean ... you mean that my annulment got approved?" her voice raised. "I'll be totally free?"

He nodded. "Yes, Father Mac called me yesterday and told me to give you a Christmas present that you'd never forget."

"Oh Ricky, I don't believe it, I'm in shock!" She held his hand tight.

"It's true! On December thirty-first all documents regarding your marriage will be expunged, and it will be as if you had never been married," he drew her closer to him.

Ricky wasn't sure what was happening as he watched her stare in silence at the Montreal view, her hand squeezing his, almost painfully. Then he knew, as tears erupted into sobs. He quickly pulled his chair around to sit beside her. He put his arms around her and took her shaking body, gently pulling her into his chest. He took out his handkerchief and dabbed at her falling tears. His voice was very consoling, while he whispered into her ear, "Let it all out, sweetheart, you deserve it. It's *finally* all over for you!"

As her tears subsided, she stared into his eyes, "You really saved my life Ricky, maybe now it's time to let me help you save yours."

Ignoring her comment, he joked, "What it's time for, pretty lady, is to get some food in you." Ricky signaled Antoine who was positioned vigilantly by the entryway.

When he arrived Ricky asked, "Is my reservation set for the B and C restaurant?"

Antoine replied, "Your table is waiting for you and the lady, just ask for Claude when you go in."

"Then please can I have the bar bill?"

Antoine handed him the bill and added, "I personally selected the best table in the house, to the left of the band. It's away from the speakers, but handy to the dance floor. Thank you, and Merry Christmas," he acknowledged the generous tip Ricky left with the bill.

Reaching for their coats, both Christine and Ricky echoed a "Thank you" to Antoine.

"Please, let me hang these in the coatroom for you," Antoine insisted.

Hand in hand, they descended the wide carpeted stairs to the entrance of the elegant Beef and Claws Restaurant, where they were greeted by the maître-de, who checked his reservation chart. "Monsieur Dean, et Mademoiselle Christine, oui?"

"Oui, Claude," Ricky replied reading his name tag.

"Votre table est prête, *Your table is ready*," he responded, leading them to a table adjacent to the dance floor.

Handing them their menus, he said, "Votre serveur sera avec vous, peu de temps." *Your server will be with you, shortly.*

Elegant was an understatement in describing the restaurant. From the huge hanging chandeliers, plush burgundy carpeting, vintage artwork by the masters, and parquet dance floor, the atmosphere was totally romantic. Each circular linen clothed table was adorned with fine chinaware and silverware. The ambiance and everything about the restaurant was perfect. And the brilliance reflected in Christine's eyes confirmed Ricky's efforts in creating the perfect setting for a momentous and adventurous evening.

As the band played a medley of the Platters and the Drifters melodies, four couples took to the dance floor. Christine scooted her chair closer to Ricky. "You know you can change the subject all you want, but we're going to come back to what to do about your life now that your divorce is in the works." The conviction in her eyes made Ricky look away.

A tuxedoed waiter with a slight limp and a broken English/French accent took their order for drinks and Hors d'oeuvres.

"There's no easy solution, Chris. The reality is that I made my bed and now I've got to lie in it. I may be able to get rid of her, but that does not change the fact that I will be a single father with a massive financial and moral obligations!"

"I don't believe you! Ricky, you've told me so many times that, 'if there's a will, there's *always* a way'."

"But sometimes things are just not that simple," he insisted.

"So, you'll work around it. Your life can't end because you made one bad mistake. God, Ricky, you were deceived by Kathy, just as I was conned by Roland. We both went into our marriages believing that we were in an honest and honorable relationship, but, neither one of them had any intention of being in an honest normal relationship. Both situations were *sick,* and I am not going to sit around and watch you wallow in your misery. We're going to do *something* about it and soon!" she flushed in anger.

"Temper, temper," he kidded.

"It's just not fair, Ricky. We're both decent people. What are the chances of two people our age, meeting and finding out we have almost identical problems? It's karma. That's what it is!"

Ricky was about to respond, when the band began to play, Frank Sinatra's "*Fly me to the moon.*"

"See, karma, that's one of my favorite songs. Will you dance with me, please?" she begged.

EATON'S – During the Second French Revolution

"My pleasure, my lady," he replied, taking her hand, and gliding her smoothly onto the dance floor.

He began in the very proper dance position, hands high, bodies apart, but was swiftly pulled into a more seductive embrace by her. She crooned the words to the song in his ear, as he inhaled the scents of her glorious body. He consciously endeavored to keep his hips a respectable distance from touching hers, but she kept snuggling her body close to his. He could feel his manhood rubbing just below her belly button and his reaction was swift and noticeable. She wasn't put off by his reaction and instead she nibbled on his ear, to show her own arousal. At that point, he wasn't sure he was going to be able to last the full three minutes of the dance.

When the song ended, she pulled him by hand back to the table as if nothing had happened.

He politely excused himself to go to the men's room to *cool* off. When he returned the waiter appeared at their table to take the meal order. Christine ordered prime rib and baked potato, while Ricky selected filet mignon and mashed potatoes. He would have preferred garlic mashed potatoes, but certainly not tonight. During their meal, they finished off a carafe of wine, and danced several more times. Ricky discovered that each dance was becoming more intimate and more difficult for him.

Over their tiramisu dessert, Christine voiced a totally unexpected comment. "You know, you don't owe Kathy anything! She didn't play fair, so you're under no obligation to play the good guy role. Just decide to do what *you* want to do, and let the chips fall where they may,"

"Whew, where did that come from? I thought we'd finished that conversation before we ate."

"Ricky, it's just that I want to be with you. I understood that when you would leave me to go home, she would be there, but I couldn't help thinking that when you were with me, I needed all of you. I always thought that I'd rather have you on a part-time basis, than not at all. And now that you filed for divorce, and she is out of the picture we can finally find something that works for both of us?" she pleaded, her eyes misting.

"I feel the same way, sweetheart, but before she left it just wasn't fair to you. I knew at your age you shouldn't be considering taking on the obligations of a married man."

"You should have let me worry about what's fair to me. I went through hell this past year, then you came into my life, and I became intoxicated and exhilarated. My days are consumed with the anticipation of just seeing you, and my nights are filled with dreams of, oh well, never mind," she stopped, totally embarrassed.

Speechless, he asked, "Will you dance with me? This is my favorite song; *I've got you Babe by Sonny and Cher.*"

He took her hand in his as he walked her to the dance floor. He elegantly twirled her in a wide circle, gliding her straight back into his waiting arms. He bent Christine in a deep dip bringing her back to join his anticipating lips. She parted her lips as his tongue licked the curvature. She pressed her body to his, this time acknowledging his manhood getting intimately acquainted with her trembling body. The moment was so intense that they hadn't realized the song had ended. Slightly embarrassed at being the only ones left on the floor, they skulked back to their table.

Before they sat, Christine staggered slightly, losing her balance.

Alarmed, he grabbed to steady her, "Are you all right?"

"Yes, I ... I just need the powder room. I'm fine." She rushed off towards the ladies' room located near the restaurant entrance.

He downed a gulp of wine, concerned about Christine. His divorce was proceeding, but not fast enough for what was happening between them.

Christine returned moments later, looking fully refreshed and perky as ever. "Sorry, I've never felt like that before. I felt like my mind had left my body and I was looking down on both of us. It was the most heavenly feeling I've ever experienced in my life. I need a drink."

"Ditto to that," he replied, pouring wine into her glass.

"Ricky, I don't want this to end, no matter what obstacles are placed in our way. It's so good for us. We need more, not less," she murmured.

"And we will, I promise," he whispered, reaching across, and drawing her hand to his lips.

"I still can't believe the sensations I experienced with you on the dance floor. I never felt those feelings before in my life." She shuddered.

"Then let's try it again. Dance with me!"

She responded breathlessly. "Yes, I think they're playing *our* song."

"*Our* song?" he questioned, leading her back onto the dance floor.

"Yes, our song. Didn't you know that Elvis wrote, *'I can't help falling in love'* just for us?" She laughed, pulling him closer to her, as they swayed as one to the rhythm of the beat.

Her inhibitions of any sexual closeness totally dissipated as her body melded with his. Her breasts freely rubbed against his chest, her pelvis readily moved with the feel of his manhood, and her tongue went in hungry search of every inch of his mouth. She displayed no fear as she exhibited only fierce desire.

Ricky had never felt this arise in his whole life. Even his first encounter with sexual intercourse, with Kathy, didn't even come close to the excitement that permeated his mind and body.

As the song ended Ricky reached into his pocket for a five-dollar bill which he handed to the band leader. *"'Fly me to the moon, again please.'"*

"Yes, sir."

"That was sweet," she responded, finding her place in his arms.

They swayed to the music and the heat of their bodies was reflected in their eyes, Ricky whispered, "I want to be with you, Christine. I really *genuinely want* to be with you!"

"If *be with me* means what I think it does, my dreams can become a reality. I want to *be with you*, too, Ricky. I Lo ..."

Ricky placed fingers to her lips, silencing her statement. Please, don't use the "L" word. Not yet anyway. It's too confusing for me. I don't know what it means, and I've truly never experienced it. Please just be patient with me!" He kissed her passionately.

As they casually returned to their table, and after a long moment of uncomfortable silence Christine looked into Ricky's eyes. "I feel like I'm going to burst, Ricky. I ... I really want to *be with you* as soon as possible!"

A million thoughts flooded Ricky's mind. "Are you sure? We would have to be incredibly careful with my divorce in the works. Maybe we should take it slow. Get to know each other better. At the very least, wait 'til your annulment is finalized." Ricky's face displayed a hint of fear."

"Am I being too forward? Am I reading your thoughts wrong? Oh God, Ricky, I'm so sorry, I think I've jumped the gun. I ... I ..." she stammered, burying her face in her hands.

"No! No!" he consoled, "It's just that you are placing yourself in a situation that could get you hurt. And I'd rather sacrifice my own feelings rather than do anything that could eventually harm you."

"I know what I feel. I know what I'm getting into. And I want to be with you! These are not new feelings for me, Ricky. These are thoughts and dreams that I've been suppressing for months. Please make it happen," she pleaded, tears flowing down her cheeks.

Ricky sat thoughtfully for several minutes, then leaned over to brush the tears from her eyes with his handkerchief.

"If you are 100% sure," he began. "I have a plan that might work, and if it doesn't work for you, or you suddenly change your mind ..."

"Please, Ricky," she interrupted, "I'm not going to change my mind. This is not sudden for me, so please tell me your thoughts."

"Well, I thought maybe, uh, we could plan for, let's say, January the third, I mean, if that's okay for you."

Christine slid her chair closer to his, gazing into his eyes and hanging on to his every word. "That would be perfect, and my annulment would even be finalized by then, so no guilt trips, eh?" She kissed his neck.

"For this to work we need to lay some ground rules."

"Only you would have a prepared list of rules for this," she chuckled. "Well, give it to me."

"It goes without saying that we need to keep our relationship to ourselves."

"Right".

"We may be getting ahead of ourselves, but," Ricky continued almost embarrassed by what he was about to say. "If something does happen uh, well, um, are you uh?"

"If what you are asking is if I'm on the pill, Ricky, the answer is no! Why would I be? I'm still a virgin with no prospects, until now. So, I guess the protection rule is yours to handle, eh?"

"Damn! I'm sorry! See what I mean, this is getting so very awkward."

"I would say more exciting than awkward! This is my dream, to be with you, and I can't believe it is going to happen on January third! In fact, if you told me right now, I had to walk on hot coals to *be with you*, I'd gladly do it. I can't wait for our little, tryst!"

Ricky laughed, casually glancing at his watch. "I'm not sure about "tryst"' but I look forward to finding out. In the meantime, I'll make some plans for the third, and let you know."

"Ricky, it's Christmas Eve and you've missed your nine-forty train. What are you going to do?" she asked, concerned.

"It's okay. My car is parked downstairs in the garage. Tonight, of all nights, I didn't want to have to rush away from you!"

"I am happy, but its Christmas Eve, shouldn't you be at home tonight?" she insisted.

He took her in his arms. "The most important thing is that I created an everlasting memory here with you, on December twenty-fourth, Christmas Eve," he emphasized, "everything else is insignificant."

Ricky paid the bill, helped Christine into her coat and exited the Place Ville Marie, with a renewed bounce in his step.

This really, really can't be happening to me! How lucky can a guy get?

⚜ Sixty-Eight ⚜

After retrieving his car from the PVM underground garage, Ricky drove Christine the short distance to her apartment on Hutchinson Street. During the trip she snuggled close to him, her arm around his neck, her hand resting innocently on his thigh. Ricky skillfully situated his car between two snowbanks in front of Christine's apartment and cranked up the heater. "So, are you still feeling okay?" he asked, swiveling in his seat to face her full on.

"What do you think?" she cooed, her dress gently sliding up her thigh, as she brought her leg up across his lap, conveniently coming to rest on his protruding manhood. "Oh, me thinks you are feeling okay, too!" she snuggled in closer.

For the first time in his life, he found himself completely immobilized, his mind cascading in a million directions, and his body paralyzed in apprehension.

EATON'S – During the Second French Revolution

She opened her lips and let her tongue wet the bright red lipstick surface. Then, slowly approached his mouth in anticipation, but instead took his hand in hers and gently placed it on her face. She guided his fingers over her eyes, her nose, then her lips, and held them there. She took his index finger seductively into her mouth, giving it a teasing nibble before leisurely sliding the whole finger into her mouth, circling it with her hot tongue.

Ricky's body tensed, then squirmed spasmodically, as the pressure of her leg on his groin became intolerable. He moved his body toward her which removed her knee, while his body continued in pursuit. Ricky kissed her deeply; his tongue thrusting in violent search for hers.

Christine drew back and looked pleadingly into his eyes. He gently drew her toward him and wrapped her in his arms, holding both their bodies in a tender embrace.

"Can life get any better?" she whispered.

"It will on the third," he assured her, "Tonight, just let me hold you."

To relax the situation, he lit two cigarettes and handed one to her, as he cracked the window open a bit, the welcome cold air helping him to settle down. They talked about what was happening between them and both agreed to delay any further advances, until the third. Reluctantly, Ricky walked Christine to her door, and gave her a goodnight kiss that left them both breathless.

"Dream of me ... and the third."

"How could I not," he heard, as he turned and left for home.

Ricky's 40-minute drive home was cruel. His thoughts kept returning to the ultra-romantic evening he'd just spent with Christine, and of course, the upcoming third of January, which would keep him awake all night!

Ricky had known for several months that he really wanted to be with Christine, but he also realized that presently he could not offer her anything more. Over those months, he'd felt uncontrollable feelings welling in his whole being, yearning just to hold her close, just once. And that "once" came tonight on the dance floor. He'd questioned himself, knowing Christine was young and incredibly attractive, and that she could have her choice of anyone.

The combination of fear welling up in his stomach, and the futility of his vivid thoughts, created an insecurity in his usually "in control" make up. He started to wonder if he could really go through with January third.

Finally, as cold, and insensitive as it may have sounded, he knew that regardless of the consequences, he had no choice, he had to see this through! Tonight, when she was in his arms on the dance floor, he realized they had turned a corner and there was no turning back! The closeness of their bodies joined with the feel of her arms firmly around him, finalized the decision that had haunted him for the past three months. He now knew he had to take the chance! His choice of rational reasoning no longer existed as he had felt the gentle heaving of her breasts against his chest, her warm breath against his neck, and her scent filling his nostrils. *No, he had absolutely no choice, he had to see this through!*

He had never in his life felt these feelings before, which raised confusing questions. *Is this love that I am feeling? Or am I just experiencing real lust, for the first time in my life?*

Ricky didn't want his thoughts of Christine to be driven by his sexual desire. He hadn't participated in any form of normal sexual relations with his wife since his marriage began, nor had he had any other normal sexual experiences, of any sort. But now, for the first time in his life, he had no conscious control over his mind, which apparently also had no control over his now yearning body. Ricky found himself consumed with thoughts of Christine in his every waking moment and even her presence would appear in his nightly dreams, as he had lay beside the wife that he loathed. He was love struck, addicted, or both, and did not like the unusual and utterly confusing feelings of being totally out of control. He had been an unemotional man with high moral values and unusual physical fortitude towards abstinence, but now, he was reduced to a babbling love-struck teenager.

At that point, regardless of how much he wanted a true answer, it was just not to be unearthed. All he knew for certain was that he had to hold this vision of beauty and begin to share with her his thoughts, his dreams, his fears ... or at the very least, he just had to feel her close to him.

And so, tonight when he finally built up the courage to unmask his carefully rehearsed proposition, he was shocked at her willingness to accept, quickly and unquestioningly.

He remembered back to the torment of the preceding months and his anticipation to rush to the store to be greeted by her smiling face, her captivating sexy presence, and her bright glowing eyes, which followed his every movement throughout the store. He had yearned daily for the stolen moments in his mind as he watched her move about her duties in the store, or as she sat before him in his private office, her short purple velour skirt enticing his sexuality as she casually crossed her shapely legs.

As the months progressed, he became incensed with himself, because his fascination with her had become so sexual, leaving him breathless and embarrassingly aroused. Her scent and body warmth stirred within him and intoxicated him, whenever she was near.

Having just spent an incredible evening with Christine, his mind began fiercely reeling to the events that had just taken place and how his life had been instantly altered from a point of mental stability into one of anxiety, fear, and desperation.

What have I just done? he thought.

The fact that he was ill prepared to follow through with his proposal came slamming into his thoughts and blurred his vision with long overdue tears. He pulled the car over to the shoulder and just sat there for a moment composing himself. He tried to concentrate on their upcoming January third date. Incredibly, he would soon be graced with both an emotional and sexual experience with the young pretty girl that had regularly consumed his nightly dreams. His dreams playout out an unbelievable scenario. He had been *Mr. Super Stud,* sexually experienced and competently knowledgeable in all the requirements of successful participation. But those had only been his dreams. This was no longer a dream! It was to become fact on January third, and he realized that he could look like a fool in front of the one person in his life in whose eyes he needed to shine. Ricky knew this was not a simple unmoving "one-night stand," Christine was too important and precious to him. He concluded that he had to make her want to know more of him and feel about him, as he had yearned. Ricky had to strive to make Christine feel desirable, aroused, and breathless for contact from his every touch. But, his inexperience, in both the areas of the heart and the body, could ultimately and forever destroy any remote chances with her.

She was young and vulnerable which necessitated Ricky developing the persona of the "macho man;" totally experienced and with incredible sexual prowess. He desperately needed to see himself shine in her eyes. He knew that he could not allow himself to fail at this, the most important mission of his adult life. He had to overcome his fears, inhibitions, and both his sexual and emotional insecurities. Ricky had been graced with this one chance to prove to Christine that, although he now desperately and hopelessly craved her body, what he craved more was her.

He saw his St. Laurent exit and, he knew, without a doubt, that these next 10 days would be an emotional conflict paramount to anything he had ever experienced. With the Christmas and New Year holiday, he knew she would be celebrating with family and friends, while he would only be with Darlene. He also knew that during these next 10 days, he would have to make a conscious choice to set all his apprehensions aside, with no turning back, and decide how he could make January third the most incredible night for her and for him. A night that both would remember all their lives!

He got off at the exit and parked his car on the side of the road. He just sat silently with the radio droning boring Christmas songs. He didn't want to go into his house. He didn't want anything to spoil his high from the last few treasured hours with Christine.

He knew Darlene would be in bed and Kathy would be waiting to go over to her parents. The trappings of Christmas eve preparations would be laid out for him. It would take him hours to set up and decorate the tree and he knew it was already late. He looked at his watch. Almost midnight. *Oh crap! Kathy is going to be pissed!*

He turned the car toward his driveway and true to form, Kathy was waiting at the front door, "Where were you until this hour? Don't you know it's Christmas Eve? I still have to drive over to my parents."

But for the first time, Ricky didn't argue. He didn't say a word. He just sat down, poured a drink, and started to set up the Christmas tree.

⚜ Sixty-Nine ⚜

Christine and Charlotte's apartment can best be described as decorated in Bohemian style, with a touch of Salvation Army mixed in. The floors were littered with a collage of old, brightly colored Persian style throw rugs and large earth-tone pillows; the furniture was mostly dark colored rattan, with mismatched tiffany style lamps. Charlotte's bedroom consisted of a single mattress on the floor, India/Pakistan blankets, two wooden crates as nightstands and simulated hurricane lamps for lighting. With clothes of psychedelic patterns and vibrant colors strewn haphazardly throughout the room, her bedroom was a natural disaster area.

In stark comparison, Christine's "private domain" was professionally decorated with all the accoutrements of an authentic Chinese bedroom. Her queen size bed sported a black onyx mirrored headboard, a burgundy oriental silk comforter with matching pillow shams, two tall side table cabinets and subtle silk paper lanterns. Her immaculate dresser was neatly accessorized with matching jewelry boxes and dressing items. All the oriental furniture was lacquered in black onyx with colorful Chinese characters and scenes gracing each piece. Her walls were adorned with her cherished oriental fan collection. Christine was a neat freak and treasured having everything in its place and a place for everything.

Charlotte's T.V. blared louder than was needed, as she sat on the floor cross-legged in front of it.

"The choice is yours, John, and you are within eight-hundred dollars of Mary." The host of Jeopardy asked.

"I'll take World Events for two hundred dollars, Art," the current Jeopardy champion said eagerly.

"Who was the first African American Supreme Court Justice?" Art Fleming questioned.

Immediately the contestant responded, "Thurgood Marshal."

"I knew that one," Charlotte shouted with glee, sitting cross-legged on the sofa. "I just didn't say it in time."

Charlotte was a T.V. addict, spending 4 to 6 hours each day watching her soaps and game shows The new game show, *Jeopardy*, being her favorite. Her part-time night bar tending job gave her plenty of time to just lay around the apartment.

EATON'S – During the Second French Revolution

Charlotte was the A-typical example of a 50's hippie. She dressed in ankle length floral dresses, open toe sandals; she wore long beads around her neck and seemed to permanently display a lilac in her hair. She was tall, 5' 8", muscular built and had a caustic disposition that didn't take shit from anyone. Her round face was draped by coal black hair, and there was a tiny heart tattoo behind her right ear. Charlotte had puffy lips which gave her the nickname, "Morticia Addams," a character from the T.V. show, "The Adams Family." She had extraordinarily piercing green eyes with a small beauty mark to the right of a sculptured nose. She was a creature of the international subculture movement where in addition to her radical hippie fashion, she also had her own characteristic music, philosophy, and way of life. Most disturbing to Christine was that Charlotte often went bra-less and didn't shave her body hair.

"I'm sure you knew that one, Char," Christine laughed, disbelievingly as she came into the living room area.

"No, no, really Chris," she pleaded, "I knew his name, I just had it turned around. I thought it was Marshal Thurgood."

"What is this show, anyway?"

"It's a new quiz show, that just came on, by Merv Griffin."

"That's not Merv Griffin, Char," she argued.

"No, No, it's one of the shows Merv Griffin produces," she corrected, "that guy is Art Fleming," she pointed at the T.V., "he's done commercials, and acted in movies, and on T.V."

The show droned on the little black and white Philco T.V. set.

"Entertainment for three-hundred, Art."

"Who had the signature song, "The House of The Rising Sun"?

I got this one. It was the Animals. I got the album right over there," she pointed to the Magnavox record console.

"The Animals," John responded.

"See I told you, Chris. I know all the answers," she pointed at the T.V. "I should audition for this show."

Christine just nodded as she walked back into her room to finish her packing.

"What's with the little red suitcase? Are you leaving me?" Charlotte asked as she stood in the bedroom doorway.

"Christ, Char, we've spent the last week talking about my rendez-vous with Ricky on January third, and today is January third, girl. We stayed up 'til four in the morning talking about it, with you imparting your vast knowledge on the subject, remember?"

"Oh yeah," her eyes scanned the clothing articles spread across the bed. "I guess I never thought of it as a rendez-vous, I just thought of it as you finally getting laid," she kidded.

"You're so crude, Char."

"I'm crude?" Christine pouted, grasping at her heart. "You're the one who is going to be doing some, what did you call it, 'rendez-vous,' with a married guy, and I'm crude," she repeated.

"I told you that his marriage was over the minute that he said, 'I do', and he's already started his divorce proceedings," she carefully folded a white night gown into the suitcase.

"Let me see, let me see," Charlotte bounded toward the bed, grasping the nightgown from the suitcase. "Wow, this peignoir set is incredible, Chris," she gazed in the mirror, holding the long white negligee and matching coving in front of her. "I'm going to need to borrow this for my next date with Billy."

"In your dreams, girl. This silk never touches any other body than mine."

"Yeah right! And your little Ricky boy."

"Give that back to me," she commanded, grabbing the peignoir set from Charlotte and refolding it into the suitcase.

"What other treasures 'ya got in there, Chris," she asked, rummaging through the suitcase.

"For my eyes only," she laughed, swatting away Charlotte's hand. "Go back to watching your 'Jeopardy!'"

Charlotte didn't move but glanced over at the T.V. to see what was happening with the game.

"World Events, for six hundred dollars."

"What year was the Berlin Wall built?" Fleming asked.

"Nineteen fifty- nine," Mary answered.

"No dummy, it was nineteen sixty-one! Christ, I should be on Jeopardy."

"Sorry, Mary the correct answer is nineteen sixty-one."

"See, told 'ya."

"You're the best, Char."

"Sure, and you're going to be all warm and cuddly with your 'Prince,' while I'll be here watching *Gunsmoke* and filling my face with vinegar chips. Maybe we should just change places and you could stay here. I've seen his rock-solid ass and, wouldn't mind sinking my nails into it."

"Oh Char, you are such a slut. If you took him on, you'd break him and then he wouldn't be good for anyone else,'" Christine teased.

"Isn't that the point! Leave them with their tongue hanging out, begging for more?"

Changing the subject, Christine asked, "Aren't you going to see Billy, this week?"

"No, he's got a run down to Nova Scotia and won't be back until Saturday night. But he did tell me I could use the vibrator and a picture of him nude, while he was away." Charlotte's boyfriend was a long-haul trucker driving for Smith Transport.

"Char! He's your boyfriend! That's just gross, even for you."

EATON'S – During the Second French Revolution

Charlotte silenced her. "Wait, I've got to get the final Jeopardy question."

"We have a real tight race going into Final Jeopardy. Our champion, John has sixteen thousand nine hundred dollars, while Mary the challenger is in second place with fourteen thousand dollars and Robert is in third place with ten thousand. I believe someone is going home with a lot of money today," Fleming said.

"The final Jeopardy category is Animals."

"And the clue is, 'There are only 3 of these animals in U.S. zoos: a twenty-eight-year-old in D.C.'s National Zoo and two younger ones in San Diego'."

"Damn. That's too easy a question for *Final Jeopardy*, everyone's going to get it. The answer is Panda Bears," Charlotte stated, waiting for the thirty second theme to end.

"We come to Robert, who was in third place going into Final Jeopardy, and he wrote 'Panda' which is the right answer. And his wager six thousand nine-hundred and one, putting him in first place, by one dollar. Mary, did you get 'Panda'? Yes, she did. And her wager three thousand bringing her into the lead, and now to our champion John, who led throughout the game. Did you have 'Panda'? Yes, you did. And did you risk enough? Oh, my! You bet it all for a total of thirty-three thousand, giving you a five-day total of ....

Charlotte got up and turned off the T.V. as she headed for their small kitchenette. "'Ya wanna sandwich?" she asked opening the refrigerator.

"Sure. What have we got?" Christine asked, closing her suitcase.

"Let's see," she answered, peering into the fridge. "We've got bologna, jam, and," she paused to smell an open can, "well, and, sardines."

"Is that all? I thought you went shopping yesterday."

"I did," she smiled holding up a case of Moosehead beer.

"Gross! Where's all the food?"

"Well let's see," she posed with her finger to her chin feigning thought. "There's Cho Lings, at the corner; Mario's Pizzeria, up the block; and Saint Hubert Barbeque, or anything else you want."

"Never mind. I'll just have a bologna sandwich with mustard."

"'Ya want that on Melba Toast, or on Saltine Crackers?"

Exasperated Christine responded, "So you're saying we have no bread?"

"But we do have this," she smiled, holding up the case of Moosehead.

"It's only seven-thirty in the morning, Char, and I've got to get to work. I wish you had told me when we came back from spending the holidays with my parent's that we were out of everything."

"Yeah, but it's 'happy hour' somewhere in the world. Cheers!" she laughed, popping the cap on the beer bottle.

"You're too much, Char."

"That's what all the boys tell me. Are you going to shower, now? 'Ya know, there won't be enough hot water for two showers."

"Hey Chris, while you're in the shower, I've got to run down to the pharmacy," she yelled, picking up her purse, need anything? How 'bout some, uh, KY Jelly and happy hats?" she joked, waiting to see her roommate's reaction.

"Happy hats, what are you talking about Char?"

"Yeah, 'ya know, safes, pappa stoppers ...,"

Christine's face still looked blank.

Uh, you know! Condoms?"

"Oh, just give it a rest, Char."

Maybe Charlotte is right! Maybe I'm supposed to handle that stuff. Damn, I don't want to screw this up, but I'm so nervous, I'm going to wet my pants if I keep thinking about it. Oh shit! If I don't get showered and dressed, I'm going to be late for work and my boss will not like that!

⚜ Seventy ⚜

Returning to work after the holidays should have been a welcome change, but instead it proved to be one of the most difficult workdays that Ricky had ever experienced at Eaton's. Because his regular babysitter had gone to Quebec City for the holidays, Ricky took part of his vacation time so that he could have the ten days between the holidays to spend with Darlene.

But now, being back at his beloved Eaton's, no matter how hard he tried he couldn't keep his mind focused on his management duties. He had meetings all day on Tuesday the second of January, and no matter how much was going on, he kept searching for just a brief glance at Christine.

The previous 10 days since their Christmas eve encounter had arduously ticked by, bringing the inevitable rendezvous of January third, ever closer. And the closer it got; the more Ricky's apprehension built. He worried about his past pre-mature ejaculation problems which had happened during the few sexual experiences he had with his wife and dreaded anything like that happening with Christine. He had only a basic literary knowledge of the female anatomy from some research he had done and had zero experience in the whole process of making love to any woman. Yet here he was trying to be Mr. Super Stud; a 22-year-old, about to have the first real sexual experience of his life! Just thinking of Christine would set his loins ablaze, his mouth dry and breathless.

During that 10 day period, Ricky had half hoped that Christine would suddenly realize the futility of her acceptance response and give him some excuse to not following through with their upcoming date. But alternatively, the other half of him would be screaming that he would die if he did not finally get to at least hold her in that special intimate way he had so long fantasized about.

When January 3rd finally arrived, anticipation seemed to paralyze Ricky's ability to function as a normal person, or even in a businesslike manner. His legs had begun to feel like they were made of rubber, and he felt as if he had been performing like a zombie in the store, since he returned after the holidays.

Uppermost in his mind was his feeling that he was going to sexually explode if Christine simply gazed into his eyes. He realized that he had to get a grip on himself and his propelling emotions and *out- of- control* body. He had to find the same confidence that had accelerated him in his successful career. He had to make everything perfect, enjoyable, and non-intimidating for her, his sweet Princess, the girl of his dreams.

Ricky had rehearsed his forthcoming performance a thousand times in his mind. He kept telling himself, *you can do this. No, you Have to do this, and do it right for just once in your life.* He had to focus on the fact that his emotional or sexual gratification was totally unimportant, and instead concentrate on Christine. Her emotional and physical pleasure must be paramount, at all costs.

By the end of his workday, Ricky had no idea what he had done all day. All he could think of was his checklist and making sure he had everything covered. He called Kathy one more time to make sure she was staying in town for one more day and was going to sleep at her parents' house that night; and that she was taking Darlene with her. *First thing checked off! Okay, don't have to worry about Darlene!*

Next item was to do the things he had pre-planned for the room. From the moment he arrived at the hotel he knew he had to put all concerns for her comfort first and foremost. He put some special things in the room and then went to pick up Christine.

I have this one incredible chance, and I will NEVER forgive myself if I blow it!'

Ricky arrived at her apartment and found her sitting quietly on the front stoop, a little red suitcase grasped in her hands.

He kissed her gently as he helped her into the car. She seemed a little nervous, so he put on some soft music and reached for her hand.

He drove to the *Howard Johnson's Motor Lodge* and parked in the back-parking lot. He had gone there earlier and checked in, purposely to shield her from the embarrassment of having to stand beside him, exposed to the questioning eyes of the reservation clerk, while he got the room.

Ricky went around and helped her out of the car and took her suitcase in one hand, and her hand in his other. His legs were shaking with anticipation, almost giving way to his fear. The time had finally arrived, but was he ready?

He walked her to the room and handed the red suitcase to her to hold while he placed the key in the door. He was unsure what she was feeling and therefore, did not want to let go of her hand. She in turn affectionately squeezed his as he guided her into the room that was to dictate their future.

Christine stood childlike holding onto her little red suitcase as he closed the heavy door. He silently criticized himself for not having secured a nice suite somewhere more special for their first intimate time together.

Ricky started to look around and thought of all the "should of's" he didn't do!

I should have had pretty flowers for her, petals lying on the bed, there should have been some sweet quiet music playing and a special card heralding her arrival, and just maybe, a special little note left for her on the pillow simply saying, thank you.

Ricky's selfish consumption with all his own wants, needs, fears, etc. had eliminated the thoughtful little touches that he now realized would have made things even better for Christine.

All Ricky had to offer was now fully exposed. He cradled her swaying body by the doorway. He knew, either one of them could run out that doorway, and disappear forever.

He pushed the bad ideas from his mind and slowly, even hesitantly moved her from his embrace. Ricky again took her little red suitcase and then led her to the intimidating double bed before them; then turned and placed the little red case on the adjoining bed.

Ricky broke the deafening silence when he turned Christine's head to face him. She reacted with a tense body and a slight smile.

"Are you okay," he whispered into her ear, feeling the intoxicating texture and silkiness of her hair, against his cheek. "It's still not too late to turn back. I'd understand completely."

She gazed deep into his eyes, then with a slightly hesitant whisper, "Y ... yes, I'm okay. Just a little nervous." Her eyes betrayed her subtle inner lie.

"Everything will be very slow and with no surprises. You can say 'stop' whenever you want," he reassured her.

He took off their coats and put them on a chair, then walked her over to the bed and eased her into a lying down position.

She watched his every move as he left her side momentarily to find some soft music on the combination TV and radio. When he walked back to the bed, Ricky had two glasses of Dubonnet in his hand, and handed her one. He sat next to her and held her hand as she cuddled up next to him and placed her head on his shoulder. The moment was full of passion for both of them, but he promised to take it slow.

He marveled at Christine's sculptured thin legs on the bedspread as he slowly removed her boots and sat on the edge of the bed next to her. He looked into her eyes and bent down to kiss her again.

They kissed and caressed in awkward silence. Each kiss became more passionate. Each caress more daring. Each touch more intimate....

By the end of the evening, they had made love numerous times. All inhibitions were thrown to the wind; all strangeness replaced with a full knowledge of each other's body and each other's wants, and needs.

Ricky could now legitimately claim to be "Mr. Stud."

EATON'S – During the Second French Revolution

⚜ Seventy-One ⚜

Still reeling from his January 3rd encounter with Christine, Ricky gingerly stepped from the Eaton's escalator onto the basement floor. His first troubling observation was his staff standing in deep conversation, paying no attention to the fact that the opening bell was about to sound.

"What the hell is going on Andrea?" he addressed his millinery manager. "The store is about to open, and everyone is just standing around talking. They haven't even taken the night covers off the tables and displays. Get it handled!"

"Sssoooo Sorry, Mister Dean," she stammered. "Everyone is stunned by the Lasalle explosion."

"Lasalle explosion?" he cut her off curtly.

"No, it's just …"

"Never mind, just get the bloody store opened," he commanded, walking towards his office. "The friggin' F.L.Q. set another bomb and the whole world stops," he muttered.

Passing teens fashions, he asked Cindy Valdez, "Where is Miss Guillaume, it's not her day off today, is it?"

"No, Mister Dean. She was just so upset about Rose Anne that she went into your office to try to recuperate."

Rose Anne? "Thanks, I'll catch Christine there," he replied, concerned about the situation.

When he entered his office, Christine was seated in a chair, her head in her hands, crying. He threw his coat on the coat rack, quickly closed the door, and grabbed Christine in his arms. "What's wrong, Princess?"

"It's just so awful, Ricky," she sobbed. "He was just a little baby, and …"

"Hold on Sweetheart. 'Ya got to calm down. Nothing we can't fix, remember?" he placated.

"This can't ever be fixed, Ricky."

Ricky locked his office door, then gently guided Christine back into the chair. He pulled another chair close to her and took her hand. "Okay, catch your breath and tell me, from the beginning, what is so terrible." He put his arm around her quivering shoulders.

"It's about the explosion in LaSalle. It, it is so terrible! I can't believe it!" she stuttered.

"Sorry, I didn't hear any details about the LaSalle F.L.Q. bombing, I just …"

"Not an F.L.Q. bombing, Ricky. A gas explosion leveled two whole apartment buildings. They say more than twenty people were killed including thirteen children. Rose Anne's baby was …" she couldn't finish her statement, and again broke down.

"What, what about Rose Anne's baby. Was he hurt, was she hurt?" concern crept across his face. "Please Christine. Try and calm down and tell me the whole story," he commanded.

Getting her emotions under control, Christine continued. "According to Rose Anne's mother, at around eight o'clock this morning Rose Anne ran down her apartment stairs to get the milk from the from porch, leaving baby Sean in his crib. She bent down to get the milk when the whole apartment complex exploded around her. She was propelled fifteen feet, onto the front lawn. When she regained consciousness, the paramedics were there, and she screamed about finding her baby. They told her that search and rescue was underway, but they needed her to get into the ambulance. Her mother told me that she passed out from severe lacerations to her arms and back before she reached the hospital. She's in stable condition, but graciously still unconscious."

"And the baby?" Ricky asked, apprehensive about the answer.

"The baby didn't make it! She said, with a sob in her voice. He was only seventeen months old. And after all Rose Anne has gone through getting a divorce from that drunken creep, I don't know how she will survive this. She wasn't only my best salesclerk, she was my friend," she sniffled.

"We'll get through this together, and be there to help her when she needs us, but now, I'm really going to need your help, Okay?"

"Yes Ricky," she replied timidly. "But what can I do?"

"First, you need to get yourself under total control, or you won't be able to help anyone. We need a plan to help Rose Anne, and as many of the other victims as possible, and as soon as possible. You need to talk with her mother soon and find out what she needs, support, money, housing, clothing, anything, understand?"

"Understood," she dabbed her eyes with the tissue he had handed her.

"Now, go to the ladies' room and repair the damage to your face and come back here, the beautiful confident manager that you are, 'cause that's what we need right now! I'm going to have a meeting with all managers and buyers immediately, so hurry."

Ricky pressed the key on his intercom, and directed his office manager, and now his secretary, "Rebecca, I want a stat alert to all floor managers, or assistant managers if the manager is off, and all buyers in my office, fifteen minutes ago. Thanks."

"Wow! You move fast," Christine commented, having already regained her composure.

"You would know first-hand, Darlin'," he winked, trying to quell the events of the tragedy.

Within minutes people flooded into his office, overflowing into the outer reception area.

"Where's Jerry," he asked.

EATON'S – During the Second French Revolution

"I'm here, boss," Jerry replied, standing on his tiptoes, in the rear of the crowd.

He noticed that Christine had returned and joined the other managers.

"Okay. You all heard about the LaSalle explosion, but what you may not have heard is that our own fashion salesclerk, Rose Anne was seriously injured, and tragically her young baby boy was killed."

Gasps and tears rang out from the assembled staff, most of whom knew Rose Anne personally.

"We are going to help her and as many of the victims as possible. Buyers, I want you to contact every single one of our suppliers for cash or clothing donations, or whatever they'll give. Andrea, I want you to contact Frank McCorcoran at Laura Secord in Toronto for a donation. He owes me from the store bombing. John, I want you to contact all your luggage people across the chain, and individual stores that you think might take up donations. The rest of you need to think of any other ways that we can raise assistance for these poor people. I will contact Catholic and Jewish Charities, and the Salvation Army, for their assistance. Oh, and Christine is going to contact Rose Anne's mother to find out about any other special needs. Now, let's get this done!"

"I just called Rose Anne's' mother, Evelyn, who told me that Rose Anne is awake, but understandably totally distraught. When I asked how we could help, she told me that Rose Anne doesn't even have money to handle the funeral expenses tomorrow, for the baby," Christine choked.

"Tell her that Eaton's Montreal will handle all the funeral costs. I'll clear it with Appleton."

The day passed incredibly well with over eight thousand dollars collected from Eaton's Montreal division staff alone. There were also over thirty-three thousand dollars from loyal Eaton's suppliers.

The next day, Ricky and Christine and a majority of Eaton's basement staff all sat in the Bagg Street Shul, the oldest congregational synagogue still operating in Montreal, since its inception in 1921. They couldn't help but stare at the solitary, highly polished, small white casket below the Bema; *known in Christian churches as an altar.*

Awaiting the entrance of the Rabbi, Ricky reflected on the story that he had read about the LaSalle explosion.

EXPLOSION KILLS 26 IN MONTREAL
SUBURBAN APARTMENT DESTROYED

Montreal (UPI) -- Twenty-six residents were killed and 37 injured Monday when a natural gas explosion leveled a 40-unit, three-story apartment building. Officials said shortly before 9 p.m. that five people were still missing. The blast lifted half the building and hurled it 50 yards from its foundation. Men, women, and children were blown from their beds and breakfast tables when the explosion erupted in the low-rent housing development. Many of them were buried alive under flaming timbers and other burning rubble.

Deputy Fire Commissioner said, "It's highly likely that a natural gas leak could have caused the explosion. Bodies were laid on the ice of a nearby hockey rink turned into a temporary morgue. One severely burned young boy was pulled out of the wreckage and doctors promptly pronounced him dead. But a policeman refused to believe it and with mouth-to-mouth resuscitation revived the youngster. The blast destroyed the three-story apartment house at 8:12 a.m. "It looked like the London blitz," one of the rescue officials said. Premier Jean Lasage and Atty. Gen. Claude Wagner rushed to the scene to help with rescue work and determine the cause of what was termed this capital province's worst disaster.

Officials said they had not yet officially determined the explosion's cause, but residents reported they noticed "the heavy sweet taste and smell" of natural gas before the explosion.

The explosion started fires that swept three adjacent buildings and turned a four-block section of the Ville la Salle suburb into a shamble. Fires sent hundreds of persons fleeing in their night clothes into the frigid Canadian morning. Fathers, who left for work a short time before rushed back to search for their families.

Factory workers, civil defense workers, and nearby military units answered the urgent calls for help which crackled out over Montreal radio stations. High schools in the area released their students so they could donate blood and help with the rescue work.

This tragedy will be remembered for generations to come.

As the Jewish funeral progressed with the traditional Memorial Prayer, called "El Maleh Rachamim," and the Mourner's Blessing, called "Mourner's Kaddish," among others, tears flowed from the mourner's eyes, and the family of Baby Sean.

Christine squeezed Ricky's hand softly saying, "We need to count our blessing each and every day!"

⚜ Seventy-Two ⚜

Ricky tried to clear his mind of the Lasalle explosion so that he could concentrate on the "Bound For Success" meeting at hand. The main topic today was to be the opening of the Metro Station directly into Eaton's basement. The ultra-modern Montreal Metro station, *Métro de Montréal*, was probably the biggest development project for the downtown Montreal Eaton's store since the 1925 purchase of the original Goodwin's store. The rubber-tired, underground metro system, was inspired by the Paris Metro subway system, and clearly mirrored their station's design and rolling stock.

EATON'S – During the Second French Revolution

The 26 stations, running on three separate lines, was to be operated by the Société de Transport de Montréal, *STM*, and destined to become Montréal's' premier form of public transport. The new Eaton's Metro station was to be inaugurated by Montreal's, Mayor, and was the subject of today's "Bound for Success" meeting.

As the last team member wandered in, Robert Appleton opened the meeting. "Today we stand at the cusp of the Eaton's of tomorrow," he began. "Every Eaton's Montreal employee shall have the privilege of embarking on an unprecedented journey into the twentieth century. The opening of our basement store, directly into the new Metro station, is destined to bring thousands of new customers into our store," he paused for effect.

Appleton continued. "But this privilege should *not* be considered a God-given right. This is a privilege earned by yourselves and our employees through dedication and hard work. Many of you had to completely restructure your departments to accommodate traffic flow, while others have had their selling areas significantly reduced. The largest area of upheaval, of course, has been our basement store operation. Almost without exception, every department has been affected. And, please keep in mind, that the basement personnel's hard work and sacrifice wasn't easy. But it is ultimately going to benefit every upper floor selling area, too! So, when one of your basement counterparts asks a favor to borrow a cash register, or a particular display, just remember that the increase on your bottom-line profits is directly attributed to their sacrifices," Appleton pointed to each individual around the table.

"Now, we have just a few weeks left to put the finishing touches on a smooth opening of the Metro, but first, we have the honor of hearing from Jacques van der Court, who has been the senior engineer of the Metro project, since it began. Mister van der Court."

"Thank you, Mister Appleton," he stood, and went over to a large flip chart. "Since I understand that you have already been through a presentation recently, I think it will be interesting to bring you through the history and development of the Metro project."

"I'm sure that many of you think that the idea for the underground Metro started just a decade ago, but you may be surprised to learn that Montreal mass-transit planning dates to eighteen sixty-one where a first line of horse-drawn cars started to operate on Saint James Street. Eventually, as Montreal grew, a comprehensive network of electric streetcar lines provided service almost everywhere. But because of urban congestion and inclement weather, the lines started to take its toll on streetcar punctuality, and so the idea of a metro was soon considered."

"The first Metro proposal, dates back to nineteen ten when the city planned for a single line to run underneath Bleury Street, at Craig Street and all the way up to Mont Royal, with several other underground expansions planned at the same time. Because of unavailable funding the plan was abandoned. However, in nineteen forty-four the Montreal Tramways Company proposed a two-line network, running underneath Sainte-Catherine from Atwater Street. to Papineau, and a second line under Saint Denis to Notre-Dame," he followed the routing on his chart. "Unfortunately, that too, never got off the ground."

"In nineteen fifty-three the newly formed Montreal Transportation Commission proposed a single line, running under Sainte Catherine from Atwater to Peel where the line would have turned south, going underneath Square Dorchester, all the way down to Saint-Jacques, where several extension were to branch off."

"In nineteen sixty-three the last proposal was the closest to what we have today. Part of the urgency was because of the Expo Sixty-Seven World's Fair, which required an underground line to serve the island site of Île Sainte-Hélène where the Expo was being held. Because of economics, I honestly believe that had it not been for the necessity of mass transit for Expo Sixty-Seven, the Metro that we are about to open, would not have come to fruition. Questions?" he asked.

John Witherspoon raised his hand, "With just the three lines that we are beginning now, are there additional lines planned for the future?"

"Yes, the city has committed annual funds to an ongoing program of developing not only new lines throughout the city but branches out into the off-island suburbs," Mister van der Court answered.

"We've all seen the pictures of new subway cars fashioned after the Paris subway, but I understand that actual station designs also simulated Parisian detail, is that correct?" Heidi Mullins asked.

"Good question. In fact, the entrances to the Square-Victoria metro station looks *exactly* like a Paris Métro station, down to an original Hector Guimard gate which is a gift from the city of Paris. Unlike other cities' metros, nearly all our station entrances are completely enclosed. Usually they are in small, separate buildings with swiveling doors meant to mitigate the wind caused by train movements that can make doors difficult to open and close. Additionally, all separate entrances are set back from the sidewalk, as well as several stations in Downtown Montreal which are directly connected to buildings, just like here at Eaton's. These entrances inside existing buildings and at street-level entrances, make the Metro an integral part of what will become, Montreal's underground city."

Ricky raised his hand.

"Yes, Mister Dean, isn't it?" Mister van der Court questioned. "You were on the *Underground City* advisory committee, representing Eaton's, were you not?"

"Yes, sir, thank you for remembering," Ricky acknowledged. "What measures have the Société de Transport de Montréal put in place to address security issues within the various stations both during and after, regular commercial store closings?"

"The M.P.D. has been tasked with developing a separate, fully funded agency to handle security, much like the transit police in many American cities. After business hours, Eaton's gates will be closed to the Metro, and passengers will be required to use the stairs to ascend and descend to the street level. Regular beat cops will be required to patrol the stairs, from the street level, and traverse each of the subway platforms."

"If there are no more questions, I look forward to seeing you again when Mayor Drapeau officially opens your station."

As he departed the group stood and gave him a round of applause.

"So, now we know how it all began," Appleton continued. "But now we have to make sure we are ready. Each of you are to have floor responsibility for making sure every ingress and egress position has clear bi-lingual signage directing people to the basement Metro entry; Every register stand is to have a supply of Metro route maps; Mister Dean, you need to delegate responsible parties to ensure that the subway advertising cases are up to date with the most recent newspaper ads, on a daily basis; and, for all of you," he looked around the room, "you need to build the enthusiasm, in every single Eaton employee, concerning the opening of the Metro. When I make my rounds, I do not want to see anything but smiling faces, understand?"

"Yes Sir," a chorus rang out.

"Then, let's get back to work!" he smiled.

⚜ Seventy-Three ⚜

"Time for coffee, Jer," Ricky grabbed Jerry Copeland's arm.

"Sorry boss, but I've already had my coffee break."

"I don't think so. Your boss ran out of cigarettes, so I don't think you've had your coffee break, yet right?"

Jerry laughed as he followed Ricky. "When you put it that way, Boss, maybe my memory is slipping."

Entering the luncheonette, Ricky filled two mugs with coffee, paid the cashier and joined Jerry in a booth overlooking the main aisle.

Jerry threw a pack of Players cigarettes across the table. "These must be yours, Boss, 'cause I've got another pack."

"Thanks, Jer, you always have my back." Ricky lit a cigarette. "Ah, that's so good. Must be just as good as sex if I could remember back that far," he joked. Even Jerry wasn't to know about Christine. Ricky had fully confided in Jerry about the problems in his marriage with Kathy, and his upcoming divorce but not of his relationship with Christine.

"I told you that Denise has a sister that would gladly clean your pipes. All you got to do is ask."

"Maybe one day, Jer."

"Anyway, do you remember that Appleton company paper project that I had you help me with a few months back?" Ricky asked.

"Yeah, I never imagined that we could accumulate so many different pieces of paper and forms. It seemed like we just kept adding stuff and never eliminated the old ones."

"Well, the end result was that we narrowed down the operating forms from four hundred and eighty-three to two hundred and twenty-nine and Appleton is ecstatic. This is going to save Eaton's a ton of money and streamline our billing procedures. And I also told him how much work you did in gathering the forms from every department in the store, then collating them to identify duplications. He was really impressed!"

"Thanks Rick, but I hope you didn't include my name in the piano scheme that you and Tony cooked up. Appleton must have busted a gut over that one. "I still don't understand how you guys pulled that off."

"The 'why' is easy. You know that Appleton is the consummate skeptic when it comes to any changes. He always wants positive proof to back up everything that we suggest. He never wants to consider that there are any flaws in store procedures that can reflect on his management."

"Yeah, so?"

"When he gave me the assignment and told me to include Tony, his final directions were that 'if we find any major security breaches in our forms, or store procedures, we will have *to unequivocally prove it to him*'."

"I remember we found a big hole in the six-part customer billing forms, right?"

"Correcto! Tony and I figured that if we just told him about how serious the breach could be, that he'd blow it off, like he usually does, like a one-time error. He'd say that it would only affect low end purchases and not be worth the expense of a complete customer form overhaul."

"And wouldn't he be right?"

"No, because if our system is flawed at one end, it's also flawed at the other. You are familiar with the destination of each of the six sections of our sales receipts, right," Ricky explained.

Jerry ticked off his fingers, "Part one goes to the customer; part two goes to the selling department. Part three remains as the salesman copy, while part four goes to the packing department. Then part five goes to the delivery department, and finally, part six goes to the accounting department for billing."

"Great! Now, what if part six never finds its way to the accounting department for billing the customer?"

EATON'S – During the Second French Revolution

"Why wouldn't it get there. As soon as we make a charged delivery sale, we send the accounting copy up the tube to the accounting office. I'm confused about where you're going with this, Rick."

"You're not thinking like a criminal, Jer. Your brother needs an overcoat, so you decide to send it to him. You fill out the total sales receipt with his name and address, charge account number, sales information, and price. You put part two, the selling department copy in the box by the register. You keep part three, the salesman copy, parts one, four and five, the customer copy, the packing copy, and the delivery copy, you pin to the overcoat and send it to the packing department. What do you do with part six, the accounting copy, Jer?"

"Send it upstairs to accounting, in the tube?"

"Jer, I want you to think like a criminal. You know what you do, you destroy part six. When the coat gets to the packing department, they keep part four and send the coat and parts one and five with the driver for delivery, the customer ends up keeping part one, the customer copy, and the free coat."

"That can't be right. The accounting office has to be looking for that missing part one."

"Why would they? They don't have anything to match it to, so they are not looking for anything."

"That's deep. The store could lose thousands of dollars with that one single sales forms breach. What's the answer? Print up seven-part forms?"

"No," Ricky responded, "just change the system. Instead of the selling department sending the charge to the accounting office, let the packing, or delivery, departments send them. That way nothing gets out of the store unless they have the accounting copy to send up."

"Got it. So, where does the grand piano fit in?"

"Tony and I used the existing sales receipt, where we destroyed the accounting copy and sent a grand piano to Appleton's house."

"For real?" Jerry was flabbergasted.

"Yeah, one guy from the packing room, an Eaton driver and Tony and I loaded the piano in an Eaton's truck and took it to his home in Laval. You should have seen the look on his wife's face when she saw the piano in the truck. When we told her the whole story of having to convince Appleton about the validity of our findings, she nearly split a gut."

"Yeah, I can see that, but how did Appleton take it. I guess that he was really pissed. That guy just doesn't 'got no' sense of humor."

"By the time we got the piano back to the store, his wife had already called him. According to his secretary, Mrs. Appleton was laughing so hard on the telephone, it took a while for her to stop long enough to tell the story. So, when Tony and I got to his office, he was looking all pissed off, complaining about the cost of labor we used to make the delivery, four guys, gas, etc. I tell him that no wages were expended, because we all volunteered our time to make the delivery and even paid for the gas. And you are not going to believe this, the old man started laughing uncontrollably. I mean he was doubling over in his fancy chair."

"I can believe everything except the old man laughing."

"But that's not the end of it! Finally, he stops laughing and he looks up at Tony and me with this real serious look that he usually has, and he says, 'If my wife gets the bright idea that she wants an eight-thousand-dollar piano, Tony and I better start looking for part time jobs to pay for it. Can you believe it, a bloody joke actually came out of his mouth!"

"Now that's really hard to believe!" Suddenly, Jerry was distracted. "I think some lovely thing is trying to get your attention."

Ricky turned to see a set of piercing blue eyes staring at him. Eyes that he'd been trying to forget, the eyes of Debbie the hooker.

She gave a quick wave, and a devious smile. Ricky waved back.

"I'm not even going to ask," Jerry commented.

"Sorry Jer, need to go!" and he left the luncheonette without saying anything more!

Jerry thought, *Yeah, I think that's a story I'd really like to hear much more about!*

⚜ Seventy-Four ⚜

Louis was both exhausted and depressed. Following the Montreal Stock Exchange bombing his handler, Mr. Smith, had advised him that his undercover work was to end with him being reassigned to Vancouver. However, the following day Smith advised him that, 'because of some developing circumstances', he would have to remain undercover a while longer.

Sure, it's my ass on the line, not his!

Louis slumped into the ragged sofa in his downtrodden apartment, totally drained from weeks of intensive infiltration into member cells associated with his own *F.L.Q. Dieppe Cell*. His days had been filled with feigned casual encounters with members of the *F.L.Q. Liberation Cell*, attempting to gather information on upcoming terror events, while secretly accumulating names and profiles of participating members in the Exchange bombing. His nights required contact with his own *Dieppe Cell* team leaders and members, usually including extensive drinking until the early hours of the morning. The reward for this sacrifice came as the members became more intoxicated and their mouths began to run with relative information about future *F.L.Q.* activities. The problem that Louis encountered of late was that with the stepped-up activities of the *F.L.Q.* there was an overabundance of information being spread around. This required him to prioritize the gathered information as to a matter of importance, or the impending danger. Where a student rally at the Montreal courthouse in the past may have garnered significant importance, now a planned bombing of a federal government target took precedent. It all came down to evaluating the actual threat level of the attack.

Louis popped the cap off a bottle of Molson's beer, propped his feet up on a wooden crate that served as his coffee table, and closed his eyes allowing his head to rest on the back of the sofa.

When I began this undercover work, it was an exciting adventure and important work, now it's just lonely and dangerous. Every day, I live in fear of discovery. If I'm ever identified as an infiltrator, I'd simply disappear, and nobody would ever be the wiser!

Louis heard the quiet ping of his pager secreted under the crate. When he retrieved it, he saw the familiar coded message stating simply, "Call mother". The old clock on the wall indicated that it was 3:48 A.M.

Shit, I've been working eighteen hours straight, now I must go back out in the middle of the night.

Louis put on his parka and boots and trudged the four blocks to a discreet telephone booth, where he contacted his handler. Going through the arduous security regimen Smith eventually came on the line. *Christ doesn't this guy ever sleep.*

"Report?" was his only comment.

"No concrete information to report since my last report two days ago," Louis began.

I wish he'd give me a little more time between reports.

"Continue Mister Jones."

"I'm getting a lot of information about F.L.Q. activities, but most are after the fact."

"After the fact?"

"Yes, I've uncovered information about Molotov cocktails being thrown through government building windows, an assault on a group of English soccer players, and a bomb that went off harmlessly at the Smith Transport depot. The problem is that I'm getting this information several days after it has happened, and not with names that I can turn over to law enforcement. It appears that so many events are happening in such quick succession that even cell members are having trouble gauging their importance."

"How so?"

"For example, the Molotov cocktails thrown at the government building, are no longer a topic of conversation, instead, the new conversation shifts to the most current event. Given this fact, from my standpoint, it would appear suspicious for me to be inquiring about these past events."

"And how do you propose getting around this obstacle?"

"There is no concrete way to get around this problem. My only course of action is to hang around with as many different cell members as I can fit into a day and hope that I will hear about something *before* it happens."

"That doesn't seem to be a very pro-active course?"

"I'm open to suggestions, Mister Smith."

It is goddamn easy for this guy to sit on his fat ass behind his big desk and tell me I'm not doing my job. His life is not on the line every day.

Mister Smith ignored Louis's statement.

"The reason I called is because we have a Priority One directive, from Toronto headquarters. All operatives are to immediately suspend their assigned operations and concentrate on gathering information on the Laporte and Cross kidnappings. This order is coming directly from Prime Minister Trudeau, who is using Canada's War Measures Act to find the kidnappers. Are you current on the case?"

"Only so far as what I've heard from the news. I heard that British diplomat, James Richard Cross, was kidnapped, but I don't know the details, then five days later Vice Premier of Quebec, Pierre Laporte was kidnapped from his front yard while playing football with his nephew."

"And have you heard anything from inside to add to this information?"

"As you can imagine, there is a lot of excitement from within the F.L.Q. about the kidnappings. This is the most daring and internationally prominent event of their reign, and as such, a lot of rumors are floating around. Unfortunately, I haven't been able to substantiate their authenticity."

"Let me worry about their authenticity. Tell me what you've heard."

"As far as I can gather, it seems pretty certain that the Laporte kidnapping was done by the Chénier Cell of the FLQ, and as such, the brothers Paul and Jacques Rose would most likely be the ringleaders."

"There were four people involved in the kidnapping."

"I haven't heard any other names mentioned, but last spring when I was at the FLQ cell meeting, at the Mont Tremblant Resort, I met Jacques Rose, who was with two other *Chénier Cell* members, Francis Simard and Bernard Lortie. I understand that the Rose brothers and these two are inseparable. So, if I had to give an educated guess I'd say Simard and Lortie make up the foursome."

"Their motivation for the Laporte kidnapping?"

"Again, just rumors, but my *Dieppe Cell* group, were joking last Friday night in the bar, about Laporte now being 'Minister of Unemployment and Assimilation', and the ransom demands were to include the release of twenty-three political prisoners."

"What about Cross?"

"Not much information there, except that the kidnappers are going to present an FLQ Manifesto, documenting a whole laundry list of their demands. I have no information on which FLQ cell conducted the kidnapping, nor which members participated."

"Is that it?"

"Just one further observation. It seems that the FLQ high echelon is extremely concerned that the kidnappings do not result in harming either Laporte or Cross. They want to use these kidnappings to gain political advantage, but not to harm and certainly not murder these prominent individuals. They don't want the blood on their hands, which would be internationally detrimental to their separatist cause."

"Okay then. As I mentioned earlier, concentrate on these men and I'll expect daily updates." He hung up the telephone.

And, you have a pleasant day, too, Sir!

⚜ Seventy-Five ⚜

After his January 3rd experience with Christine, Ricky was looking forward to his therapy session with Doctor Markovitz, which he hoped would be his last. Ricky plopped down on the sofa adjacent to the doctor.

"Richard, the last we heard from you, was that you had canceled your sessions indefinitely. I was fearful that you had abandoned my assistance. Was there a development that caused your cancellation?"

Ricky related all the Eaton's events that had transpired that had kept him busy since his last session.

"So, you were part of this foiled robbery attempt at the store that I read in the paper? That had to be frightening, yes?"

"Yes, that along with all the other stuff that I was trying to handle made life extremely stressful during that same time."

"That was probably when you needed to see me most of all! But I'm sensing a new calmness from you, and less stress. So, I also believe that something maybe, something good, has happened in your life, yes? I've never seen you look so happy. Am I reading something that is not there?"

"There's been a nice change to my normally turbulent life, but we can get to that later," Ricky smiled coyly.

"If you remember, I thought I detected that same excitement at the end of our last session."

"Yeah, it was there, but, well, now it's much better."

"I'm intrigued! Anything that finally makes you happy, is progress."

"Well, then I guess I have really progressed, Doc."

"Good! Good! So, Now, tell me. Last session I wanted you to concentrate on your present home life situation, your feelings of sexual inadequacy, and any outside interest that may be occupying your mind, yes?"

"To start with my home life, Doc, my wife has moved out of the house, and I have filed for divorce and custody of Darlene, so that issue is about to be solved."

"Excellent. And how do feel about this burden being lifted from your shoulders?"

"It was a situation that I always considered hopeless. Something I thought that I would be saddled with for the rest of my life. And then, with the help of some friends the problem was solved. I sleep better, eat better, and smile more. I now know what happiness can be. I always lived as my personal morality dictated, which was that I had made my bed and had to lie in it, as the old proverb says."

"But not all proverbs are made to cover all circumstances, Richard. Yours was unique. You had a wife who seemed to have a mental illness, or at the very least, a deep psychological disturbance that she refused to acknowledge, or seek treatment for. Her actions were destructive to you, your daughter, and your marriage in general, yes?"

"Yes, that's right, but ..."

Markowitz interrupted. "There are no *'buts'*, my boy," he raised his voice, "there was just what were you prepared to do about it. Somewhere deep down you realized that this couldn't go on forever. It would have continued to cause damage to everyone, including your wife. Your analytical mind thoroughly identified the problem and formulated a viable solution. I'm proud of you Richard."

"Thanks, Doc."

"This positive result has been a long time coming. How did you handle the wife separation situation?"

"I devised a systematic plan of action and then checked off every aspect as I achieved each of the goals. For example, you helped me to better understand my wife's illness, and that helped me to be more tolerant of her actions. That was step one towards reaching my end goal. I spent considerable time analyzing the positives and negatives regarding my marital situation. The result dictated that a divorce was the best resolution for all three of us, regardless of my moral position on the marriage."

"Very good. But just like every other person facing divorce, accept the losses but focus on the ultimate emotional gains for your future. You are too young to have your life destroyed by circumstances beyond your control. From what I understand of your growth at Eaton's, if your life were presented to you as an overwhelming Eaton's problem that needed to be solved, you would already have a one-hundred-page brief on how to resolve the issue, yes?"

"When you put it that way, I guess."

EATON'S – During the Second French Revolution

"There is no guesswork here, young man, there's only action and results," he lectured. "And I knew that you were much too smart to allow your marital problems to defeat you."

Doctor Markovitz checked his notes before making his next statement. "I also sense that there is some other revelation that you have on your mind."

"You could say that," Ricky hesitated.

"Ah, a secret love, my boy?" the doctor's eyes questioned. "Well, let's hear it. I'm not going to leak your secret to the *Montreal Star*, yes?"

"It's kinda' complicated, Doc," Ricky offered.

"As they say, Richard, 'life's complicated, what else is new?' so let's have it!"

"That's not quite as the saying goes, but yeah, it's something beautiful, but confusing at the same time."

"Something that is creating more pressure for you?"

"No, actually someone that has been the answer to my prayers."

"Now, I am fascinated," he leaned forward, "give me the whole story."

"Well, I met this girl. Actually, I didn't just meet her, she's worked for me for some time, and ..."

"So, a workplace romance?"

"I guess." Ricky hesitated, gathering his thoughts. "We went out several times, first just to discuss business matters, then our meetings progressed into personal matters, and finally we developed a relationship." Ricky sighed. "Now, it consumes my every thought and fills my brain with trepidation."

"So, *trepidation*. Now that's a big word. Richard, you sound like you are giving a medical thesis. Be yourself. Express your emotions clearly and honestly. This is not a third-party presentation, this is Richard Dean, live, in person, this is you, yes?"

"Sorry Doc, old habits die hard. Anyway, this girl's name is Christine. She's beautiful, compassionate, sexy, and most important, she seems to want me in her life."

Ricky relayed the details of his relationship with Christine from their very first business meeting at the Place Ville Marie, offering only the PG version of their interlude on January 3rd. He included the full story of her marriage, annulment, and her move in with her friend, Charlotte. And how their closeness developed with each contact.

"I see. Very interesting," Doc jotted down notes. "Earlier, you stammered and stuttered when you were describing the things that you love about your life, and I think you left out one very important part which is actual love, yes?"

"It's because I can't use the word *love* concerning Christine, Doc, it just wouldn't be fair. First, I don't know a damn thing about love. What's it supposed to feel like? How it's supposed to be shown, and what would be the effect of using the word *love*, on the other party. I desperately need help here, Doc."

Doctor Markovitz thought in silence for a moment, before responding. "First, I believe you are kidding yourself because you do know what it feels like to be in love, because you are in love. I can see it on your face, yes?"

"Aside from my daughter, it's a feeling I've never encountered before."

The doctor nodded his understanding. "When you are with this Christine, does her actions show you love?"

"Yes, but that may be part of the problem."

"How can someone loving you be a problem? It is a gift, yes?"

"Of course, I realize the importance of her showing love towards me, the problem is that I'm not sure that I can honestly reciprocate."

"You're using the *big words* again, Richard," he admonished. "I think that in order to separate yourself from a difficult topic you slip into your business mode with big words, and emotionless comments, yes?"

Ricky laughed, "You're not the first person to tell me that."

"Let me be perfectly blunt, Richard, my boy! Your relationship with Miss Christine, has it progressed to a point of a pending sexual relationship, or has it already happened?"

"It happened on January third," Ricky blushed.

"Good, good! And does this fact embarrass you? Why? Do you regret what happened?"

"No! no Doc, not at all. It's just that I'm not used to talking about my intimacy, because I've never had any real intimacy."

"Well, it's about time my boy, about time." Again, Doctor Markovitz collected his thoughts before continuing. "But why do you say that you can't express your love to this young lady?"

"If I express what I'm truly feeling for her, it will give her false hope that there is actually a lasting future for us."

"So, this relationship with Miss Christine is meaningless. As they say just a 'one-night stand', yes?"

"No, no Doc! Not at all. She is the most important thing to come into my life since the birth of my daughter. I care too much for Christine to ever hurt her."

"And you think because you never speak the actual word, she won't realize that you do love her."

"If I never speak the actual word, I can never be accused of leading her on."

"How noble of you! You'll show her love, but if you never use the word you'll be exonerated from any future blame. There's a psychological term for that called C.Y.A.," he laughed, sarcastically.

"C.Y.A.?"

"Yes, my boy, C.Y.A., 'cover your ass'. It means if everything hits the fan, down the road, perfect Mister Dean, will not be held to blame."

Doctor Markovitz got out of his chair and for the first time since Ricky knew him, he came to stand at Ricky's side. "Richard, listen to me. You need to break out, you need to be adventurous, to live life to the fullest by expressing what is really in your heart. Do you think the deception doesn't exist just because you show her love, but don't express your love in words? Do you think if, God forbid, this relationship ends she won't be just as hurt because you didn't use the word? Give the girl the pleasure of knowing what is truly in your heart today, and stop worrying about what may, or may not, happen in the future. You don't just owe it to her, but you also owe it to yourself. Can you just imagine how beautiful a relationship with Miss Christine can be, if there is nothing taboo between the two of you? You have utopia in your grasp, Richard, don't be so arrogant that you let it slip through your fingers, because I can guarantee that *that* is something that *will* take you ages to get over, yes."

"When you put it that way, Doc, it seems so simple!"

"Okay, then," the doctor looked down again and checked his notes, "we've addressed, and hopefully solved, what love feels like, how to show it, and using the love word. This is great progress Richard, my boy. Great progress indeed, yes?"

"Yeah, I feel like a load has been lifted from my shoulders."

"In our first session we talked a little about your feeling of sexual inadequacy, do you remember?"

"Yes, it was a very short discussion," he joked.

"But very important, yes?" Doc added. "Perhaps we could discuss that issue today, since that seems to be your final unresolved problem," Doc smiled.

"Sure, I, uh, I guess," Ricky hesitated, not sure if he was ready to explore that area.

"Okay, then let me recap what we already know about your feelings of sexual inadequacy," Doc started checking off a list on his fingers. "Your high school sexual dating relationships were non-existent, your first sexual encounter with your wife-to-be was a disaster. Then your honeymoon sexual activity never happened, and your marital sexual actions have been minimal and unrewarding. The best part was the sex that produced your daughter, and that was the only bright light that you can perceive concerning sex with your wife. More recently, your sexual activity with Miss Christine, was great. Does that about cover it all?"

"Sadly, Yes, except for Christine. That has been fan-friggin-tastic!" Ricky glowed.

"I'm not sure that is the proper physiological term, but I bow to your enthusiasm, Richard. So, where do you see yourself now, with this new Miss Christine addition to your life?"

"Our January third rendez-vous eliminated any concerns about my sexual inadequacy. Although I was initially worried about premature ejaculation, and my sexual inexperience, everything came off great. No, let me correct that." Thinking how to rephrase, he added, "Everything was beyond my wildest dreams. She put me so at ease, and our lovemaking coupled with the emotional feelings of love were absolutely overwhelming," he gushed. "I no longer question my sexual abilities, nor the fears of non-performance."

"That is outstanding, my boy! You are ninety-nine percent better than when you first arrived on my doorstep. And you even used the term, 'lovemaking' instead of sex."

"So, I'm cured, Doc?" he questioned.

"You know quite well, Richard, that nobody is ever one hundred percent cured. If we admitted that to our patients, we would be putting ourselves out of business," he laughed.

"So, I don't need any more sessions?" he looked hopefully at Doctor Markowitz.

"Not in the immediate future, but if you reach a trauma stage of not being able to choose between salted and unsalted cereal in the supermarket, we can schedule an emergency consultation," he smiled.

Then, Doctor Markowitz stopped and turned serious, "I'm proud of you, Richard. You've made great strides in a truly short period of time, and as they say, 'you took the bull by the horns. Although we are never completely cured, I'm assured that you now have the knowledge and commitment to bring yourself to the level of understanding that will benefit your mental health. And, if you are feeling regression at any point, you can still call me any time to talk."

"Thanks for everything, Doc," Ricky extended his hand.

To Ricky's surprise, Doctor Markowitz flung his arms around him. "You should know, my boy, that you were my very last patient in a career of thousands of patients, and I'm grateful to you that I'll be retiring on an incredibly positive note. My son will be taking over my whole practice, next week, but you will be among the very few patients that I'll retain for future consultations. So, if you feel you ever need me, I will be available to you. You know, you can also just give me a call periodically to let me know how you are progressing."

"Thank you again, Doc. I'm honored that you chose to include me as a patient during your retirement. I wish you nothing but happiness and long life."

"And thank you, uh, Ricky. It has been my pleasure to try and help you. And remember, from this old doctor, if you don't take anything else away from our sessions, live every day to the fullest, and find happiness instead of defeat, because every day is precious, yes?"

"I will, Doc, and you do the same."

Ricky exited his office, a renewed skip in his step.

That is the first time Doc has called me Ricky instead of the usual my boy, son, or Richard, yes?

EATON'S – During the Second French Revolution

⚜ Seventy-Six ⚜

Louis stopped at the reception desk of McFadden & Holmes Consulting on his way to his meeting with Mr. Smith.

"I'm Louis Jones and I have a meeting with Mister Smith," he addressed the pretty receptionist, bearing the nametag, Samantha.

"Why yes, Mister Jones, Mister Smith is expecting you. Go right in," she pointed to a door marked Chief Engineer.

"Before I see Mister Smith could I trouble you to use a telephone?"

"Sure. You can use the one over on that vacant desk," she indicated an empty desk piled high with telephone books.

He dialed a number for Eaton's department Store. "Mister Dean, please. He's a basement manager."

"Yes Sir. His extension is 1818 for future reference.

He waited while he was being connected.

"Basement manager's offices."

"Mister Dean, please," he repeated.

"I'm sorry, Mister Dean is in a meeting right now. Can I take a message, sir?"

"Yes, could you have Mister Dean call his brother at this number," he gave her the number he dialed so often.

"Certainly, Sir. I'll put the message on his desk immediately!"

Louis returned the telephone to the cradle and walked back to the cute receptionist. "There will be a telephone call coming in for a Norman Dean, could you transfer that call to Mister Smith's office, please."

"Of course, Mister Jones," she replied, with a smile.

No questions? I believe that this girl is certainly used to handling clandestine operations.

Louis had spent the last two days in the second and last Montreal Stock Exchange most-mortem debriefing, with his handler, Adjutant General Magnus Ferguson, better known to Louis as Mister Smith. Louis was awfully familiar, through his training, of the need for multiple debriefings and numerous witness follow-up statements that many times bring forth additional information.

And, since the Laporte and Cross kidnappings had been taken over by the R.C.M.P. Terrorist Crimes Unit in Ottawa, Louis was free to end his Quebec F.L.Q. undercover assignment.

Louis documented the last eight months of his undercover infiltration of the F.L.Q.; ending with his final assignment regarding the stock exchange bombing, his collection of onsite blast photographs, Laporte and Cross kidnappings, and his extraction from his false life as an undercover F.L.Q. operative. Ferguson assured him that his supported documentation would, no doubt, result in the arrest and conviction of several prominent cell members.

"You did an outstanding job, Agent Dean. "As this was only your second undercover assignment, you surpassed all my expectations."

What? Suddenly this guy develops a personality.

"Thank you, Sir. It wasn't easy."

"I know, my boy, I know. I spent four years in my early career undercover, and it cost me both my marriage and my health. It's the price we pay for the vocation we have chosen. Pursuing justice is never easy, but results like you achieved are reward enough, right?"

"Yes, Sir, but I can't help but wonder if I should have remained in *Dieppe Cell* a little while longer. I could have found out so much more. And we could have put away more!" Norman reflected.

"And you could have ended up floating in the Saint Lawrence River. No son, you got out at exactly the right time."

"Yes Sir. May I ask, if I am still slated for Vancouver, as my next assignment, as you mentioned earlier?"

"Yes, that's still the plan. I wish I could give you some well-deserved time off to regroup, but we have a dire situation in Vancouver that requires your immediate attention."

"Vancouver sounds great, and the weather is terrific out there."

"Do you remember Inspector Lee Yung?"

"Yes, he was my training instructor at the R.C.M.P. *Depot*. Why do you ask?"

"Well apparently, he has kept up on your undercover work here and in Hamilton, Ontario, and is extremely impressed. When I told him that your assignment was over, he immediately requested that you be assigned to his narcotics squad. It seems he has an Agent Zhāng that is also a close friend of yours?"

"Yes, Paul and I survived *The Depot* training together," Norman laughed, "and, remained in contact thereafter."

"Inspector Lee Yung advised me that he has Agent Zhāng under deep cover within the Triade Chinese mafia in Vancouver's Chinatown. He is in desperate need of a partner to pose as a major American drug dealer. If this can be accomplished, we can destroy the largest organized crime operation in all of Canada and ultimately fracture their organization back in China."

"I'm ready, Sir. The only obligation I have left in Montreal will be a brief meeting with my brother, then I'll be ready to go to Vancouver."

"Wonderful! Then, my boy, it will take you about six or seven hours to get out west, so here's the file on the China operation to bring you up to speed."

Ferguson handed Norman a thick accordion file. "Since the drug sting is already in play you'll be at a disadvantage, so I suggest you memorize every detail, so you can hit the ground running when you arrive."

"I have a photographic memory, Sir." Norman scanned the file. "When do I leave?"

EATON'S – During the Second French Revolution

"You have a place aboard our R.C.M.P. Canuck One, leaving for Toronto at four tomorrow afternoon. From there, you'll be ticketed on a direct commercial flight to Vancouver."

When Norman was leaving McFadden & Holmes, he noticed that a different receptionist was occupying the front desk.

"Did a call come in for a Norman Dean?"

"Well, yes Sir, just a few moments ago," she hesitated, obviously flustered. "I checked the employee roster, and found no one by that name, and, well, Samantha is out to lunch and ..."

"Didn't she leave a message on her desk?" Louis questioned, pointing to a pink telephone message lying on top of the I.B.M. Selectric typewriter.

"Oh, I'm so sorry, Sir," she flushed. "I just got here to relieve Samantha, and I didn't see the note."

"No problem! I know who called, so I'll just use that telephone to call him back." *I'm not going to let anything screw up my good mood!*

⚜ Seventy-Seven ⚜

Advance preparation and instrumenting the Trans-Canada sale throughout his departments had been a grueling task. But the rewards for Ricky's efforts had been satisfying. His group of departments had exceeded their budgetary goals by over 12%, within every department, including the troubled lingerie department, showing a substantial bottom line profit. Most important was the fact that during the three-day sale there hadn't been any major trauma or disturbances that he had to address. His staff's performance was exemplary.

Ricky sat with his feet propped up on his desk and smiled at his good fortune. His smile was more for his relationship with Christine. Where he had always believed that his Eaton career would always be the most important thing in his life, he now realized that Christine had taken over that important position. His dreams were no longer filled with trepidation of his sad life, but now with the treasured contact that he had daily with Christine. No longer the doom and gloom of being trapped in a life that saw no future, but a renewed breath of fresh air where he could control that future. A future that he could change from negative to positive. A future that could make Christine his, forever!

And much of this elation was thanks to the positive direction set by Dr. Markowitz. He hadn't felt the need to talk to the doctor since but admonished himself for not at least making telephone contact with him. He removed his feet from the desk, checked his Rolodex for the number, and dialed the number.

"Harold Markowitz and Associates," came the crisp answer.

"Yes, this is Richard Dean, I was a patient of Doctor Markowitz. Do you have a number where I can reach him, he asked me to stay in touch?"

The receptionist hesitated. "Could you stay on the line, Mister Dean?"

"Sure, no problem," he replied, presuming she was searching for Doc's contact number.

After a few moments, a man came on the line. "Mister Dean this is Harold Markowitz. I'm Doctor Markowitz's son."

"Yes, Doctor Markowitz. Your father mentioned that you would be taking over his practice. How is he enjoying retirement?"

Dr. Markowitz remained silent for several moments.

"Are you there, Doctor Markowitz?" he questioned, thinking that they'd been disconnected.

"Uh, yes, well, sorry," he stammered. "Yes, Mister Dean, I know who you are. Without discussing details of your sessions, Dad had mentioned you were a past patient of his."

"Yeah, I had my last session several months ago, but Doc asked me to stay in touch, is all," repeating what he had said earlier.

"Are you in need of further therapy, Mister Dean?" he asked cautiously.

What the hell! Is this guy writing a book?

"No, just a touch base conversation with your Dad." Ricky was losing his patience.

"I'm sorry to have to tell you, but uh, my dad passed away ten days ago," his voice quivered, the hurt no doubt fresh in his mind.

The telephone fell from his hand with a resounding crash on his desk, an anxious voice spilling from it, "Are you there, Mister Dean? Are you all right? Hello. Hello ...."

Ricky slowly brought the telephone back to his ear, "I'm so, so sorry for your loss."

"Thank you. He passed peacefully in his sleep." Dr. Markowitz regrouped into his therapist mode. "Because I took over the practice, Dad left his files with me, yours included, but only for me to reference if you ever needed further therapy, and of course, only with your permission. If I can ever be of assistance to you, you need only call."

"Thank you, but I don't think that will be necessary!"

"Mister Dean, one more thing. Dad spoke fondly of his relationship with you. He mentioned that you were his last patient and that because of your final session, he boasted that he left his practice on a positive note. And for that, I thank you!"

"Yeah! Uh, thanks! I'll call if I need any help," Ricky abruptly ended the conversation.

He sat at his desk, head in his hands, tears streaking down his cheeks, as he murmured to no one in particular. "Well Doc, you always wanted me to shed some tears! I guess in that, you were finally successful, yes?"

Ricky remembered back to his final conversation with Doc.

"And remember, from this old doctor, if you don't take anything else away from our sessions, live every day to the fullest, and find happiness instead of defeat, because every day is precious, yes?"

Yes Doc. And thank you because you most certainly saved my life!

⚜ Seventy-Eight ⚜

Ricky and Jerry Copeland stopped for lunch at the *Shamrock Pub* on their way to see Ultimate Sportswear about a closeout of sport jackets.

"I just love this place," Jerry hung his coat on the coat rack.

"The best Irish Pub in Canada," Ricky replied.

"Dere's me wee cousin," Paddy roared in his fake Irish brogue.

"Hi Paddy," Ricky acknowledged. "Where's Agnes today?"

"She's in the kitchen preparing her Irish stew for our dinner menu. She'll be out in a minute."

They settled into their usual booth by the dart boards.

"I was in an Irish pub just like this in Belfast, last year." Jerry told Ricky, as he offered him a cigarette.

"That's right, you went on that buying trip with your mother, right?" Ricky in turn offered Jerry a light.

"Yeah, she had been invited to tour the plant where she buys all her crystal home décor items. It was really great."

"Did you get to see much of Ireland?"

"No, we were only there for three days, so we mostly toured around Belfast. But I'll tell you, it felt just like home."

"Belfast felt like Montreal?"

"Yeah, they had soldiers in full combat gear roaming the streets, bombed out cars and buildings, and warnings from the locals to watch out that you didn't get murdered. Ain't that just like *our* Montreal?"

Ricky laughed. "You got that right. I don't know how, or when all this F.L.Q. shit is ever going to end."

"I'm not sure who is worse their I.R.A., or our F.L.Q. They're all a bunch of sick bastards killing innocents, as far as I'm concerned."

"Shh! Jerry, someone will hear you, for Christ's sake."

"So?" Jerry asked, looking around the bar. "I've never met a Frenchman yet that I can't beat the crap out of."

Ricky nodded toward the bar, where Paddy was busy washing some beer glasses. "'Ya' think you can take out that big guy behind the bar?"

"You mean Paddy? Why the hell should I worry about him?"

Ricky motioned Jerry closer. "Keep your voice down. The rumor around here is that Paddy was a former member of the I.R.A. before he immigrated to

Canada. And the fact that he is from a prominent family, with a large lumber business, makes you wonder why he would leave all that to come here. Don't 'ya think?"

"Wow, I didn't know any of that, Paddy, really?"

Ricky nodded.

"What'll ye lads be drinkin'," Agnes asked, placing two shamrock coasters on the table.

"Oh, hi Agnes. I'll have a Guinness Draught, and Jerry will have his usual O'Hara's Celtic Stout, right?"

Jerry nodded.

"So, what's the story? You guys are never gunna try something different? Back in two shakes," Agnes laughed, as she walked to the bar.

"Talking about the F.L.Q., what do you think about this Laporte and Cross kidnapping crap?" Jerry asked.

"I think the stupid F.L.Q. shot themselves in the foot this time, by pulling this stunt. Both Canada and the international community are not going to look favorably on the kidnapping of government dignitaries. They may have thought that they could garner support for their cause with their rallies, or even their idiotic bombings, but when they purposely murder some innocent person, they are totally screwed."

Agnes returned with the two beers. "Enjoy."

"Yeah, Jer, I heard that the *Chenier* cell killed Laporte and stuck him in the trunk of a car which they abandoned near the Saint-Hubert Airport. And James Cross was finally freed unharmed after sixty days in captivity."

"That's right, but the F.L.Q. is claiming that the strangling of Laporte was accidental due to him struggling to escape. Can you believe that shit?"

"How the hell do you accidentally strangle someone?"

"That excuse is what is making the F.L.Q. look like assholes. Mark my words, they're never going to survive this."

"But we'll still have the politicians in the Quebec government making anti-English policy, right?"

"The problem is never going to completely disappear," Ricky sighed, "And, the old Quebec that we grew up in, is never going to return to what it was.

"I guess," Jerry relented. "I also heard that this '*Shadow*' character was instrumental in passing along information to the R.C.M.P. Terrorist Unit that resulted in the arrests of the Rose brothers, for killing of Laporte.

"Yeah. The R.C.M.P. should find out who he, or she, is and hire him, or her, as their chief investigator," Ricky laughed.

Agnes returned with two menus. "So, what are we eating today boys?"

"I'll have the bangers and mash and a piece of your fantastic Irish cream Bundt cake for dessert. How 'bout you, Jerry?"

"I'll have the Irish shepherd's pie and the Bundt cake, also."

EATON'S – During the Second French Revolution

"Oh, and can you bring us a couple of regular coffees, with lots of cream, please?"

"You got it Ricky."

"So, what's going on in your life?" Ricky changed subject."

"Home life is the same except Denise and I are moving into a larger apartment in Verdun. My mother is pressuring me to quit Eaton's and come work for her in the furniture store, and I'm still as poor as ever!"

"So poor that you're driving a brand new Trans-Am?"

"We boys must have our toys," Jerry laughed.

"What's the rumor saying these days about our basement floor?"

"For me, I love working for Amed, he's great guy, but I think I'm ready to handle my own department."

"More than ready, and plans are in the works," Ricky stated, bringing a wide smile to Randy's face.

"Let's hope. Anyway, as far as the floor personnel, Serge is still mooning over Susan in Millinery. I don't think that boy will ever get the nerve to make his move. John Baker, in upstairs appliances, got nailed by his wife for having an affair with our very own, Rebecca Snyder, and Steve Fortuna's wife packed up the kids and moved back to Naples, Italy."

"Thanks Agnes," Ricky said, as she placed their entrees, desserts, and coffees on the table.

Ricky added cream and sugar to his coffee. "I've got to pay closer attention to what's going on. I was aware of Serge and Susan, but Baker and Becky, that is a total shock. How long has the affair been going on?"

"About sixteen or eighteen months."

"That long, and no one clued me in?"

"Maybe your interest was directed elsewhere," Jerry winked, digging into his shepherd's pie. "I've noticed that you've been walking with a little bit of bounce in your steps these past few months my friend."

"Meaning?" Ricky cut into his bangers.

"Meaning my best friend has turned in his scowl look, for a happy face. That can only mean that there is love in the air."

"Screw you," Ricky shot back, changing the subject. "I thought Becky was happily married to that military guy?"

"They are both married, but apparently not happily, or they wouldn't be jumping in the sack. Do you know Baker well?"

"You could say that," Ricky started to say.

"Spit it out, Buddy."

"Well, do you remember Johnnie Baker from high school? Well, our John Baker, Senior is Johnnie's father, and you could say my surrogate father. I just about lived at their house during my senior years."

"Right. Denise and I went to a party at Johnnie's house, in Montreal East. Boy, this thing must bring everything close to home for you."

"'Ya think? Mrs. Baker is a nice lady and was always like a mother to me. She has got to be devastated."

"Sorry." Jerry dug into his Bundt cake.

"And Steve lost his wife and kids? Wow, his life revolved around them. He never even seems like he has any problems."

"I guess you never know what's really going on in someone's life, eh? So, do you want to go back to the conversation about your happy face, and tell your best buddy all about it?"

"I guess you missed the part where I told my best buddy to screw off."

"Does that mean that it is really serious?" Jerry prodded.

Ricky didn't answer.

Why the hell am I keeping the most important part of my life from my best friend? Ricky thought.

⚜ Seventy-Nine ⚜

The following day Ricky spotted Jerry Copeland idly hanging a selection of the newly arrived Nero sport jackets. As he tapped him on the shoulder Jerry looked up startled. "Oh hi, Rick. I guess I was off daydreaming someplace."

"And here, I thought you were dreaming about naked men," he kidded, "are you ready for lunch?"

"Are you kiddin'? With my boss ready to dig into his pockets to spring for lunch in the fancy-dancy ninth floor restaurant, who wouldn't be ready?"

"Well, for sure I wouldn't, if I hadn't lost the bet to you on that bloody hockey game. And, if Henri, *the pocket*, Richard hadn't gotten that high sticking penalty in the final minutes of the last period, you'd be the one springing for lunch."

"Excuses, excuses!" Jerry looked over his shoulder at his manager. "Amed, I'm going to lunch."

"Enjoy. I'll be leaving for Consolidated Sweaters when you get back."

"Okay. Local or express Rick?" Jerry asked about the elevator.

"Let's get the express, since I see you chomping-at-the-bit to stick me with a massive restaurant bill."

They headed up the escalator, and across the main floor, to the express elevator to the 9th floor dining room.

"You realize that I haven't eaten anything since the Saturday night hockey game in anticipation of this gourmet meal, don't you?" Jerry offered, as they arrived at the elevator.

"Don't feed me that crap. Gourmet to you means a double burger with

EATON'S – During the Second French Revolution

peppers at Dilallo Hamburgers, in Verdun, at three A.M."

"Yeah, well" Jerry started to respond when the elevator door opened.

"Hey Sharron," Ricky addressed the operator. "Ninth Floor, please."

"Oh hi, Mister Dean, Mister Copeland. You're in luck, the restaurant isn't swamped today."

Ricky marveled at how Sharron's burgundy dress uniform, pillbox hat and crisp white gloves complimented the dining experience for Eaton's shoppers, employees, and downtown businesspeople. For these diners, the experience began immediately as they stepped off the elevator into the restaurant's elegant foyer.

Exiting the elevator was like stepping out of a time machine. The stark transformation from the dimly lit antique elevator, with its stylish chrome doors, into the brightly lit restaurant foyer was truly breathtaking. The main focal point was the huge circular skylight perched high above a large round Persian rug covering a dark brown parquet floor. The fine art deco atmosphere was accented with a multitude of matching dark brown heavily stuffed living room chairs and loveseats, wall and art décor hangings, mirrors and a center glass table bearing fine crystal vases and floral arrangements. The tall windows throughout the foyer area, accompanied by old Art Deco benches in front of the windows offered a panoramic view of downtown Montreal, and the adjacent hills of Mount Royal.

On the east side of the foyer were a series of circa 1920's-1930's style phone booths which were built into the wall with glass doors on them so you could sit down inside the booth in privacy. Although they had functioning telephones, the booths were more a source for regular local customer and tourist's photographs, and those who reveled in the pristine condition of these antiques.

If the foyer accoutrement image was not enough to tantalize the restaurant patrons, then stepping through the huge chrome doors and descending the half-dozen steps into the 650-seat dining room, with its 40-foot-tall ceiling and enormous center glass skylight, was truly overwhelming. The architecturally coved ceiling sported a full surround array of paned glass windows cascading natural light throughout the vast expanse. Everyone, no matter how rich or poor, could experience a world of luxury, ambiance, and grace, and although the room was large, the way that it was specifically divided in its original design did not make it feel in any fashion, impersonal.

The restaurant was first inspired by a 1920's ocean voyage taken by Eaton's company matriarch, Lady Eaton, aboard the transatlantic luxury liner *Île de France*. She had the luxury liner's elegant dining room and supporting facilities incorporated into the architectural plans when Eaton's decided to expand its Ste. Catherine Street store to nine floors from the original six in 1928, following the purchase of the Goodwin Department Store. This unique setting evoked simulated adventure and romance of true transatlantic travel.

Originally, the dining room opened on January 25, 1931, named as *Le François Premier*, but regular patrons who dined consistently referred to it as simply, "The Ninth Floor Lounge." That name caught on and the actual *Le François Premier* name was eventually abandoned.

The dining room was the work of interior designer, Jacques Carlu, the French-born professor of advanced design at the Massachusetts Institute of Technology. He was also responsible for the celebrated "Trocadéro," *in Paris*, and the famed "Rainbow Room" in New York's Rockefeller Plaza.

The restaurant was an elegantly proportioned space measuring, 130 feet long, and 175 feet wide, with two smaller dining rooms off to the side; the Gold Room and the Silver Room, generally used for private banquets, meetings, and affairs. Elegantly bracketing either end of the main room were two allegorical cubist floor-to-ceiling murals, "Pleasure of the Chase" and "Pleasures of Peace," painted by Carlu's wife, Natasha.

Most impressive were the collection of paintings and statutes set off by the marble columns, sheet marble wall panels, marble stairs and huge floral arrangements. Music played over the cascading sound of a small water fountain prominently positioned in the center of the room. This was truly an architectural jewel destined to create a striking legacy for the Eaton's empire, and the crown jewel of the downtown Montreal Eaton's Department Store.

Ricky and Jerry selected a secluded table in the corner of the dining room as Ricky acknowledged the approach of the waitress dressed in an old fashioned black and white staff uniform.

"Bon jour, Nicolette. Comment êtes-vous, aujourd'hui?" *Hello. How are you, today?*

Nicolette had worked in the ninth-floor dining room for what seemed like forever. She was in her fifties but carried her trim body as that of someone half her age.

"Très bien, merci, Monsieur Dean, et vous?" *Very good, Mister Dean, and you?*

"Very good, thank you," Ricky reverted to English. "Is Mister deGraff here today?

Ernest deGraff was the manager and chief chef of the 9th Floor dining room and graduate of the renowned Ferrandi French School of Culinary Arts, in Paris France.

"No, it is his day off," Nicolette, also reverted to English. "Can I get you some coffee to start?"

Ricky looked to Jerry who nodded. "Sure, that would be great."

Placing the menus on the table she said, "Today our Italian day specialties are a choice of our baked rigatoni with marinara sauce and garlic bread, chicken parmigiana with garlic bread sticks and lasagna with ricotta cheese and bruschetta. And, for dessert we have Tiramisu and an excellent Panna Cotta."

EATON'S – During the Second French Revolution

Jerry replied, "I'll have the baked rigatoni with marinara sauce and garlic bread, and a garden salad with ranch dressing.

Nicolette wrote his order on her service pad. "And you, Mister Dean?"

"I'll have the lasagna with ricotta cheese and bruschetta, and a garden salad with thousand island dressing. And bring a side order of bruschetta for my hungry friend, here."

Certainly. And, for dessert?"

"Tell me. What is this Tiramisu and Panna Cotta?" Jerry asked.

She began her spiel that she'd probably related thousands of times throughout the years. "Tiramisu is a layered cake, consisting of a flogged mixture of egg yolk and mascarpone cheese flavored with cocoa and liquor. It is dipped in coffee and garnished with bitter cocoa to balance the sugared cheese mixture. Panna Cotta is a rich Italian pudding made by simmering together cream, sugar, and milk, mixing this with gelatin, and letting it cool until set. You can choose special toppings such as caramel, chocolate sauce, fruit coulis or wild berries.

Jerry's eyes lit up. "I'm sold. I'll have the Panna Cotta with chocolate sauce, please."

"And, I'll have the Tiramisu, Nicolette."

"Very Good. I'll bring your coffees right up."

Lighting a cigarette, he whispered to Jerry. "So, back in your department, we were talking about the naked man, yes?"

"Shit, not you, too. I thought you forgot all about it." Jerry replied embarrassingly, as Nicolette arrived with the coffees.

Ricky put two sugars and lots of cream in his cup. "Not on your life, good buddy. Come on now, did you think that I was going to be the only one in all of downtown Montreal who hadn't heard of your quirky homosexual experience?"

"Rick, let me tell you, if I had it to do all over again, I'd say screw what's happening on the floor, and I'd have hightailed it for the safety of the stockroom. All I've done, all goddamn day today, is listened to jokes about the incident. You're lucky it was your day off, or the joke would have been on you, my friend" he sighed. "'Ya got an extra smoke?" he asked, drinking his coffee black.

"Sure," Ricky offered, throwing his cigarette pack across the table. "So, give me the whole story, from start to finish, and I'll see what I can do about glossing the incident report for you."

"Okay Rick, but some of the story is what I've been told second hand, and the rest, unfortunately, I was part of."

"Just the facts, Jerry boy, just the facts," Ricky imitated Sgt. Joe Friday, from the Dragnet T.V. show.

"Okay, okay, so this weirdo starts to completely undress on the main floor of Simpson's Department Store until one of the managers there tries unsuccessfully to catch him. The guy runs out of their store onto Saint Catherine Street heading east towards Eaton's, wearing just a pair of white underwear, one sock and a half torn white shirt. He knocks over several people as he plows along while removing the rest of his clothes. Oh, yeah, I forgot, all along he's laughing uncontrollably and making sexual remarks at every female he passes."

"That paints one hellava picture," Ricky interrupted.

"Oh, it gets better," he nervously took a deep draw on his cigarette. "That new blonde-haired security kid that Tony just hired told me later, 'that the guy came careening,' his words, 'through the Metcalfe, Saint Catherine Street revolving door, flinging bodies everywhere.' By this time, he's completely naked, and this security kid is all alone trying to corral him, but the guy is a maniac. So, when the kid tries to grab him, the crazy bastard jumps up on one of the glass showcases in the cosmetic's department, and of course, he goes through the glass tipping the showcase and him onto the floor. The kid dives for the guy now sprawled on the floor, screaming in a pool of blood and glass shards, but the guy must have seen the kid coming, and kicks him straight in the balls," Jerry stopped. "Please stop laughing, Rick. It's *not* funny!"

"Sorry," Ricky tried to control his laughter, as Nicolette arrived with their entrees.

"Enjoy, Gentlemen."

Taking a bite of his baked rigatoni, Jerry continued, "Anyway a male customer tries to jump in to help the security kid, but the guy sidesteps him and heads down the escalator. Before this, I hear all the racket and screams coming from the main floor, and the security chime rings, so I know something bad is happening. I see Rene Beaudreaux, in his boy's wear department, and he's looking around, all confused about where the yelling is coming from. So, I yell at him to get his ass over with me by the escalator, just as I see, out of the corner of my eye, this bloody red streak plummeting down the escalator, toppling everyone in his way," Jerry takes a deep breath.

"Don't stop now, dude." With a mouthful of lasagna, Ricky placed a hand over his mouth trying to suppress his laughter.

Jerry ignored Ricky. "Just as Rene gets to me, I grab this guy's arm and pull him away from the escalator, so more people won't fall over him, and he's fighting me like a bitch. Rene immediately punches the guy, and it doesn't even faze the guy. Because he's got blood all over his arm it's slippery and I lose my grip, and the guy goes running nude down the main aisle towards lingerie. With a combination of shrieking female customers and screaming female staff, Rene and I go tearing after the bastard and corner him in the lingerie department. The stupid idiot starts playing with us hiding behind columns, behind mannequins until he finally decides to jump up on one of the wooden sale tables, dancing and singing for everyone to witness. His thing swinging wildly in the breeze. The guy is totally bonkers, but I'll tell you one thing, he was having one happy time."

Holding back a snicker, Ricky asked, "Why didn't one of you grab a clothes rack and knock his legs out from under him?"

"Not so fast, it's my story, Rick."

"So, I've got one of the guy's bloody legs in my grasp, but I can't keep a good hold on it. Finally, Rene decks the guy on the head with a heavy wooden girdle display and the guy topples off the table into my arms, so I'm able to get an arm around his neck. I yell at Rene to get one of the dressing gowns to throw over the guy before he comes around and I tighten my grip around his neck. Rene threw the dressing gown over the guy and gets ready to pop him again if he tries anything. He was watching the guy's face, as I choke him, and didn't notice the guy's hands raising the front of the dressing gown, grabbing his dick, and pissing all over the front of Rene's suit and shoes. Rene punches him in the face, and I drop him."

Ricky could not hold it anymore and burst out in uncontrollable laughter. "Stop, Stop, please," he begged, "I've got to catch my breath."

Jerry's face remained totally serious, as he stopped eating and reached for another of Ricky's cigarettes.

"Sure, go ahead and laugh. Here Rene and I have blood all over our clothes, Rene has piss running off the front of his suit, and an unconscious nutcase in a pink dressing gown, lying on the floor. And, about fifty or more customers applauding our take-down. No big deal, right?"

"The guy was unconscious?"

"Well yeah. You didn't think Rene was going to let someone piss on him, and not take him out, did you?"

Nicolette removed the salad and dinner plates and replaced them with their desserts.

"So, how did it end?" Ricky dug into his Tiramisu.

"Finally, the new security kid shows up, limping badly, by the way, with a bunch of MPD and they haul the guy away. Apparently, the guy escaped from some funny farm and the cops had been looking all over for him, for days. Lucky me!" Jerry finished off his Panna Cotta.

Regaining control Ricky offered, "If you and Rene need any reimbursement for cleaning bills or replacement of clothing, fill out a six-thirteen and submit it to me."

Picking up the check Ricky patted Jerry's shoulder, "Oh, and just because we've been friends for so long, I'll sanitize the incident report, so your folly won't be sent all across Canada as employee entertainment," he joked. "Can I laugh now?"

Ricky returned to his office and finalized the previous day's incident report, chuckling as each word of Jerry's naked man incident was typed.

⚜ Eighty ⚜

Ricky had just returned to his office following his weekly *Bound for Success* meeting where he found a telephone message from his brother, Norman, on his desk. He filed his meeting notes in the file cabinet, grabbed a cup of coffee and dialed '9' for an outside line, then the number on the message.

"McFadden and Holmes Consulting," a pleasant female voice answered.

That seems like an unlikely place for my brother to be.

"I'm returning a call from Norman Dean."

"One moment, please." Ricky heard the shuffling of papers. "I'm sorry, sir. We have no one here by that name!"

"Are you sure?"

"Yes sir, I just checked the employee roster and there is no one by that name with McFadden and Holmes."

"Okay, thank you," Ricky hung up the telephone. He sat for several moments studying the message, then placed it in the corner of his blotter.

I guess if it is important, he'll call back again.

He had just begun to review the millinery ad scheduled to appear in the Montreal Star on Thursday when his intercom buzzed.

"Dean."

"Mister Dean, you have a call on line two."

"Thank you," he pressed line 2.

"Good afternoon, Richard Dean, here."

"Hey, bro. How are they hanging?"

"For Christ's sake! Where the hell have you been? I've been trying to find you for the last six weeks. Mom and Dad are worried, 'cause they can't find you either."

"Calm down, big bro! I just talked with them and explained that I was on assignment and couldn't be reached."

"Assignment! Shit, you make it sound like you're working for the goddamn C.I.A."

"Nothing so adventurous. I'll tell you all about it when I see you."

"By the way, I just returned your call to some friggin' consulting firm and they said they didn't know who the hell you were?"

"Yeah, I'm sorry about that. I had a meeting here with one of the staff and told the receptionist that I was expecting your call, but she went to lunch and didn't tell the other receptionist."

"No problem. It's great to finally hear from you."

"I'm heading out to Vancouver and wanted to meet with you before I go. Are you free tonight?"

"Uh, no, sorry, I've got a security meeting scheduled for tonight?" Ricky lied, to cover his late-night date with Christine.

"Bullshit! I can always tell when you're lying cause your voice cracks. So, what's up."

Ricky remained quiet for a minute.

"Come on. Spill! What's going on?"

"Just an engagement with a friend," Ricky stammered.

"Male engagement, or female engagement?"

"Female, but she's just one of my employees. Totally innocent!"

"Sure, it is! You can fill me in on all that when we meet. How about lunch tomorrow?"

"That I can do. Where?"

"Your choice, but somewhere in the north end. I'm flying out of Cartierville Airport at four tomorrow afternoon."

"Cartierville? Why aren't you flying out of Dorval? Cartierville is only for private charter and small local aircraft."

"I'm flying on a company plane to Toronto, then commercial into Vancouver."

"A company plane? You mean an R.C.M.P. plane?"

"Yeah. I can't explain details over the phone. Anyway, is there a decent restaurant up here where we can get a brewski, and fantastic food, my treat?"

"Yeah, Spiros Italian Bistro, eighty-six seventy-five Decarie Boulevard, in Notre Dame De Graf. It's in a strip mall, but you can't miss it. How about one o'clock? Does that work for you?"

"Lookin' forward, big bro! One tomorrow, it is. See 'ya," Norman hung up.

Something fishy is going on with him.

⚜ Eighty-One ⚜

Ricky cleared his desk of all pending chores and prepared for his lunch meeting with his brother. He'd arranged for John LeClerke to take over his floor duty responsibilities, so he wouldn't have to rush back and could spend some quality time catching up. Putting on his overcoat, he bounded up the stairs to the University Street exit.

Typical of every winter season in Montreal, the whole city was bracing for the annual major ice storm that was destined to plunge the major metropolis into mayhem, for days to come. The temperature was already well below freezing, with the wind plummeting the cold chill well into the single digits. Welcome to Montreal!

Already the sand and salt plow trucks were positioned on the major arteries ready to facilitate traction on the coming slippery road surfaces. In readiness, fleets of Hydro-Quebec utility trucks were strategically stationed throughout the city to address downed power lines, and the multitude of expected exploding transformers.

As taxi after taxi passed him on University St. all filled with passengers, Ricky became concerned about making his meeting with his brother on time. Finally, an older taxi, displaying no affiliation with any of the major cab companies, slid to a stop, acknowledging his waving hand.

"Eight six-seven five Decarie Boulevard, in Notre Dame De Graf," he commanded, hopping into the back seat. "Take Guy Street over Mount Royal to Decarie."

"Yes Sir," the driver replied in a heavy Pakistani accent, while spinning his wheels to gain traction. The colorful turban on his head was a dead giveaway.

"This must be a harsh transition from the weather in your home country?" Ricky stated.

"Yes, veather very, very bad, kind Sir. I only see snow and ice on mountains far, far away, no like dis," he replied.

Watching the cab slide uncontrollably as the driver rounded the turn onto Sherbrooke Blvd., he asked, "Have you been driving taxi for a long time?"

"Oh, yes Sir. Very, very long." He regained control from the slide.

"So, this is not your first winter?"

"Yes, I drive one month and one-half month. I very good driver. Snow, ice, water, no problem. I good driver, only two accidents."

Christ on a rubber crutch! Two accidents in a month and a half.

"Okay, don't rush. Let's just get there safely," he cautioned.

"No rush. Get fast. Yes, kind Sir," he countered, avoiding another spinout rounding on Cote Des Neiges Blvd.

Finally, arriving at Spiros on Decarie Blvd., Ricky quickly thrusts ten dollars into the driver's hand and exited the cab, braving the howling wind. Thrilled to have made it there in one piece, he quickly raced across the street to the sanctuary of the warm restaurant.

The owner, Spiro Terrazopoullos, was waiting to welcome him at the register stand by the front door.

Spiro's eyes lit up and a broad smile flashed across his face, "Ricky, my boy. So good see you," he said in his broken English.

"Yes Pappa, you, too. Did you have a good visit to your family home in Greece?" Ricky put his arm around Spiro's broad shoulders.

After numerous laments by Spiro, in conversations with Ricky in his original downtown restaurant, he realized that although he loved his daughter, Angelina immensely, deep down he pined for a son to share his thoughts and dreams. He also told Ricky that he was the exact type of person he would want as his son. After that Ricky began calling Spiro, *Pappa*, a name that was always accepted with pride.

EATON'S – During the Second French Revolution

"Yes, good. But not so good with no Magdelaine, or Angelina. Next time I go, they go too." Spiro looked him in the eye and asked, "I hear you take my Angelina to work your store, so it good between you too?"

Ricky tried to respond in the kindest way. "Pappa, you know I love Angelina like a sister and while you were away I kept an eye on her at work." Ricky motioned towards the back of the restaurant, "Oh, sorry Pappa, I just spotted my brother, Norman, sitting at the bar. We'll talk more later!"

Following Ricky's gaze, Spiro asked, "you meet bruddah, here?"

"Yes, Pappa, he's sitting at the bar," he pointed to Norman.

"Your bruddah? No, he no look like you," he exclaimed.

"Yes, that's my brother, Norman," he replied, threading his way through the maze of tables, to reach the bar.

Spiro followed Ricky, "Is Mamma Magdelaine, in the kitchen?"

"No, she go market.

Arriving at the bar Ricky embraced Norman. "Pappa Spiro, this is my brother, Norman. Norman, this is Spiro, the owner, and my Pappa!"

"Hello. You have good bruddah," Spiro responded, wrapping his both hands warmly around Norman's hand. "You want table?"

"Sure Pappa. The booth in the corner will be great," Ricky replied, guiding Norman across the room. "Two Molson, tall bottles, please."

"Okay, you have good food, yes? Angelina brings you, today."

When Spiro returned to the bar, Norman offered Ricky a cigarette and settled into the bright red leather booth. "Been a long time, big bro, how have you been?"

"Well, I've been busy, life's been exciting, the F.L.Q. are trying to blow me up with bombs in the store, I'm divorcing Kathy, I'm getting custody of Darlene and I have a new young lady in my life. So, nothing much is new with me, how about you?" Ricky lit a cigarette and took a long drag, sending smoke rings into the air.

"Whoa! Slow down. Too much information at one time. I'm really surprised that you finally had the balls to get rid of that bitch and, get custody of Darlene. That is a great bonus, and also finally getting laid. Wow!"

"I didn't say that. You are always such a crude prick," he joked. "Christine is a very special girl who is managing my teen department and we've been on a few dates," he lied.

"Ah, come on now, big bro, ya gotta fill me in with more details."

Ricky spent the next 20 minutes recounting everything about his personal life, his financial life and his Eaton's life in war torn Montreal. He even disclosed the story of the new love of his life.

Norman slapped his hand and clinked beer bottles. "I'm so happy for you, man! If anyone deserves happiness, after all the shit you've been through, it certainly is you. Who knows, I may finally get a sister-in-law that I like," he laughed?

"Let's not rush stuff, Norm."

"Okay. Just know that I'm happy for you and I'm always there for you, no matter what! But seriously, bro, did you get laid, yet?" he roared.

Ricky was saved from responding by a presence he felt towering over him and when he looked over his shoulder, he saw Angelina's piercing eyes and long dark hair holding two bottles of Molson's.

"Hi Angie," he acknowledged her presence, "you snuck up on me."

"Sorry Mister Dean," she smiled, "I have the two extra beers compliments of Pappa."

"Thank him for me, and remember Angie we're not in the store now, so you can drop the Mister Dean, okay?" Ricky passed one of the Molson's to Norman.

"By the way, Angie, this is my brother, Norman. Norman, Angie."

"A pleasure, Angie," Norman responded, grasping her hand. "And where do we know this beautiful creature from?"

"Hi Norman," she blushed. "I work for Ricky part time in his teens fashion department."

"Well, he's a very lucky man."

"Can I take your order, or do you want to wait?" she ignored Norman's forwardness.

"We'll just wait a bit. Thanks Angie."

Angie went to serve another table and Norman's eyes hungrily followed her every step. "That, my friend is what I genuinely want for Christmas. She is an absolute beauty!"

"Knock it off!" Ricky barked with slight anger in his voice. "She's just a friend! Actually, she's more like a baby sister. I've known her, and her Mom and Dad, for almost ten years."

"Boy, that's your loss. If it were me, and she ain't related by blood, I would go for her, all the way." He took a large gulp of his beer.

"Christ, you'd screw a snake if I held its head." Ricky changed the subject. "Enough about me, let's hear what you've been up to and why you're running off to Vancouver. Don't they have translators out there?"

"It's a little more complicated than that, so I better start at the beginning. And if you want me to get the whole story told in time for my plane you better try to hold your questions 'til the end."

"All right, but, before we start, perhaps we should order," Ricky signaled Angie. "You still favor baked rigatoni, right?"

Norman nodded.

Angie appeared with her order book ready.

"I'll have the spaghetti with meat sauce and two meatballs; Norman will have your baked rigatoni with a side of sautéed mushrooms, a basket of garlic bread and cheddar cheese bread, and you can bring us another couple of Molson's," Ricky handed her the two empty bottles.

"Sure thing, Ricky. The meals will be up in about ten minutes," she acknowledged. "Do you want me to save you some cannoli for dessert."

"Yes, thank you, Angie, that would be great."

"Okay, you have the floor little brother."

"First, I need to preface the conversation with a sincere apology to you for my deception over the past year plus, concerning my job."

"Shit I knew it," Ricky joked, "you're not a translator! You do work for the C.I.A."

"Actually, in truth, you're not that far off."

"What!" Ricky began, but halted, as Norman raised his hand in silence.

"I do work for the R.C.M.P. but not as a translator, as an agent."

"You mean like those U.S. Secret Service guys with speakers in their ears that protect the president and dignitaries?"

"Not quite so glamourous. If you remember when I first got out of the service, I was lost, I had no direction. I was so used to having someone tell me what to do and when to do it, that I had to think hard before even going to breakfast. So, the natural progression was to join something that gave me that direction, and that was law enforcement. And the best law enforcement agency in Canada is the R.C.M.P. When I originally talked with the recruiter, he zeroed in on the fact that I had had training as a provost marshal in the service, therefore my R.C.M.P. training, at the *Depot*, was concentrated primarily on investigation and apprehension. The *Depot* is the counterpart to the F.B.I.'s *Farm* in Virginia, where in addition to full law enforcement training, I attended four weeks of special classes on undercover techniques. And they were friggin' grueling!"

"Actually, I don't remember you being lost after the service. What I do remember is you banging every broad that was just over the legal age," Ricky laughed.

Angie brought their two new Molson's. "Your order will be out in just a minute," she piped in, scurrying back towards the kitchen.

Norman took a sip of beer, lit another cigarette, and paused to gather his thoughts. "I realized early on in my training that the fastest way to advancement was through undercover work, which would take me from agent to special agent in about eighteen months, so, that was my goal. I finished my *Depot* training, gaining 'first in my class honors', and without any fanfare, I was immediately assigned to a drug operation in Hamilton, Ontario. That only lasted ten weeks, so, because I was perfectly fluent in French, I got assigned to the Montreal counter-terrorism task force. There I was posted as an undercover agent."

Angie returned with their entrees, "Be careful, the plates are very hot! Enjoy!"

Norman took a mouthful of the steaming rigatoni. "Um ... this is great!" This gave Ricky a chance to ask a question.

"So, this task force was all undercover agents?" Ricky reacted, twirling the spaghetti on his fork, as he stabbed at a meatball.

Profoundly serious, now, Norman continued, "Not exactly. But first, I need you to swear that you will never relate anything that I'm telling you to anyone, and I mean anyone. The repercussions could cost someone their lives. I could get myself in deep shit if anyone found out what I am about to tell you. It's just that, well, I believe I owe you an explanation for my secrecy these past months."

"I swear!" Ricky responded, feigning crossing his heart.

"You remember the name McFadden and Holmes Consulting?"

"Yeah, that's where I called you yesterday."

"Well, that's a front for our counter-terrorism task force headquarters and my base of contact with my handler. For legitimacy purposes, we have several engineers on staff, in a separate part of the building, and they do consult on mining operations. Even they have no idea that this company is actually a ruse."

"So, let me get this straight. They have a legitimate company working within the confines of a R.C.M.P. operation, and no one is the wiser. That sounds impossible."

"Not really. The real McFadden and Holmes Consulting operation runs totally autonomously. They have their own hierarchy of management and staff and never interact with our area. They are even a lucrative profit center. They operate on their side of the building, and we, on ours. This has been going on for six years without incident."

"Do you have a desk and stuff at this Fadden place."

"No, for security purposes, only my handler, Mister Smith, knows who I am. This is as much to preserve the integrity of the R.C.M.P. front company, as to protect my undercover persona."

"Wow! I'm just blown away," Ricky clinked Norman's bottle. "So, your handler places you undercover, and you what? You sneak around and discover who the bad guys are that are dealing drugs?"

"It's a lot more complex than that. What is the biggest danger problem that you personally face every day in Montreal?"

Ricky thought for a moment, "Getting my bloody ass blown up by some friggin' F.L.Q. bomb," he answered.

"Right! And that was my assignment. To prevent, or at least uncover potential threats to the citizens of Quebec, or even Canada. My job was to infiltrate the radical student organizations, and the F.L.Q., and relay any threats back to my handler for police action. At the same time, I had to protect my own ass from getting found out. Not an easy feat!"

"How does an English looking, ex-Canadian champion wrestler infiltrate a large provincial organization like the F.L.Q., without getting his ass blown off?"

EATON'S – During the Second French Revolution

"It ain't easy." Norman viewed the other assembled diners to ensure no one was within earshot. "A complete bona fide package was prepared for me with a bogus social insurance card, driver's license, passport, etc. Additionally, comprehensive documentation to cover my education, work history, and even an arrest record for petty larceny and civil disturbance. My new undercover persona was accurate down to the finest detail."

"So, with this new identity you just call up the F.L.Q. and say, 'I want to join your screwed-up organization?'" Ricky kidded.

"I wish it were that simple. You don't ask to join; you need to be invited to join. And these guys are very wary of everyone they allow into their midst, particularly someone who has no one inside their organization who can vouch for them. I spent several months hanging around local bars, before being invited to my first rally. Even then, aside from being allowed to shout obscenities, I was usually only permitted as an observer to make the crowd look larger, and not to be starting damage. Only after several rallies was I given an active role in initiating mayhem. I was given a baseball bat, and a couple of Molotov cocktails."

"You actually had to firebomb stuff with Molotov cocktails?" Ricky was astonished.

"Yes. To gain credibility with my group, I threw Molotov cocktails at the target buildings, or empty cars. But, when possible, I tried to direct my assault harmlessly at brick facing so as not to create significant damage. However, at the Lafontaine Park rally, I finally gained full credibility by smashing a police van window, which ultimately led to my arrest. Apparently, this arrest brought me to the attention of the team leader of the Montreal North *Dieppe Cell,* of the F.L.Q. After that, I became privy to almost every event that was to transpire within my cell, and rumors of activities in other cells like the Laval *Liberation Cell,* and many others. The information that I filtered back to the task force was instrumental in thwarting several serious altercations and bombings throughout the province. And" he swirled his bottle of beer, "I'm sorry I wasn't in time to save your department from the locker bombing."

Confused, Ricky ignored the comment. "If it took you so long to get deeply entrenched in the F.L.Q., why would your handler be transferring you to Vancouver?"

A grim look flashed across Norman's face. "I was about to get burned."

"Burned?"

"Yeah, I'd uncovered so many events that were leaked to my handler, the press, and the police about planned terrorist targets, that the investigative branch of the F.L.Q. was combing all the cells to discover who the traitor was in their midst. They narrowed it down to nineteen individuals within the *Dieppe Cell and the Liberation Cell*, and it was only a matter of time before they pinpointed me as the culprit."

"That is bloody scary!"

Angie arrived carrying two cannoli's and two shot glasses of ouzo, the most popular Greek libation. "Pappa sent these as an after-dinner aperitif, on the house. Enjoy," she smiled, clearing the finished meals.

Ricky waved a "thank you," to Spiro who was beaming behind the bar.

"Your damn right it was scary. It was actually terrifying, thinking that at any moment I could be silenced by the F.L.Q. So, my handler decided that as soon as the Exchange operation was completed, I was to be extracted from the F.L.Q., my persona made non-existent and transferred as far away from Quebec as possible. Thus Vancouver. He determined that as soon as they discovered the true identity of the traitor a bounty would be placed on my head. Although I was slated to head to Vancouver immediately after the Exchange operation, because of the Laporte and Cross kidnappings, the powers that be directed me to dig up information on the suspects within the F.L.Q. cells to which I had gained access."

"Christ, what have you gotten yourself into, Norm. They're not going to give up looking for you. You'll be on the run for the rest of your life."

"Not really. My appearance has totally changed from when I worked with these guys, and my identity is completely scrubbed, so the chance of them tracing me is nil. We figure that they'll surmise that I might have been an investigator but after that, they'll probably give up and go on with their murders, kidnapping, and bombings."

"What is this Exchange operation that you mentioned?"

"The bombing of the Montreal Stock Exchange."

"You were part of that!" Ricky was noticeably shocked.

"You could say that since I was the one who alerted the authorities through my handler and made the phone call to the Exchange advising that a bomb was going to explode, yeah, I guess I 'was part of that.'"

"That was you? I read that in the paper. It said that although short notice was given before the blast, the leak may have saved numerous lives."

"I don't know about that, but I only had twenty minute's notice before the blast to notify everyone." Norman lowered his head. "If I had had more time, we might have been able to find the bomb's location, evacuate the trading floor before hundreds of people would not have been injured."

"You can chastise yourself all you want, but your actions were nothing short of heroic. I'm proud of you, little bro." Ricky reached across the table and affectionately squeezed Norman's hand.

"Thank you," was the silent reply.

Taking a swig of his beer Ricky asked, "How did you leak all that stuff to the press and police? Did your Mister Smith pass it on?"

Norman smiled slyly. "My handler and I decided early on that I had to have a tag to give credibility to the leaks that I was submitting. The cops get false leaks all the time that have them chasing their tails and wasting valuable manpower. They came to realize, with a little prodding from my handler, that when they received a threat from *C'est l'ombre*, they were to take it as gospel truth. And, don't forget Eaton's."

Ricky put up his hand to stop Norman. "Hang on. This is too much to digest. What do you mean about Eaton's? That's the second time you mentioned the store.'"

Norman smiled coyly, "Eaton's also got regular tips from *C'est l'ombre*, but even my big brother didn't know they were from me."

"*C'est l'ombre* means, '*The Shadow*', in English, right?" Ricky was flabbergasted. "How could you be '*The Shadow*'?"

"Hang on a minute Ricky," he cut him off. "Everyone was told not to allow, 'The *Shadow*,' tag to become public knowledge, so that would keep the information credible. Everyone was advised never to divulge the source when they received tips from *The Shadow*. And *The Shadow* tag has remained a well-kept secret to this day. And before you bust a blood vessel," he looked at Ricky's crimson face, "yes, I was the one giving *Shadow* notes to you, and your Tony Cartwright, in security, about events that were to happen within Eaton's. I had to protect my big bro, yes?"

"I can't believe I missed it! I was the one who played the part of *The Shadow* when we were kids. I'd hide in the closet and jump out at you, and scare the crap out of you, yelling, '*The Shadow* is going to kill you'."

"How can I forget. I still have nightmares every time I get near a goddamn closet," he laughed.

"But *The Shadow* is a common myth, everyone uses that name. Why did you choose it?"

"Simple! Using it was my only tie to the real world, to.my family, and to you. I was sure that you would eventually put two and two together but, I guess I was wrong. In fact, I gave you a clue. Do you remember the last thing I told you at Dorval Airport before going for my Quebec City flight?"

"Uh, goodbye?"

"No dummy. Remember, I told you to, '*stay in the shadows, Bro!*'"

"Shit Yeah, I do now. But remember, you were the straight A student, not me," Ricky laughed, offering a cigarette to Norman.

"Yeah well, that's the whole sordid story and now I'm off to Vancouver. No rest for the wicked, I guess."

"And I suppose you can't tell me about that assignment?"

"If I tell 'ya, I'll hafta kill 'ya," he joked. "All I can tell you is if this operation is successful, it'll put a hell of a dent in Canada's drug traffic." Norman looked at his watch, throwing two twenty-dollar bills on the table. "I got to run, Bro. I've got to catch a four o'clock flight out of Cartierville Airport."

Ricky embraced Norman warmly before he raced out the door to get a taxi. Ricky then said his goodbyes to Angie and Spiro before heading back to Eaton's. His mind was still reeling from the revelations his brother had revealed to him.

That little bugger kept all that to himself, all this time. How completely alienated and frightened he must have felt. The Shadow strikes again!

⚜ Eighty-Two ⚜

Twenty-two months had passed since Ricky had filed his divorce decree application to the court, complete with his sordid adultery evidence with Debbie "the hooker."

That time frame saw little change in the political climate within Montreal, or the Province of Quebec. The FLQ terrorist were continuing their regime of bombings, dissent, and intimidation, while Quebec politicians continued to regularly spew independence rhetoric to the ever-growing population of French supporters.

Previously benign procedures now also evolved with the changing climate. The English-speaking employees at Eaton's were now immersed in mandatory French language classes, and store security was beefed up by thirty percent, with a special squad trained to search for bombs, instead of the previously unqualified employees. Eaton's management had been reduced through early retirements, with the remaining management given more responsibilities to fill in the gaps. Cash transfers to local banks were now handled by Brinks trucks entering a secure locked delivery bay, instead of their usual street parking procedures. Store advertising was structured to downplay English language newspapers and promote sale merchandise in *LaPresse*, the sole French language publication.

Eaton's was no longer the happy-go-lucky employer of bygone years, but through necessity had morphed into a place of fear and discontent. French customers no longer were tolerant of a struggling English-speaking salesclerk. Mr. Timothy Eaton would have been appalled by the transformation of his dream empire.

On a personal level, Ricky's relationship with Christine ignored the negativity of these situations, and instead they built a solid impenetrable, loving future together. Their efforts had been rewarded a hundredfold. Ricky no longer felt the need to hold back expressing the "love" word to Christine, thus galvanizing their intimacy beyond anything each of them could have expected. Darlene had become accustomed to only seeing Kathy sporadically, and really enjoyed her nanny-time with Mrs. Cote. But the best part was that she had become quite close to Christine, now calling her Auntie Chris. Although enjoying their Eaton's-time working together, their private time turned into a world-wind of loving adventure and romance.

Because of the pending divorce, Christine could not move in with Ricky, but they spent many nights secreted in each other's arms in his St. Laurent apartment, or her apartment, where they made love and lists of their future goals together. They went on buying trips together to Toronto and New York and enjoyed the paid luxuries of quality hotels and splendid meals. They spent a glorious three days at the Mont Tremblant ski resort, sipping hot brandy before a roaring fire and pursuing nights of romantic ecstasy buried beneath a bearskin comforter. They even had a treasured July 4th long weekend at the lakeside lodge in Rawdon, Quebec, where they went horseback riding, the first time Christine had been on a horse.

With Radford away in Toronto, Ricky had assumed his responsibilities and was filling out some paperwork at his large oak French Provincial desk. The office was lavishly decorated, not only with the expensive desk, but also a heavily tufted chaise, Parisian lamps and a collection of fine-art tapestries and European prints.

Ricky sat alone at the spacious desk, looking at the large manila envelope that he had received in the mail that morning and finally decided to open it. He was already fully aware of its contents. But this was not his alone, but rather, a collective effort that must be shared with the girl of his dreams. A document that was as much a part of her as it was of him. A simple piece of paper that would change the course of their lives, forever.

Scanning the document again, Ricky absently picked up the telephone receiver and dialed the number for Mrs. Cote.

"Hi Celine. This is Ricky, just checking in. How's Darlene doing with her sniffles?"

"Her cough is all gone, and I have her down for her nap, right now."

"I wanted to tell you again, how much I truly appreciate you keeping her overnight."

"No problem, Ricky. We love having her here and it gives little Andrew someone to play with. And anyway, you spend too much time alone in your apartment. You need to get out more with friends."

"I should be there around noon tomorrow to pick up Darlene."

"No need. Let her stay overnight tomorrow again too! Remember Andrew's third birthday party is at one o'clock so why not just come then and enjoy the party with Darlene?"

"That sounds great, Celine, but would it be okay if I brought my friend Christine, again?"

"Christine is such a sweet girl. She's welcome here any time."

"Thanks. Yes, she is wonderful, and if I get my wish, I may have some special news I want to share with you."

"I love secrets! I'll see you tomorrow."

Hanging up, Ricky placed the document back in the envelope with reverence, as if it were a million-dollar stock certificate. He picked up the telephone again and dialed the teens fashion department.

The phone was answered on the first ring. "Teen Fashions, Lori Robinson, here. How may I assist you?"

"Hi Lori, Mister Dean calling. Is Miss Guillaume around?"

"Let me check, Mister Dean," he heard, as she placed her hand over the receiver. "Sorry. She just left for her break in the luncheonette."

"Fine. Have her call me when she gets back."

Lori interrupted. "Before you hang up, Sir, while you were at your meeting with Mister Appleton, Maggie told me to tell you, and I'm quoting her, 'that a mysterious package was delivered for you, by an even more mysterious beautiful young lady, and she put it in the closet in your office'. Geez, I hope I got that right or Maggie will kill me."

"I'm sure you did Lori," he laughed, "and remember to give Chris, uh, Miss Guillaume my message."

Not two minutes later his phone rang.

"Dean, here."

He heard a breathless Christine on the other end of the line. "You called?"

"It wasn't that important that you had to get the message, right away. Why are you out of breath?"

"Lori caught me just as I was returning from the west side ladies' room, and I ran back to use the luncheonette cashier's phone."

"That wasn't necessary but thank you. I was wondering if, uh, whether we could get together at the Windsor Lounge, at The Queen Elizabeth Hotel, after work tonight?" he stammered. "I have some news that I'd like to share with you."

"I don't know. The last time you were all serious about sharing news with me, you ended up telling me that you were getting a motel room to sleep with a hooker." Ricky heard her giggling.

"That is going to be a story between us, forever, isn't it?"

"Well, yes! But I do like the word *'forever'*."

"And the answer to my original question is?"

"Why certainly, Mister Dean, I'd be honored to meet you for cocktails. Shall I bring my little red suitcase?" she laughed.

"I sure hope the cashier is not standing there listening to you."

"No, dopey. She's at the express register! Now, you were saying about the suitcase?"

"What I was saying is that if *you* get lucky tonight, you won't need the contents of the little red suitcase," he teased.

"Why, Mister Dean, I do declare," she was putting on a southern accent, "you'll be turning the head of this Southern Belle," she laughed, then continued, "the Windsor Lounge, right after work."

"Lookin' forward!" he hung up.

Ricky got up from Radford's desk and went around the corner to his own office, where he opened the closet to find the package Maggie had put there.

EATON'S – During the Second French Revolution

Thank you, thank you, Charlotte.

With his cherished envelope in hand, he left his office and started across the floor, where he saw Rene Beaudreaux approaching. He took his pager off his belt and handed it to Rene.

"Hi Rene. I'll be 10-7B for about a half hour," referencing the pager call code for, *out of service, personal.*

"Sure, I'll run a floor circuit while you're away." Rene attached the pager to his belt.

"Any emergency, you can reach me at gift wrapping, extension, four three, two, two."

"Sure 'nough," Ricky heard, as he ran for an elevator disembarking several customers.

"Thanks, Mandy." He leaned against the handrail at the back of the elevator. "Fourth floor, please."

"Express, Mister Dean?" She batted her eyes at him, closing the accordion gate, then the sliding elevator doors, before the ascent.

"No, local only, Mandy. Remember the customer is the most important person in this store."

"Main floor, cosmetics, jewelry, luggage and ..." she announced, opening the doors.

Man, do I have a lot to do before I meet Christine. And everything has to be perfect 'cause 'there ain't no do-overs'.

"Second floor, boys wear, third floor, bedding."

Where the hell did I put the Burke's box? Panicked, Ricky slapped at his pockets, finally hitting what he was looking for. *There it is, thank goodness.* Ricky sighed loudly.

"Fourth floor, ladies' shoes, gift wrapping."

"Thanks Mandy." Ricky stepped off the elevator and headed to the gift-wrapping department.

"Hey Julie, how do you like your new job?" Julie had worked for him as a salesclerk in his corset department, but after a few months she had told her manager, Rebecca Snyder, that 'she hated fitting old fat ladies with corsets'. Snyder was going to fire her, but Ricky intervened, finding her a job in gift wrapping.

"Fantastic, Mister Dean," she gushed. "Thanks to you!"

"Don't mention it. I need a special gift wrap, for a special friend's gift, for this evening, and I count on your expertise."

"You'll get the best I have to give," she blushed, tucking a loose strand of hair back into her hair band.

"I'll need a gift box with a lid about ten inches by twelve inches by four inches deep."

"Got exactly what you need right here." She searched the wide selection of boxes grasping a white box with a floral pattern. "Is this design, okay?"

"That's just perfect." Ricky placed the envelope on the counter and retrieved the Burke box from his jacket pocket. "But that was the easy part," he laughed.

"Well, we do wonders here. What do you need?"

"I need you to build a platform in the bottom of your gift box to conceal this Burke box, so when my friend opens it, it will not be seen."

Confusion flashed across Julie's face.

"Bear with me until I finish, Julie."

She nodded.

"Okay, then I want you to wrap this manila envelope in matching paper and lay it on top of the platform, so that when the box is opened the only thing visible will be the wrapped manila envelope. Does that make sense to you?"

"Now it does. You want your friend to open the box and think that the only thing in the box is the gift-wrapped envelope, then later you'll have him or her search the box for something more."

"Why did it make so much more sense when you said it?"

"Because you transferred me here to be a professional, Mister Dean. Now, the last thing we need is a great bow. What are your friends favorite color?"

"Purple. And can you get it ready for me before closing?" he asked.

"It will be ready in a half hour," she replied proudly, "and I'll even bring it down to your office."

"You don't need ..." Ricky started.

"No arguments. I owe you Mister Dean. Anyway, I'm going down to see Susan in millinery on my break, so I'll bring the parcel down with me then. And I'll put it in a large brown paper bag so no one will notice that it is a gift."

"I knew I made the right choice getting you a job up here," Ricky laughed, as he headed back to the basement floor.

Ricky retrieved his pager from Rene and called Duane to tell him that he'd be leaving early. As promised Julie arrived within the hour with his gift in a large brown paper bag. He packed up the gift, the parcel from Charlotte and headed for the garage to pick up his car. His suitcase was already in the trunk of his car as he headed for the Queen Elizabeth Hotel.

Sure, as hell, I've forgotten something.

⚜ Eighty-Three ⚜

Christine was just coming through the revolving doors as Ricky exited the Queen Elizabeth elevator. They each ran toward the other with Christine propelling herself into Ricky's waiting arms.

"I've missed you so much," she breathed into his ear. "I wish we could act like this without the fear of constantly being discovered."

EATON'S – During the Second French Revolution

He guided her towards the Windsor Lounge. "Be patient, Princess. Your dreams may be fulfilled when you least expect them."

Ricky placed Christine's coat and handbag on an adjoining chair and pulled out a large wrap-around burgundy leather chair for her.

"Good evening. May I get you a cocktail," the waitress asked in a very distinctive British accent.

"You may," Ricky quickly responded, "and where in England do you hail from?"

"A little town called Borewood, just north of London, But I spent most of my time working in London. Have you ever been abroad?"

"Yes, I spent a few days in London. Stayed at the Dorchester Hotel."

"Been there many times, actually worked at the Pilsener Bar in the hotel," she corrected.

"Yeah, great place and great Scottish music. Do you have any sweet champagne by-the-glass?" he asked.

"Yes sir. We have a Korbel Brut, a Segura Viudas and of course, a Dom Perignon, all available by-the-glass."

Ricky smiled at Christine. "So, I don't have to float a loan for Dom Perignon, I think we'll have two glasses of your Korbel Brut," he joked.

"Be right up," the waitress said, heading back to the bar.

"You do like champagne, don't you?" He asked, biting teasingly at Christine's earlobe.

"I don't know. I've never had any champagne, but always wanted to try it." She drew his lips to hers, tracing her tongue around the perimeter.

Ricky held her kiss and then slowly moved back to look at her. "Are you ready for the night of your life?" he asked, lighting two cigarettes.

"I thought our January third had been the 'night of my life?'"

"That was the appetizer, this is the main course."

"I think maybe you've bit off more than you can chew, Ricky. I don't think it's possible for anyone to beat your record of that date, and certainly not sitting in a bar."

The waitress arrived with two fluted glasses of Brut.

"Will you be dining with us tonight, Sir."

"We will. Is there an orchestra playing in the Buckingham Restaurant, tonight?"

"Yes Sir, a five-piece horn, string, and piano group. They are good. They play all the favorites and take special requests. Can I make a reservation for you?"

"Please. A table for two, in the back corner, around seven thirty."

"Yes Sir." She headed for the dining room.

Ricky raised his glass in a toast. "To us. May the woes of the past become the blossoms of our future. And may the Princess find everlasting happiness with her Prince. I *love* you, Christine Guillaume."

Tears flooding her eyes, Christine clinked glasses with him. "I need the ladies' room," she stated hesitantly, rushing off towards the lobby. On her way there all she could think of as the tears flowed was, *I never thought I would hear those words from this man that I love so much!*

Ricky at the same time was concerned that he made her runoff crying and wondered, *I sure hope I'm not overdoing this whole thing.*

When she returned, she looked fresh and as beautiful as ever.

"Whew, that's better," she sat back into her chair. "Now, Mister Dean, you had me waiting all day for your big news, ply me with celebration champagne, and you are about to feed me in one of Montreal's best restaurants. It's time to fill me in on the big secret, don't you think?" She took a sip of her champagne, the bubbles twinkling in her nose. "Wow, that is *so* good."

Ricky waved two fingers at the waitress signaling two more glasses of champagne.

"Well, my darling, there have been some big changes in our Eaton's home, today. You know that Jeremy Radford has been slacking off over the past few years and that has come to the attention of Appleton. Radford was offered early retirement or dismissal, and of course, he chose retirement. Appleton promoted me to basement merchandise manager with buying control responsibilities over all basement purchases Canada wide."

Christine's eyes lit up with glee. "Oh Ricky, really? That is the best news I could ever have hoped for you. You certainly deserve it since you've been covering for Radford all this time. And I have to say that the guy gave me the creeps. Every time he passed; I could feel his eyes staring at me."

"Well, I can't fault him for that."

I sure hope you don't really believe that 'that is the best news you could ever have hoped for'.

"There's more. With this promotion Appleton asked me to do a basement reorganization, so effective Monday, Duane takes over as manager of all footwear, Rene Boudreaux takes over management of the flooring department, Jerry Copeland is promoted to manager of boy's wear, with Andrea Bardot as his assistant manager, and Charlotte Henderson takes over as manager of notions and sundries. What do you think?"

"Hmmm," was her only response.

Ricky could see that she was trying to place all the individuals in the appropriate departments as the waitress placed new cocktail napkins and two glasses of champagne before them.

Finally, she surmised, "That leaves both the millinery department, purses and the leather goods department without managers."

"Not exactly," he smiled, raising his glass.

"How do you figure?" Their glasses clinked together.

EATON'S – During the Second French Revolution

"Well, if Christine Guillaume took over both those departments in addition to teens fashion, well then, you see, problem solved, yes?"

"Oh yes, Ricky, yes, yes! Thank you, thank you. You won't be sorry. I'll make you proud."

"You don't have to do anything more to make me any prouder than I am of you already, Princess." He held her in a long embrace, sharing her sobs of joy.

He blotted her eyes and then handed her his handkerchief. They talked for a long time about Eaton's business until the waitress returned advising them their seven thirty reservation was ready, and the bar bill would be passed along to their restaurant server.

"Do you think I am dressed properly for this fancy-dancy restaurant," she questioned."

"Yes. And regardless of what you wear you will be the most beautiful woman in the room."

They were seated at a prime table in the rear with a partially screened enclosure shielding them from the view of the rest of the diners. As Ricky shook out a linen napkin and placed it on Christine's lap, a tuxedoed waiter arrived, handing them royal blue leather-bound menus.

"Good evening Miss, Sir. My name is Germaine, and I will be at your service tonight. May we begin with a libation to tease your palate?"

Ricky was concerned about eating up more time that would cut into his planned evening. He looked at Christine, who shook her head. Then, whispered in his ear, "I'm the only one that gets to tease your palate."

"Thank you, Germaine, but we've had sufficient cocktails in the Windsor."

"Very well, Sir. Perhaps an appetizer before you begin, then?"

Ricky looked at Christine who nodded. He knew exactly what she loved in the way of food. He scanned the menu.

"The lady will have the shrimp cocktail, and I'll have the French onion soup. And you can bring us some coffee with lots of cream."

As Ricky lit two cigarettes, passing one to Christine, the band began its first set of the evening beginning with Duke Ellington's, *It Don't Mean A Thing, If It Ain't Got That Swing.*

"Very good Sir. And have you decided on your entrée? We have Chicken Alfredo, Steak Diane, Curried lamb ..."

Ricky held up his hand. "The lady will have a queen cut prime rib au jus, baked potato with sour cream, chives and cheddar cheese, and the vegetable medley. And, I'll have the filet mignon, rare, with the same baked potato and vegetable medley as the lady."

The waiter scribbled on his order pad.

"And for the salads, Sir?"

"The lady will have a salad without mushrooms or tomatoes, with blue cheese dressing on the side. I'll have same with ranch on the side."

"Your appetizers and hot baked bread will be along shortly, Sir." He headed for the kitchen.

"Ricky, this is all too much," she whispered. "It'll cost a fortune."

"And you are worth every penny, my darling," he responded, kissing her waiting lips. "Anyway, I figured with the big bucks you'll be getting for your new department responsibilities, you'd be picking up the check," he teased.

She punched his arm playfully, as Ricky got up from his chair and headed for the bandstand.

When the band finished the song, it had been playing, the band leader announced that he had a special request.

Ricky returned to the table, and took Christine's hand, "May I have this dance, Mademoiselle?"

"Enchante, Monsieur," she cooed.

Before they reached the dance floor. Christine froze in her tracks. The band began playing her favorite Frank Sinatra song, "*Fly me to the moon."*

"Ricky, you did that for me. No matter how long I live, I know I'll never be able to tell you how much I really, really love you. You are my everything!" Tears streaked down her cheek.

Ricky turned her face to his, licking her tears, offering the one word that would remain with Christine forever. "Ditto!"

They danced and ate their delicious meal and topped their meal off with raspberry cheesecake for dessert. Their evening on-the-town seemed to be never ending.

Ricky finally paid the bill and was ready for the next part of their evening.

While waiting for the waiter's return with the change, Christine tenderly placed both her hands enveloping his, and asked pleadingly, "Can you be with me for a while, tonight. Charlotte's away, and I have the apartment to myself."

"Well, I don't know," he teased, kissing her neck, "I was planning to *be with you* all night."

"Really," she gushed, her eyes as big as saucers, "all night, really?"

The waiter returned with his change and Ricky gave him a generous tip.

"But first, I need to pick up a security proposal for Tony, from a Mister Bestway at nine o'clock tonight. He has a suite on the twentieth floor, and you're welcome to come up with me if you like."

"That would be awesome. Can you see the city lights from way up there?"

"Sorry, I don't think so. There are no windows in the hallways," he rose from his chair to help Christine.

He grabbed their coats and headed for the elevator. As they began their ascent Christine pressed her hot body into Ricky. "Do you suppose there is enough time in a twenty-floor elevator rise to get a sexual rise out of you?"

"When you are near me, I always have a sexual rise, darlin'," he positioned her hand on his upper leg.

EATON'S – During the Second French Revolution

She swooned, taking a firm grasp of his manhood through his thin pants just as the door opened on the twentieth floor. They walked together down the long hallway to room 2018, where Ricky took a key from his jacket pocket.

"What are you doing?" she questioned, looking suspiciously back down the hallway.

"Picking up the report," and before she knew what was happening, he grasped her behind her knees and propelled her up into his arms, kicking the door open at the same time. Crossing the threshold with this confused girl, he murmured, "Happy Anniversary, Princess," as he gently placed her on the bed, his mouth searching for hers.

"But wait, our anniversary is on January third, and this is March fourteenth," she protested.

"Until now!" was his only response.

She sat for several minutes on the corner of the bed where Ricky had placed her, watching the flickering candles changing shadows on the wall. Ricky stroked her hair, as her head swiveled aimlessly, scanning the entire room, from the raised hot tub to the elegant cityscape art on the walls, to the breadth of the bed, and finally settling on the floor to ceiling windows overlooking the glimmering lights of their city, below. Finally, and slowly, she rose from the bed, took Ricky's hand in hers and guided him toward the windows.

"Did you do all this for us, Ricky?" she muttered softly, squeezing his hand. "I've never seen anything this beautiful in all my life. And it's only beautiful because I'm sharing it with the man that I love with my whole heart." She pulled his head down to meet her lips, and without the appearance of sexual overtones, slowly slid her tongue into his mouth, caressing his tongue, then biting his lip gently.

"Ditto," he responded.

"But first my lady, we're going to soak in the hot tub." He picked up the two terrycloth robes from the bed, and guided her to the tub, then positioned her on the rim as he turned on the water. Ricky poured in some bubble bath salts and adjusted the water jets to the desired temperature. Her eyes remained fixed on the view through the small window.

Ricky retrieved two fluted glasses, and the silver stand with the chilled Dubonnet, and placed them by the tub. He popped the cork and poured two full glasses of the wine, bringing one to her lips for a taste. She grabbed the other glass and did the same for him. Then, Ricky intertwined their arms with the wine glasses in a short toast, "To forever, and tomorrow. May they be ever as glorious as tonight!" They silently drank their wine.

Ricky put his wine glass down; bent to his knees and seductively lowered the long zippers on her knee length boots, removed them, and stood them beside the tub.

Christine's eyes took in his every movement.

He stood up and gently gathered her pink blouse above her head not to mess her hair; carefully folding it, then placed it on the shelf by the tub. He slid his thumbs into the waistband of her black skirt lowering it down across her slender hips and across her milk-white thighs. He continued slowly from her perfect knees to her ankles.

"You are an absolute goddess," he sighed, noticing a slight tremble in her body. "Are you cold, Princess?"

"Nnnn ... no," she stammered. "Just totally and unbelievably happy!"

He pulled her into his arms as his hands enveloped her slight frame. He expertly removed the rest of her clothing, followed by his own, as they slipped into the waiting warmth of the bubbling hot tub. They drank their wine, holding each other close, while admiring the view of the city below. Eventually their kissing and petting lead to lovemaking, a treasured repeat of January 3rd

⚜ Eighty-Four ⚜

As they left the warmth of the bubbling hot tub, Ricky carried Christine's still trembling body to the sanctity of the yet unused king size bed. He pulled down the red velour comforter and the sheet underneath, placing her within its warmth. He propped a pillow under her head and brought the ice bucket, Dubonnet, and glasses to the bed, where he poured each of them another glass.

She watched in fascination as he strutted his nude body across the room. "I don't know how much more of this I can take." Her voice cracked as she downed a long swig of wine.

"Well, I don't either, but I sure hope there's room for a few more surprises. The night ain't over yet, Darlin."

"I don't think I have the strength for anymore. I don't even think I could walk if I had to."

"Believe me, the next surprise doesn't require you walking, in fact, it just requires enjoying." Ricky moved Christine to the center of the bed. "I'm going to place this towel over your eyes so that you can savor this experience without seeing. It is not going to take awfully long, and I want you to visualize everything that is happening. Do you trust me?"

"So, mysterious! Of course, I trust you." She positioned the small towel over her eyes."

Ricky went to the hall closet where he retrieved the parcels, bringing them back to the bed, as he slid under the sheets, his body touching her still smoldering skin.

He handed her the first large brown bag parcel, which she peeked into.

"What? How? Who gave you my little red suitcase?" She pulled the suitcase from the bag.

"Who do you think. I talked to Charlotte, and she told me that you have duplicates of all your personal needs in the suitcase, along with freshly washed clothes. She added some girlie essentials, and I asked her to pack that little black dress that I enjoy so much. End of story!"

"Ricky, you are just too much?" She took his face in her two hands, crimping his lips and laying a big kiss on him. "You went to all that trouble just to surprise me? And the black dress, why."

"Because pretty soon we're going back downstairs to celebrate, and I want my Princess in my favorite black dress."

"That would be a great ending to an incredible everything! I don't even have the words." Christine placed the suitcase on the floor beside the bed. "Okay, do you want me to start getting ready?"

She began to climb out of bed but was stopped by Ricky reaching for her wrist. "Not so fast, we're not finished here." He slid the other brown bag toward her. "You need to open this first. This is the most important surprise."

"Ricky, there's nothing more you need to do, you have surprised me with each thing, and I just can't believe all you've done, and ..."

" Shh! Just look in the bag!"

"It's gift wrapped!" She pulled the gift from the bag. "And in my favorite color."

"Well, don't just gawk at it, silly. Open it."

She pulled on the bow which released the ribbon. Then she curiously lifted the lid and retrieved the thin wrapped package. She carefully removed the gift wrapping which exposed the brown manila envelope. "This is a copy of my promotion letter from Appleton, right?"

"I don't think so. But you can keep guessing, or just open it!"

She undid the clasp and peered cautiously inside, as if something was going to jump out at her. She slowly pulled the document from the envelope revealing the seal of the Province of Quebec and displayed, in bold words across the header, "Décret de Dissolution de Mariage," *Marriage Dissolution Decree.*

Christine froze in place, her breath seeming to stop, her eyes fixed on the paper, her tears rolling down her face. She jumped from the bed and ran to the bathroom.

He raced after her, finding her curled up in the corner of the cold tiled floor, her shoulders quivering as she sobbed uncontrollably.

Ricky sat on the floor beside her taking her in his arms and rocking her like a baby. "This is not the reaction that I expected." He lifted her chin, so he could see her face. "I love you honey, I wanted this to be joyous for you. Are you okay?"

She whimpered and tried to get her sobbing under control. "Oh Ricky, I thought this day would never come." She grabbed a Kleenex from the commode and blew her nose. "You've had delay after delay and I was sure somewhere Kathy would show up, take Darlene, and destroy everything."

"Listen, Little Miss Princess, nobody, can ever destroy what we have together, understand?"

"Yes Sir," she answered getting up from the floor, "but I need to pee."

Ricky closed the bathroom door and got back under the covers, taking a large gulp of wine.

If this almost made her pass out, how is she going to react to the final surprise?

Christine came out of the bathroom, dabbing her eyes, as her nude body tiptoed across the deep pile carpet. She leaped under the covers and surrounded Ricky's body with hers.

"Ricky, I am so happy I think I'm going to burst." She intertwined her legs around his. "I don't want this day to ever end."

Ricky threw the covers back so that both their bodies were nude on top of the crisp white sheets. Pointing to the divorce decree in his hand. "You know what this means, don't you?"

She nodded.

"This means I'm finally a free man and can do whatever I want."

Christine looked at him curiously as he rose to his knees. "And Christine Roberta Guillaume, I want you to be my wife for as long as we both shall live. Will you marry me, my Princess?"

Her reaction was so fast, he was knocked from his knees, with Christine lying on top of him on the floor, smothering him with kisses, sobs, and tears. "Yes, I would be honored to marry the man of my dreams," she finally offered, rolling off his body. "I wonder how many people get proposed to, totally nude?" she laughed.

"Not too many, I'm sure." Ricky helped her off the floor and back onto the bed. "There are a few things that we need to discuss." Ricky checked off his fingers.

"Number one, we have a new anniversary to add and celebrate. March fourteenth, our engagement date, and number two, we need to get the bride-to-be a ring, and number three, we need to set a wedding date. I was thinking how about, October sixth, that should give us enough time and yet it's not too far away?"

"Well," now Christine checked off her fingers. "Number one, I'll never forget March fourteenth, so an extra anniversary date would be great, and number two, we don't have to rush into buying a ring, a cigar band would do fine, just as long as it is from you, and number three, October sixth sounds absolutely perfect, but out of curiosity, why that date."

"Ah, how fast the lady forgets." He pushed the hair away from her eyes. "October sixth was the first day that we laid eyes on each other. You came down to my office from Junior fashions upstairs, to apply for the position in my Teen Fashions Department. That was the day I knew I had to have you as my own."

EATON'S – During the Second French Revolution

She cradled his hands in hers. "That's incredible, because as much as I tried, you know with us both being married, I just couldn't help falling for you, but I never could have believed you would ever give me a second look!"

"Well, my beautiful, I had pretty much those feeling, too!"

He pulled the box and lid across the bed. "So, to get this straight we have number one and number three solved, right?"

She nodded.

"Was that it for stuff in the box? Did you see anything else?" he asked, pushing the box toward her.

She looked quizzically inside what appeared to be an empty box. "I ... I think I got everything. The box looks empty. She looked again and ran her fingers around the inside. "Why?"

"I don't know. You never know what else you might find in a big box like that! Why don't you look again, please?"

As she looked closer, she discovered the false bottom which she removed to unveil a blue velvet jewelry box with the word Burkes Jewelry printed in gold letters across the top. "Is this what I think it is?" She clasped both hands around the box secreting it from sight. "No, it can't be!" she stammered.

"Can't be what, Christine? I'm not sure I know what you think it is, but maybe I'll open it just to see what's inside!

Ricky gently pulled her hands apart and opened the box to reveal a one-carat diamond engagement ring with four large diamond baguettes, two on each side of the solitaire. He took her hand, disregarding the shocked look on her face, and placed the ring slowly on her finger. "Christine Roberta Guillaume will you be my bride?"

She stared for a long time at the ring in disbelief, then answered quietly and simply, "Ricky, my husband to be, please make love to me!"

An hour and one half later, both totally spent, Christine lit two cigarettes, placed a glass of Dubonnet in Ricky's hand, and snuggled back into his waiting arms. "You know, with all that Eaton's has been through, and all the craziness surrounding Quebec's separatist efforts, it's a thankful miracle that we found each other to *love*."

"Thank God for miracles!" Ricky whispered in her ear.

They made love again, then she dressed in his favorite little black dress. They left their dream room and went downstairs to dance the night away, into the wee hours of the morning, as Mr. Richard Dean, and the future, Mrs. Christine Dean.

From where my life was, to this magic moment, I never would have believed that this could have happened to me!

⚜ Eighty-Five ⚜

It was June 14th, three months to the day since Ricky had proposed to Christine and just about everyone knew of their upcoming marriage. Ricky had cleared any conflict of interest of working with Christine with Appleton and had been given a green light to continue regular operations as his new responsibilities dictated.

Ricky couldn't put his finger on it, but he knew something was seriously out of whack in his life. Now, with Christine moved in with him and Darlene, permanently in Ville St. Laurent, his ex-wife permanently out of his life, and finances no longer a problem because of his promotion, as old Doc Julie would have said, 'you have it all, my boy. Now enjoy, yes?' But, although thankful for all these blessings, when away from Christine and Darlene, all he seemed to be exposed to was negativity.

F.L.Q. where still violently active, Quebec government more than ever excluded Anglophones progressive legislation, and the most grievous negative of Ricky's loss of interest in his dream job at Eaton's Montreal. This was a negative that he never thought he would ever endure. Now, all he wanted was tranquility, family, love and now a new goal of being his own boss to support his growing family. Christine and Ricky had talked in depth about their plans for the future and were totally aligned on a common goal of moving west to a more secure and stable environment.

And, with their new addition on the way, there is no better way for them to welcome this treasured creation addition into the world.

⚜ Epilogue ⚜

The new decade of the 1970's brought significant changes for the separatist plight in the Province of Quebec, the corporate climate of The T. Eaton Canada, Ltd. and the personal and business life of Ricky Dean and his family.

With the 1960's F.L.Q. debacle surrounding the kidnapping of British diplomat, James Richard Cross and the kidnapping and murder of Quebec politician, Pierre Laporte, national and international indignation resulted in rapid decline in support for the terrorist organization. This separatist vacuum was replaced by non-violent rhetoric and policy making by Quebec cabinet ministers and leaders. But the perpetuation of the original goals of the F.L.Q. to strip Anglophones of their constitutional rights continued without the necessity of further terrorist actions.

The T. Eaton Canada, Ltd., was still under family management and had made numerous development errors that subsequently would lead to the ultimate

EATON'S – During the Second French Revolution

road of bankruptcy. And, with the Sears Company already making in-roads to buy out Eaton's, it was only a matter of time before the original company no longer existed. Additionally, part of Eaton's rapid demise can be directly attributed to the actions of the F.L.Q., both in anti-Quebec sentiment and directed violence against the once predominant Canadian retailer.

But on the positive side, the business and personal life of Ricky Dean transcended the changing times.

Ricky's brother, Norman, who had thankfully survived his undercover internship within the R.C.M.P. and became a special agent in charge of the Vancouver narcotics division, met and married his Chinese sweetheart and had two children. And because they were just a few hundred miles apart remained in regular contact with each other.

Ricky's ex-wife, Kathy's mental condition further deteriorated to a point that she could not hold down a job and eventually became a "bag lady" roaming the streets of Toronto. Her father gained court sanctioned conservatorship over her and her finances, eventually moving her back into the family home. She never had any further contact with her daughter, Darlene.

As the decade transitioned from the late 60's into the early 70's, Ricky had become more and more disillusioned with Eaton's and the radical policies and procedures that were contrary to the original doctrine of its founder. The company was no longer a family, but rather an impersonal corporation floundering for survival. His participation in Eaton's growth activities became more painful than exhilarating, and as years went by, Ricky realized that the original vision of Timothy Eaton no longer set precedent or commanded any importance in today's Eaton's organization, or in him.

Subsequently, watching the slow decline of the Eaton's organization, Ricky began a small part time management consulting business that eventually blossomed into an international entity catering to developing Canadian businesses, both at home and abroad. Although Ricky had initially fantasized that Eaton's would be his lifelong career, eventually he realized he needed to abandon that goal and pursue his consulting business on a full-time basis.

In 1969, Ricky and Christine, had a large wedding officiated by Father Mac, at St. Patrick's Cathedral, in Montreal. They left their childhood home province of Quebec to settle on the shores of Lake Louise, in Banff, Alberta, Canada. Christine became a part time columnist for the Canadian Women's Wear Daily, Teen Fashion section, and a full-time mother to her treasured Darlene and their newborn son, Dean Robert.

Many of Ricky's friends and co-workers had also, "seen the writing on the wall" and had, over the waning years, abandoned Eaton's Montreal for greener pastures out west.

During Eaton's Montreal waning years and because of Tony Cartwright's numerous security department achievements in the Montreal store, Tony was promoted to National Security Administrator for the Canadian Eaton's chain, based out of Toronto. Ray Archambault was promoted to head of security for the Montreal store and eventually succeeded in changing all the store detectives to French only employees. Kate Middleton, seeing the French only trend, took early retirement.

Jerry Copeland joined his mother's business, eventually expanding it into the United States as a publicly traded company, on the New York stock exchange.

Duane Hutchinson stuck it out as department manager until the Montreal store closed, sadly leaving him unemployed.

Maggie Hilbert married Myron and followed her dream of moving to Florida to be close to her daughter and grandchildren.

Steve Fortuna returned to Italy where he was reunited with his wife and children.

Unfortunately, John LeClerke passed away four days after taking early retirement from Eaton's.

The Calabresee family was dissolved when they were caught up in *RICO*, the *Racketeer Influenced and Corrupt Organizations Law*, conviction connected with the five crime families in New York. Canada approved extradition to the U.S., incarcerating the family heads to life sentences.

Spiro and Magdalene expanded their restaurants into Laval, St Jerome, and Ville Lasalle. Their daughter, Angie completed her medical residency at the Royal Victoria Hospital, eventually taking a position at an Albany New York hospital.

Throughout the 1970's English Quebec businesses continued to leave the province for Toronto and western provinces sinking Quebec into financial chaos. Quebec became 100% French only, with all the rights of the Anglophones being suspended.

And, of course the biggest tragedy was the eventual demise of the once grand Montreal Eaton's Store and the Eaton's national chain. The early beginnings of Ricky and Christine's *not-to-be* life had miraculously become a life of, *to-be-forever* ... a fact that lives on to this day!

They had survived "The Second French Revolution!"

EATON'S – During the Second French Revolution

Historical Resource Information
About Eaton's

The T. Eaton Canada, Ltd. chain, which had controlled 60% of all department store sales in Canada in 1930, had been reduced to a market share of 10.6% by 1997, and had subsequently filed for bankruptcy protection that same year. At that time, the company had an estimated 24,500 employees and over 90 retail outlets. The plan was to close 31 underperforming stores, including two-thirds of its stores in Alberta. George Eaton, the last surviving family member to be involved in management, resigned as chief executive in 1997, being succeeded by George Kosich. In September of that year, creditors approved the bankruptcy restructuring plan that would eventually fail.

In 1998, George Kosich resigned as chairman of the board and was succeeded by Brent Ballantyne, under whom the company was taken public for the first time in its history. The chain finally folded in 1999 after operating for 130 years. Though it had reduced its retail outlets to 64, it finished 1998 with a net loss of $72 million, and it announced further closures, and another corporate restructuring plan. This was also unsuccessful, and the company declared bankruptcy in August 1999.

Eaton's corporate assets were acquired by Sears Canada in a 50-million-dollar deal. Sears purchased all the shares of T. Eaton Co., eight of its stores, with the option to buy five more, and the Eaton's name, trademarks, brands, and Web site. For the first time in its history, Sears held the leases to several prime locations in Toronto, including the Eaton's Centre and Yorkdale Mall, Vancouver Pacific Centre, and the Victoria, Winnipeg, Ottawa, Calgary stores. Sears had intended to obtain the former downtown Montreal store, although it lost out to the incumbent, Les Ailes de la Mode.

Sears Canada closed some Eaton's stores, converted others to Sears stores, sold others to The Bay or Zellers, and kept a number of downtown stores with the intention of relaunching Eaton's in 2000 as a more high-end, modern brand, retail organization. Sears also launched a new Eaton's catalogue, with the intent of complementing the Sears moderate catalogue assortment with something more upscale and urban. According to Rick Brown, senior vice president at Sears Canada, merchandise was supposed to be priced above the level of Sears Canada and The Bay, but below that of competitor, Holt Renfrew.

Sears had trouble securing name brand merchandise consistent with the image of the new chain. This was mainly because of doubt in Sears' ability to manage an upper-end chain, since until recently their merchandise was of lower price and quality compared to the old Eaton's and The Bay. George Heller, then-president of the rival department store; The Bay, publicly warned vendors not to supply the new Eaton's with merchandise. Many mid-to-upper tier brands, particularly in clothing, feared reprisal and avoided the new Eaton's.

The new Eaton's was scheduled to open September 1, 2000, but was pushed back three times, eventually opening November 25th. Consequently, Eaton's had missed much of the lucrative holiday season and opened with merchandise already marked down. Construction was haphazard; all stores opened unfinished, and renovations were to continue well into 2001.

The seven-store experiment was not successful, and Sears Canada President, Paul Walters was forced to resign. He was replaced by a former rival and Sears Roebuck executive from the U.S., Mark Cohen, who prioritized Sears over Eaton's and cut back aggressively on markdown strategies. By March 2001 Sears announced they were ceasing publication of the newly resurrected Eaton's catalogue "due to a lack of interest". Although Mark Cohen officially announced that the Eaton's chain had seen an impressive rebound in June 2001, by 2002 he retired the "Eaton's" name. The remaining stores were converted to Sears, including the flagship Eaton's Centre store located at the Toronto Eaton's Centre in downtown Toronto.

A new modern Eaton's Centre was constructed on the original Ste.- Catherine St. property of the Montreal T. Eaton Company, Canada, Ltd., and is still in operation today.

The Eaton's 100+ year legacy had ended,
But Ricky Dean and his family had prevailed!

EATON'S
During The Second French Revolution

CONTENT DISCLAIMER

Fact or Fiction

As a first-time author it was my intention to document the events that I experienced in the 1960's as seen through my eyes as the fictional character, Richard (Ricky) Dean, a young manager of Eaton's Montreal basement departments.

Even though this book is based on actual events, for the purpose of this book many events may be embellished, or even fictionalized.

The following is an explanation of what is true and what is fictionalized.

Prologue: This historical information about the Canadian confederation, the development of the Province of Quebec and the transition from Anglophone to Francophone dominance is accurate as to resource content.

Timothy Eaton History: All the details considering founder Timothy Eaton and the development of the Eaton chain are factual.

Richard (Ricky) Dean: Ricky is based on my life and times at Eaton's Montreal through the 1960's. The events depicted, traumas, interaction with Eaton's staff, love affair, personal family history, etc. were based on my experiences during that period of time.

Westmount Bombing: Although the names have been changed this depiction is offered as a factual account of the Canada Poste mailbox bombings that sadly maimed, and many years later, took the life of a Canadian bomb disposal agent. The ATV reporting of the events were gleaned from my personal recollection of T.V., radio and newspaper reports and articles.

In-Store Bomb Searches: Although it may seem unfathomable, during the time of widespread F.L.Q terror and bombings, Eaton's staff members were regularly tasked with searching for potential bombs, as each threat was communicated to the store.

In-Store Accidents, Crimes And Interaction With Customers And Staff: All these instances are true events which were experienced by me during this period, including: the man dying, man running nude through the store, shoplifting stories, employee crimes, department organizing, escalator accidents, contact with MPD, and interaction with customers.

J.F.K. Assassination: The day of the J.F.K. Assassination is detailed as the event unfolded in my basement shoe department.

"Norman" R.C.M.P. Undercover Agent: This is a totally fictional person, however, most of the depictions of the conduct of The F.L.Q. terror events such as the Montreal Stock Exchange bombing, Black Watch Armory bombing, La

Fountaine Park demonstrations, and the Laporte & Cross kidnapping and murder are all factual accounts. The Norman character is loosely based on my own brother who did serve in the U.S. Airforce in Vietnam, attended Rosemount High School, and was a successful HS wrestler.

The Montreal Forum Riot: This was a factual event resulting from the suspension of Maurice (the Rocket) Richard.

Montreal Crime Families: Although there were indeed two prominent crime families controlling east and west Montreal; including several other competitive factions, the stories concerning The Westies and the Calabrisee families are pure fabrication.

Vinney (the Truck) Calabrisee: The stories of the 'Liftermob', the Eaton's cash office attempted robbery, truck high-jackings, man in the truck of the Cadillac by the dock, etc. are all factual accounts of Montreal crime events, but not directly connected to my fictional "Vinney" character.

Montreal Landmarks: For historical value I have included many Montreal landmarks, many of which have disappeared over time, and some which still remain prominent to this day.

Eaton's Locker Bombing: This is a factional account of a successful bombing attack by the F.L.Q. that destroyed our antique wooden escalator, a band of lockers, my notion department, and the Laura Secord Chocolate store.

Montreal Night Of Terror: The events surrounding the police and firefighter strike, which resulted in crimes throughout the city and the political handling of these events, are based on personal knowledge and media coverage. The actual radio reporting coverage, although factual in content, is not the actual comments by the reporters.

Eaton's Store F.L.Q. Attack: These are the actual events that I experienced, on the Montreal Night Of Terror, when the F.L.Q. took advantage of the police and fireman strike to terrorize downtown and attack the Eaton's store directly.

Murray Hill Limousine F.L.Q. Attack: During the Montreal Night Of Terror police and fireman strike, rival cab drivers took advantage of the lack of law enforcement to set fire to the Murray Hill Limousine Company with the result; killing one person. The discord had to do with Murray Hill having a monopoly on fare pickups at Dorval airport.

Historic Fashion Show: This was an event that had never been done in Canada before. All the development events surrounding this Ten Fashion Show are accurate and the use of my non-professional teen models gained acclaim across Canada and the U.S.

Quebec Divorce: The information regarding the restriction on gaining a divorce in Quebec during that time is factual; requiring the necessity to fake a case of infidelity to qualify.

"Vinney's" Funeral: Although the full story of development of St. Joseph's Oratory is factual, general funerals are not conducted at the Oratory.

LaSalle Gas Explosion: Factual - Twenty-six residents were killed and 37 injured when a natural gas explosion blasted a 40-unit, three-story apartment building. A young salesclerk in my ladieswear department's child was killed in the explosion.

KENNETH A. BRAY

AUTHOR'S BIOGRAPHY

Kenneth A. Bray was born in Montreal, Quebec, Canada in 1943, the son of an engraver and a homemaker. His first job, at the age of fourteen was a runner for a sportswear manufacturer, followed at sixteen as a carrier boy in the Montreal Eaton's store. That began his career at Eaton's, which spanned approximately eleven years. He quickly rose in position to merchandise manager status, supervising numerous basement departments and over one hundred and twenty-five personnel. One of his greatest achievements within his basement departments was the creation of the historic Teen Fashion Show, featuring amateur models from his various departments. He was also one of the youngest managers ever in all Easton's Canada.

In nineteen sixty-nine, he moved with his family to the United States to take a position as President of Tana Company of America. In later years Bray owned a Canadian fashion import business, general contracting business, built over one hundred houses, an international consulting business, consulted on the creation and development of over forty international businesses, and finally a Greetings on Gold greeting card and art manufacturing business.

Upon retirement, at the age of seventy-five, he began writing his book about his time at Eaton's during the turbulent 1960's. His primary motivation for documenting those years was the preservation of facts surrounding the waning years of Eaton's and the historic account of Montreal under FLQ threats.

EATON'S – During the Second French Revolution

Final Word From The Author

I sincerely hope you have enjoyed *Eaton's the Second French Revolution* and will let me know your comments.
I can be reached on social media:
info@ goldenquillpress.com Subject Eaton's

You can also connect with me on **Face Book** * at Eatons Montreal Department Store | Facebook
http://www.facebook.com/Eatons-Montreal-Department-Store-106388181378702

LinkedIn (EATONS Montreal Department Store: About | LinkedIn
https://www.linkedin.com/company/Eaton's-montreal-department-store/about/?viewAsMember=true

As a "Thank You" For Your Purchase of Eaton's
Receive a
SPECIAL 20% DISCOUNT
When you
ORDER Any Book (s) AT GOLDEN QUILL PRESS
On any of our books (print and/or e-books)
STEP #1 Visit **https://goldenquillpress.com/bookstore**
STEP #2 Choose what you want.
STEP #3 email **info@goldenquillpress.com Subject Eaton's reader wants an additional 20% discount.**
list what you want, and we will arrange your discount - it's that easy!

KENNETH A. BRAY

BOOKS BY
GOLDEN QUILL PRESS

DOGGY DEMENTIA & ALZHEIMER'S: SHAMROCK'S STORY FROM HURRICANE KATRINA TO By: F. Barish-Stern
A rescued dog's journey through life and the stages of dementia are interwoven with guidance from 50 + experts to help any pet parent from puppy to senior dog to know how to understand this disease that can threaten any dog.

CODE 47 to BREV Force - Trilogy By: F. Barish-Stern
The adventures of The BREV Force: College Students fighting to defeat a virus that threatens to take over the world.

FROM AN IDEA TO YOUR FINISHED STORY
By F. Barish-Stern and Bobbi Madry
A writer's journey with an editor, a writer and a publisher helping you follow interactive maps to custom tailor your idea into a finished manuscript.

SEEING THE UNSEEABLE By: Ruth Cefola
A 16-year-old first time writer needs to find a way to help a friend who may be going blind, and she decides to write her a story with the possibilities of a good future – that labor of love is Ruth's story, "Seeing the Unseeable."

TELL IT TO THE FUTURE BY: Cefola (Barish-Stern) & Bobbi Madry
TELL IT TO THE FUTURE-Have I Got A Story For You, about the Twentieth Century leaves personal messages with timelines and stories about our hopes, dreams, or events that impacted on, or changed our lives. Each story focuses on events from a specific decade of the twentieth century with descriptions that reflect the color of the times. Some are witty, some filled with wisdom, while others pull at your heart strings.

TELL OTHERS BY: Marjorie Struck
A family torn apart by over 10+ suicides; while one woman has the courage to stand up and speak up and not let this family history keep going in silence. For the future and for all who suffer from depression, addiction, and eventual suicide, she says, "Tell Others" this is a disease and needs to be discussed and dealt with.

LOVE MAKES A DIFFERENCE BY: Mary Bianchini &Bobbi Madry
Arriving as an immigrant with her mother in the early 1900's, Mary grew up to become one of the most influential figures in Rockland County, N.Y. Honored by four Presidents and in the Congressional Record, Mary shares her advice about family, community service and reaching her dreams.

NEW HORIZONS - BY: F. Barish-Stern) & Bobbi R. Madry
Poetry is the art that speaks to our hearts and minds. Like a beautiful painting or a musical composition, this collection of poetry will take you into worlds limited only by your imagination ... from the splendor of a sunset to tasting

candy, to memories from a rocking chair. These Poems Take You To Your Own New Horizons!!

CHALLENGING MESSAGES FROM BEYOND BY: Marjorie Struck
Does the Spiritual World have a message for us? Can we learn to understand that communication? Marjorie Struck certainly believes. This is her personal story of how a message from Beyond changed her life. Informative, at times shocking but ultimately a journey that reveals a side of the spiritual world that can transform you forever. Marjorie invites you along to witness how this revelation helped her understand the connection between life and beyond- and how souls in the afterlife help us to find the Light!

COMPASSION'S LURE BY: Kathleen Lukens
This is the story of a visionary. Kathy Lukens founder of Camp Venture - advocate for all people with special needs standing up for the rights and deeds of those who could not fight for themselves. With words backed by tireless efforts, Kathy made the impossible happen for the developmentally disabled- a home and the proper attention to their needs. She was truly one of the Great Women of our times.

the GRANPA SPIDER stories BY: Granpa Spider
A delightful story for children of all ages. Granpa Spider weaves a web of adventure and intrigue, mystery, and fun! Along with his Arachnid friends, Penelope, The Colonel, and others we journey into the exciting world of the web. As Shamrock McGee says, "May the wind be at your web. May your web be in the trees. May cicada be chattering. May there be a host of bees. And may the web that you spin be serving all your needs."

MAE SINGS ABOUT SHORT VOWELS BY: Karen A. Coleman
was developed as a method for teaching music, while learning vowel sounds. The book uses songs and a vowel recognition technique in an interactive way to help students improve reading skills while learning musical notes.

OPENING THE DOOR TO A BRIGHTER FUTURE BY: Daniel Windheim
Marjorie Windheim writes, "After my son, Dan sustaining a traumatic brain injury and the efforts he made to recover and build a productive life, we decided that many of the lessons both Dan and I learned from that experience might have relevance to others recovering from injuries or illnesses. We therefore set out to write a book detailing ten key strategies that could help individuals in their recovery efforts and to share the experiences of some survivors as they struggle to return to a healthy life. As Dan notes, 'There is not time to waste focusing on the negative, but we need to take what we have and make the most out of things.'"

THE POEM BOOK BY: Daniel Windheim
A brain injury victim of a car accident young Daniel Windheim's life is turned upside down. He turns to poetry to express his frustration, anger and to take the

reader on a beautiful journey through recuperation and new life challenges. Daniel Windheim is truly a shining hero, overcoming life's worst experience. "I remain practical but a realist and accept what I am. Life is good and there is goodness in life."

SWEET MERCY BY: Rebecca H. Cofer

Katherine Ryder peels away the decades of family secrets to tell her story of growing up in Fairburn, Georgia at the turn of the century - 1900. She battles many obstacles to free herself from small town life and her autocratic mother and moves to Atlanta. In the big city she is betrayed by the man she loves. But her generous heart and hard work pay off, bringing her joy and fulfillment in the end.

THERE IS HOPE BY: Debby Paine

There Is Hope is a collection of religious poetry about the struggles, pains, questions and fears we all face. Debby's love of family, church and community is portrayed as she searches for and reaches toward God to find hope. These poems from the heart-for the heart, will reach out to everyone searching for hope. "Reach for it. Hold on to it. 'Hope is There.'"

Other books marketed by Golden Quill Press:

YOU ARE WHAT YOU WEAR BY: William Thourlby

"First impressions" are lasting. YOU ARE WHAT YOU
WEAR will help you make the right "first impression." Develop skills that are cost effective because they not only increase the quality of life in the workplace, contribute to employee morale and embellish the company image, they play a major role in developing a person's self - image and generating profits. The lack of these skills can be highly visible and costly for any person or company in every day and age.

PASSPORT TO POWER BY: William Thourlby

Part practical, part primer, part visionary, Passport to Power, gives the reader background and formulas to follow to acquire and master international communication skills and provide the keys to unlocking human potential for success as a leader in the new global village of today.

www.ingramcontent.com/pod-product-compliance
Lightning Source LLC
LaVergne TN
LVHW021220080526
838199LV00084B/4294